The New Era in U.S. National Security

The New Era in U.S. National Security

An Introduction to Emerging Threats and Challenges

Jack A. Jarmon

ROWMAN & LITTLEFIELD
Lanham • Boulder • New York • Toronto • Plymouth, UK

Published by Rowman & Littlefield
4501 Forbes Boulevard, Suite 200, Lanham, Maryland 20706
www.rowman.com

10 Thornbury Road, Plymouth PL6 7PP, United Kingdom

British Library Cataloguing in Publication Information Available

Library of Congress Cataloging-in-Publication Data

Jarmon, Jack A., 1951-
The new era in U.S. national security : an introduction to emerging threats and challenges / Jack A. Jarmon.
p. cm.
Includes bibliographical references and index.
ISBN 978-1-4422-2410-0 (cloth : alk. paper) -- ISBN 978-1-4422-2411-7 (pbk. : alk. paper) -- ISBN 978-1-4422-2412-4 (electronic)
1. National security--United States. 2. United States--Military policy. 3. Civil defense--United States. 4. Terrorism--Prevention--United States. 5. Weapons of mass destruction. 6. Computer networks--Security measures. 7. Arms control. I. Title.
UA23.J35 2014
355'.033073--dc23

2013049335

♾ ™ The paper used in this publication meets the minimum requirements of American National Standard for Information Sciences Permanence of Paper for Printed Library Materials, ANSI/NISO Z39.48-1992.

Printed in the United States of America

To
My son, Kyle
My wife, Barbara Diane
Robert and Mary Jarmon
Gordon and Stacy Gemma
&
In loving memory of
George P. Bundy
Gertrude Berman
Jonathan B. Weiss

Contents

List of Tables, Figures, and Maps   ix

Abbreviations   xi

Foreword   xv

Introduction   xvii

Part I: The Establishment and the National Security Environment   **1**

1   The National Security Establishment   3

2   Policies and Processes in the New Geopolitics   17

3   Industrial Age Warfare and Information Age Weapons   37

4   The New Arena of Conflict and Economic Competition   55

Part II: Current, Emerging, and Impending Threats and Challenges   **73**

5   The Maritime Supply Chain: Vast, Diverse, and Anarchic   75

6   The Gatekeeper's Challenge   103

7   The Cyber War: New Battlefronts, Old and New Enemies   121

8   Cyber Guerilla War   145

9   Terrorism Versus Crime   163

10   Building a Global Network   187

11   Chemical Biological Radiological & Nuclear: The Chemical Threat   203

12   Chemical Biological Radiological & Nuclear: The Biological Threat   217

13 Chemical Biological Radiological & Nuclear: The Radiological
    Nuclear Threat   239

Part III: Policy Implications and the Public—Private Partnership   **253**
14 Industrial Policy and Defense Policy   255

Glossary of Terms   275

Index   281

About the Author   287

List of Tables, Figures, and Maps

TABLES

Table 1.1 The National Security Establishment
Table 1.2 The Homeland Security Establishment
Table 2.1 Amount of Jobs Created by Sector Per $1Billion
Table 5.1 The Layered Approach to Maritime Security
Table 5.2 Potential Consequences of Terrorist Attacks, Scenarios on Container Shipping
Table 6.1 The 20 Biggest Suppliers of Officers and Ratings in 2010
Table 8.1 Techniques Used to Commit Cyber Crimes
Table 11.1 Characteristics of Chemical and Biological Agents
Table 12.1 Hemorrhagic Fevers
Table 12.2 Category A Biological Agents

FIGURES

Figure 4.1 Container Cargo Vessel and Gantry
Figure 5.1 Maritime Shipping Density
Figure 5.2 Growth in International Maritime Trade
Figure 5.3 Supply Chain Process
Figure 5.4 Container Security Initiative Ports
Figure 5.5 War Game—Economic Impact
Figure 6.1 Regional Breakdown of Container Throughput for 2005
Figure 6.2 International Containerized Trade Growth
Figure 7.1 Internet Architecture
Figure 7.2 U.S. DoD Reported Incidents of Malicious Cyber Activity, 2003–2011

Figure 13.1 Non-ionizing and Ionizing Radiation

MAPS

Map 6.1 Major Trade Routes, Container Traffic—2007
Map 9.1 Heroin Flows to West and Central Europe, 2009
Map 9.2 Main Global Cocaine Flows, 2009
Map 10.1 Tri-Border Area of Argentina, Brazil, and Paraguay
Map 12.1 Reported Cases of Human Plague in the United States, 1970–2012
Map 13.1 Status of States with Nuclear Capability

Abbreviations

NSA — National Security Agency
NRA — National Reconnaissance Agency
DIA — Defense Intelligence Agency
NSC — National Security Council
FEMA — Federal Emergency Management Agency
DNI — Director of National Intelligence
OSINT — Open Source Intelligence
HUMINT — Human Intelligence
SIGINT — Signals Intelligence
MASINT — Measurement and Signature Intelligence
IMINT — Imagery Intelligence
GEOINT — Geospatial Intelligence
NATO — North Atlantic Treaty Organization
SEATO — Southeast Asia Treaty Organization
ANZUS — Australia/New Zealand/United States
RMA — Revolution in Military Affairs
C4ISR — Command Control Communication Computers Intelligence
  Surveillance Reconnaissance
QDR — Quadrennial Defense Review
PPBES — Planning Programming Budgeting Execution System
HSC — Homeland Security Council
NSC/PC — National Security Council/Principals Committee
NSC/DC — National Security Council/Deputies Committee
NSC/IWG — National Security Council/Interagency Working Group
PCC — Policy Coordinating Committee
GWOT — Global War on Terrorism
IW — Information Warfare

NGO — Non-Governmental Organizations
TQM — Total Quality Management
CSR — Corporate Social Responsibility
CERT — Computer Emergency Response Team
CSIRT — Computer Security Incident Response Team
DHS — Department of Homeland Security
NCSD — National Cyber Security Division
ISAC — Information Sharing and Analysis Centers
NIPC — National Infrastructure Protection Center
CIP — Critical Infrastructure Protection
BENS — Business Executives for National Security
INSA — Intelligence and National Security Alliance
SAFE — Standards to Secure and Facilitate Global Trade
CBRN — Chemical Biological Radiation Nuclear
IND — Improvised Nuclear Device
ICBM — Inter-Continental Ballistic Missile
MANPADS — Man-Portable Air-Defense System
SAMS — Surface-to-Air Missile
IMF — International Monetary Fund
LTTE — Liberation Tigers of Tamil Eeslam
WMD — Weapon of Mass Destruction
OECD — Organization for Economic Cooperation and Development
CBP — Customs Border Protection
NII — Non-Intrusive Inspection vehicle
VACIS — Vehicle and Cargo Inspection System
CES — Container Evaluation Facilities
UNCTAD — United Nations Conference on Trade and Development
ATS — Automated Targeting System
LNG — Liquefied Natural Gas
RFID — Radio Frequency Identification
TIR — Trans-International Routier
PIRA — Provisional Irish Republican Army
C-TPAT — Customs-Trade Partnership Against Terrorism
DCMA — Defense Contract Management Agency
DCAA — Defense Contract Audit Agency
PMA — Private Military Army
NORAD — North American Aerospace Defense Command
IAEA — International Atomic Energy Agency
GAO — Government Accountability Office
CSIS — Center for Strategic and International Studies
ICT — Information-Communication Technology
EM — Electromagnetic
VPN — Virtual Private Networks

TCP/IP — Transmission Control Protocol/Internet Protocol
DNS — Domain Name System
URL — Uniform Resource Locator
ICANN — Internet Corporation for Assigned Names and Numbers
ARPA — Advanced Research Projects Agency
DARPA — Defense Advanced Research Projects Agency
NSF — National Science Foundation
NSFNET — National Science Foundation NET
ISP — Internet Service Provider
VoIP — Voice over Internet Protocol
PTN — Public Telecommunications Network
NRC — National Research Council
NCSI — National Cybersecurity Initiative
PRC — People's Republic of China
PLA — People's Liberation Army
NCPH — Network Crack Program Hacker
CENTCOM — Central Command
HSIN — Homeland Security Information Network
SCADA — Supervisory Control and Data Acquisition System
COTS — Commercial Off-the-Shelf
CNCI — Comprehensive National Cybersecurity Initiative
DTO — Drug Tracking Organization
IED — Improvised Explosive Device
RPG — Rocket Propelled Grenade
CREATE — Center for Risk and Economic Analysis of Terrorism Events
KLA — Kosovo Liberation Army
IMU — Islamic Movement of Uzbekistan
HT — Hizb-ut-Tahrir
ROC — Russian Organized Crime
FARC — Revolutionary Armed Forces of Colombia
FTO — Foreign Terrorist Organization
ELN — National Liberation Army
TBA — Tri-Border Area
CPC — Communist Party of China
AEO — Authorized Economic Operator
FATF — Financial Action Trade Force
MLAT — Mutual Legal Assistance Treaty
ROI — Return on Investment
LMF — Large Multinational Firm
SME — Small Medium Size Enterprise
ITC — Investment Tax Credit
LAN — Local Area Network
OMB — Office of Management and Budget

HSPD — Homeland Security Presidential Directive
ICT — Information/Communication Technology
BW — Biological Weapons
BWC — Biological Weapons Convention
CDC — Centers for Disease Control
SME — Subject Matter Specialist
PFLP-GC — Popular Front for the Liberation of Palestine—General Command
HF — Hemorrhagic Fever
RNA — Ribonucleic Acid
WHO — World Health Organization
TOPOFF — Top Officials Emergency Services
CW — Chemical Warfare
HR — Sulfur Mustard Gas
HN — Nitrogen Mustard Gas
TIC — Toxic Industrial Chemical
AG — Australia Group
OPCW — Organization for the Prevention of Chemical Warfare
eV — Electron Volt
HEU — Highly Enriched Uranium
RDD — Radiological Dispersion Device
NPT — Nuclear Proliferation Treaty
NWS — Nuclear Weapons States
NNWS — Non- Nuclear Weapons States

Foreword

Contemporary national and international security organizations and agencies must manage global challenges such as organized crime, weapons proliferation, cyber attacks, bio-terrorism, catastrophic disasters, forced migration, and radicalization. But their bureaucratic frameworks, strategic doctrine, organization processes, and security tools and tactics are poorly suited for these challenges. Many are rooted in the World War II era and adapted to demands of the Cold War, even though today's international environment requires new approaches.

The New Era in U.S. National Security provides a helpful guide for understanding the turbulence of 21st Century and how the U.S. national security establishment is striving to adapt to the complex array of threat and challenges that confront the global community. To an extraordinary extent, providing for the common defense requires a command of a complex set of transnational issues and expertise that draws on multiple academic disciplines. Quite simply, the traditional concepts of security, centered on nation-states, conventional armed conflicts, nuclear deterrence, and arms control, must be broadened to include asymmetrical warfare and other risks to the global community.

Lives and property are increasingly in the crosshairs of non-state terrorism, cyber attacks, disease outbreaks, mass migration, transnational crime, and catastrophic storms and droughts associated with climate change. These risks require institutions, policymakers, and academics to reconsider long-established patterns for managing security challenges. Similarly, ethnic and religious conflict and chronic shortages of food, water, and employment opportunities within a state can overwhelm domestic institutions with consequences for neighboring countries. In short, both the practice and study of national and international security must undergo profound change.

In the pages that follow, Jack Jarmon serves as a modern day reconnaissance scout, surveying the global landscape and reporting back on the emerging dangers. Importantly, he identifies the new and widening array of participants who are empowered to pose new threats. At the same time there are also new actors who must be enlisted to confront those threats. The days when national security could be left almost exclusively in the hands of uniformed professionals is long over. Indeed, defensive strategies rooted in industrial age warfare are hopelessly out of alignment with information age challenges.

The race is on for national security policies to catch up with contemporary circumstances. Part of the challenge is that while there are ample new threats and vulnerabilities, old forms of warfare have by no means disappeared. Defense planners have to be prepared to prevail against both familiar and emerging hazards and to do so against the backdrop of resource constraints. This requires making difficult choices that, in turn, must be informed by a sophisticated understanding of the critical foundations of the international system that adversaries may exploit or target. Supply chains, cyberspace, and critical infrastructure have become new battlefields. Safeguarding them requires enlisting their designers, owners, operators, and stakeholders. The private sector and civil society cannot be relegated to the sidelines when it comes to providing for the common defense.

While we continue to live in a perilous world, there is no reason to believe that building a safer, more prosperous and sustainable international community lies beyond our reach. Two things are required. First, we must be clear-eyed about the dangers we face. Second, we must be willing to harness our collective capacity to think and act anew in confronting those dangers. *The New Era in U.S. National Security* provides essential reading towards achieving these two goals.

Stephen E. Flynn, Ph.D.
Professor of Political Science
Northeastern University
Boston, Massachusetts

Introduction

The main focus of this book is U.S. national security and the challenges created by the processes of globalization. Although the discussion is U.S.-centric, the context is global. The American military and security establishment are hegemonic, but its impact takes shape in response to many forces and pressures beyond its control. Therefore, when we speak of U.S national security we are speaking of a paradigm in constant flux. It is a mutable system of new complexities with a grander range of actors and a brand of asymmetry never before known. In this environment it is more difficult for the United States to act unilaterally despite its military and political dominance.

The term "globalization" in this text refers to the highly connected state and manner by which populations link economically and politically. Technological advancement has resulted in a compression of time and space. The consequence has meant an unprecedented interconnectedness and interdependence never before known among peoples and locales. As the world transforms, as it moves toward a mode of existence resembling a single space, the possibilities of market relations and political responses are heightened and intensified. This new geography that pressures commerce to respond to exact quality and price demands of the market, similarly, imposes a historical transformation on the national security establishment to adapt to the precision weaponry and information technology of modern warfare. Whether the target is a market or a battlefield, no territory is beyond reach at, ideally, any time. As James Mittelman puts it, globalization is more than a process of forming a new structure of international relations. It is also a "domain of knowledge."

For the defense and national security community the impact has been seismic. The responsibilities for securing the homeland and advancing U.S.

xvii

interests overseas are under new pressures. In the post-Cold War environment globalization has meant a re-envisioning of priorities, adapting the force structure, and devising new ways to network with civic society, the private sector, and other organs of government—at home and abroad.

In his 1960 book, *International Politics of the Atomic Age*, John Herz wrote: "political authority is based upon the power of protection." The ability to assure U.S. survival by protecting the nation's economic strength and competitiveness is no longer in defending the strategic markets in Western Europe and Japan and the remote territories from which we access valuable resources to feed the economic engine. The prime target is the economic engine itself. It includes the critical infrastructure, intellectual property, and the stability of the markets. The ironic twist to the arguments is while Herz claims the "permeability of the state" is due to the "all out onslaught of the new (nuclear) weapons," the argument of this book is that a similar porosity is exploited by a different kind of onslaught—an asymmetric onslaught that exists despite the advantage a nation may have in strategic nuclear weapons. The primary differentiator is asymmetric attacks do not aim for total annihilation or to establish an area of pacification as had security regimes of previous eras. Rather, the goals are either parasitical, as often is with cyber attacks, or to drain the country ("the protection unit" as Herz would say) financially and psychologically through unending conflict. The pacification of an area or over a group is unproductive and plays into the hands of those who seek unending war. The erosion of markets means the erosion of political influence.

In the sense that weaponry has overtaken the security apparatus of the age, Herz's argument aligns with that of this book. However, the United States, its allies, and adversaries have entered a new age and face a new generation of weapons. The struggle is not necessarily in fending off annihilation but rather avoiding marginalization. In addition, the scope of the threat matrix not only includes the nation state, it spans the arc of criminal syndicates, entrepreneurial terrorists and to the level of the disgruntled employee. Therefore, national governments and militaries are limited in their capacity to provide a protection force.

Adjustment to the new order of world affairs has, and will continue to be a process of trial, reorientation, missteps, and lapses. Inhibiting progress are not only the present institutions and embedded interests, but also a policy-making apparatus and a preference for large-scale maneuver warfare, which are rooted in a fluctuating interstate system. As mentioned above, it is a system that has been reshaped by technology and the demands of an ever expanding and intensifying global economy. The advanced skills' revolutions in science and commerce require harmony with a global marketplace that operates by the requirements of "just-in-time processing" and disregard for borders. These same "megatrends" have made information accessible in waves of tsunami proportion. Today, we do not mine data—we are bombarded by it. Management of information of such grand scale is key. The riches of information come with a double edge, however, which can either be used for empowerment or in exploitation of one group over another.

As these developments have drawn populations closer, they simultaneously create opportunities for collaboration and tension. At the same time emerging technology and the undermining of borders compel militaries to adapt force structures to a new generation of weaponry and the need to be more flexible, agile, to operate in smaller units, to adjust objectives and maneuver by different rules of engagement. Similar demands are not only put upon diplomatic efforts, but also the imperatives of economic and social corporate responsibility as the private sector confronts its revised role in national security.

These developments have given way to a different structure and level of interaction. For the national security establishment it involves a break from the state-centered international system and contending more with national and subnational governments, quasi-states, ethnic groups, rivalries among traditional allies, criminal gangs, diasporas, nongovernmental organizations, and the new phenomena in media. In the post-Cold War arena of conflict the security framework of past power alliances and strategies based upon a notion of collective security has become outmoded. The organizing principles of U.S. national security strategy reflect less a threat from peer military competitors and more of an "all hazards" approach to counter transnational forces that emanate from criminal enterprises, terrorists, pirates, and events caused by natural catastrophes. Yet, while these emerging threats exist, the primary competitors of the Cold War are still major players. Russia and China are participants and innovators in this asymmetric war. They compete politically and economically with the United States and continue to prosecute the remains of a conflict born from the previous era, but with variation in mission and rationale adapted to the realities of the post-Cold War period. Adding to the enigma and burden of the American security establishment is the need for the United States hegemony to support global commerce and defend the global commons. The Pacific Rim countries, including the People's Republic of China, need the U.S. Navy to protect the shipping lanes. Other nations, particularly Saudi Arabia and Japan, buy U.S. federal debt instruments as indirect payment for a security force. These and other governments can justify the investment as being more favorable than the alternative of developing their own capabilities and militarizing their domestic economies. Similar rationale applies to many other security issues, including cyberspace, outer space, the arctic poles, and human security in times of war and natural disaster.

The result of these upheavals is that the familiar ground of a few decades ago has become a changing landscape. Furthermore, we see now trends develop and events unfold at a historic pace. Yet, before they have a chance to take hold we have watched as they reverse their course or, in some cases, disappear altogether. Most of the U.S. national security establishment was taken by surprise by the fall of the Soviet Union at the time, and no one could have predicted how much the world has changed since September 11, 2001. The array of failed states, the crime—terrorist nexus, jurisdictional arbitrage, attribution and response, and the role of multinational firms are only some of the issues that create and impact the global security paradigm. The pattern shift signals the emergence of a new perilous world. The reorientation in national security portends an era of an asymmetric environment that is—in effect—non-asymmetric. Disorienting features of the new conflict are the unfamiliar objectives that dominate a new strategy of warfare and competition by statal and non-state actors. In these new wars mass disruption rather than destruction can be acceptable goals. The preference of endless conflict over final victory is another strategic objective that forces a reshaping of the accepted wisdom on preparedness and offensive planning.

The impact of technology has been a key driver. The compressing of time and space has made populations more accessible, whether they are markets or political constituencies. Just as economic globalization has opened the field of play to new actors and opportunities for creating wealth, global warfare has given many competitors frequent openings for plunder and exploitation. The motives can be political or economic. The risks can be low for the attacker, and the losses to the targeted group can be substantial.

On these subjects much has been written. Modern weaponry, cyber-terrorism, corporate espionage, the corruptibility of failed states, and other various themes are often discussed as instruments of hard power. Each topic has specific issues, vernacular, and circle of noted authorities and subject matter experts. The purpose of this book, however, is to provide the reader with an upper aerial view of the threats to national security and a survey of the attack surface that threatens U.S. national interests abroad and at home. Too often books on national security view the subject from the perspective of a specific niche or based upon the analysis of a particular field of expertise, be it military, cyber terrorism, political risk, et al. This effort hopes to provide the reader with an understanding of the broad array of elements that form the global threat vector and the basic principles and concepts that distinguish and define them.

This book is intended as a core text for courses of security studies. Upper level undergraduate and graduate students will gain an understanding of the morphing threat and the forces driving change. Readers will also learn about the current apparatus in place to counter the vulnerability. In contrast, much of the literature on security studies is anthologies. Many of these edited volumes provide an overview of a broad subject area from the perspective of individual viewpoints and experience. Although they unearth some profound questions and relevant themes facing the current global security paradigm, the sum is often nothing more than the assemblage of separate and distinct parts. Unlike most texts on this subject, this book is more than a collection of readings. It is an attempt at a sustained analysis of the current arena of conflict and the competition over political and economic control by state and non-state actors, as well as how instruments of the new warfare have leveled the playing field for a broader range of participants.

The book begins by addressing the contemporary setting and context for security issues today. After some historical background, we look at the problem of asymmetry—the effective use of weaker force against a superior advantage in material and manpower. One theme the book raises is that because of the legacy structure and system of a national security and defense establishment, which resulted from the demands of World War II and developed in response to the perceived imperatives of the Cold War, we still practice industrial age warfare in the information age. The chapters in Part 1 discuss the current national security establishment and explore issues regarding the incompatibility between the threat and the structures organized to meet the challenges. A central problem is that most national militaries are locked into an outdated system of governance, protocols, and jurisdictional and philosophical boundaries. Policy lags behind precedent under these circumstances. Defensive strategies lag behind a morphing offensive.

Part 2 turns to the emerging challenges. The chapters on the maritime supply chain discuss the nature of the threats and the vulnerability they pose to political and economic stability. Eighty to ninety percent of world trade is seaborne. The maritime trade transport system remains a major integrant of the global economy and source of unending concern for logistic specialists, security professions, and proponents of frictionless trade. In order to provide sharper relief to the dilemma of security versus trade, the section examines topics on containerization, targeting methods, risk calculation, and the issue of commercial transparency within a democracy. In calculating the dangers and risks, these chapters investigate not just the vulnerabilities but also the solution set from sensor technology and tracking software to research in algorithmic theory and data exploitation methodology.

As a result of competing concerns and special interests, security approaches in maritime trade often rely on layered defense and consequence management. However, while these regimens have been in place for years, the debate on their effectiveness and future utility is reviving. Many subject matter experts question the current security framework and their arguments appear in the discussion. Meanwhile, the supply chain remains at risk and its security is an evolving art as world commerce grows in volume and intensity.

Chapters 6 and 7 examine the key threats to cybersecurity. Cyberspace has become the new field of battle. Because it is the core of critical infrastructure and industrial control systems, the electronic medium is a target for adversaries, whether they be hostile states, criminals, terrorists, or disgruntled employees. The power grid is decentralized, aging, and susceptible to blackouts. The U.S. reliance on these systems and the increasing demand of the digital economy make the quality of life vulnerable. Overall, the cybersecurity threat is outpacing the attempts at a solution. Cyber war and cybercrime employ the same weapons and require the same skills. However, the skills and weapons may now be for sale. The world may be at the onset of an interstate war among past Cold War rivals and, simultaneously, engaged in an asymmetric conflict of non-state players who all have access and the means to become peer forces.

The collusion between terrorism and cross-border crime networks is the topic of chapters 9 and 10. This is a critical area often given short shrift in most standard texts in courses on national security. Although there is no evidence of any grand strategy of terrorists and criminals locking arms against their legitimate counterparts, motives and opportunities exist around the world for their collusion. The growth of the global economy, communication/computer networks and the volume of information transmitted have fueled scientific advancement, but also complicates the threat vector as crime insinuates itself in the political process and terrorists become more entrepreneurial. The struggle to adapt to a new and perilous environment has strained the capacity to think anew and to form efficient partnerships within government and between the private and public sectors. These changes arose from the natural and irresistible forces of technological development and advancement and high volume trade. Yet, those outside the law have benefited as well. Terrorists and criminals take advantage of the same tools and mechanisms of the global economy as do legitimate actors. Therefore, the opportunity to create wealth and engage in plunder exists side by side.

As the last entries among the list of new threats and challenges to national security, chapters 11 through 13 survey the issues and vulnerabilities relative to the chemical, biological, radiological, and nuclear threat. These agents and their weaponized devices represent impending perils. Unlike the supply chain, electronic networks, and the collaboration of crime and terrorism in undermining licit markets and political stability, CBRN threats are not routine and their use has been mostly seen in isolated instances. Since World War I bio-chemical warfare has not been deployed on a mass scale. There was limited use in World War II, some noted regional conflicts in the Mid East, and a few foiled terrorist events. However, the 1994 Bhopal industrial leak from a Union Carbide production plant that affected nearly 600,000 people demonstrated the potential for disaster that a commercial facility can pose from accidents or by mismanagement. Contributing to the risk is the fact that duel-use applications of these substances make them easy to purchase and smuggle. Usually, small amounts are all that is needed to create a strategic event and raise public alarm to a level of mass chaos and even political instability. Compounding the CBRN threat are the advancements in chemical and biological sciences, which are aided by advancement in information/communication technology. Never has so much information been available. Never has there been a greater instance of commoditization of duel-use goods and technology. Never has there been a greater opportunity for misuse of technical expertise and potentially hazardous material.

This is true for nuclear weapons production as well. Since the first deployment of a nuclear bomb nearly seventy years ago, the basics in the manufacturing of crude nuclear weapons devices are reasonably well known and available through research. Furthermore, as with many other hazardous agents there exists a black market in radioactive and fissile material. Designs, real-time technical advice, and thousands of sensitive parts are also accessible through similar channels. Hence, the rate of progress is accelerating in all sciences and, therefore, the volume of information increases and the level of expertise expands. As skills and hazardous materials commoditize, the ability to defend against CBRN attacks is under pressure to gain ground. In this scenario the strategic edge may gradually favor the ability by terrorists to launch an assault and escape capture and retaliation.

In the background of these events, many population segments have become victims of poverty. Economic globalization policies from above, such as structural adjustment programs, privatization strategies, and other IMF and World Bank-imposed reform projects, are often agents of this spreading poverty. The debt trap now being experienced by the developing world has unleashed global migration on a mass scale. Ethnic groups, indigenous populations, religious sects, etc., have the ability to traverse the globe while maintaining ties with identities, cultures, belief systems, and devotions or hatreds. They remain connected with their communities and worldviews by the instruments of technology and globalization, which reduce the importance and relevance of geographic distances and the effectiveness of borders. The same tools that can inspire and empower marginalized populations can also make them prey to terrorist and criminal enterprises and conspiracies.

As a partial solution to the new security dilemma, Part 3 examines and suggests policy recommendations to existing industrial and defense strategy. The private sector can play a key role in national defense; however, pressures of just-in-time processing often crowd out the concerns for security. Financial constraints and the absence of a perceivable, overt threat often leave fallow the will and actions to commit resources. The infrastructure is aging. The threat is growing and morphing. Under such pressures government and commerce are partners. The convergence of functions should, therefore, reflect a confluence of policies—industrial, defense, fiscal, and diplomatic.

The concluding chapter also discusses the potential benefits of merging industrial policy and defense policy into a more holistic approach. The forces of globalization and international trade, persistent hatred, and an environment of economic and democratic deficits create unfamiliar security threats and smoldering tensions. National defense, worldwide, might be better served when security becomes a part of the core business process. However, incentives are still lacking and security investments are not seen as directly converting into earnings. With some well-known and time-tested industrial improvement processes, this chapter suggests there is opportunity to change the business model so that it serves the purposes of national security and, at the same time, the enablement of commerce. The section suggests a combination of tax incentives, market mechanisms, and a stricter application of regulatory oversight as the possible start of a new direction and restructuring of national defense. The hope is that under the right conditions a refreshed collaboration between government and industry might emerge to strengthen a vital public good—national defense.

While focusing on these threats to national security, globalization is a fixed theme and subtext to these separate threat topics. In addition to its myriad interpretations and nuances, the process of globalization also means a reordering of notions of governance and claims of authority as well as the hyper-connectivity of human relations in commerce and social life. The topics discussed above are the main issues that make and influence the current global security environment. These elements are organically linked, and the purpose of this research is to introduce readers to the broad array of threats and the vulnerabilities of a sclerotic system that often finds conflict within itself and reactive more often than self-enacting. It is also hoped that this book will encourage students and professionals to consider their particular expertise, experience, and skills against the backdrop of the greater reality of a perilous world. The concepts discussed, hopefully, provide a stronger grasp of the factors that contribute to the inner rhythms of state-to-state relations, the threat and competition from state and non-state actors and that it does so in a way that is informative and with a language that makes new concepts accessible.

Part I

The Establishment and the National Security Environment

Chapter One

The National Security Establishment

The nightmare of the modern state is the hugeness of the bureaucracy, and the problem is how to get coherence and design in it.
—Henry Kissinger

The function of national security and the responsibility of its establishment are to create and maintain a favorable environment for United States' national interests—in times of both war and peace. Those interests include the defense of the country's territory, access to global commodity and goods markets, and the pursuit of American values. It is a vast enterprise. The U.S. homeland occupies a continent with a territorial coastline of over 12,000 miles. The U.S. border with Canada is the largest unguarded border in the world. The national economy is approximately fifteen trillion and represents one quarter of world GDP. The U.S. economy also represents 16 percent of global imports and supplies nearly 9 percent of the world's exports.[1] Adding further onus to the responsibility is the fact that the term *American values* can be elusive. It undergoes interpretations as time advances, advocacy groups express their social views with discordant voices, and events abroad affect politics at home. Former Secretary of State Dean Acheson attempted to give definition to the expression, *American values*, by asserting it involved the fostering and preservation of: "an environment in which free societies may exist and flourish."[2] The standards of freedom, however, are left open and in the mind of the assessor. Amid these pressures the national security establishment rose. It designs policy and pursues its goals in the face of rising tensions and a freely flowing system of goods and ideas. At the same time a skills and technology revolution has been taking place affecting human affairs across the globe.

National defense includes a wide swathe of the U.S. economy. Today the U.S. defense's industrial base is worth trillions and employs millions (over

3.5 million direct, indirect, and induced workers in the aerospace industry alone[3]). Deputy Defense Secretary William J. Lynn III told a crowd in May 2012: "Today's defense industrial base is more global, more commercial and more financially complex and competitive than ever before."[4]

To understand how the national defense and security establishment has evolved we must remember that prior to World War II there was neither a national military industrial base nor a standing military. Upon the outbreak of World War II, the United States military ranked sixteenth in the world and on par with Portugal in terms of readiness and capacity. From 1812 to World War II the government relied on its own arsenals to produce and supply its shipyards and ordnance requirements. The private sector filled the gap during surge periods and demobilized during times of peace. During World War I the United States would have to depend on French and British industries to supply its military needs. Eventually, this "arsenal system" would be replaced to meet the demands of a two-front war with Germany and Japan. A paradigm shift and a break with history occurred when U.S. weapons production and design shifted to private firms and universities. An "enduring partnership of science, industry, and the military"[5] formed to create Franklin D. Roosevelt's *Arsenal of Democracy*, and abides today but is on the brink of another paradigm shift.

The onset of the Cold War and North Korean dictator Kim Il-sung's invasion of South Korea initially forged this "enduring partnership." U.S. leadership response to the postwar era was a determination to create "an international system with American power at its center."[6] The chief architects of the grand strategy were President Harry Truman, Dean Acheson, George Kennan, George Marshall, and Paul Nitze. Irving Stewart, deputy director of the wartime Office of Scientific Research and Development, wrote in 1947 of the effort to bring civilian science into the field of arms development and strategy:

> Modern science has progressed to the point where the military chieftains were not sufficiently acquainted with its possibilities to know for what they might ask with a reasonable expectation that it could be developed. The times called for a reversal of the situation, namely letting men who knew the latest advances in science become more familiar with the needs of the military in order that they might tell the military what was possible in science so that together they might assess what should be done.[7]

Part of the postwar reorganization included the establishment of the county's first "think tank," the RAND Corporation. Originally, RAND (a contraction for research and development) was a subsidiary of Douglas Aircraft. As a result of discussions within the U.S. War Department and industry leaders, a project was born to connect military planning with R&D. RAND was established, and from that point forward civilian strategists began to take leading roles in not only the development of weaponry, but also the philosophical ideas concerning their use. The partnership between government and the private sector was taking shape and its interdependency becoming permanent. Today the scale and range of U.S. contractors are vast and international. One half of the DoD's budget, over \$300 billion, goes to private sector contractors.[8] That number may grow proportionately as the Department of Defense comes under pressure to reduce its budget by cutting personnel.

As the events unfurled during this reorganization, the United States' tradition of non-involvement in international affairs was coming to an end. On March 12, 1947, President Harry Truman laid down his appeal and outline before the U.S. Congress for the postwar era. His argument for an aggressive response to the emerging communist threat would become known as the *Truman Doctrine*. It was a call to resist the efforts of totalitarian regimes wishing to impose their systems on free countries and, thus, destabilize international peace and the security of the United States.[9] The Truman doctrine, hence, set the justification for American intervention in foreign affairs. The same basic rationale has been used by succeeding administrations—even after the collapse of the Soviet Union and the fall of communism in Eastern Europe.

Today the U.S. military is charged with not only defending the homeland and its country's interests abroad, but in addition often serves as a peacekeeping force in violent regions around the world. The U.S. Navy also protects the sea-lanes and defends the shipping routes. As a result of the above, the sprawl of U.S. defense contractors seems endless. Furthermore, in a commercial age when nearly all manufactured goods have dual use application (consumer and military usage) the situation and culture becomes more complex. The structure, strategy, and policies of U.S. national security have impact for nearly every nation, and the numbers reflect American dominance. The International Institute for Strategic Studies estimated in 2011 that the U.S. defense budget "accounts for 45.7 percent of total spending by the world's 171 governments and territories."[10] Furthermore, not only are the suppliers to the American arsenal U.S. companies, but procurement also involves a global list of foreign manufacturers and service providers.

Over time the relationship between the military and the private sector has evolved and been politicized. Privatization of many government functions, technological innovation, and the reassessment of national interests have changed the nature of the attack/defense surface, altered the character of risk, and reoriented strategic focus. Through these crosscurrents, American national security navigates its way and seeks its appropriate levels of urgency alongside other national imperatives and competing interests. Additionally, as it rises to the challenge of a changing global political landscape, the national security establishment often finds adjustment difficult. Agility in policy formulation is not an intrinsic feature for democratic governments or the large institutions that provide the framework. The instinctive resistance to change is a prime contributor to "the nightmare of the modern state" Kissinger evokes. The challenge is made more difficult by the breakneck speed of technological advancement. In this environment, policy trails events more so now than at any other previous time.

A BRIEF HISTORY OF THE STRUCTURE

The end of World War II placed the United States in a position of unrivaled superiority. The United States was untouched by the destruction and scourge of the war. Its industrial base was healthy and eclipsed all others in capacity. Technologically, the United States was also unsurpassed. The strategic edge of its modest atomic weapons arsenal made its military position unchallengeable and the collective security apparatus of the United Nations seemed to signal a period of relative peace—despite the growing tensions between the East and West.

The country was eager to demilitarize. From 1945 to 1947 the United States reduced the number of those in uniform from a wartime peak of 12 million to the level of 1.4 million. However, the weakened condition of postwar Europe led to fears of Soviet expansion. The annexation of Eastern Europe into the Soviet sphere and the USSR's aggressive intentions toward Turkey, Greece, Iran, and the Far East forced the United States to consider new strategic options as it attempted to demobilize from the war. The National Security Act of 1947 was an outcome of those pressures. Once passed, the legislation fundamentally reorganized the structure of the defense and national security community. A prime element of the transformation was the creation of the office of the secretary of defense to replace the War Department. The successor organization now had oversight of the military establishment and the authority and responsibility to provide overall strategic vision. [11]

Under the Secretary of Defense, an alignment of the military services with foreign policy making and intelligence operations took form. The new configuration represented a conceptual overhaul of the American approach to national security. Each branch of the military had its own department and an independent Air Force was added as a separate armed service. [12] The act also established the Central Intelligence Agency (CIA), the National Security Agency (NSA), the Defense Intelligence Agency (DIA), the National Reconnaissance Office (NRO), as well as other intelligence and reconnaissance related agencies within the Department of Defense (DoD). Establishing a clear line and unity of command, removing duplicate functions, and coordinating research and engineering efforts was the goal of the bill's sponsors and the planners of the reorganization.

As part of this reorganization, the bill created the National Security Council (NSC) as a forum to assist the president in coordinating defense policy and foreign policy. Presently, the council's statutory members are the president, the vice president, the secretary of defense, and the secretary of state. Statutory advisors are the Director of National Intelligence and the Chairman of the Joint Chiefs of Staff. The National Security Advisor, formally known as the Assistant to the President on National Security Affairs, is a member with unique status.

While the president chairs the NSC, the National Security Advisor is a special counsel. Appointed by the president without the need of Senate approval, the freedom from the constraint of congressional consent allows the National Security Advisor to offer counsel with some degree of independence from partisan politics. As well, because of the proximity to the president, the holder of this position often has protection from the inner politics of the executive branch. Over the course of various administrations, the influence of this position depends upon the force of personality of the office holder and his relationship with the president. McGeorge Bundy, who served under presidents Kennedy and Johnson, was the first National Security Advisor to wield considerable power. However, his influence paled compared to that of Henry Kissinger and Zbigniew Brzezinski, which many observers claimed often undermined the sitting secretaries of state.[13]

The NSC also includes the Director of the CIA, other key officials when subject matter falls under their jurisdiction (i.e., Treasury, economic policy, Office of Budgetary Management, Attorney General, etc.), and various presidential appointees, which must be approved by the Senate. The role of the NSC is to help coordinate the country's security assets and formulate policy. Together with the Department of Defense and the Department of State it is among the three power clusters, which form what is known as the "policy triad." Their interaction with the president and with each other establishes the direction of national security policy. Put into other words: "The policy triad is the fulcrum around which the policy process revolves."[14]

Ideally, the council gives the president a structure and system for weighing strategic and policy options. It also is a roundtable for harmonizing diplomatic and military issues. In reality, depending upon the leadership style and view of the world, each administration puts its stamp on the NSC with respect to its role, influence, and the nature of its interaction with the office of the President and the larger national security community. In establishing their distinct *modus operandi*, presidents cast the NSC according to their own predispositions. President Truman mostly relied upon advice from Dean Acheson, his Secretary of State, for foreign policy decisions, whereas Dwight Eisenhower put into place a more elaborate staff structure that mirrored his military experience. Succeeding administrations from Johnson to the present fluctuated between collegial, informal styles of management and formal policy-making machinery and modes. In more recent history, the Bush administration came to value the loyalty and advice of a close circle. Critics claimed this approach diminished the benefits of dissenting views in shaping foreign policy and military operations.[15] Regardless of its varying nature, the NSC has played a central role in the policy decisions that impact U.S. national security. For over sixty years and throughout ten presidencies, the NSC continues to be a driver in the policy-making process; where prior to its founding, national security policy was uncoordinated or existed in a void. Despite improvements over the previous structure, internal problems still arise.[16] The dilemma resulting from a diffused and uncoordinated bureaucracy is hard to overcome and will probably be a systemic problem for at least the near future.

As opposed to the National Security Council whose chief advisor is appointed and serves independently from political pressure, the Department of State and the Department of Defense have substantial ties to Congress. For better or for worse, these linkages bring to bear the pressures of domestic politics to the national security policy-making process. While the State advises and conducts operations related to foreign policy and DoD performs the same functions with regard to defense policy, the two bureaucracies often clash on policy when there is overlap. By the nature of their history, organizational culture, and institutional orientation, the departments of State and

Table 1.1 The National Security Establishment

Defense can find themselves in stark disagreement. This is particularly the case as DoD has become more focused on organizing the military as an instrument of flexible response rather than a purely retaliatory force. Since the end of the Cold War, the U.S. military has found itself involved in more frequent multilateral efforts, humanitarian missions, and law enforcement operations. These assignments require diplomatic skills in addition to combat readiness. As a result, many experts in the national security field see the marginalization of the State Department within the policy triad.

The current U.S. national security structure is from the same blueprint as the one drawn over half a century ago. With some exceptions, the Goldwater-Nichols Reorganization Act being the most notable,[17] the apparatus that stood throughout the duration of the Cold War remains basically intact today. Until September 11, 2001, structure and strategy aligned according to the framework designed by the architects of the Truman administration. The jolt of the catastrophic attacks on the World Trade Center and Pentagon, however, shook the establishment and nation to the core. During the investigations of the attack on the World Trade Center, the 9/11 Commission Report uncovered findings, which were startling revelations to some, and yet, the confirmed fears of others. Among them was the following observation: "As presently configured, the national security institutions of the U.S. are still the institutions constructed to win the Cold War."[18] Despite the warnings, the United States was mostly organized and prepared to fight the last war. The 9/11 Commission report went on to say that the new conflict requires a quicker, more imaginative, and agile response.

In response to the 9/11 tragedy the United States would attempt to reorganize its national security establishment again. In terms of personnel and adaptive strategies, the largest reorganization of the security community since 1947 occurred in 2002. The founding of the Department of Homeland Security (DHS) created a new cabinet level department. The move intended to place the responsibility of homeland security under a single organizational body that would improve information and intelligence sharing, enhance national preparedness and resiliency, and incorporate an all-hazards approach as a constituent element. Such extensive reorganization came with fears of governmental overreach, abuse of power, and questions of whether a federal administrative body was up to the task of such a managerial challenge. Since the creation of DHS, there have been successes but critics still point to weaknesses in program development, interoperability, execution, and even organizational culture. Although the size of the restructuring was on a grand scale, the foundations of the earlier national security edifice are still in place, and it is yet to be determined whether the presumed effectiveness has been achieved.

THE NEW SECURITY REORGANIZATION

The month following the attack of 9/11 President George Bush signed an executive order establishing the Office of Homeland Security and the Homeland Security Council. Headed by Tom Ridge, former Governor of Pennsylvania, the Office of Homeland Security became the central agency in charge of coordinating and implementing a national strategy for securing the United States from future terrorist attacks.[19]

The Homeland Security Council was and is an advisory body that meets at the discretion of the president. Its function is to advise the President on all matters relevant to homeland security. Its membership includes the assistant to the president on homeland security, the vice president, the director of the CIA, secretary of defense, secretary of treasury, secretary of health and human services, attorney general, director of the FBI, secretary of transportation, and the director of the Federal Emergency Management Agency (FEMA). It is an entity within the Executive Office of the president and is counterpart to the National Security Council. As with the NSC, membership includes statutory and non-statutory members.

The 9/11 attack and subsequent creation of these organizations lifted the concept of homeland security to a new level of comprehension and sense of apprehension in government and among the American public. During the Cold War, the purview of homeland security belonged to the realm of federal, state, and local agencies. Border protection, public health, disaster management, law enforcement, and counter-espionage were mostly themes and terrain separate from the notion, undertaking, and study of national security. However, events of the 1990s spawned a concern within government over the potential of terrorist attacks. The 1993 bombing of the World Trade Center, the bombing of the Murrah Federal Building in Oklahoma City in 1995, attacks on U.S. embassies in Kenya and Tanzania in 1998, and the 2000 assault on the USS *Cole* in Yemen created a conclusive body of evidence of a growing threat from networks of terrorist groups who could strike from anywhere in the world and within the United States. Suddenly U.S. national interests were no longer in Europe, Japan, or in remote corners of the world, but rather at the ports, along the energy and communication grids, within the food supply, the health system, iconic structures, and anywhere an attack would mean a destruction or disruption of life and daily routine.

Also at large in the world was access to the materials and expertise required to assemble weapons of mass destruction. The disintegration of the Soviet Union boosted the potential threat from the proliferation of chemical, biological, radiological, and nuclear (CBRN) materials. The leakage of trained scientists and engineers from defunct government programs as a result of a bankrupt economic system led to the dissemination of technical personnel circulating the world in search of new homes for their skills. A global black market (currently in an estimate range of $10 trillion[20]) and the availability of information through open sources or via corruptible channels heightened the sense of alarm. Against the backdrop of these events and circumstances, the security community began to consider the nation's ability to avert and mitigate the consequences of terrorist attacks. Those concerns concretized on September 11, 2001.

In 2002, Congress signed into law the establishment of the Department of Homeland Security as a new cabinet department (subsuming the Office of Homeland Security). The reorganization of national security assets aligned to fight a Cold War now were being reassessed and restructured to combat the global war on terrorism. In all, twenty-two existing federal agencies re-formed as sub-departments under DHS. A total of over 180,000 employees made the new department, instantly, the third largest in the U.S. government. The Office of Homeland Security dissolved under DHS and the 2001 PA-TRIOT (Providing Appropriate Tools Required to Intercept and Obstruct Terrorism) Act was being implemented to grant the government new security and surveillance powers. Expanded authority under the PATRIOT Act in-cluded the legal right to monitor credit card transactions, telephone calls, academic transcripts, drug prescriptions, driving licenses, bank accounts, air-line tickets, parking permits, websites, and e-mails.

The re-mobilization also involved the creation of the U.S. Northern Com-mand. USNORTHCOM is one of the nine combatant commands under the Department of Defense and operates to centralize homeland defense activ-ities. It provides military assistance to civil authorities on the continental United States, Alaska, Puerto Rico, the U.S. Virgin Islands, Mexico, and Canada. The *Posse Comitatus* Act, which restricts the role of the U.S. mili-tary in domestic affairs, regulates its operations.[21] However, Congress can allow for exceptions to *Posse Comitatus* in the event of a national disaster or emergency.

Another outcome from the recommendations by the 9/11 Commission Report was the establishment of the office of the Director of National Intelli-gence. The Intelligence Reform and Terrorist Prevention Act of 2004 created the position of the Director of National Intelligence (DNI), in effect, replac-ing the director of the CIA as the principal advisor on intelligence matters. With its implementation, the bill created another layer of bureaucracy atop the intelligence community structure.[22] How this will provide a centralized coordination process and a more efficient pattern of operation for intelligence gathering remains, yet, unanswered.[23] A major criticism of the reorganiza-tion is the fact that the NSA and the Defense Intelligence Agency (DIA), although having reporting responsibility to the DNI, are outside the control of that agency. The illogicality is apparent to many. Combined, these two organizations, NSA and DIA, account for 80 percent of the government's intelligence budget.[24] Together, they represent a major constituent and contribution to the intelligence community. Part of the DNI's role includes control over the national intelligence budget, but the main collection agencies remain within DoD. As Senator John Rockefeller put it:

> We gave the DNI the authority to build the national intelligence budget, but we left the execution of the budget with the agencies. We gave the DNI tremendous responsibility. The question is, did we give the DNI enough authority to exercise his responsibility?[25]

Nevertheless, although the CIA continues to be the primary intelligence agency, the Director of National Intelligence is the chief coordinator and chief advisor to the president on intelligence matters. The responsibilities of this office are quite considerable. Not only must the DNI maintain a coordinated working relationship across the broad spectrum of all U.S. intelligence-gathering agencies, he or she must also establish working relationships with foreign intelligence services. These may include, occasionally, adversary states as well as allies. The new structure, for now, depends upon the managerial and diplomatic skills of the director.[26] Until an atmosphere of trust and familiarity settles in, tensions will haunt the arrangement, the structure, and inhibit efficiency.

A constant of the intelligence community, regardless of structure, is the intelligence-gathering process itself. What is referred to as the *intelligence cycle* is a process of five steps for converting raw information or data into actionable intelligence for use by policy makers in decision making.[27] Those steps include (1) planning and direction, (2) collection, (3) processing, (4) analysis and production, and (5) dissemination. Requests for intelligence are either *ad hoc* or standing requests. Usually they originate with the National Security Council, but other agencies and departments are also natural clients. The methods of intelligence gathering are standard as well. They include:

- Open source intelligence (OSINT)
- Human intelligence (HUMINT)
- Signals intelligence (SIGINT)
- Measurement and signature intelligence (MASINT)
- Imagery intelligence (IMINT)
- Geospatial intelligence (GEOINT)

Prior to the global war on terrorism, intelligence gathering has mostly been a matter for foreign policy rather than domestic policy.[28] However, the events on 9/11 revealed a new urgency. The Bush administration recognized a need for effective information sharing and integration of intelligence from not only foreign and electronic surveillance operations, but also links with local law enforcement. There are constitutional restrictions about spying on U.S.

citizens. Therefore, the PATRIOT Act's expansion of government authority in redefining terrorist-related crimes and facilitating information sharing between local law enforcement and the intelligence communities—raised harsh criticism.[29] The act provides for congressional oversight, yet despite this provision opponents warn of the possibility for abuse of individual privacy rights.[30] These arguments have been tested in the courts, successfully in varying degrees.

Although the FBI is the primary government agency charged with counter intelligence responsibilities, several other government offices provide assistance to that effort. Within DHS is the Office of Intelligence Analysis. This department oversees operations throughout DHS and works to coordinate all elements of the intelligence community and between state and local authorities. Additionally, state and major area fusion centers are intelligence-gathering stations at the sub-federal level that focus on situational awareness and threat analysis. Not only do fusion centers concentrate on working to pursue, disrupt, and identify precursor crime and activity relative to emerging terrorist threats, they also work with private-sector personnel and public safety officials on critical infrastructure protection, disaster recovery, and emergency response events.[31]

These methods of police-led intelligence operations are unique to the traditions of a previous era. Although a panoptic view of the entire arrangement of disparate parts of the intelligence-gathering process is not yet in place according to vision, glimpses of what may be possible are emerging. One benefit to this bottom/up approach to intelligence gathering is it can be a check against the reverse procedure of the top/down regimen, which can lead to a system of self-serving conveniences "enmeshed in meaningless operations, committed more to bureaucratic efficiency than to the purpose of intelligence."[32] We have seen through past examples, such as the Cold War arms race and the invasion of Iraq, how the mixture of policy formulation and policy advocacy at the top have corrupted the process and contorted it into a situation of tails wagging dogs.

It was originally hoped that by employing the perspective of local authorities, such a method might ease that risk at the center and the potential for adverse outcomes based upon distorted analysis. Unfortunately, according to a U.S. Senate subcommittee, these sub-federal intelligence fusion centers have not fulfilled their touted promise. A 2012 report accused the majority of the nationwide network of seventy-seven centers as producing "irrelevant, useless, inappropriate intelligence reporting to the DHS"[33] The debate continues between the detractors and defenders of police-led intelligence. The rift underscores the coordination problems across the intelligence community and the patience required if these issues are going to be resolved.

A BALANCE BETWEEN DOMESTIC AND FOREIGN AFFAIRS

National security policy must also justify the commitment of domestic resources to the international sphere for the benefit and security of the homeland. Therefore, the policy decision-making process is subject to pressures
from both domestic and foreign affairs.

As Samuel Huntington puts it in describing the sources of influence on
policy making:

> One is international politics, the world of balance of power, wars and alliances,
> the subtle and brutal uses of force and diplomacy to influence the behavior of
> other states. The other world is domestic politics, the world of interest groups,
> political parties, social classes with their conflicting interests and goals. [34]

Department of Homeland Security	President Director of National Intelligence			Homeland Security Council
Management	-Deputies-			• Homeland Security Advisor
Science & Technology	•Collection•Analysis•Acquisition			
Policy	•Policy plans & requirements			• Vice President
National Protection & Programs				• Secretary of Treasury
General Council	CIA	Army	NGO	
Legislative Affairs	DIA	Navy	DEA	• Secretary of Defense
Public Affairs	NSA	USM	FBI	
Inspector General	NRO	C	DoE	• Attorney General
Health Affairs	INR	USAF	Treasury/	• Secretary of Health and Human Services
Operations Coordination	DHS/	USCG	TFI	
Citizenship & Immigration Serv.	Intel			• Secretary of Transportation
Chief Privacy Officer				
Civil Rights & Civil Liberties				• Administrator of FEMA
Counter Narcotics Enforcement				• Director, FBI
Federal Law Enforcement Training				• Director, CIA
Domestic Nuclear Detection				
Transportation Security Administration				
US Customs & Border Protection				
Immigration and Customs Enforcement				
US Secret Service				
US Coast Guard				
Federal Emergency Management Agency (FEMA)				
Intelligence & Analysis				

Table 1.2 The Homeland Security Establishment

Reconciling the two imperatives is a delicate political balancing act. Despite the constructs, structure, and mechanisms in place to coordinate implementation, operations, information sharing, and consensus, national security policy is a changing organizational panorama with many elements. This phantasmagoria is subject to the onslaught of crises, turnover of administrations, the public discourse, and the bureaucratic "nightmare." It relies on a labyrinthine system of formal and informal meetings by top-level principals and senior advisors, subordinate councils, and working groups. Unlike the budgetary process, it is a system of processes without any strict adherence to rules or timelines. Adding to the intricacies of its coordination nightmare: "The processes used to support major decisions have differed significantly across administrations and even within the same administration on different issues."[35] It is as complex as it is fascinating.

Aggravating the policy-making process is the friction between the State and the DoD. Over the years the relationship and tension between the State Department and the Department of Defense has evolved and devolved. Founded in 1789, the Department of State is the older organization, while the current structure and mission of Defense has only been in operation since 1947. Because of the influence of technology and the preference to use the military as a diplomatic instrument in peacekeeping missions, many suggest the DoD is the more adaptable and flexible. These assessments and the view that the State Department is less agile and innovative in policy formulation due to the changing landscape of classic interstate relations, has helped to further marginalize it.[36] However, these historical trends are more cyclical than linear and we have already noted that events not only influence circumstances but also can influence personalities. The calculus of the future roles and mass of working parts of the national security establishment is that they are as subject to alteration as are the forces around them. The unending waves of technology and a less visible adversary create greater challenges that "surpass the boundaries of traditional nation-states."[37] How well the U.S. security establishment reorients will depend upon its leadership, a vision, efficiencies and competencies, and perhaps a modicum of luck.

NOTES

1. WTO, "World Trade in 2005—Overview," in Amos A. Jordan, *et al.*, American National Security, Sixth Edition, Johns Hopkins University Press, Baltimore, MD, 2008.

2. Dean Acheson as quoted in "Ends and Means," *Time Magazine.* December 18, 1964. Also see Jordan, p. 233.

3. The Aerospace and Defense Industry in the U.S.: a financial and economic impact study, Deloitte, March 2012.

4. American Forces Press Service, May 12, 2011, http://www.defense.gov/news/newsarticle.aspx?id=63913.

5. *Ibid.*

6. Deloitte.

7. *Ibid.*

8. Ben Freeman, *Third Way*, interview with author (29 July 2013).

9. Henry T. Nash, *American Foreign Policy: A Response to a Sense of Threat*, Dorsey Press, 1973 in Jordan.

10. Winslow Wheeler, "The Military Imbalance: How the U.S. Outspends the World," http://defense.aol.com/2012/03/16/the-military-imbalance-how-the-u-s-outspends-the-world/.

11. Amos, p. 45.

12. To help quell inter-service rivalries the law was later amended in 1949 and reduced the service departments from cabinet posts to military departments, which reported to the chairman of the Joint Chiefs of Staff.

13. Sam C. Sarkesian, John Allen Williams, Stephen Cimbala, *U.S. National Security, Policymakers, Policies, and Politics*, Fourth Edition, Lynn Reinner Publishers, Inc., 2008, p. 83.

14. *Ibid*, p. 92.

15. *Encyclopedia of United States National Security*, Sage Publications, Thousand Oaks, CA, 2006, p. 501.

16. Sarkesian, p. 79.

17. The Goldwater-Nichols Department of Defense Reorganization Act of 1986 required the president to report to Congress, annually, the administration's national security strategy. The bill called for a streamlining of the operational chain of command and was a response to the failed rescue operation in Iran in 1980 and the 1983 invasion of Grenada.

18. *Final Report of the National Commission on Terrorist Attacks upon the United States*, W.W. Norton & Co., Inc., New York, 2002, p. 399.

19. *Encyclopedia of United States National Security*, p. 327.

20. Robert Nuewirth, The Shadow Superpower, *Foreign Policy*, October 28, 2011. http://www.foreignpolicy.com/articles/2011/10/28/black_market_global_economy

21. *Posse Comitatus* Act of 1878 restricts the use of U.S. troops in law enforcement operations. It was originally enacted to prevent local authorities from using federal troops in the post Civil War South to avoid the effect of an occupation army.

22. Jordan, p. 128.

23. Sarkesian, p. 145.

24. *Op. cit.*

25. Senate Select Committee on Intelligence, "The Nomination of Mike McConnell to be Director of National Intelligence," 110th Congress, First Session, February 1, 2007, 3.

26. Sarkesian, p. 148.

27. CIA, *Fact Book on Intelligence*, p. 13.

28. *Encyclopedia of United States National Security*, p. 358.

29. Jordan, p. 128.

30. Mark A. Sauter and James J. Carafano, *Homeland Security: A Complete Guide to Understanding, Preventing, and Surviving Terrorism*, McGraw-Hill, 2005.

31. http://www.dhs.gov/state-and-major-urban-area-fusion-centers.

32. Sarkesian, p. 155.

33. "DHS 'fusion centers' portrayed as pools of ineptitude, civil liberties intrusion" *Washington Post*, October 2, 2012.

34. Samuel P. Huntington, *The Common Defense*, Columbia University Press, 1961.

35. Jordan, p. 209.

36. Sarkesian, p. 102.

37. *Final Report of the National Commission on Terrorist Attacks upon the United States*, p. 399.

Chapter Two

Policies and Processes in the New Geopolitics

Policy founded upon error multiplies, never retreats.

—Barbara W. Tuchman

As discussed earlier, at the end of World War II, the U.S. found itself at the center of world affairs. In order to counter the Soviet threat, the authors of NSC-68 reassessed American foreign and defense policy and determined conditions required a long-term military buildup in "righting the power balance." Today the United States still holds center stage. However, the conflict arena is unfamiliar. It not only involves asymmetric and non-asymmetric armed conflict, but also cyber war and climate disruptions. It is, in a very true sense, an "all hazards" defense strategy. Poverty, migration trends, ecological disasters, organized crime, terrorism, regional conflicts, and disruptive technologies all have impact on U.S. national security. Any attempt to re-shape the future through foreign policy or national security strategy must consider the new geography of violence and upheaval within a mutating security structure of continuous political tension.

Under such conditions, the policy-making process is complex. Nonetheless, the 9/11 Commission Report emphatically made clear that the generation that experienced the 2001 catastrophe must match the effort of the earlier generation of Americans who restructured government to meet the challenges of the 1940s and 1950s. That security structure created a generation ago suits a world that no longer exists. The authors of the report also warn that incremental and *ad hoc* adjustments are inadequate. To date, the overhaul of the system has taken time and success is difficult to measure. The size of the bureaucracy, the scope of national security, and the forces of globalization all contribute to the enormity of the challenge. Despite the obstacles, the national security strategy has to stipulate, as accurately as possible, the nation's preparation against any of the potential onslaughts.

Among the challenges is the fact that the new era of warfare occurs in areas of failed or frail states. In these jurisdictions there are the virtual opposite conditions of legitimate functioning states. They can hoist a national flag, issue a national currency, and declare a right to sovereignty, but control over territory and their monopoly of violence erodes as the administrative apparatus collapses and becomes corrupt.[1] Modern warfare was an interstate battle between nations, which had no such issues, and hence victory was basically achieved with the military capture of territory. However, the mere capacity to "kill people and break things" no longer is the essence of these new military conflicts. The purpose of the asymmetric war effort is to continue the violence. Rather than the Clausewitzean motive to "compel an opponent to fill our will," the objective, often, is to spread panic and create disorder so that the conditions for economic, political, and criminal exploitation remain apposite. Civilian targets surpass military targets as strike objectives, while the military needs to respond as more than simply a combat force. To be effective, it requires diplomacy, law enforcement capabilities, technological skills, and the ability to administer humanitarian aid. Adapting national security policy to meet the needs of the new conflict arena requires flexibility and foresight.

THE EVOLUTION OF THE STRATEGY

To further understand the current form and substance of the U.S. national security establishment and processes it is important to understand the evolution of strategic policy. Since the Cold War, despite the influence of technology and the upheaval in inter-state relations, many institutional elements of earlier times abide compositionally and culturally. The structure erected to compete against former foes has deep roots. The challenges of communism as ideological alternative, Europe's state of exhaustion, and the economic and military dominance of the United States created a natural precondition for the United States to fill the hegemonic vacuum. At the end of World War Two policy elites scurried to address America's new responsibilities and advantages.

An intellectual consequence of the new international post-World War II environment was the strategic policy known as *containment*. The aim of containment policy was to restore the balance of power in postwar Europe, curtail the projection of Soviet power, and ultimately modify their conception of international relations.[2] George Kennan, the American diplomat and scholar, was the author of containment policy. Identifying himself as "X," Kennan laid out the details of his policy option in an article in *Foreign*

Affairs magazine. He wrote: "The main element of any United States policy toward the Soviet Union must be that of a long term, patient but firm and vigilant containment of Russian expansive tendencies."[3][4] He believed the USSR's fixed ideology, aging and inflexible state apparatus constrained the system and held it captive. The demands of allegiance and sacrifice placed upon the Soviet people at the costs of personal liberties and a demilitarized economy were too high. Therefore, Kennan viewed the Soviet system as fragile, and also predicted that any disruption of the "unity and efficacy" of the Communist Party was a political instrument to be exploited.[5] With the appropriate application of hard and soft power, Soviet Russia's institutionalized fortress mentality would, eventually, push the system to the brink of collapse. In order to facilitate the course of these events, Kennan counseled the United States to identify and defend only its most vital spheres of interest—Western Europe and Japan. Rather than engage in direct military confrontation, containment policy recommended the United States should use overt propaganda, covert operations, and even economic assistance to outlast its ideological foe.[6]

Containment policy attracted both controversy and appeal. Among its detractors was a group of policy analysts known as the *idealists*. These strategists felt containment did not go far enough in meeting the Soviet challenge. Their worldview was partly shaped by the events of 1948 and 1949. The forced communization of Czechoslovakia, the blockade of Berlin, and the conquest of mainland China by Chinese Communists raised tensions and re-ignited fears of another world war. The Soviet Union's detonation of their first nuclear device in August 1949 removed America's monopoly on atomic weapons and changed the dynamic of international relations with a single stroke. To these policy makers, experience was proving that containment was an inadequate response to the Soviet threat and required some intellectual revisionism.

The idealists felt containment lacked the militarization necessary to counter the Soviet Union's world ambitions, and the concession of peripheral interests imperiled United States access to production and supply markets in the developing world. These losses, they reasoned, would not only endanger the nation's defense posture, but also signal psychological defeats in the ideological struggle with communism.[7] They urged that the United States should create a force structure proportionate to its grand strategy of challenging Soviet aggression. Hence, in 1950, the government released a report known as NSC-68 (National Security Report), which set in motion a military buildup that would be sustained for decades. Its principal author was Paul H. Nitze, Director of Policy Planning for the Department of State. The secret document was a joint project of the State and Defense departments "to make an overall review and reassessment of American foreign and defense policy."[8] It advocated:

> An immediate and large scale build up in our military and general strength and
> that of our allies with the intention of righting the power balance and in the
> hope that through means other than all out war we could induce a change in the
> nature of the Soviet system.[9]

It was a plea, in other words, to raise defense spending far above the levels
originally set and committed to by the Truman administration at the close of
World War II. The Korean conflict applied the final pressure. Truman approved a new defense budget and the United States re-militarized. The Korean War put on the table three strategic goals for the defense community: (1)
immediate prosecution of the war in Korea; (2) the creation of a military base
ready for long-term mobilization; and (3) the development of a deterrence
force to keep in check Soviet attempts at expansion.[10] Within the few immediate years following the end of World War II, new circumstances forced a
mobilization of permanent war economy and the buildup of an imposing
national security structure. NSC-68 also declared the United States had the
right to claim scarce resources anywhere in the world in the name of national
security.[11] It was the basic U.S. foreign policy document of the Cold War. It
eventually put forward the concept of *deterrence* as the underlying principle
in foreign policy.

Rational deterrence theory posits the assumption that the target/player of
the deterrence is able to recognize the probability and benefits of an action
versus the cost of retaliation by its opponent if it does not comply with their
demands. The theory assumes the players are rational actors and the retaliator
has both the means and political will to carry through with its threat. To be
effective the threat must be clearly communicated and the retaliation costs
must outweigh the benefits resulting from the action—if perpetrated. In his
classic work *The Absolute Weapon*, Bernard Brodie expressed the new logic
of the Cold War: "Thus, far from the chief purpose of our military establishment has been to win wars. From now on its chief purpose is to avert them."

Tandem to the concept of deterrence is the idea of collective security.
Two historic instruments of the postwar era were the European Recovery Act
(ERA), or known more familiarly as the Marshall Plan, and the North Atlantic Treaty Organization (NATO). The Marshall Plan sought to rebuild an
economically devastated and war-ravaged Western Europe into a bulwark
against Soviet expansion. The judgment being that an economically robust
Europe would have an easier time resisting Soviet incursion, politically and
ideologically. With the benefit of $13 billion of U.S. economic aid, between
1948 and 1951 Western Europe experienced the fastest period of growth in
its history. During that time, industrial output rose by 35 percent and agriculture rebounded above prewar levels.[12] The program not only restored the
European economy, but also undercut the ideological appeal of communism,
which was growing in parts of southern Europe. Early observers claimed the

plan an unalloyed success. Critics claim it was an attempt by the United States to cast Europe in its own image. The consensus is the ERA program had a significant effect on European recovery, and is the definitive example of the benefits possible through soft power—in this case—economic assistance. [13]

In 1949, during the administration of the Marshall Plan, the United States and its European allies established the North Atlantic Treaty Organization (NATO). The NATO alliance institutionalized the doctrine of containment and placed the United States in the center of alliance politics. The organization saw itself as a collective security arrangement, where an attack on any member would be viewed as an attack upon all. It provided a joint command structure with joint planning capabilities and operations. [14] It relied on joint ground forces and the U.S. nuclear arsenal for strategic advantage. NATO was the first in a succession of pacts, which the United States formed and led. SEATO (Southeast Asia Treaty Organization), ANZUS (Australia/New Zealand/United States), and the Baghdad Pact are some of the strategic military pacts that would follow. Various bilateral defense agreements flourished and added to the collective security webbing intended to contain communist aggression.

Over time, while other alliance pacts and defense agreements may have withered away in influence and significance, NATO remains. It not only has outlived the Cold War, which was its original *raison d'être*, it expands. Since the collapse of the Soviet Union, NATO has increased its membership from twelve to twenty-eight, and extended the mission beyond its initial purpose. In addition to the task of defending member states it has moved into the area of crisis management. [15] The creation of the NATO Response Force and the organization's involvement in the conflict in the Balkans, the global war on terrorism and international piracy represent key developments and the evolution of the alliance. Upon its creation the alliance emphasized a challenge to Soviet aggression through collective security and deterrence. Since the end of the Cold War, NATO and the former Soviet Union have held discussions on a partner status. In 2002 the NATO-Russia Council (NRC) formed to address such topics as global terrorism, missile defense, and the proliferation of weapons of mass destruction. Many barriers and questions remain. Among them are not only the future of this potential partnership, but also the future of NATO. As the international arena changes, NATO and Russia will most likely undergo more stages of evolution.

As asserted above, underlying the entire security apparatus of these arrangements was the theory of deterrence. The earlier adherents of deterrence theory claim it helped the United States eventually prevail in the Cold War. Skeptics argue that the point is impossible to establish since the ultimate success is determined by non-events. Research into cognitive psychology contributes to the debate by suggesting that not all actors are "rational" in moments of crises. Furthermore, foreign policy decision makers are often subject to misperception, miscalculations, and prejudices, making the claims of deterrence theorists harder to substantiate.[16]

As an additional counterpoint, doubters of deterrence theory suggest that these approaches have had the opposite of the intended effects. The Cold War may have been extended by exaggerated threat assessments, which thrust the United States and the USSR into a protracted and, at times, irrational arms race.[17] In his farewell address, Eisenhower warned of such miscalculations and misallocations of power. The interplay between the "immense military establishment" and "a large arms industry" harbored, in his appraisal, a dual threat. Referring to the "military-industrial complex," the retiring president expressed his concerns about the cost of an arms race to the national economy and to democratic ideals.

In the councils of government, we must guard against the acquisition of unwarranted influence, whether sought or unsought, by the military-industrial complex. The disastrous rise of misplaced power will exist, and will persist.[18]

Any notion taken to the extreme runs a certain risk of miscarry. The security structure that stood for over fifty years was destabilizing above a shifting landscape. The shocking reality that burst forth violently from the 9/11 attacks exposed vulnerability in the force structure and an obsolescence of mindset. In the post-9/11 world of asymmetric conflict involving state, quasi-state, and non-state actors, George W. Bush cited the current shortcomings of deterrence at the 2002 graduation speech at West Point:

> deterrence . . . means nothing against shadowy terrorist networks with no nations or citizens to defend. Containment is not possible when unbalanced dictators with weapons of mass destruction can deliver those weapons on missiles or secretly provide them to terrorist allies.[19]

Alliance politics, collective security, and the definition of deterrence, as previously imagined, need rethinking. Inter-agency cooperation and interoperability across borders is a main focus. Conflict is asymmetric. U.S. adversaries are no longer solely other nation-states. They include stateless cell members, criminal organizations, entrepreneurial terrorists, and traditional allies and enemies. As well, U.S. vital national security interests are no longer as much the foreign markets and the remote corners of the world from where it extracts critical resources to support the economic machinery. The national interests are much closer to home. They dwell in data and computer banks, at the ports, along the supply chain, and in personal files. Defending them is not a matter of containing the enemy by limiting the rationale for an attack by dint of fear from retaliation. It will be, rather, a question of whether the United States can dissuade attacks due to its ability to restore functionality and recover from assault. In the post-Cold War era, resilience is the new deterrence. Retaliation is secondary when the aggressor's identity is uncertain, counterattack raises questions of legality, and the entire principle of *jus ad bellum* (a just war) is debatable.

AN ERA OF NEW WEAPONRY AND GEOPOLITICS

At a Unity Luncheon in Atlanta, Georgia, in 2002, George Bush said: "It used to be that the oceans would protect us. But that was all changed on September 11th." The president was referring to the global war on terrorism, and by implication announcing that the geopolitical rivalry was morphing into a new reality where the entire planet was a potential battle space. Using its own words, the *Quadrennial Defense Review* (2006) concurred with Bush's assessment:

> Throughout much of its history, the United States enjoyed a geographic position of strategic insularity. The oceans and uncontested borders permitted rapid economic growth and allowed the United States to spend little at home to defend against foreign threats. The advent of long-range bombers and missiles, nuclear weapons, and more recently of terrorist groups with global reach, fundamentally changed the relationship between U.S. geography and security. Geographic insularity no longer confers security. [20]

As technology was making the world smaller by crushing time and territory, it was also enabling state and non-state adversaries with the same tools. The incorporation of the latest technological advancements has always been a challenge for all militaries. In the post Cold War era, however, never has the pace of technological change been so great or geopolitics so complex. The term *Revolution in Military Affairs* (RMA) is a recurring and loose theme to describe the process of integrating technological innovations in weapon systems. In the discourse over RMA, primary focus is on the important changes created by computer technologies and communication systems. [21] The array of new generation weaponry was on display during the 1991 Gulf War. The use of "smart" weapons, which were supported by global positioning navigation systems and the latest IT technology allowed Allied forces in Operation Desert Storm to outmaneuver the opposition, destroy targets, and limit casualties. [22] This technology not only wrought changes in military arms, but also in military organization and culture.

Revolution in military affairs began to gain notice during the 1970s. The increasing accuracy and effect of new munitions at the end of the Vietnam War and in Middle East conflicts was observable. One noted observer was the Soviet Chief of Staff, Marshal Nikolai Ogarkov. In the 1980s Ogarkov wrote about the "military technical revolution" he was witnessing. He viewed the trend as a threat to Warsaw Pact forces whose major advantage was in the number of military assets, not in the technological or computerized sophistication of its weapons. Experts often cite Ogarkov's writings and warnings to his government as the genesis of the current thinking on RMA.[23] However, his views were not singular to him. In 1970, two years before the invention of the microchip, General William Westmoreland, testifying in Congress, reported on the USSR's fear of the United States' mounting advantage. He outlined his expectations for the nature of prospective military conflict:

> On the battlefield of the future, enemy forces will be located, tracked and targeted almost instantaneously through the use of data links, computer assisted intelligence evaluation, and automated fire control.

Thus, RMA refers the precision weapons and information technology of modern warfare needed to attain decisive military action without the need for large mobilized land forces. It is a "system of systems" often referred to as C4ISR (command, control, communication, computers, intelligence, surveillance, reconnaissance). C4ISR combines information collection, analysis, and transmission and weapons systems to create perfected mission assignment—or what others sarcastically have called "precision violence" or "just-in-time warfare."[24] The evolution of warfare technology creates a new fast-paced battlefield. Success on this battle-scape, ideally, requires an integration of hyper-accurate reconnaissance, seamless intelligence, the most advanced standoff munitions (laser or TV guided missiles), and computers.[25,26]

The key elements to having this advantage are enhanced command systems and situational awareness. Remote sensors and computer tracking of numerous targets allow for smaller, more flexible units to cover more distance by having the ability to interoperate and form into joint operations. This means a shift away from division-centric command structure to take advantage of precision navigation systems and precision air power.[27] This sort of flexibility comes from not only the ability to adapt to technology, but also adapt change management strategies operationally, organizationally, and according to regional and local environments (as in Afghanistan where special forces units used horse transportation and laser targeting technology to track enemy movements). Theoretically, it also means, no territory is remote, and anywhere on earth is within reach—at nearly any time. Geopolitics in this arena is no longer framed by an interstate system of borders and inviolates state sovereignty. Rather it implies a field of global conflict involving state and non-state actors, of disparate regional and strategic contests, and a struggle that targets political and economic objectives without the ideological passions of the past. Former cleavages are irrelevant, and the opposing force can be reduced to the operational unit of an aggrieved employee or an unstable individual.

When Bush made his pithy comments he was simultaneously discussing the new military arena, the "transformational military" his Secretary of Defense, Donald Rumsfeld, was advocating, and the terrestrial and earth orbit technology that was driving events. The reorganization of the armed services into smaller brigade-sized units makes possible rapid deployment surges into global flash points and trouble spots. Therefore, the traditional organization of the service branches into separate missions and roles yields to a new priority based upon joint operations.[28] However, despite the technological superiority of U.S. forces, the dependency on C4ISR systems makes the "transformed" military vulnerable. The ability to react faster because of superior intelligence-gathering and synchronization methods comes with a risk. The disruption of the hi-tech military infrastructure can affect the delicate efficiencies of space-based communication and monitoring satellites and, in turn, on the coordination of ground conditions and operations.

These same strategies also put homeland security on alert. As a way of compensating for the U.S. technological lead, peer competitors may choose to adapt strategies directed at non-military targets. In commercial and in private life, Americans have become highly dependent upon technology. The critical infrastructure of financial systems, energy grids, communication networks, commercial transportation, supply chains, and the food supply are strategic targets. These new asymmetric threat assumptions pertain to not only non-state actors but also with respect to near peer competition with established and rising states. As the United States' dependency on these systems has grown, economic, social, and security stability is targeted and made more vulnerable. The use of cyber terrorism, bio-chemical attacks, and the acquisition or development of WMDs can be a part of strategies, which conjecturally, and in reality, pose counter and preemptive strike options. An opposition force that is in a position of weakness, conventionally or technologically, will have these alternatives to consider. The overall national security strategy must reflect these contingencies and provide for the systemic redundancy and resiliency needed to sustain and attack, as well as having in place the capability to deter and retaliate.

RMA also makes the process of budgeting and planning for future conflict more complex. The advent of breakthrough or disruptive technology can erupt any time and tilt the balance of power in one direction or another. Despite the degree of impossibility, national security policy has to find a way to prepare for such events. Forecasting the future is even more challenging given the pace of technological advancement and the pattern of change where the ability to defend is trailing the capability to attack.

BUDGETING AND PLANNING IN SUPPORT OF POLICY

The National Security Strategy (NSS) is the document outlining U.S. world-wide interests and foreign policy. Once approved by the president, the secretary of defense and the joint chiefs work together in compiling the *Quadrennial Defense Review*. This report details the fundamentals and essentials required to actively support the NSS. Such elements include military force structure and modernization, business processes and supporting infrastructure, funding, and manpower requirements.[29] The recommendations of the QDR provide the foundation for federal budget planning for the Department of Defense. By law, the DoD conducts studies and releases the QDR findings every four years. The first report appeared in 1997 under the Clinton administration and confirmed the U.S. orientation according to conventional war paradigms. Traditional doctrine and funding percentages among the branch services remained in place. The 2006 version, completed after the attack on September 11, on the other hand, called for the preparation of a "long war" against terrorism. Defeating terrorism, preventing the development and acquisition of WMDs, homeland defense, and helping to democratize politically fragile states were the basic principles. In a break from previous canon the report also emphasized the need for a more agile military, more advanced weapons systems, and new bases in many parts of the world to make possible the rapid deployment of forces into emerging conflict zones.

However, deployment from the Cold War has not been simple. Many weapons procurement programs for submarine, carriers, and fighter jets continue to exist.[30] Furthermore, although the QDR clearly states that expeditionary forces will be based mostly on domestic territory, it acknowledges that the United States maintains a presence in 130 countries. The inconsistencies have drawn criticism. In response to the findings of the 2010 QDR, the Center for Strategic and International Studies notes that key decisions about force structure and procurement programs remain vague.

If the United States is supposed to be able to defeat peer competitors in conventional war yet also deal with hybrid threats from non-state actors, how should forces be sized? What high-technology weapons systems will be necessary to defeat peer competitors? Is there a stable, cost-effective procurement path to achieve them? It is unclear the extent to which the 2010 QDR will answer these questions.[31]

In the absence of a unified agency or department to act as the legal machinery that controls decisions over national security objectives and ways and means to achieve these goals, the process of setting national security goals and budget planning is left to a complex method of negotiation between the legislative and executive branches. The creation of budgets and planning of programs for national security involve thousands of staffers and bureaucrats. The ordeal is repetitive and sequential, and often bitterly contested.

There are obvious reasons for the rancor in Washington over budgets. Special interests and politics are in a proverbial state of conflict. However, some arguments are resistant, such as the "guns verses butter" dilemma. Opportunity costs occur when national resources are diverted to national security and other public sectors and the commercial sector go lacking. The capital invested in national security assets is not available for ordinary production of consumer goods or other socially beneficial programs. The return on investment to the public is in the form of a "public good," which is the comfort and the assurance of the nation's security. Jobs are created, but studies repeatedly show that employment as a result of military spending is nowhere as robust as investment in other areas. The following analysis compiled by the University of Massachusetts in 2009 reflects the opportunity cost of military investment and upholds the claim that cutting domestic programs can limit job creation.[32]

Therefore, the balancing act is to estimate the most security the nation can achieve for each available dollar spent, given the amount of acceptable risk and the needs of other government programs. Without a centralized command system to establish policy and the approaches toward achieving policy goals, agencies and departments simultaneously cooperate and compete to define needs and recommend funding limits. Yet, by meting out tasks and expectations, setting deadlines, and putting limits on the range of items for deliberation, the overall process of federal budget procedures allows the system to work despite a highly charged political environment.[33]

Saving the process from complete chaos is the requirement that the president must present a budget to Congress by the first Monday in February each year. In the spring prior to that date, the Office of Management and Budget (OMB) conducts a study of the economy and presents the president with its projections. As a result of these findings, individual agencies revise current program budgets based upon the guidelines recommended by the OMB. After reviewing these projections, the OMB makes an analysis of programs and budgets. National security policy formulation occurs as budget levels

SECTOR	NUMBER OF JOBS	PERCENT OF INCREASE
Military	11,600	---
Household consumption	14,800	Up by 28%
Clean energy	17,100	Up by 48%
Health care	19,600	Up by 69%
Education	29,100	Up by 151%

Table 2.1 Amount of Jobs Created by Sector Per $1Billion

and projections are being prepared. During the following summer, the president establishes guidelines and targets. The various agencies then review. Agencies make their projections and re-submit them to the OMB, which in turn makes recommendations to the president. The president then makes the decision regarding agency budgets and overall budget policy. The final budget document emerges after agencies conform to the president's decision and the OMB makes a final review.

On the legislative side, another iterative process is taking place. The Constitution requires that Congress authorize appropriations. The *budget resolution* is an agreement between the House and Senate and an initial step in determining the overall size of the budget and how it breaks down among the various functional categories. It is essentially the blueprint for the actual appropriation process. It is, however, a resolution, not a law. In some years if no agreement is reached, then the previous year's resolution stands. Actual appropriation occurs through the House and Senate Appropriations Committees and their subcommittees. The review process consists of meetings and hearings involving agency spokespersons, lobbyists, and expert witnesses. Finally, money becomes available through an appropriations act. This legislation originates from the Appropriations Committee with the recommendations of the defense subcommittees. The process is programmed, sequential, arduous, and often contentious. Consensus between the legislative branch and the executive branch is the aim, but not always the result. The fragmented nature of the national security apparatus[34] and the absence of any unified command system to plan, manage, and control spending and operations leaves the process open to inefficiencies. The NSC can coordinate and make recommendations, but Congress advises and consents.

In order to establish a link between the civilian budgeting process and integrated military planning of the Joint Chiefs, a systematic methodology called PPBS (Planning, Programming, Budgeting System) was conceived during the administration of Secretary of Defense Robert McNamara. Renamed the PPBES (Execution was added to the acronym): "It is a formal, systematic structure for making decisions on policy, strategy, and the development of forces and capabilities to accomplish anticipated missions."[35] PPBES analyzes the value of fund allocation on force structure, weapons procurement, and mission objectives. The QDR is the base document for PPBES, both of which mainly coincide with presidential terms. Admittedly imperfect, it remains a primary tool for linking expenditures to national security objectives and as a way to evaluate change requests.[36] Connecting budget requests and performance results is an elusive task. When the scope of national security is vast and the return on investment vague because of the lack of precedence and incident experience—efficient management of the national security process is often elusive and policy formulation is more conjectural than in other areas of government.

The growth of the federal government has not made life inside the national security establishment easier, either. As more agencies and departments take on responsibilities for homeland and national security, the response has been additional layers of staff to fill roles on committees, bureaus, offices, centers, etc. The widening attack surface that put soft targets and critical infrastructure components at risk drew in the departments of Agriculture and Transportation, the Environmental Protection Agency, the United States Coast Guard, and other offices and entities as part of the defense umbrella. The expanding panoply created a Herculean task of coordinating and implementing policy. The complexity in national security affairs is not only administrational, but also thematic. Cultural, diplomatic, economic, technological, and military issues figure prominently. As the authors of *American National Security*, the core text in the security studies field, state in their reference to the 9/11 Commission Report:

> . . . even given the national security professionals commitment to collaboration, it has become harder to get agencies to act in concert. The NSC and the HSC systems must untangle these interconnections to forge coherent policy. [37]

To provide some structure and stability to the inter-agency process of consensus building and policy making, an array of tiered committees was formed in the late 1980s to support the NSC. As stated, these forums include the following: [38]

The NSC Principals Committee (NSC/PC)

At the cabinet level is the NSC Principals Committee (NSC/PC). It is the senior interagency forum for considering policy issues affecting national security. The NSC/PC reviews, coordinates, and monitors the development and implementation of national security policy. It is a forum where cabinet-level officials meet to discuss and resolve issues not requiring the president's participation.

The NSC Deputies Committee (NSC/DC)

At the sub-cabinet level is the NSC Deputies Committee. This body focuses attention on policy implementation. The DC holds periodic reviews of the administration's major foreign policy initiatives and works to ensure they are being "implanted in a timely and effective manner." It also makes recommendations regarding the revision or withdrawal of existing directives. Crises management is also the purview of the DC.

Interagency Working Groups (IWG/DC)

The Interagency Working Groups convene on a regular basis at the discretion of the Deputies Committee to review and coordinate the implementation of presidential decisions in their policy areas. These IWGs may be permanent or *ad hoc*. The participants, timeline, and decision-making paths are subject to strict guidelines according to the Presidential Directive.

Policy Coordination Committee (PCC)

The PCC is a fourth interagency committee. These committees relate to either specific geographical areas or functional policy areas. PCCs focus on advance planning on political and strategic issues.[39] They facilitate teamwork, policy integration, and politically acceptable solutions. For these reasons, PCCs sometimes sacrifice decisive action for the sake of consensus.

The complexity of national security policy formulation grows with time. As the bureaucracy expands, missions overlap. Programs become scattered and uncoordinated. At the same time the tide of events outpaces the policy-making process and the bureaucracy's ability to adapt. The move to more specialized functions within government creates a greater need for integration. Furthermore, the additional layers of bureaucracy intended to assist the coordination of policy often add to the complexity of the process. Despite the effort to establish a system of responsibilities, accountability, guidelines, and time frames, nothing goes "according to the book." There is no "book." These influences plus the need to strike a balance politically and economically come together in a mill of government machinery where opinions anneal around national security policy.

THE ROLE OF THE PRIVATE SECTOR

Since the launch of Roosevelt's *Arsenal of Democracy*, despite the apprehension over Eisenhower's "military industrial complex," the partnership between government and the private sector has lasted through generations of conflict and taken assorted shapes. Its interdependency has become even more permanent as the revolution in military affairs and the rise of surveillance society entwines both spheres in a shared threat and a mutual reliance upon technology.

The old arsenal system would never have offered the U.S. War Department and the allied effort the personnel, innovation, and energizing force required to prevail in a world war fought on two fronts. The United States would also not have maintained its economic and political hegemony during the Cold War without the enterprise and efficiencies of the market system. Today, when disruptive technologies are possible in more frequent cycles and lesser time scales, the interdependency between government and industry is a foundational strength. The manpower and skill sets each control and contribute are essential for national security. The relationship is more inextricable than before and even more complex. The privatization of security and defense functions has created a more multi-layered connection. Additionally, decades of deregulation, government outsourcing, and privatization placed more and more critical infrastructure assets under private-sector control and responsibility. These assets are strategic and political targets in the post Cold War arena and need defending as well as maintenance and upgrade. As a result of these events and circumstances, the role of the private sector has grown considerably. Over five million military and civilian personnel hold security clearances. The sprawl of defense contractors includes U.S. national and foreign firms and employees. The attack matrix has expanded and become more technologically based. The number of government contractors has increased precipitously since 9/11. The relationship between DoD and its civilian force morphs and eventually often creates morass.

Over time, careers moved back and forth between government and the private sector. The interchange can be seamless, and critics claim it might also be incestuous. Interests embed and policy follows in accommodation. Outcomes are unanticipated.

Originally forecasted as a cost saving to the DoD budget, outsourcing to the private sector removed the financial and staffing onus from government payrolls. With the private firm's ability to hire and fire correspondingly to surges in demand and economic cycles, it was reasoned that these efficiencies would transfer to government. However, contracts were renewed, extended, or never "fully completed." Contracted employees became permanent fixtures on projects and government programs. In addition, for reasons mostly to do with the delays in the security clearance process and bureaucratic cumbrance, there comes a slightly ironic twist. Recently the term *insourcing* in government parlance came to mean not transferring the task from an outside contractor to an internal division or employee, but rather transferring the employee or unit of the contractor to government. The arrangement could be considered a form of conscription and the prudence of the initial intent now stands on its head.

Half of the U.S. Department of Defense budget goes to defense contractors.[40] According to the U.S. government website, usaspending.gov, over $361 billion went to private firms in fiscal year 2012. At a rate of $1 billion per day in defense contracts, critics of this symbiosis argue, and defenders admit: "Can the government follow that much money?" The Government Accountability Office (GAO) expressed its doubts in several reports. Because of manpower shortages, the Defense Contract Management Agency (DCMA) was deemed limited in its ability to provide the oversight required to ensure the products and services to the Department of Defense are delivered on time, within budget, and in conformity to agreed performance requirements. The DCMA supplies contract administration services for DoD procurement. According to the GAO, the agency is understaffed and relies heavily upon the Defense Contract Auditing Agency (DCAA), which a 2011 report claims: "has its own workforce struggles."[41]

The post-9/11 spike in defense contracting occurred without a corresponding increase in staffing by the DCMA and the DCAA. To compensate, the DCAA raised the dollar amount threshold of contracts that triggers an automatic audit. Not only was the contractor's incurred cost proposal hoisted from $15 million to $250 million, the agency revised the criteria used to determine a proposal's risk level, and significantly reduced the number of low risk audits to be randomly sampled.[42] The policy change plus the backlog of audits (which have a closing statute of limitations window) means that billions of dollars in defense contractor payments will escape scrutiny. Under current projections, the Commission on Wartime Contracting predicts by 2016 the backlog will be as high as $1 trillion.[43] There has been progress in making the government's acquisition process more accountable and efficient. However, according to Eric Auner, a senior defense and national security analyst at Guardian Six Consulting, this is more the exception than the rule.

DOD has taken steps to enhance the competence of its acquisition workforce, which had been allowed to decay, both in numbers and experience. With more reliance on private contractors, the acquisition workforce is important not only in terms of holding firms accountable, but also in terms of helping companies to navigate the complex acquisition system in some kind of timely manner.[44]

Accountability is not only a matter for budgets, it is also an issue for military operations. The rise of private military armies (PMA) raises serious questions in war zones and creates command structure issues. Since the end of the Cold War, the United States employed these services in many major military operations, including operating the computer and communications systems for the U.S. nuclear response at North American Aerospace Defense Command (NORAD), and as proxies in Colombia and Liberia. Their presence and possible inappropriate use in Iraq and Afghanistan drew the most attention. The question of: "Where do these units fit?" extends to questions of international law. These corporate units, independent of war conventions and, in some cases, international norms, fall within the legal gap, and, therefore, another problem concerning the deployment of PMAs relates to the potential abuse of human rights laws and the difficulty in effective prosecution against abusers.[45]

Despite these examples of recent and historic problems, the partnership between the private sector and government is vital to national security and inextricable. Inextricable, also, is the mutual benefit both share in a strong industrial economy and robust technological advancement. The revolutions in computers, communications, and information occurred as a result of "entrepreneurial spirit and inventiveness in the private sector." They did not hatch from incubators in government research labs.[46] Without these breakthroughs, the American military dominance would not have been sustained. Thus, economic and security goals are often mutual. However, in an era of intense economic competition and global industrialization, technology dispersion is fluid. The diffusion of technology can influence the international redistribution of power.[47] These developments have also set in motion the forces and aided conditions for asymmetric warfare and economic competition. In such an environment networks are more suited than hierarchies. These are also areas where entrepreneurial skills excel more than the bureaucratic and political strictures of government.

Maintaining the partnership is critical. Finding a balance in the triangle of influence of Congress, defense contractors, and the military has been a delicate act. Corruption and abuse will hamper efforts to create an environment of transparency and accountability. However, a partnership between national security and private-sector innovation is central to having a strategic advantage. A more diffused international power structure and security regime may, eventually, limit the politicizing of policy and the acquisition process. Global economic competition is fierce. Human skills and product innovation will originate from more diverse and remote sources. The military advantages, which the United States formerly enjoyed, are losing relevance. Hopefully, the special interests that influenced the national security framework and process in the past will lose some relevance as well. Finally, the bureaucracy Robert Gates described as having "the fine motor skills of a dinosaur"[48] and which oversees and manages these relationships will find a way to adapt.

CONCLUSION

Following World War II an immediate and large-scale rearmament program followed based upon an interstate geopolitical landscape rooted in a strategy of containment and deterrence. However, with the collapse of the Cold War world order, geopolitics morphed from a concern with European battlefields and nuclear standoff into a global war on terrorism. Potential foreign battlefields could be anywhere and the range of the attack surface could be virtually boundless as military instillations, government buildings, iconic structures, the commercial infrastructure, and civilians become targets. While World War II took an estimated toll of upward of fifty million lives, in the time since the 1950s casualties from military violence in developing parts of the world have equaled approximately five million per decade. The overwhelming proportion of these deaths has been civilian.[49] We have now also moved from the times of "war as an instrument of policy," as von Clausewitz would have it, to a time of a series of wars whose outcomes may not be winnable—unless endless war is the objective.

If the national security interests of the United States included, as Dean Acheson asserted, "creating an environment in which free societies may exist and flourish," then those responsibilities required "the long war" of defeating terrorist networks, limiting the proliferation and development of WMDs, and influencing the options of fragile and failed states. It also infers that any-where on the entire planet is a potential battlefield. The defense of the United States and other nations must also take into account assaults of nature and the consequences of ecological disaster. How does a nation, then, defend itself in an all hazards environment of potential natural and human inflicted catas-trophes when the national security establishment is often fighting the bureau-cratic inertia of fighting the last war? This becomes the systemic challenge.

The *Arsenal of Democracy* as FDR imagined needs re-imagining. The "enduring partnership" needs to include civic society's participation in the community of science, industry, and the military to create an effective na-tional defense public good. The industrial capacity and technical advantages the United States enjoyed after World War II remain still. However, these conditions are fluid. The former arrangement of alliances fluctuates, as well. As national borders lose their significance, diaspora groups play a more dominant role, criminal networks expand, and terrorists become more entre-preneurial due to the opportunities of illegal commerce and the mechanisms of globalization—the U.S. national security establishment will need to be more flexible and adaptive. The process and structure, which the framers of NSC-68 hoisted as the new national direction may require the same level of effort. However, the bureaucracy and the imbedded interests that resulted remain in many quarters of government and arise on many occasions.

NOTES

1. Kaldor, Mary, Beyond Militarism, Arms Races, and Arms Control, speech prepared for the Nobel Peace Prize Centennial Symposium, December 2001.

2. Jack Jarmon, *Encyclopedia of United States National Security*, Sage Publications, Thousand Oaks, CA, 2006, p. 160.

3. *Ibid.*

4. Amos A. Jordan, William J. Taylor Jr., Michael J. Meese, Suzanne C. Nielsen, *American National Security*, sixth edition, Johns Hopkins University Press, (2008) p. 44

5. *Op. cit.*

6. Jarmon.

7. *Ibid.*

8. Warner Schilling, Paul Hammond, Glenn Snyder, *Strategy, Politics, and the Defense Budget*, Columbia University Press. 1962, p. 292.

9. Paul H. Nitze, "The Need for a National Strategy," address at the Army War College, Carlyle, PA, August 27, 1958, in Amos.

10. Jordan, p. 47

11. *Encyclopedia of United States National Security*, p. 531–32.

12. Jarmon, p. 446.

13. *Ibid.*, p. 447.

14. Jordan, p. 490

15. *Ibid.*, p. 490–94.

16. *Ibid.*, p. 204–5.

17. *Ibid.*

18. National Public Radio, http://www.npr.org/2011/01/17/132942244/ikes-warning-of-military-expansion-50-years-later.

19. George W. Bush, "Address Delivered to the West Point Graduating Class (June 1, 2002), www.whitehouse.gov/news/releases/2002/06/20020601-3.html. Also see Amos, p. 63–64.

20. *Quadrennial Defense Review*, 2006.

21. Simon Dalby, "Geopolitics: The Revolution in Military Affairs and the Bush Doctrine" in *International Politics, Beyond Bush: A New Era in US Foreign Policy* (Palgrave MacMillan, March 2009).

22. *Ibid.*

23. Gary Chapman, "An Introduction to the Revolution in Military Affairs," LBJ School of Public Affairs, University of Texas, Austin (XV Amaldi Conference on Problems in Global Security, Helsinki, Finland, 2003).

24. Kaldor.

25. Jordan, p. 318

26. Christopher Bolkom, "Missiles for Standoff Attack: Air-Launched Air-to-Surface Missile Programs" *CRS Report for Congress* (Congressional Research Service of the Congressional Library, update, October 2000).

27. Jordan, p. 318.

28. Jordan, p. 318

29. Jordan, p. 202

30. *Ibid.*

31. Anthony Cordesman, Erin K. Fitzgerald, "The 2010 Quadrennial Defense Review, A+, F, or Dead on Arrival?" *Center for Strategic and International Studies* (8 September 2009), http://csis.org/publication/2010-quadrennial-defense-review.

32. "Protecting American Power and Keeping the Pentagon on the Table." *National Security Network* (12 November 2012), http://nsnetwork.org/protecting-american-power-and-keeping-the-pentagon-on-the-table/.

33. Jordan, p. 193

34. *Ibid.*, p. 205.

35. Acquisition Community Connection website, https://acc.dau.mil/CommunityBrowser.aspx?id=160404.

36. http://mrsi.usace.army.mil/Shared%20Documents/Heath/Executive%20Primer%20-%20DoD-Army-PPBE.pdf.

37. Jordan, p. 212

38. Organization of the National Security Council, Presidential Decision Directive, PDD2, http://www.fas.org/irp/offdocs/pdd/pdd-2.htm.

39. Alan G.Whitaker, Frederick C. Smith, Elizabeth McKune. "The National Security Policy Process: The National Security Council and the Interagency System." *Research Report, Annual Update,* National Defense University (2007), p. 27.

40. Ben Freeman, "Don't Fall for the Pentagon Spin," *Salon*, March 12, 2013.

41. John Hutton, "Defense Contract Management Agency: Amid Ongoing Efforts to Rebuild Capacity, Several Factors Present Challenges in Meeting Its Mission," General Accountability Office, GAO-12-83 (November 2011).

42. Scott Amey, "Billions of Defense Contract Dollars May Go Unaudited," Project on Government Oversight (July 24, 2013), http://www.pogo.org/blog/2013/07/20130724-billions-of-defense-contract-dollars-may-go-unaudited.html.

43. *Ibid.*

44. Eric Auner, interview and email from author (July 8, 2013).

45. Nathanial Stinnet, "Regulating the Privatization of War: How to Stop Private Military Firms From Committing Human Rights Abuses," *Boston College International and Comparative Law Review*, Vol. 2, Iss. 1 (2005), p. 211.

46. Sam C. Sarkesian, John Allen Williams, Stephen Cimbala, *U.S. National Security, Policymakers, Policies, and Politics*, Fourth Edition, Lynn Reinner Publishers, Inc. (2008), p. 267.

47. Robert Gilpin, *War and Change in World Politics*, Cambridge University Press, (1983), p. 177.

48. Ben Freeman, "Today's Military: The Most Top-Heavy Force in U.S. History," *Project on Government Oversight* (November 29, 2011), http://pogoblog.typepad.com/pogo/2011/11/todays-military-the-most-top-heavy-force-in-us-history.html.

49. Kaldor.

Chapter Three

Industrial Age Warfare and Information Age Weapons

We haz 0 smoke stacks, dude!

—Anonymous hacker

In 2008 a cyber attack destroyed a CIA website created to intercept terrorist communications and monitor movements of mideast extremists. The website was a joint venture between the Central Intelligence Agency and the Saudi government. These "honey pots" are online forums clandestinely organized to entrap participants. Plotters exchange information and assist in operational planning to conduct attacks, sabotage missions, and pass along useful intelligence to accomplices. The traffic generated over the site, in turn, is closely studied and used to support counterintelligence operations. The CIA and its Saudi partners regarded the multiyear project as a boon in its efforts to stem terrorist activity and hinder the enemy's effectiveness in the region. They claimed to have captured a good number of radicals and foiled their attacks as a result of the valuable data retrieved from its online source. Such sites are valuable assets in today's covert wars. As pipelines of information they can be helpful in blunting militants' attempts to marshal followers, recruit, and spread their message. They not only are a mechanism for gathering actionable intelligence, but also can be a conduit for implanting misinformation. The successful attack, which took down the website, consequently "led to a significant loss of intelligence" according to CIA assertions.[1]

However, despite the value to counterintelligence operations, the project did not upend as a result of the efforts of a rival group or an exploited enemy looking to dismantle the program. The assault to halt the operation came from a source far closer to home. The decision and successful attack eliminating the website originated from Fort Meade, Maryland—headquarters of the National Security Agency and home of another program called Countering Adversary Use of the Internet.[2] In other words, the U.S. military attacked and disabled a successful U.S. intelligence operation.

Pentagon officials claimed the program was putting the lives of American personnel at risk. As useful a tool as the website was to intelligence gathering, it was also deemed to be serving the logistical needs of foreign fighters and jihadists flowing forth from Saudi Arabia into Iraq. The internal debate over the fate of the website involved the National Security Agency, CIA, National Security Council, Department of Justice, Department of Defense, and the Office of the Director of National Intelligence. Absent from discussions were a well-defined policy for the conduct of cyber warfare and the legal machinery for assigning proper authority to make a decision and execute a plan. As former CIA Director Michael Hayden commented in a *Washington Post* article: "Cyber was moving so fast that we were always in danger of building up precedent before we built up policy."[3]

In addition to exposing the obvious anarchy in national security policy and interagency and departmental turf battles, the incident also unleashed a diplomatic storm. Saudi officials, despite being previously notified, expressed outrage. Several Saudi princes and persons within the intelligence communities were alarmed by the loss of a valuable counterintelligence tool and the impact it could have on their country's national security. Compounding these consequences was the blow back on bystander organizations. Unintended outcomes involved over three hundred affected servers in Saudi Arabia, Germany, and Texas. Diplomatic tensions arose alongside private-sector collateral damage.

This clash between industrial age tactics and information age technology claimed its own casualties far apart from the global war on terrorism (GWOT). The entire episode conjures up the tableau of a circular firing squad involving state militaries, private-sector interests, bureaucratic territories, diplomatic protocols, and legal jurisdictions. Adding insult to the injury, the coda to the operational tragedy is that the process of mobilizing attackers and assets against U.S. forces in Iraq continued. The elimination of the website did no damage to the terrorist logistical apparatus. Within an estimated forty-eight hours, information stored in servers around the world appeared on alternate and replacement websites. Data and users migrated to new loci and a useful terrorist tool remained in service. In the final accounting, some American lives may have been spared. However, the side effects were the rise in diplomatic tensions, the loss of a valuable counterintelligence weapon, and further damage to the war effort, which may yet, have included the further loss of American life.

Throughout the ordeal of this incident it becomes apparent that while we may be technically prepared to fight new-age wars, we fight them encumbered by the apparatus and machinery of a bygone era. Old protocols and a degrading security framework from the previous century prevailed over the decision-making process. Policy naturally follows precedent. However, time lag is critical along this curve. As opposed to preceding times, the ability to defend now trails the offense in efficiencies. The terms of battle have changed. Attackers can choose the time and space (either real or virtual) of attack, and the adjustment to the new logic and requirements of war has been difficult. The disconnect, frustration, and disorientation caused by blare and brawl of foundational national security institutions struggling with the paradigm shift is, perhaps, best expressed in a simple exchange between two bloggers on the subject of cyber war. In a comment to the *Wall Street Journal* an unnamed military official wrote:

> If you shut down our power grid, maybe we will put a missile down one of your smoke stacks.

To which an anonymous hacker responded:

> LOLZ . . . We haz 0 smoke stacks, dude![4]

ASYMMETRIC WARFARE

As the world's most dominant conventional military the United States knows no rival. Hence, no state would pit its armed forces against the U.S. supremacy. The overwhelming advantage of armed force is a great deterrent. So great is the deterrence that it will most likely never be tested. The option to "kill or capture our way to victory,"[5] as General David Petraeus commented to the International Security Assistance Force in Afghanistan, is no longer a strategic opportunity. Foes would sensibly circumvent confrontation rather than engage it. Their strategy is to take the conflict to another field of battle under a parity of power where the terms might more benefit non-state actors lacking national resources as well as weaker states lacking the corresponding military might. Those battlefronts are in cyberspace, along the supply chain, communication networks, transportation systems, power grids, and places where people congregate, such as malls, parks, schools, and near iconic or symbolic structures.

Not only is destruction an objective but also disruption and chaos. The cost of the disruption would have to be measured in terms of direct material costs due to equipment replacement, emergency healthcare, and spoilage. However, collateral costs can have a cascading effect and their impact could have greater severity. Those costs could be over extended time periods and include:

- Damages due to market panic and political instability, particularly, if the event were terrorist induced
- Contingency and restorative operations
- The impact on insurance markets
- The strain on infrastructure sectors
- The expense of future investment in security

The economic and political toll is almost impossible to estimate. The capability to quantify thresholds of acceptable loss is difficult to establish because of the interdependence and complexity between sectors. In this conflict the objectives are political and economic. The targets are not necessarily military. The repercussion from a single incident in this hyper-connected economy could be global.

In today's arena of asymmetrical conflict the United States finds itself shackled to many outmoded institutions, policies, and embedded interests. Economic relations and notions of governance have felt the pressures of globalization and the breakneck speed of technological advancement. With respect to national security, the dissonance is most apparent. The incompatibility between the threat and structures organized to meet the challenges clash more often than they align. All the while technology hurls populations, cultures, and institutions headlong into the information age. These sets of circumstances bring us to a time in the age of information when, despite the demands, we are still organized to fight Industrial Age conflicts. The knowledge and familiarity with the new battle landscape is evolving. The battle terrain is blurred, the weaponry is in a constant state of upgrade, and the enemy is indistinct and ubiquitous.

The rivalry is among states, tribes, crime organizations, corporate interests, religious and political sects, and even allies. Persistent hatred and an environment of economic and democratic inequality have created a security threat and a challenge to authority and claims to legitimacy as to the right to rule (at the time of this writing the U.S. Congress' approval rating among Americans is 13 percent). In many areas, states are losing their monopoly as primary actors in international relations. In addition to non-state actors, failed or quasi-states are becoming influencers of events as populations are exploited through corruption and these countries become safe havens for terrorism and crime. As part of that understanding of failed states the United States should, too, recognize that these legal or alternative spheres of authority are not only in far flung corners of the world, but also inhabit spaces along and within its own borders. They sometimes include neighbors and involve fellow citizens and coworkers.

THE PHENOMENON OF SOCIAL MEDIA

The example of the CIA honeypot illustrates how the transformation from industrial age war to an era of information warfare (IW) can be precariously fought, and for the security establishment fraught with unexpected consequences. On a grand scale the "World Wide Web" is a marvelous tool of empowerment. Social media, also known as social software or Web 2.0, adds to the dynamic. Users interact across many devices and fluently transfer between author and audience states—in real time and with outreach to millions. Electronic venues such as Facebook, Twitter, LinkedIn, etc., have become drivers of the information flow. By 2009, Wikipedia had four million articles and YouTube had about 100 million videos.[6] Social networking services now exceed web-based e-mail usage.[7]

The potential consequences for national security are also dynamic. As the CIA honeypot episode demonstrates, too, social media can mobilize sympathizers, associates, and armed insurgents into action in support of causes or combat. The same virtual pageant functions to bring nonviolent protestors, business people, and consumers together for the sake of peaceful interaction and the steady continuance of commerce. Obviously, the blade has dual sides. The use of social media has been responsible for exponential growth of e-commerce and e-government, and at the same time, has been a catalyst of events in many well-noted conflicts.

The power of social software not only tracked the political situation in Egypt but also influenced it. In 2008 a Facebook group launched a pro-democracy protest that attracted tens of thousands of followers and exposed the government's brutality tactics. A few years later it contributed to the forced removal of President Hosni Mubarak. Mubarak's successor and Muslim Brotherhood representative, Mohamed Morsi, fell to similar pressures in 2013. As it expands, the machinery of social media has not lost timing and its political force only gains vigor. The Arab Spring, which was unofficially launched in 2010, can credit much of its momentum in Egypt, Yemen, Syria, Tunisia, and across the Arab world to the information sharing functionality and activism organized through social media. However, it is a phenomenon with phantasmagoric properties that often places it astride the thin line between public empowerment and mob rule.

The cyber attack on Estonia in 2007 may have been instigated and conducted by freelance Russian hackers with the collusion of government authorities. The same suspected sources are accused of disabling and defacing Georgian government websites in 2008 while a simultaneous military invasion was in process (see chapter 7). These "cyber riots," as they are known, are becoming a new way of waging war. One such conflict occurred in 2001 between China and the United States as a result of an incident involving a U.S. EP-3 reconnaissance and surveillance plane and Chinese F-8 fighter jets. When the EP-3 approached Chinese airspace near Hainan Province, two F-8s scrambled to meet it. A mid-air collision forced the reconnaissance plane to land in Hainan and resulted in the death of one of the fighter pilots. An exchange of cyber attacks between "unidentified activists" arose across the Pacific.[8] A cyber war was even declared for the dates of April 30 through May 8.[9] Hackers from both sides launched denial of service attacks and defaced websites. In homage to the lost fighter jet pilot, a Chinese hacker wrote: "You may have fallen but millions like you live on to fight for the motherland." A less worshipful notation by an American counterpart read: "Bagel—morning coffee—and a Chinese website. Nice little routine."[10] Both governments took the hacker war seriously. During the hostilities the National Infrastructure Protection Commission Watch and Warning Unit established a hotline. The U.S. Navy also announced it was at INFOCONAL-PHA: a cyber equivalent status of a physical threat condition.[11]

Other examples of social web activities with national security implications include:

- An online counter-revolution against the FARC (*Fuerzas Armada Revolucionarias de Colombia*) enlisted over a million participants to protest the Colombian-based guerilla groups' terrorist and criminal activities. An international event in 2008 called "One Million Voices against the FARC" drew attention and world condemnation of FARC atrocities.
- The Mumbai terrorists' attacks in 2008 streamed online and in real time. As the tragedy unfolded, unverified accounts co-mingled with facts. The pace of the information flow put added pressure on the security services and the element of misinformation may have hindered the government's ability to respond effectively.
- In 2007, the Pakistani government imposed a state of emergency as justification for shutting down privately owned television stations. In reaction, activists, lawyers, professional and amateur journalists kept record of their government's actions. Once formed and mobilized, the virtual social network worked to assure accountability and in 2009 successfully helped to reinstate the nation's Chief Justice.[12]
- The People's Republic of China has long appreciated the use of social media as an effective propaganda tool and an instrument of national security policy. It has not only enlisted thousands of professional propagandists to influence online blogs, chat rooms, message boards, and other types of social networking sites. It also is developing offensive capabilities to access proprietary databases, sensitive foreign government information, and infiltration into command and control facilities (see chapter 7).

Over the past decade, the growth in social networks has been enormously robust. The processes and relationships that govern them are complex. The benefits to national security can be significant, even critical. It is a valuable enabler of information sharing between governments, government agencies, government and its citizenry, individuals in government and communities of interest, and researchers and government data sources. Web 2.0 is a connective tool and an intellectual force multiplier.[13] Not only is it useful as a general networking apparatus for expressing and advocating policy, it can identify emerging trends and influencers. As missions overlap between DHS, DoD, state, and law enforcement and emergency management agencies, these capabilities can be essential in forming a seamless connection for diverse missions.

Combat personnel and first responders rely on situational awareness to improve operational effectiveness. Extraction of geospatial information from maps, satellite images, and textual information from news articles, websites, and Twitter can assist war fighters and emergency personnel as well as analysts. This information can be retrieved in real time and shared in distributed manner. In this regard, social networks like Twitter form a real-time on-the-ground distributed sensor network for whoever has the power to filter and classify the messages appropriately.

In general, social networks are a resource for the Intelligence community who can use software programs to help them integrate and distill data in order to create holistic actionable intelligence. This information can reflect a particular incident at a particular time, like a revolution or earthquake, or reflect the knowledge, interests, and activities of an individual or group over periods of time. Crisis responders, emergency managers, and military leaders tend to focus on the former, while intel analysts concentrate on the latter. In both cases, natural language processing programs can be used to analyze, filter, classify, and otherwise process human language, whether it is news articles, e-mails, tweets, reports, recorded conversation, or any other genre.[14]

Eduard Hovy of Carnegie Mellon University further explains that this field includes programs that perform information retrieval (Google), speech recognition (IBM's ViaVoice), information extraction into databases, automated summarization of one or more texts, question answering such as IBM's Watson system (featured in the TV quiz game *Jeopardy!*), and many other applications.

Frequently these engines create a characterization of a word, concept, topic, person, organization, or even an entire document that comprises a list of the most relevant words and phrases associated with that object; each word or phrase is given a strength or weight score. Even though they do not fully describe the nature of the object in question, these so-called "topic/word signatures" are useful for a variety of purposes.[15]

The field also includes so-called inference engines, which combine rules and old facts to deduce new facts to aid analysts in filling knowledge gaps and finding inconsistencies in oral or written texts. From these programs come data analytic techniques such as anomaly detection and pattern learning that help interpret subjective text, opinions, and attitudes of authors and other agents. A key approach in information retrieval and disambiguation (natural language processing that governs which sense of a word may be applicable to its use in a specific sentence) is textual entailment. Textual entailment captures the semantic variability of texts and performs inferences as it moves from a lexical to relational context.

When Edward Snowden, the former CIA employee and NSA contractor, revealed details of the United States' and Britain's mass surveillance programs in 2013, he unleashed a global controversy and had some even accusing him of treason. His revelations, nevertheless, do not focus on the core issue of these programs. The main challenge to governments is not in gathering data but, rather, managing it. The estimated amounts of data produced each year are almost beyond comprehension. The growth of social networks has added to the situation and intensified the imperative of controlling the massive flows of information. How to sift through these immense amounts of records to find the relative minute sets of data that could potentially have relevance for national security is more than a task—it is an industry. In addition to the above examples of data extraction, integration, and analysis are programs designed to assure anonymity. Programs built upon privacy-sensitive algorithms for data streams, allow for precise privacy guarantees for individuals while in support of accurate and useful data analysis.

The tools for making social media an effective component part of the apparatus of national security are available and constantly evolving. It is possible to have an effective administration for extracting valuable information in the interest of national security while at the same time assuring privacy rights. Analysts and public opinion are divided on these issues, however. Hindering the use of social media, some also say, is the institutionalization of old practices and the hierarchal structure of the chains of command.[16] The inflexibility of governmental bureaucratic structures runs in contrast to the self-organizing, horizontal nature of social media. There as well exists a cultural divide between many military commanders and entrenched bureaucrats whose understanding of social software is comparatively blurred, versus junior members of the security establishment whose familiarity is more immediate and crystalline. There are observers who claim that until a coherent information strategy forms, the great potential of social media may go unmet.[17]

PUBLIC GOOD—NATIONAL DEFENSE AND CRITICAL INFRASTRUCTURE

While these events take their course, the U.S. infrastructure ages to a point of collapse. During this time, decades of deregulation and privatization placed vital assets under private-sector ownership. Private interests now own between 85 and 90 percent of the U.S. critical infrastructure. Resources for long-term infrastructure upgrade and security investment are strained by the demands for profit whose time horizons are only from quarter to quarter. These pressures of the global economy skew the perception of threat as being too abstract to justify the diversion of funds away from profit centers toward what strategy teams and corporate boards view as cost centers. These assets, however, are at the base of daily life and represent the core of U.S. national defense.

Although the ownership of these vital assets may be corporate, the burden to protect them is also a shared responsibility of government and civic society. Since all depend and benefit from the power grid, ports, communication networks, rail, healthcare, food, and supply chain systems, the need and obligation to involve all of society is both necessary and moral. National defense is still a public good and by definition—all-inclusive and absent of "rivalness." There are no free riders. Under such assumptions, corporations fund security and make it part of their core business process. The government assists by updating legislation, creating new frameworks for international cooperation, offering tax incentives for additional investment, and mandating standards. Finally, the public can contribute as not just taxpayers, but also by their demands at the ballot box and in the marketplace. The public can also participate as concerned citizens representing their industries and their communities through involvement in the many non-governmental organizations (NGOs) involved in national security themes and topics. On this last point it would be wise to remember that the run-up and early prosecution of the U.S. war in Iraq was conspicuously lacking of any real public debate. The result has been a decade-long war, a cost to the treasury in the trillions of dollars, and the incalculable price of the loss of life.

In a conflict that is asymmetrical there is parity of risk. The security challenge extends to business, government, and the public. How a national defense strategy responds to the challenge will depend upon the ability to rethink national security policy and recreate the security infrastructure. Success relies on how well policy makers identify national interests and the way to enlist appropriate stakeholders.

ENLISTING THE STAKEHOLDERS

In a 2008 book a team of four top executives at the consulting firm Booz Allen Hamilton put forth the idea of "megacommunities." *Megacommunities* describes the concept that calls for an integrative approach to solution solving and governance. According to the idea, the three great power sectors: government, business, and civic society, use a cross-sector dialogue that creates a "recurring pattern of communication" to address challenges. In much the way a computer network operates, the system makes use of distributive capabilities to manage the simultaneity and complexity of large-scale environments. In this type of schema, an adaptive control system adjudicates problems and displaces a central decision-making process. It is a departure from the old hierarchical command and control organizing principles of the industrial age. Rather than administering decision making from the top down, the framework aligns with circumstances through the collective behavior of all stakeholders.[18]

> With sustained connections and combined interactions, the members of the megacommunity develop bonds, intellectual pathways, enhanced linguistic abilities, and even a higher capacity for critical thinking and problem solving around the set of interests that prompted the megacommunity to form in the first place.[19]

The concept of the megacommunity requires that the stakeholders in these sectors work to optimize interests as opposed to maximize positions. Maximizing a position is a zero-sum game. It assumes winners only win at the expense of losers (such as in kinetic conventional warfare, where one player can only benefit by taking territory from another player). Optimization, on the other hand, "refers to the recognition and actualization of benefits to the larger system as a whole."[20] Actors, in this context, acknowledge an overarching mutual interest in the system's robustness superseding their roles as competitors. Variants of the notion have been used in labor disputes and international negotiation practices for many years. Applying it to national security means deconstructing the present framework and dismantling sectoral silos. Intelligence sharing, agreeing to some form of regulation, and committing to the sea change in organizational management are a few ways for a new security environment to self-enact. It is a way to reset response to the evolving global threat, rescale national defense to suit the nature of asymmetric warfare, and restructure a public good. The results would not only make the nation safer, but also save billions of dollars of investment in obsolete offensive weapons designed to fight the last war. The approach unifies the interests of all in government, business, and the public.

Similar to the philosophy of the megacommunity are management approaches conceptualized to establish higher standards of quality and ethics across partner organizations. Total Quality Management (TQM) and Six Sigma are organizational improvement processes conceived to reach across vertical markets and involve other sectors to improve products and processes. Providers and end users in such paradigms are mutual beneficiaries. For business they create a common good by forming targeted applications and identifying well-defined disciplines. Consumers get higher quality products that more exactly meet their consumption needs. Ideally, the commercial infrastructure operates more efficiently and the demand economy functions more flawlessly. The ultimate aim of these integrative management philosophies is to enlist participation of the greater society, not only in satisfying consumption but also in addressing corporate social responsibility (CSR) demands. These methods also have use in helping to form national security policy and structures. By regarding all participants as partners, if applied prudently, these concepts make the supply chain, electronic communication networks, and the production and trade of duel use technology more secure and efficient.

FORMS OF COLLABORATIONS

Working examples of collaborative efforts in national security exist. They reach beyond the single sector environment and function to combine capabilities from disparate sources into a whole-cloth network of stakeholders and solutions. Many have been operating for years and more are taking form. A sampling of a few includes the following initiatives.

Computer Emergency Response Team, CERT (also known as CSIRT— Computer Security Incident Response Team), refers to groups of computer experts who handle computer security incidents. CERT's inception originated with the early appearance of computer worms. The first "team" formed in 1988 in reaction to the Morris Worm (named after its author, Robert Tappan Morris, a Cornell graduate student). At that time the federal government contracted with Carnegie Mellon University to help monitor activity and coordinate responses to cyber threats. The Carnegie Mellon site remains a chief coordinating center and point of contact for corporations and other university and research institutions around the country.

The U.S. government partner US-CERT was established in 2003 and is located in Washington, DC. It is the operational arm of the National Cyber Security Division (NCSD) at the Department of Homeland Security (DHS). Its stated mission is to "improve the nation's cybersecurity posture, coordinate cyber information sharing and proactively manage cyber risks to the nation while protecting the constitutional rights of Americans."[21] Around the world more than 250 organizations using the name CERT or CSIRT focus on cybersecurity threat issues and response. US-CERT acts independently of these organizations, yet maintains relationships for information sharing and coordination purposes. It works with its partners to control the abuse and misuse of technology across cyberspace. Those partners include private-sector cybersecurity vendors, academia, federal agencies, Information Sharing and Analysis Centers (ISACs), state and local governments, and domestic and international organizations. In cyberspace, CERTs might be an example of an attempt to build a megacommunity. Yet given the exponential growth and pace of the morphing threat, there is much potential still to fill.

Another initiative is a program founded in 1996 by the Federal Bureau of Investigation. InfraGard, as it is called, originally worked with the information technology industry and academia to defend against cyber crimes. Upon the founding of the Department of Homeland Security, it and its parent organization, National Infrastructure Protection Center (NIPC) came under DHS authority and expanded its mission to include physical as well as cyber threats to critical infrastructures. Since 2003 InfraGard has been supporting DHS's Critical Infrastructure Protection (CIP) mission, despite still being an FBI-sponsored program.

InfraGard is an association of businesses, academic institutions, state and local law enforcement agencies, and other participants who share information and intelligence to prevent acts of terrorism, espionage, and other various forms of crime. Chapters extend across the United States and are linked with FBI field office territories. An FBI Special Agent Coordinator is assigned to each chapter based on geographic proximity and works closely with a Supervisory Special Agent Program Manager at the headquarters in Washington. The main goal is to promote dialogue and an atmosphere of trust between the private sector and the FBI. The "recurring pattern of communication" so important to the megacommunity concept is promoted within InfraGard. In addition to intelligence sharing, program members form liaisons and participate in training and education forums. A barrier to previous efforts of collaboration has been the fear by firms that submitting information to the government could compromise their competitive position in the market. One of InfraGard's objectives is to allay those fears.

There are also organizations in the private sector creating forums for dialogues and avenues of thought. Business Executives for National Security (BENS) refers to itself as a "member-driven" organization committed to applying best business practices to national security. [22] The themes where they attempt to draw focus include cybersecurity, defense acquisition reform, energy conservation, terrorist finance tracking, and any area where there is an opportunity for business input on collective security. Business has experience in adapting to rapid change and channeling cutting-edge technology. Its advice to the military and the defense community has always been welcome.

However, in these times their contribution becomes *sine qua non*. BENS outreach not only tries to offer advice to the architects of grand strategy but, more importantly, to connect government with local representatives. As civic-minded citizen-business leaders they often "understand the unique challenges their cities and towns encounter when preparing for and protecting against an attack in their community."[23]

Another example of effort is the Intelligence and National Security Alliance (INSA). INSA is an NGO providing *fora* and venues for discussions on national security and intelligence community topics. Former and current high-ranking members of the intelligence community, the military, government agencies, and analysts from the private sector and academia collaborate to form networks to develop policy recommendations and solutions. Their work is nonpartisan and nonprofit.

INSA and BENS are just two examples of NGOs and think tanks working on research and ways to bring the debate on national security to the public domain. The others are too many to mention but help filter and form the public contribution to what might be a nascent megacommunity for national defense. As with all NGOs, they encourage involvement and offer a means of collective empowerment. Bear in mind, terrorist cells and their affiliates also might be considered a form of NGO at times. They use the same technology to advance their beliefs, marshal support, and foment ideas and policy. Such is the nature of twenty-first-century asymmetric warfare.

PREPARING FOR THE NEXT WAR

The end of the Cold War signaled an end of a historical epoch. The conflict over ideology with the Soviet Bloc mobilized enormous financial resources as well as harnessed generations of populations and technology. During these times the United States prided itself on the openness of its society and willingness to defend individual liberties anywhere in the world. With the collapse of the USSR, however, the post-Cold War reality may have stripped the United States of that identity. The cessation of East-West rivalries deprived America of a clear, present, and common enemy. Because group identity often defines itself by its opposition, without an ideological and international rival, the notion of nationhood became a more fluid term. Globalization and advanced technology limited the importance of borders as political and ideological drivers gave way to economic imperatives. Security became a barrier to trade and economic development. As the United States ascended to the role of the last great superpower, it may have reveled in the "triumphism" too early. The new enemy circled the globe without a native territory, was ill defined if not invisible, void of any single ideological bent and, therefore, thoroughly enigmatic. However, it proved to be just as deadly and perhaps a greater threat than previous foes to an open society with a tradition of civil liberties. It posed a greater threat not by its intention to impose its will, but by creating an environment of chaos and influencing a public to react in contradiction to its traditions and democratic ideals.

Because of the great wealth opportunities the global economy offered, many constituencies may have turned their natural competitiveness inward and from the great "bastion of democracy" created a nation of interest groups. The pace of technology, the fragile hyper-connectivity of the global system, privatization policies, and the obsession with deregulation drove U.S. national policy. Success in this environment is relative and best measured in terms of the zero-sum game where actors adhere only to their positions rather than being motivated by shared best interests. These are the principles by which the U.S. waged war and developed policies in the past age. Therefore, the transition from the current national defense structure, imagined and implemented during World War II, will be difficult to reconfigure because of entrenched institutional interests and the inertia to adapt to new threats and corresponding business models.

While the country metes out its differences in an implacable political climate, the role of government is debated. Rather than representing a unity of command and arbiter in the solution-finding process, government is often in stalemate as the political process wrenches over questions about its appropriate function. However, the structuring of a reliable national defense that protects the quality of life and, at the same time, facilitates commerce will require an engaged public and active government. The timing is important. These national defense issues erupt at a time when the U.S. critical infrastructure is becoming obsolete, and as the needs of national security and infrastructure upgrade overlap. A neglect of these issues makes a nation vulnerable and subject to catastrophe. The United States may have reached an inflection point and faces the choice between short-term conveniences and long-term planning and benefits.

Despite the changing paradigm, the responsibility of national defense is a shared one. The efforts sustained in the previous century will possibly need renewal with the same vigor. The public good of national defense requires broad-based support and participation. The initiatives and organizations mentioned above only represent a scant sampling of examples where industry, government, and civic society can participate and collaborate. The final chapter of this book discusses possible mechanisms for impelling change toward a secure national defense framework. These options include:

- The suggestion of investment tax credits for firms that upgrade or deploy security enhancements for their business
- Stricter interpretation and application of Sarbanes Oxley
- The use of IRS regulations to set and enforce security standards

- Market mechanisms to encourage compliance with state-of-the-art security benchmarks.

Additionally, programs discussed in later chapters, such as the Customs-Trade Partnership Against Terrorism (C-TPAT), the World Trade Organization's SAFE Framework, and various international pacts reveal how security might become a non-intrusive integrant to frictionless trade. These programs were formed as a result of input from the private sector. The security measures reflect established industry best practices standards. However, in the spirit of deregulation, compliance is voluntary.

In the meantime, despite the abstractness of the threat, the United States might do well by regarding national security with an unrelenting sense of urgency. As the following chapters warn, the system is under daily assault. Adversaries include past foes and allies, disparate groups of criminals and terrorists, and insider threats from coworkers and community members. The threat is more than an abstract fear. If policy makers must rely on a high impact event to ultimately force themselves to act, the result would most likely be a set of solutions that are a response to rage rather than a response to the problem. If this becomes the case, a vengeful United States will only help to make the world a more dangerous place.

As the above CIA honeypot account appears to confirm, warfare in the information age plays out under different rules and strategies. Cultural, operational, jurisdictional, and psychological silos abide. Aligning defenses to meet the challenge of the post-Cold War era threat means dismantling some old barriers before erecting more efficient fences and gates. Many of the technological weapons are out of development and prepared for deployment, but are the legal system, international commerce, or the present scheme of national and global governance in a position to put them in place? While the question remains unresolved, understanding the true nature of the threat is crucial while waiting for the gap between precedent and policy to narrow.

Although each has separate functions and even exists and operates with tension, government, industry, and civic society are organs of the same body politic. Despite the fact there is no unity of command, the threat and onus of national security has forced a pari passu partnership between the public and private sectors. Technology is responsible for drawing these spheres more tightly together. The mechanisms and immediate connections of the modern machinery and process of globalization created a more level playing field for participants on either side of the law. Asymmetry, in the competition for power and pelf, has offered up both boon and bane. It tenders empowerment to the under-represented and disconnected as well as to the corrupt. Its other underside is that it makes populations, systems, and organizations more easily accessible and exploitable.

The opportunity to engage pertinent segments of society over national defense is an opportunity to advance interests outside the defense community and marshal the assets of the greater society. Broad-based participation in rebuilding of the public good of national defense may also be a chance to erase some of the effect of the creeping democratic deficit, which over recent decades has yielded much authority over to non-elected central bankers, rating agencies, and corporate strategy teams. Hopefully, it will force policy makers to think and plan for the long term—not only in the United States but also among its allies. The obsession with quarter-to-quarter results has had its costs and the bills for a porous defense and a neglected infrastructure are coming due. Mark Gerencser, Executive Vice president at Booz Allen Hamilton writes:

> Deregulation, which began in earnest in the mid-1970s and accelerated into the 1980s and 1990s, may well have bequeathed short-term economic benefits, but it has also made long-range management, planning and investment decisions for infrastructure systems far more difficult. . . . At the same time, the globalization of finance and capital flows has changed the stakeholder landscape almost beyond recognition in only the past twenty years. The infrastructure-related industries of the United States used to be part of a relatively stable public utilities market, but deregulation, corporate mergers and acquisitions, and outsourcing trends have put an end to that stability. [24]

Modernizing the defense infrastructure will be more difficult than building it from the ground up. It will also involve a great cross section of talent and industry. To hearken Gerencser's words, the task will be composed "not just of invention, engineering and construction, but also of finance, management and planning." The transition from the current array of defenses will be problematical because of entrenched institutional interests and the inertia to adapt to new business models. The focus of restructuring the present system into an effective national defense program requires input from manufacturers, consumers, service providers, the military, the scientific community, and infrastructure policy experts in various fields from energy, healthcare, transportation, agriculture, and food processing, etc. The process would mean a refreshed collaboration of government, industry, and academia that could help make these entities more representative, more efficient, and more responsive to the public's needs in education. This kind of alliance, taken seriously, would be a form of renewal with spillover potential into other areas of society. The goal of structuring a reliable national defense that facilitates commerce is in the same spirit as the ambition of forming "a more perfect union"—as stated by the founders of the American republic. To some, national security is a basic right. Because of its intensifying insinuation with private and public interests it is an issue with impact for democratic market principles as well as daily routines. It is a daunting task, not alone because of its scale, but because it requires a redefinition of the role of government and, consequentially, an attempt to insert more stability to the marketplace.

Such is the theme of the following pages. In surveying the threats and vulnerabilities, the book attempts to underscore the most acute dangers to national security. In the final chapters of Part 2 the text discusses the danger from chemical biological radiological nuclear (CBRN) incidents. They represent impending threats and the placement of their discussion at the end of this section does not imply that they are less serious issues. Rather, the choice of an early focus on the commercial supply chain, cybersecurity, and the rise of the crime-terrorist network is a way to emphasize the most immediate perils. These struggles are already underway, and whether obvious or not, their effects are occurring every day. Some issues, such as the threat to the food supply, the consequences of alternative energy source development, and the frailty of the public health infrastructure deserve more attention than they are given in this work. For the consideration of space and time, those topics have been temporarily set aside.

The book also does not aim to be a text for experts in supply chain logistics, computer science engineers, life science professionals, or policy wonks. The level of depth required by students of those specialties is found in other sources. This is intended to be a non-technical piece, which attempts to explain a few basic technology issues and some aspect of the complexities of a dangerous world. The view is wide-angle and the vernacular is layman. The purpose in the writing is to describe events and activate debate. To the extent it achieves those goals is the measure of the work's success.

NOTES

1. Ellen Nakashima, "Dismantling of Saudi-CIA Web site illustrates need for clearer cyberwar policies," *Washington Post*, 19 March 2010.

2. *Ibid.*

3. *Ibid.*

4. Lawrence Husick, Senior Fellow at the Foreign Policy Research Institute, presentation in Washington, DC on 11 July 2011.

5. Christopher Paul, "Winning Every Battle but Losing the War against Terrorists and Insurgents" in *The Long Shadow of 9/11: America's Response to Terrorism*, Rand Corporation, 2011.

6. Mark Drapeau and Linton Wells II, "Social Software and National Security: An Initial Net Assessment," Center for Technology and National Security Policy, National Defense University (April 2009), p. 1.

7. Gregory C. Wilshusen, "Social Media: Federal Agencies Need Policies and Procedures for Managing and Protecting Information They Access and Disseminate," General Accountability Office, GOA-11-605 (June 2011).

8. *Op cit.*

9. Timothy L. Thomas, "The Internet in China: Civilian and Military Uses," *Information & Security, An International Journal*, Vol. 7 (2001), Fort Leavenworth, KS.

10. *Ibid.*

11. *Ibid.*

12. Darapeau and Wells, p. 21.

13. *Ibid.*, p. 34.

14. Eduard Hovy, Language Technologies Institute, Carnegie Mellon University, conversation with author (17 July 2013).

15. *Ibid.*

16. James J. Carafano, "Social Media and National Security: A Wake Up Call," *Joint Force Quarterly* (March 2011), http://archive.atlantic-community.org/index/items/view/Social_Media_and_National_Security:_A_Wake-Up_Call.

17. *Ibid.*

18. Mark Gerencser, *et al.*, *Megacommunities* (Palgrave MacMillan, 2008), p. 38–82.

19. *Ibid.*, p. 74.

20. *Ibid.*, p. 87.

21. http://www.us-cert.gov.

22. http://www.bens.org.

23. *Ibid.*

24. Mark Gerencser, "Re-imaging Infrastructure," *The American Interest Magazine*, March, 2011.

Chapter Four

The New Arena of Conflict and Economic Competition

The United States confronts a very different world today. Instead of facing a few very dangerous adversaries, the United States confronts a number of less visible challenges that surpass the boundaries of traditional nation-states and call for quick, imaginative, and agile response.

—9/11 Commission Report

So intoned the 9/11 Commission Report. The statement reflected the realities of a new period of history and suggests the focus of U.S. national defense was disoriented and disproportionate. The document further recommended the United States should direct its energies on combating threats that originate from the string of failed states left in the wake of the Cold War.[1] The report, or, as it is formally titled, "The National Commission on Terrorists Attacks upon the United States" was the public disclosure that the world had changed. Amid the triumph of overcoming communism and the emergence of the United States as the only standing superpower, was the fact that everything, in actuality, was vulnerable. Despite the apparently enormous creation of wealth, the nation was, and still is, exposed to great risk. The end of the Cold War power alignment and the new era of globalization had produced a hyper-connected world driven by technology and based on commerce. No rival ideology or military force posed an apparent threat. However, in truth, the world was rife with enemies. The technological supremacy, which had invigorated the U.S. ascent was more accessible and was leveling the battle-field. Furthermore, our ever tightening over dependence on networks, which had made us more efficient, had also made the country more susceptible to danger. In the rush to create a global economy that would produce great streams of wealth, Americans created a system designed to guarantee freely flowing capital and trade, but not one built to safeguard their country from attack and utter disruption. Many pundits and planners also failed to realize that rather than remote territories of potential satellite states and sources of raw capital to feed the economic engine, at stake was the homeland. Its defense against attack, which could occur from within as well as afar, was the most vital national interest.

During the period of the Cold War, countries across the earth mostly fell within either one of two orbits. The conclusion of the superpower hostilities, however, left behind a string of failed states and quasi-states. As the USSR fell, new states in the region from central Asia to Eastern Europe rose to take its place. Unstable economic and political structures stood where harsh security frameworks had governed. Across the globe, once the aegis of mutual assistance programs, treaty organizations (with the exception of NATO, which expanded) and military pacts was tossed aside, new tensions emerged unleashing a massive wave of migration from within Europe,[2] as well as in Africa, Asia, and south/central America. The end of the "orderly" Cold War system of power alliances blurred the divide between East and West and reduced the roles and importance of borders. These developments ushered in a new era of cross-border crime and terrorism.

As the state loses its monopoly over control of its border and loses the ability to regulate economic activity, control information flow, and control violence—armed networks of non-state actors expand where the state is unraveling. The Balkan Wars in the 1990s, for instance, forced a collapse in law enforcement and opened the field for linkages and opportunities for criminal networks. The regional combatants there had, and maintain, arrant ties with organized crime.[3] Terrorist cells, organized criminal groups, mercenaries, and para-military groups in many parts of the world form to challenge the supremacy of the modern state. Taking advantage of the anonymity and ubiquity of the virtual world, new opportunities for criminal and terrorist activity arise and continue to expand. Within this world, crime and terrorism comfortably nest. Their groups take advantage of the dynamism of globalization by exploiting the lacunae in global governance and law enforcement.

While the trend toward de-borderization created opportunities for criminals and terrorist organizations, it did not do the same for state law enforcement organs and their sanctioned agencies. The work of countering and coordinating activity to defeat crime and terrorism often comes up against layers of diplomatic protocol and claims of sovereign rights. The trend of territorial "unbundling" or "de-bordering," which has made borders more porous, at the same time can have the reverse effect when it comes to interstate cooperation as nations struggle to update their legal codes and previous ways of thinking. National borders can be upheld as traditional boundaries of authority when groups or individuals seek safe havens from legal prosecution and for their illegal activities. These issues of sovereignty can inhibit collaborative, interstate efforts when matters of extradition, jurisdiction, and diplomatic relations erupt. Such "jurisdictional arbitrage" (using legal discrepancies between jurisdictions or states in order to have advantage over government law enforcement agencies) allows crime organizations and other renegade groups to continue to operate with impunity.[4]

Meanwhile, the virtual world is borderless and, perhaps, boundless. In our era of modernity, time and space has been crushed by advancements in communication, automation, simulation, and information technology. Microelectronic and skill revolutions have—and will continue—to reduce the importance and relevance of geographic distances and limitations. The relevance is that the struggle over territory has gradually given way to a struggle over systems and networks. People find kinship through ethnic ties, religion, tribal traditions, shared narratives, and worldviews. They are less defined by their place of residence, than by the rhythms and experience that connect them with others who share in their understanding of the world around them. In this light, national borders lose their magic over group identities and conventional militaries their effectiveness. It raises legal questions and complications about the role and mission of national armed forces. For example, the October 2011 killing of Anwar al Awlaki, an American-born al Qaeda leader, was considered a military success by most. To others it was a political assassination of an American citizen by the U.S. government. Both views are valid and, hence, create an internal moral and legal conflict for a nation that, throughout most of the duration of the wars in Iraq and Afghanistan, appeared disoriented as to its goals and divided about its commitment.

TECHNOLOGY, INFORMATION AGE, AND THE COSTS OF WAR

Technology is often the driver of events and the nature of human relations. Ironically, it was the efforts from the laudable work in science and technological advancement, which helped to shape our political and economic systems—and the perilous state of global security. The pace of technology will only increase and its impact will be a reckoning force. How the social system harnesses this momentum is critical and requires a delicate balance of the interests of commerce, security, and the protection of property, sovereignty, and human rights.

The Internet is presumed growing at the rate greater than one million pages a day. Within one year, the use of e-mail has expanded by the same extent as it took the telephone in forty. New computer technology anticipates the deployment of a chip, which is ten billion times faster than the current generation.[5] The amount of data we generate and transport annually will soon be at exabyte rate (an exabyte = 1 billion billion bytes. Putting the amount in more real-world event terms, 5 exabytes are considered to be equal to all words ever spoken by human beings).

Advances in computer, communication, information technology, and transportation have helped launch the recent patterns of change. These trends will also either transfigure the state of education, healthcare, and the quality of life worldwide or leave behind a growing generation of unskilled workers consigned to exist along the edges of poverty. Asymmetric conflict has been an outcome and integrant of the new arena.

In the military theater, the logistics of asymmetrical warfare has forced traditional militaries to adapt or become irrelevant. As mentioned earlier, the rise of the information age, the decline of the importance and effectiveness of national borders, our overdependence on fragile infrastructures, and the global reach of virtual paramilitary, crime, and terrorist networks created new battlefields. As a consequence, new adversaries with diverse objectives can stake out a terrain alongside conventional foes. Therefore, traditional state militaries and defense communities are rewriting their war plans. Robert Keohane of Princeton's Woodrow Wilson School of Public and International Affairs and Joseph Nye of the John F. Kennedy School of Government of Harvard noted how the impact of globalization has transformed and redefined military tactics in a "thickening" arena of increasingly intensive and extensive web of international relations. According to their assessment,

> At a tactical level, the asymmetry of global military power and the interconnections among networks raise new options for warfare. For example, in devising a strategy to stand up to the United States, some Chinese officers are proposing terrorism, drug trafficking, environmental degradation, and computer virus propagation. They argue that the more complicated the combination—for example, terrorism plus a media war plus a financial war—the better the results.[6]

As mentioned in the 9/11 Commission Report, at the time of the attack the United States defense community was still poised against a rival, which had since departed the field.[7] However, while Pentagon bureaucrats built theories and quantified war material in a struggle where the goal is to destroy the enemy's capacity to wage war, al Qaeda was in preparation for their offensive based calculations on the goal of establishing chaos. "Aborting the American economy is not an unattainable dream," proclaimed *Al-Anser*, an al Qaeda journal. The author based his assumption, not as much on the direct material costs of absorbing an attack, but also on calculations relative to the cascading economic effects of security expenditures, business disruption, psychological impact, and market shock.[8] Many have claimed, prior to and since the World Trade Center attack, that plunging the economic structure in turmoil was an important element, if not the primary aim, of Osama bin Laden's mission. Aware of the intensive and efficient dimensions of the world trading system, reports stated al Qaeda placed a specific emphasis on this aspect of war. Repeated calls to followers expressed the importance of waging assaults against Western economic targets. These targets are more than simply symbolic. The attack on the twin towers and the Pentagon had an emotional and market impact and unleashed a sensation that created a previously unknown state of public panic in the political arena and the marketplace. The plotters also recognized the fragility of the financial system and understood the criticality of infrastructure components such as the commercial supply chain. In *The Guardian*, Paul Eedle wrote in 2002:

> Certainly there have been repeated statements attributed to the Saudi renegade [bin Laden] and his major cohorts post-September 11, which have explicitly denigrated America as a paper tiger on the verge of financial collapse, with many further urging young Muslims to wage their jihad against Washington by focusing on targets that are likely to have a disruptive economic effect including shipping.[9]

Two years after the monstrous tragedy of the World Trade Center, *Al-Anser*'s exhortation seemed a reasonable calculation. The estimated loss to the economy due to direct and collateral damage was $120 billion.[10] The bombing incident in Madrid in 2004 was placed at $55 billion.[11] Using the same metrics to approximate potential economic loss, most estimates claim a single megaton improvised nuclear device (IND), detonated in the vicinity of Manhattan, may result in losses equal to $1 trillion. In quantitative terms, expert estimates project a macabre reality. Depending on such factors as the size, placement, and atmospheric conditions at the time, the detonation of a radiological device with the lethality approximate to the Hiroshima bomb could cause between fifty thousand to one million deaths.[12] The chilling economic consequences roughly equate to $1 million per death.[13] The latent effects of the fallout could extend across several decades.

Economic destruction and disruption would be an appealing objective to a terrorist organization as it exacted revenge in exchange for what they perceive as injustice. This could pressure sovereign states into some sort of political submission or regime change through the ballot box. Either tactic could fulfill such an aim. The physical destruction of the economic infrastructure, or the operational disablement of the system due to fear might achieve the same goal. Many security experts claim the reaction to such an attack would force governments to impose strict security measures, which could be costly and profoundly constrict commerce. The effect on the global economy would be devastating. The consequences resulting from a catastrophic physical attack or a global shutdown of commerce would be relatively equal in impact. Therefore, since the political objective is economic, a security regime, which does not enable commerce and ensure business continuity, is neither practical for business nor actionable politically.

A WORLD OF WEAPONS

Distressingly, warhead delivery has equally low technological and economic barriers as conventional devices and *materiale*.[14] According to Mohamed El Baradei, the Director General of the International Atomic Energy Agency (IAEA), there exists a "Wal-Mart of private-sector proliferation" in nuclear materials, designs, and technologies.[15] These products have been available on a worldwide black market for decades. With the former Soviet Union being the lead supplier, other chief sources of procurement come from Russia, Pakistan, North Korea, Ukraine, and Uzbekistan. In 2003, former Senator Sam Nunn commented, "There are 100 nuclear research reactors and other facilities in 40 countries using highly enriched uranium—the raw material of nuclear terrorism. Some of it is secured by nothing more than an underpaid guard sitting inside a chain-linked fence."[16] As testament to Nunn's remark, in June 2007, the London *Observer* reported that British intelligence services intercepted an effort by a group of British citizens to sell weapons-grade uranium to Iran. Prior to their arrest, the smugglers had successfully acquired the material from the Russian black market. The lethal contraband was *en route* to a middleman in the Sudan before authorities interdicted.[17]

Dispersed over fourteen of its bygone republics and across eleven time zones, the former Soviet Union had 22,000 tactical nuclear weapons in its national arsenal at the time of its collapse. Despite the assurances by the Russian Ministry of Defense that tactical weapons were to be removed from all its forces around the world, the odds of following through with the plan at a 100 percent success rate were minute. Given the state of the Russian economy, the condition of its crumbling ministries, and the level of corruption and crime at the time, one would be credulous to think that Russia could complete a successful removal of these weapons within the announced timeframe. At the same time, inventories from around the former USSR were expropriated into the hands of enterprise managers by these officials' own authority. Accounts abound of plant workers, scientists, and high-ranking government and military officials attempting to sell nuclear material and weaponry on the black market.[18] During the period of Russia's privatization programs of the 1990s, "a nuclear heist at many Russian facilities would be easier than robbing a bank,"[19] claims Graham Allison, founding dean of Harvard's John F. Kennedy School of Government. Therefore, less than a few decades after the Cold War, non-ICBM attacks constitute a much greater risk than a launch from an ICBM system.[20]

Within the maritime trade network, these conditions offer a range of possibilities and theaters of operation. As great a potential for disaster as might be, shipping containers may not be the only weapons delivery platform of the maritime security threat. The ships, themselves, can be used as weapons. Incidents such as the USS *Cole* in 2000 and the attack off the coast of

Yemen on the French tanker *Limburg* are illustrations of how the hypothetical threat from an explosive-laden sea vessel can become a deadly event. The attack of a commercial target, such as the *Limburg*, is a "minor" demonstration of the previously cited al Qaeda objective of "aborting the American economy." The suicide assault in October 2002 resulted in three deaths (two of which were the assailants). However, in addition to being merely symbolic, the event led to the short-term collapse of the international shipping business in the Gulf of Aden and the nearby region. Brent crude rose and war-risk insurance premiums for the shipping industry tripled. Among the losses for the Yemen economy was an average of $3.8 million a month in port revenues.[21] Although the numbers are not enormous the incident demonstrates the causal chain of events, which can reverberate from a relatively simple, low cost, and crude attack. These acute and wholesale exposures to attack make ports attractive targets to terrorists. The same traits make them financially prohibitive to defend. Whether as launching pads or as weapons, Hezbollah, al Qaeda, Indonesia's Jemaah Islamiyah, and the Popular Front for the Liberation of Palestine are known to have sought and/or acquired cargo vessels and achieved maritime capability, including the capability to transport contraband and illegal weapons.[22]

As opposed to the limited damage done in Yemen, an attack on a major terminal or a strategic chokepoint such as the Straight of Hormuz, the Straight of Malacca, Bab el Mandeb, or the Bosperous could have severe consequences for the global economy. Small freight and even fishing vessels can be used as launching pads for cruise missile attacks to unleash an assault hundreds of miles from shore. The risk of detection for assailants would be moderate. Approximately 70,000 cruise missiles are in arsenal around the world and their technology is economically and physically accessible.[23] In addition, and more menacing than sophisticated cruise missiles, are man-portable air-defense systems (MANPADS). MANPADS are very affordable and widely available. These are shoulder-launched-surface to air missiles (SAMS) and can be purchased on virtually any black market in the world for as little as a few hundred dollars. They are lightweight (between 35–40 pounds) and have an engagement range of 4 miles. Kill ratios are high and the proliferation of these weapons is in large numbers. Military aircraft are highly vulnerable and civil aircrafts are sitting ducks.[24] Despite some systematic use of codes and controls in place to monitor and limit their illegal sale and use, smugglers have the choice of moving these weapons around the global network of ports either legitimately or clandestinely.

Figure 4.1.   Container Cargo Vessel and Gantry *(Source: CREATE Homeland Security Center at the University of Southern California)*

WARFARE AND GLOBALIZATION

Ideology is not only found in politics but also in economic theory. By the time the Thatcherite and Reagan administrations had reached full momentum, an era of deregulation had triumphantly arrived with, what some might also say, an aura of spite and vengeance following the inconsistent years under Carter. In later decades, as the Cold War wound down, neo-liberal economic policies launched a dramatic new—or, perhaps, revived—dogmatic approach to economic development.[25] Taxes and regulations came under pressure around the world. Concurrent, or rather, synchronized with the *laissez faire*–Washington consensus policies, is the fact that trade tariffs for industrialized nations fell between 1980 and 1999, while tariffs for Lesser Developed Countries declined over the same period.[26] According to a 2004 study, four times as many varieties of goods were imported to the United States in 2002 as were imported in 1972 during this time.[27]

The thrust of this political energy found its way into American Grand Strategy. During the fall of the Soviet Union and through the period of the war in Iraq, U.S. foreign policy included a strong prescription of neoliberal treatment. In the preamble to the 2002 *National Security Strategy* President George W. Bush, in hardly veiled terms, set down the administration's economic principles and declared its underlying vision:

> We will actively work to bring the hope of democracy, development, free markets, and free trade to every corner of the world. . . . Free trade and free markets have proven their ability to lift whole societies out of poverty—so the United States will work with individual nations, entire regions, and the entire global trading community to build a world that trades in freedom and therefore grows in prosperity.[28,29]

Thus, James N. Rosenau, who studies globalization and analyzes how the process pervades the routine of daily life, states: "Virtually no one contests the proposition that the worldwide turn of countries toward free trade and neoliberal economic policies has had vast consequences."[30] Although the debate over the benefits and consequences of neo-liberalism still persists, there is no doubt that its ascendance in policy guidance signaled a radical departure from a previous era. According to Joseph Stiglitz, former chief economist at the World Bank, these policies have altered the roles and interrelationships between the IMF and the World Bank[31]—as well as their clients.

Hastened by the effects of these "altered roles" the international trading system was undergoing change. The impact of free trade policies, financial liberalization, and the internationalization of production resulted in a new commercial environment of high-volume, unfettered movement of goods.[32] As crossings become bridges for economic activity rather than security checkpoints and control sites, a new stimulus was influencing and shaping international relations. These events coincided with political changes in Moscow, Peking, and continued to extend across the globe.

At the time of the disintegration of the USSR, the failure of the Communist Party trumpeted proof for proponents of neoliberal economic policies that government was fallible and the market was not. Hence, a disdain for intervention into economic affairs by national governments grew, while a belief in the efficiency of markets (as expressed in the 2002 *National Security Strategy* above) gained fervor. Less government regulation and more business, it was reasoned, would generate a cycle of economic growth and a sustained attack on poverty, worldwide. Coinciding with these policies and beliefs are the data that trade tariffs for less developed countries declined to 11.3 percent from 27.6 percent over the same period.[33] As trade barriers withered away, trade volume responded with growth. Privatization and deregulation further contributed to the momentum of the self-regulating market, as disciplinary powers became the province of credit rating agencies and currency speculators. Countries formed into economic blocs and obliged the system with lax border controls and facilitated capital flow. Although not totally unencumbered by concerns for security, the goals of free trade policy were always to make trade as frictionless as possible.

To these forces, include advancements in transportation and communication technology. Since World War II the average ocean freight costs have declined 50 percent, air transport by 80 percent, and transatlantic telecommunications by 99 percent.[34] Collectively, these influences shape an emerging new world system. This revolution in the communication and transportation industries made possible disaggregated production schemes, allowing for firms to gain economies of scale and more highly organized inventory and asset management control. These changing patterns opened the way for just-in-time manufacturing processes. From these forces the business model of the extended enterprise arose. The truth that the majority of trade is in intermediate goods is further evidence confirming the paradigm shift in the production model. A new international trade paradigm took form. Remote production sites and points of sales are more tightly linked than before. A new self-enforced market discipline drives business planning, inventory, and asset management.[35] Production and labor are mobile (in some cases, nomadic). Capital and customers can be sourced and tapped from anywhere depending upon political and economic environments. No markets or places are inaccessible. The system strives to commoditize products, services, and access.

The result for a global security framework is an open world system, where traditional linkages between states become more indistinct as political priorities yield to economic imperatives.[36] What arises is a network designed to accommodate the voluminous transfer of financial flows, trade in goods, and manufacturing processes, which uses the supply chain network as a way to warehouse goods simultaneously as it moves them to market. Yet, these very principles of unfettered trade and open participation, which have been responsible for the extraordinary gains in prosperity and economic growth, are also at the heart of the system's vulnerability. This demand for unfettered trade still drives commerce. Yet, the economic benefits are unequally shared, and the uneven pace and apportionment of the distribution of basic humanitarian goods and services breeds tension.

During the recent decades, the promise of some that economic globalization would reduce poverty failed to deliver. Despite the enormous increase in wealth of the latest period, the creation of riches has not cast back an equitable arrangement of distribution. Figures tend to confirm that coinciding with the rise of liberal economic policies has been the widening divide between the haves and have-nots. Throughout this period an additional 100 million people across the earth were driven into abject poverty. A shroud of marginalized populations of people who are either unemployed or underemployed covers much of the globe. While at the same time, world income grew, in aggregate, at an annual rate of 2 percent.[37] Poverty and population segments marginalized by economic policies create a fertile ground for recruitment and plunder by transnational criminal and terrorist organizations. The result is that tensions abound.

Many analysts claim the drive for free trade and open markets, deregulation, and the privatization of former public assets has created opportunities for participants from both sides of the law. Accessible technology gives criminals and terrorists options for grander panoramas of competition and warfare. As asymmetrical warfare spreads, it breeds an environment of opportunity for anonymous and pervasive power by illegal contestants. This occurs while the obsolescence of traditional militaries as a protection force inhibits legitimate state actors. The transformations in warfare and global competition trap these forces within an obsolete security framework and mindset. Imaginative forms of intelligent weaponry are in development and being deployed at a rigorous rate. The field of conflict and competition is morphing into an unfamiliar terrain. The new landscape is rife with mounting and unforeseen threats while many struggle to adapt to the new contours with no comprehensive or collaborative policy guidance or vision.

The intricate problems of securing national interests, which include a fragile infrastructure of utility networks, energy delivery lines, communication systems, and supply chain webs against sabotage raises many questions about the "public good," ownership, and governance. With the private sector owning over 85 percent of the U.S. critical infrastructure, profit incentives often clash with the needs for investment in security. The traditional and legal boundaries of national security lag behind the change curve, too. Yet, at the same time, the matrix of state defense, private-sector interests, and economic forces is more multi-layered. As well, their relationship is more interwoven and their interaction more rhythmic than any other time in the past. These related elements flow more deeply and bewilderingly as a result of technological advancement and the rise of asymmetrical, modern war. The composition of the modern security framework reflects both the cacophony and the harmony. All the while, the gathering and uneven momentum of globalization provide a growth mechanism for legitimate and non-legitimate actors alike.

CRIME AND TERRORISM, INTERNATIONAL

Aided by advancements in communication technology and adoption of the organizational logic of multinational companies, crime and terrorism have been allowed to thrive. Transnational crime and international terrorism exploit the mechanisms of globalization much the same way private-sector actors do. The regional conflicts in the Balkans, Chechnya, Central Asia, South and Central America, et al., revealed that as legitimate actors mastered the technological tools of globalization, so can those who choose to manipulate the economic and political system for their own, outlawed or terrorist benefit. The very institutions, international codes, practices, and policies that have enabled economic globalization have offered criminals and terrorists opportunities for exploitation as well. They have advanced their agendas quite effectively adapting to the organizational philosophies of multinational companies. Multicultural, multi-operational, geographically diverse, techno-logically savvy, and highly mobile, terrorists and criminals are the obverse image of their legitimate counterparts. Their ability to manage the system to their use and benefit has allowed them to survive and be successful while, at the same time, their illegal operations mirror the lawful. The result is a world of international and transnational relations where voids of authority exist spasmodically among legitimate actors. As failed states populate the planet affording crime and terrorism opportunities for corruption and exploitation, these elements can find accommodating and sympathetic host governments. These criminal organizations are often extended enterprises themselves, forming partnerships, entering into licensing agreements, and lobbying governments.

If they cannot manipulate the state, terrorist cells, organized criminal groups, mercenaries, and paramilitary groups in many parts of the world can also form to challenge its supremacy. Taking advantage of the anonymity and ubiquity of the virtual world and asymmetric wars, new opportunities for terrorist/criminal activity arise and continue to expand while law enforce-ment and military organizations face greater challenges. Places such as Af-ghanistan and Chechnya are obvious examples. That said, those outside the law do not always restrict themselves to criminal activity. Legitimate com-mercial operations are sometimes a source of revenue for not only pirate and criminal gangs, but also terrorist groups. The Liberation Tigers of Tamil Eelam (LTTE) had been waging war against the Sri Lankan government for decades. They also have been operating a profitable network of freight for-warders and ship operators since the mid-1980s. Operating under Panama-nian and Honduran registry, the LTTE maintained a fleet of ten to twelve bulk cargo freighters hauling such commodities as cement, hardwood, tea, and fertilizer. Although the bulk of the cargo was legitimate, reports claimed that at least 5 percent might have represented arms, ammunition, explosives, and other military-related supplies. An unsettling revelation is the allegation that the LTTE used its maritime companies to transfer arms to other terrorist groups, including the al Qaeda linked Harkat-ul-Mujahideen of Pakistan.[38] It is believed that al Qaeda had a fleet of cargo vessels of its own and may have used it to generate revenue.[39] The obvious possibility is that a terrorist group could establish a reputable record after years of legitimate maritime commer-cial service while it waits for its moment to launch a highly coordinated and catastrophic assault on one or more population centers.

Throughout such unfolding of events, the evolution of transnational crime and terrorism may have entered a new era of symbiosis. The growth of the global economic system has widened the scope of opportunities for crime and terrorism to converge, collaborate, and emerge. These two outlaw groups traditionally are separated by motives, time/action horizons, and their relationship with the state. Now they share the same *modus operandi* and, in many places, similar motivations to oppose authority. Where once the fault line between crime and terrorism was distinct, today those contours are becoming indistinct.[40] The post-Cold War period and the development of the uneven process of globalization have generated a rising criminal economy. Wherever shadow economies are allowed to prosper the politicalization of economics and the criminalization of politics have accelerated their rise. In states where tax systems, trade, investment, and security infrastructure have collapsed, new opportunities emerge for criminal organizations through illegal trade, drug trafficking, extortion, and other forms of plunder. Rather than pay taxes to guarantee safety and equity, citizens pay protection money and rely on the black market as an alternative allocative mechanism for goods and services. For an economy that Mary Kaldor of the London School of Economics describes as "the underside of globalization," these activities not only draw financial support trading in contraband substances and predatory activity, but also backing from sympathetic states and networks. These "alternative, exploitive forms of financing"[41] are made more problematic by the dynamism that accompanies globalization.[42] In an editorial in *The New York Times*, journalist and author Robert Wright offers up an ominous appraisal:

> A confluence of technologies, from the Internet to biotechnology, is making it easier and easier for far-flung hatred to assume organized form, intersect with weapons technology and constitute unprecedently potent terrorism. This growing lethality of hatred may be the biggest long-term problem we face.[43]

Not only the advancement but also the versatility of modern technology brings further complications to the security dilemma. Adding to the disorientation of an unfamiliar environment, few private high-tech areas produce technologies solely for civilian application. Today, nearly all technical product development has military potential. From delicate medical instrumentation to social networking tools, the application potential can be useful to traditional militaries and also terrorists, criminal elements, and other nonstate actors. A case illustration occurred in 2004. An Israeli businessman from South Africa was detained in Denver. The reason for his detention was the discovery of 200 devices used in hospitals to break kidney stones apart. He had ordered these instruments from an American company on behalf of a Pakistani concern. However, U.S. authorities alertly observed that hospitals routinely require only a small handful be in supply in order to meet their infrequent demands. Suspicions rose because these same medical instruments are also used to detonate nuclear explosions. To weapons builders they are triggering devices for bombs and are a classic example of "dual use" application. [44]

The above instance only points to the fact that companies and their research teams are becoming more multinational and multicultural while they continue to develop and produce security relevant goods and technologies. [45] Surely, such factors only work to make the task of national security more challenging and complex. The blurring of demarcations between legitimate boundaries, whether it concerns governance, ownership, or technological application, has created a very perilous world for global security. The example above also underscores the issue that in addition to the transit of goods, there also needs to be a more universal and reliable system of export controls as part of a global security scheme.

In addition to those exploitation tools and methods already cited, the opportunity of asymmetric war provides the criminal and the terrorist with political, social, technical, and tactical laboratories. Flashpoints such as Afghanistan, the Balkans, Chechnya, Iraq, Pakistan, Sri Lanka, or South America offer proving grounds and fields of operation where terrorism and crime can ply their crafts in combat, oppressive rule, illegal trafficking, hostage taking, and murder. These conditions along with the imperatives of global commerce, the spread of multinational firms, the implementation of privatization programs, the rise of civil society, the unbundling of borders, a democratic deficit, [46] and the momentum and politicalization of transnational crime organizations may head us toward an era of resilient terrorism and crime. The mechanisms of global commerce, advancements and confluence of technology, and the ability of outlaw elements to intersect with these forces, may present the twenty-first century with a challenge, which may rival in consequence and gravity the future problems of an energy crisis, global recession, and the prospects of environmental disaster.

CONCLUSION

The events of 9/11 exposed a new field of conflict. The definitions of national security and threat acquired new meanings. Interstate wars declined as the driving force behind policies that formed alliances, created treaties, and marshaled technology. Competition subsided over control of territory in favor of objectives less defined and more enigmatic. Hence, the new web of international relations, issues of governance, the role of the state, and the organizing elements of politics and economics set a complicated context for security policy. Given the sea change, at what point would it be too late to warn against falling into the trap of assessing our situation in terms of preconceived accepted wisdoms? We disregard or deny the contradictory signs of conventional thinking at our own peril. Despite the U.S. hegemony in the world, to paraphrase the 9/11 Commission Report, "the system alarms were flashing" before the planes hit the World Trade Center.

The shift from interstate wars to the Bush administration's "war on terrorism" was the natural reaction to the new state of international relations. The devastation of the World Trade Center forced the U.S. federal government and the traditional military to come to the private sector seeking help in developing domestic security regimes. In addition to the challenges raised by groups officially unaffiliated with sovereign governments, the decades of deregulation, government outsourcing, and privatization policies made it apparent that the private sector must take some ownership in providing the public good of national defense by protecting its own assets. As principal owners and operators of the nation's critical infrastructure and vital interests, the private sector came into a position of new responsibility. However, old business models and praxis basically went, and remain, unchanged. The system of commerce still remains resistant to the intrusion of regulatory oversight. Mandates for security standards will be difficult to implement—particularly in times of economic hardship. It is counter-intuitive for private enterprise to want the added cost of security investment, as it is for firms to welcome the prospect of encumbered trade flow and the risk of lawsuits should they fall out of compliance with government regulations.

Voluntary programs such as the ones presently in place are unlikely to succeed since they would only produce competitive cost disadvantages for enrollees. Yet, perhaps more importantly, they leave the integrity of the system still unsecured because of the lack of full participation. Private-sector actors who voluntarily decline to upgrade their security regimes are the "free riders" that might benefit, but at the same time allow their organizations to become breaches in the overall security system due to the inter-connectivity of commerce. Security, as with any public good, is only effective if its aegis is non-exclusive. Benefits of security investment, unfortunately, often appear to boards and audit committees as abstract as the fears they are at work to neutralize. In today's environment, without some tangible return, justification for enterprise security investment will have to rely upon the motivational stimuli found in traditional asset protection, competitive market pressures, some prospect of organizational efficiency, and the indefinite advantages of good corporate citizenship. While business struggles with itself to establish enough justification to commit to a reliable, whole-cloth security infrastructure, the pressures of just-in-time processes drive the decision making. Security divisions will have to compete with other departments for corporate resources and funds. The conflict between commerce and security may create a dilemma for strategic planners at the enterprise level and, eventually, a strain upon the principles of a demand market economy.

Hence, national security, often cited as the textbook example of a public good, became subject to a paradigm shift after 9/11 and a victim to an outmoded mindset and established arrangements and embedded interests. The nature of the "non-excludability" of a public good means that when a "good" is provided to one, it is provided to all. This "non-rivalness" helped propel and justify the scale and enormity of U.S. defense budgets in the past. The structure and mechanisms of the old order, unfortunately, hold hostage the forward motion necessary to meet and align against the new set of threats.

Additionally, when a public good such as the commercial infrastructure is under the control of private owners—who bears the financial onus and rightful accountability for its protection? It is not easy to convince a stakeholder public of diverse backgrounds, interests, motivations, and goals that these privately owned assets of the commercial infrastructure are their responsibility. Despite being a political and strategic target, on whose reliability all depend, policy makers will have a difficult time justifying public funds to cover private-sector asset protection. The argument in the United States that the system privatize profits while it made risk a public burden has been politically sensitive since the financial crisis bailout in 2008. However, the question of who should share this onus is important and unavoidable. Which entity, the individual taxpayer, the corporation, or a combination of both, bears the weight of national defense? In short, how do we restore a "non-rivalness" view that engages all government, private sector, and civil society stakeholders under the circumstances of economic hardship, a fractious electorate, and the overhang of an abstract threat? At the same time, the political system needs to assure property and privacy rights, encourage fair competition in the marketplace, and preserve democratic institutions.

Despite the fact that the collective homeland, quality of life, and daily routines are the objectives under attack, a natural constituency and central U.S. policy has yet to form. The process of globalization has offered up an amazing range of possibilities, and also opened up a commensurate array of complex questions and opportunities for exploitation. Unfortunately, criminals and terrorists know the systems' weaknesses well and are in position to take advantage.

Making gain of the "mechanisms of globalization" and the lapses in global governance, criminal organizations have the reach and capability of many international organizations. Yet, lurking within the complexity of the pattern in global affairs, a future widespread, catastrophic event may be only a question of at what point will an "entrepreneurial terrorist" decide that merely exploiting the system is not enough. The dream of "aborting the American economy" could be overwhelming to some soul and his followers. The opportunity to apply knowledge of the system and fulfill a passion to avenge a feeling of injustice may be too tempting. If one such person or group is determined enough, another assault upon us all similar to the catastrophe in 2001 is not unrealistic.

The rise of private armies, the contracting to private companies of many military support functions, the new options of global military power and the asymmetry of the conflict complicate standing notions of traditional warfare. Complicated, too, are notions about the proper role of government and the obligation of the corporate citizen to meet the challenge of the new array of adversaries. Finally, the perception of national defense is a public good, which needs support and is an idea due for re-envisioning.

NOTES

1. *The 9/11 Commission Report* (W.W. Norton & Company, New York & London, 2004), p 367.

2. T. Koppel & A. Szekely "Transnational and organized crime and conflict in the Balkans" in Philip Reichel (Ed.), *Handbook of Transnational Crime & Justice* (Sage: Thousand Oaks, CA, 2002), p. 12.

3. *Ibid.*

4. Phil Williams, "Organized Crime and Cybercrime, Synergies, Trends, and Responses," in *Global Issues 2001,* US Information Agency.

5. James N. Rosenau, *Distant Proximities: Dynamics Beyond Globalization* (Princeton University Press, 2003), p. 54–55.

6. Robert O. Keohane, & Joseph S. Nye, "Governance in a Globalizing World," in *Power and Governance in a Partially Globalized World*, Robert O. Koehane (Routledge, London & New York, 2002), p. 201.

7. The 9/11 Commission Report, p. 399.

8. Abu-Ubayd Al-Qurashi, "A lesson in War," Al-Anser (Internet, 19 December 2002), as quoted by Anonymous, *Imperial Hubris: Why the West is Losing the War on Terror* (Brassey's Inc., Washington, DC, 2004), p. 102.

9. Paul Eedle, "G2: Inside Story, Terrorism.com: How does al Qaida stay organized when its members are in hiding and scattered across the world? Easy—it runs a website, says Paul Eedle," *The Guardian,* London, 17 July 2002 in Michael D. Greenberg, "Maritime Terrorism: risk and Liability" Center for Terrorism Risk Management Policy, RAND Corp. Santa Monica, CA (2006), p. 16.

10. Philippe Crist, "Security in Maritime Transport: Risk Factors and Economic Impact," Prepared for the Organization for Economic Cooperation and Development (2003).

11. Barrie Stevens, "The Security Economy," Prepared for the Organization for Economic Cooperation and Development, 2004, pp. 12–13.

12. C. Clark, "The Economic Impact of Nuclear Terrorist Attacks on Freight Transport System in an Age of Seaport Vulnerability," Cambridge, MA: Abt Associates, Inc. (2003).

13. Michael D. Greenberg, *et al.*, "Maritime Terrorism: Risk and Liability" Center for Terrorism Risk Management Policy, RAND Corp. Santa Monica, CA (2006), p. 120.

14. James M. Loy, Robert G. Ross, "Global Trade: America's Achilles Heel," in *Defense Horizons*, Center for Technology and National Security Policy, National Defense University (February 2002).

15. Graham Allison, *Nuclear Terrorism: The Ultimate Preventable Catastrophe* (Holt & Co., New York, 2004), p. 61.

16. http://www.sgpproject.org/NunnKazakhstan.pdf.

17. "UK Stops Iranian Nuclear Smuggling Effort," *Global Security Newswire*, posted 6/11/07 on Nuclear Threat Initiative website, www.nti.org.

18. One celebrated case tells of the Russian Pacific Fleet Admiral, Igor Khmelnov, selling off sixty-four decommissioned ships including two aircraft carriers, which he reportedly received $5 million each from India and South Korea.

19. Allison, p. 86.

20. *Ibid.*

21. Greenberg, p. 16.

22. Gal Luft, Allen Korin, "Terrorism Goes to Sea" *Foreign Affairs* (November/December 2004), Vol. 83, Issue 6.

23. Greenberg, p. 16.

24. "Man Portable Air Defense System (MANPADS)," GlobalSecurity.org, May 2011, http://www.globalsecurity.org/military/intro/manpads.htm.

25. Joseph E. Stiglitz, *Globalization and Its Discontents* (W.W. Norton & Co., 2003), p. 16.

26. Peter Andreas, "Redrawing the Line: Borders and Security in the Twenty-first Century," *International Security*, Vol. 28, No. 2 (Fall 2003), p. 83.

27. Marc Levinson, *The Box: How the Shipping Container Made the World Smaller and the World Economy Bigger* (Princeton University Press, 2006), p. 3.

28. *The National Security Strategy of the United States* (2002), p. IV–V, http://www.whitehouse.gov/nsc/nssintro.html.

29. Ian Shapiro, *Containment: Rebuilding a Strategy Against Global Terror* (Princeton University Press, 2007), p. 23.

30. Rosenau, p. 19.

31. Stiglitz, pp. 13–15, 74.

32. Philip G. Cerny, "Mapping Varieties of Neoliberalism," presentation to the International Studies Association annual meeting, Montreal (March 2004), p. 8–9.

33. Andreas, pp. 81–82.

34. Byron G. Auguste, as cited by Koslowski, Rey in "Border and Transportation Security in the Transatlantic Relationship," Anja Dalagaard-Nielsen and Daniel Hamilton, *Transatlantic Homeland Security? Protecting Society in the Age of Catastrophic Terrorism* (Routledge, forthcoming).

35. Levinson, p. 256.

36. *Ibid.*

37. "Global Economic Prospects and the Developing Countries 2000," Washington, DC, World Bank 2000 in Stiglitz, p. 29.

38. Peter Chalk, "Liberation Tigers of Tamil Eelam's (LTTE) International Organization and Operations—A Preliminary Analysis" Commentary No. 77, Canadian Security Intelligence Service (17 March 2000), as cited by Crist, pp. 15–16.

39. Philippe Crist, "Security in Maritime Transport: Risk Factors and Economic Impact," Prepared for the Organization for Economic Cooperation and Development (2003), p. 12.

40. Walter Laqueur, *The New Terrorism* (Oxford University Press, 1999), p. 211.

41. Mary Kaldor, "Beyond Militarism, Arms Races, and Arms Control." Talk delivered at the Nobel Peace Prize Centennial Symposium, Oslo, Norway (6 December 2001).

42. James H. Mittelman, *The Globalization Syndrome* (Princeton University Press, 2000), p. 208.

43. Robert Wright, "The Neocon Paradox," *New York Times* editorial (24 April 2007).

44. Allison, p. 77.

45. Allyson J. K. Bailes, Business and the Security Agenda: "Victim, Accomplice, or Ally," Center for Transatlantic Relations (2004), p. 7.

46. Democratic deficit refers to the lack of democratic accountability and control over the decision-making process. Although the number of legitimate and self-proclaimed "democracies" has risen around the world, it is the claim that too much authority has been delivered into the hands of bodies such as The World Bank Group, the IMF, central banks, corporate boards, and via the influence of powerful lobbies and other rent seeking activists.

Part II

Current, Emerging, and Impending Threats and Challenges

Chapter Five

The Maritime Supply Chain: Vast, Diverse, and Anarchic

... there is no doubt that containers are going to be exploited as a poor man's missile. The question is when, not if.
—John Meredith, Managing Director of Hutchinson Port Holdings

In assessing the challenges from a threat in terms of direct economic and commercial costs, the greatest exposure of risk is probably along the maritime transportation system. It has the greatest number of breach points and the potential for the most serious damage. Because ports are located at the intersection of transportation, communication, and human traffic flows, they are prime targets for terrorist groups. Moreover, the vast, un-policed, and under-governed nature of the maritime system is another reason making it a particularly attractive target for terrorists. The seas cover 130 million miles of the earth's surface. No sole state or hegemony is powerful enough to command over it. The international maritime supply chain is a web of transport routes that intersect at thousands of points and among as many intermediaries. Amid the webbing of international affairs and global commerce is this stateless, anarchic realm, beyond the jurisdictional reach and control of politicians, law enforcement authorities, intelligence agencies, and international regimes. It is an environment open to exploitation by terrorists and crime. The major concern for authorities is that terrorists will not only exploit this potential successfully, but also do so with dramatic economic and political effect.

Ports can be either gateways into foreign territory or targets for terrorists. Attack scenarios are multiple and varied. The most commonly suggested is the possibility that terrorists will smuggle a WMD into a shipping container at a major port. The pathways used by criminals to bring in drugs or illegal

aliens are a matter of routine. Certainly terrorists have adequate knowledge
of the same methods and tactics. The proliferation of these weapons and the
intensification of global trade have raised the odds and created ample opportunities for such events. It has been assumed that the explosives used in the
bombing of the U.S. embassies in Kenya in 1998 were brought into the
country by a vessel controlled by al Qaeda.[1] In March 2004, the same week
as the commuter train bombing in Madrid, a suicide attack at the Israeli port
of Ashdod killed ten Israelis. The terrorists involved may have been let into
the port via a specially equipped container. The *Jerusalem Post* reported that
Palestinian operatives might have made the trip from Gaza with their arms
cache in an undetected, hidden compartment.[2]

Seaports pose a particularly serious risk as high valued targets because
they lie at the heart of our economic and societal vital interests. We must bear
in mind, too, that the circulatory system of the global supply chain is also the
inventory warehouse of the just-in-time manufacturing process. Should an
attack occur at a major intermodal juncture of the transportation system, the
disruption could be disabling to international trade and the world economy.
Some even suggest that a single attack on a prime container port could spawn
a global recession.[3] This contention rests partly on the assumption that all
commerce would come to a halt due to a public demand for inspection rates
of cargo to rise to 100 percent levels. These measures would strangle world
trade and essentially grind world commerce to a halt. As the crises spread, all
sectors would be affected and all markets would reflect the fears of a system
thrown into chaos. The rush toward the safe havens of cash and precious
commodities could be furious. Investors' tolerance for securities with only
the slightest modicum of risk could be tested.

Within two weeks, these analysts claim, the economic and market shock
would be global. An event would be a severe test of business resiliency. The
2002 ten-day labor lockout at the Port of Los Angeles/Long Beach cost the
U.S. economy $1 billion per day.[4] These numbers are an insufficient bench-
mark, however. They only reflect pure economic costs without the impact of
market panic, political volatility, and the price of higher investment in security. In the event of a terrorist attack, the political fallout might be destabilizing. Ironically, the theory posits the opinion that the misdirected resources
devoted to military supremacy would be a foundational factor in ultimately
weakening our national security.[5] The policies that created this "Maginot
Line" of defense would ultimately be an Achilles heel because of their strategic obsolescence. Whether this hypothesis is accurately predictive or simply
alarmist is open to much debate. Nevertheless, no matter how uncertain may
be the severity of the degree and nature of such a significant event, it is clear
the cost will be high and by then it may be too late to design ways to organize
national defenses along an appropriate strategic tract.

The increase in world trade has increased the strain and our dependency on the maritime supply chain. Analogously to the growth of the Internet, when the seaborne trade network expanded—so did the population of nodes and breach points. As previously noted, neo-liberal economic policies paved the way for unfettered trade and assigned to security concerns the same category of disregard as regulation. Trade tariffs over the world fell and the volume and variety of goods rose exponentially. Deregulation, borderless trade, and accessible technology and weaponry marked a new era of competition and conflict. According to a report by the Organization for Economic Cooperation and Development (OECD), "the world paradigm for global prosperity has been predicated on near-frictionless trade."[6] The statement's implication for the trafficking of weapons, illegal drugs, cash, and human beings brims with the obvious logic that these forms of capital circulate within the global supply chain as well. Rather than yield global prosperity, however, their returns are in the form of political instability, crime, danger, and mounting threat.

CONTAINERIZATION

At the core of the commercial and technological revolution in the global marketplace and its environment of frictionless trade is an uncomplex, dull assembly of wood, steel, and/or aluminum. The shipping container, despite its lack of sophistication, is arguably a main reason for the transformation of the world economy. Its standard dimensions, ubiquity, and inexpensiveness have changed our conception of the geographic economy in much the same way as has the Internet. By making shipping cheap it has made capital more mobile, facilitated just-in-time manufacturing, extended the enterprise, and created new market centers as it has eliminated or forced the decline of old ones. How did a simple device become such a fundamental agent of change and driver of events? Its importance is not associated with what it can do, but with how it can be used.

Marc Levinson, an economist and writer, has written authoritatively on how this basic low-tech tool has enabled globalization with as much force and impact as the computer chip. He reminds us that prior to its use, production sites needed to be located close to markets. In the period immediately following World War II, the world was abundant with factories selling directly to local markets. Transportation costs were high. Then as now, inventory required financing (carrying costs), and was susceptive to vandalism and theft. Therefore, idle inventory is a drag on company assets. By the late 1950s, however, all this changed with the introduction of containerized shipping. When a trucking entrepreneur, named Malcolm McLean, purchased a steamship company to merge sea and ground transport of containerized goods he set in motion a revolution in commercial trade. The efficiencies he introduced reduced transportation costs while simultaneously eliminating delays. Low-cost transportation changed the geography of business forever. Not only did it nullify the commercial advantage urban locations had over their country cousins, it shifted the terms of trade in favor of enterprises who enjoyed paying cheaper wages, lower taxes, and utility rates in more remote areas.[7]

Today the equivalent of more than 300 million containers are handled each year around the world. In 2011, approximately 10.7 million containers arrived in U.S. ports.[8] The loading and unloading process is highly automated. Computers choreograph container movements as cargo is discharged from vessels and outgoing cargo is simultaneously loaded with the aid of preprogrammed container cranes. Transport has become inexpensive, frictionless, and predictable. Yet, before containers, freight terminals were choke points. The most expensive part of the journey occurred at the inter-modal junctures where cargo was transferred between ship and ground carriers.[9] As mentioned above, these operations not only translated into costs, but also delays. Presently, however, these former choke points are a boost to trade. Rather than delayed, lost, or pilfered, cargo is now seamlessly re-routed and commerce accelerates. Between 1957 and 1966, when shipping containers were put into service, international trade in manufactured goods outgrew total world production in volume by more than twice as much.[10] Today, the continued amplification of trade has brought the number of containers in circulation to approximately 12–15 million.[11] According to published estimates of Maersk Sealand, "If all the containers in the world were lined up, it would create a container wall of 108,000 kilometers, or 2.7 times the circumference of the world." If these statistics were not already staggering, it is worthwhile to note that the number of containers in operation is expected to increase to 30 million over the next twenty years.[12]

The growth and impact of containerization did not simply have an effect on the manufacturing industry. The shipment of commodities and raw materials was subject to this revolution in global commerce as well. In the effort to lower costs by enhancing efficiency, containerization eventually led to segmenting maritime commercial traffic, ships, and ports into specialized subsystems.[13] Rather than a port being a general facility for all cargo, maritime trade's throughput is accelerated, broadened, and intensified by uniquely designed ships and handling facilities. Containers and container ships transport high-value cargo. Tankers carry liquid petroleum and gas products between liquid bulk facilities. Other bulk terminals receive and disperse bulk cargos of grain, ores, fertilizers, etc. Hence, the network of the modern maritime supply chain flourishes with automated and specialized nodes for loading and unloading. John Harrald, Director of the George Washington University Institute for Crises, Disaster, and Risk Management, offers up a brief but

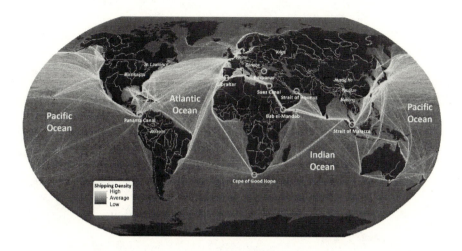

Figure 5.1. Maritime Shipping Density *(Source: Rodrigue, J-P et al. (2013) The Geography of Transport Systems, Hofstra University, Department of Global Studies & Geography. Shipping density data adapted from National Center for Ecological Analysis and Synthesis, A Global Map of Human Impacts to Marine Ecosystems)*

forceful comment: "the general purpose terminals that marked the waterfront of all U.S. port cities became restaurants, condominiums, and shops."[14] His observation reflects upon the transformation of sea trade and how its current character barely resembles the previous era when general purpose ports and fleets dominated.

In addition to transforming the face of waterfronts, this focus on specialization and efficiency has forced a pattern toward more capacity and a greater volume of trade. The trend is for even more containers, larger ships, and terminals. As justification, the underlying rationale states that in order for container shipping to be more efficient, it needs to be larger in scale. Container shipping thrives on volume. The greater the throughput, the lower the cost per box. Naval architects envision the next generation of container ship to be a quarter mile long and 190 feet wide. It will carry 18,000 TEUs (20-foot equivalent unit) and a cargo whose value could be as much as $1 billion. The line of trucks needed to off-load a full shipment would extend for 68 miles.[15] The only constraint along the path toward the construction of such a vessel is the Straights of Malacca.

"Malacca-Max" is the designation given to this future standard. Beyond these dimensions, a ship would be too large to pass through the vital shipping lane between Malaysia and Indonesia. If this standard is reached, it will require even larger and deeper ports creating yet more economies of scale.

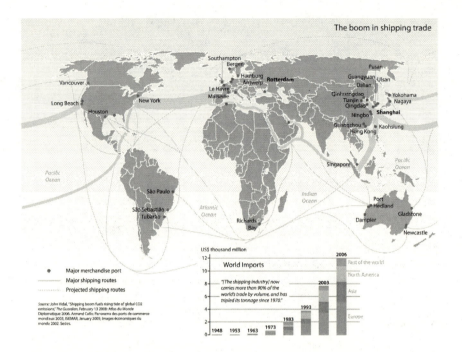

Figure 5.2.   Growth in International Maritime Trade *(Source: GRID-Arendal http://www.grida.no/graphicslib/detail/the-boom-in-shipping-trade_5cb7)*

The result will be still lower transportation costs, faster time to market, and more vibrant trade.[16]

This revolution in the transportation industry made possible disaggregated production schemes, allowing for firms to gain economies of scale and more highly organized inventory and asset management control. Thus, the changing patterns opened the way for just-in-time manufacturing processes and the new business model of the extended enterprise. Remote production sites become part of a seamless network linked to intermediate and end users. Inventories are lowered and quality control is heightened by a self-enforced discipline, which is a consequence of the production pressures and standards of just-in-time manufacturing processes.[17] Furthermore, these new global corporations can shift production around the world as dictated by costs, exchange rates, market conditions, or political environments. All manufacturing and business partners are "local," as are customers.

Yet, as the revolution occurs in the shipping industry, creating new possibilities for importers and exporters, it also offers up severe security challenges for law enforcement and counterterrorism officials. Due to the volume of traffic and the demand pressures for frictionless trade, risks are inherent and abound. Container inspection rates are fractionally low. There is no authority, which can verify or guarantee that the items on record match the contents of the container. As Levinson remarks: "Containers can be just as efficient for smuggling undeclared merchandise, illegal drugs, undocumented immigrants, and terrorist bombs as for moving legitimate cargo."[18]

Anyone can lease a container box and fill it with 65,000 pounds of cargo. There are no standard accounting features to describe the contents. Despite that, on average, overseas containers pass through seventeen intermediate points between their place of origin and final destination, the manifest will usually reveal only the details known by the final destination carrier. Therefore, the documents on a container being loaded in The Netherlands, shipped to Canada, and eventually destined for Chicago, may report that the contents came from Rotterdam and arrived in Halifax. The fact that it originated in central Asia and passed through several interior ports on its way through continental Europe may go unreported or hidden in the paper trail. Frequently, the items inside the container appear on documents in the most generalized terms and descriptions. Intermediary operators, or consolidators, know only what their customers allow them to know about their shipments.[19] Manifest records can be inaccurate, corrupted, or falsified. Transparency is denied and risks to security abide.

Adding to the difficulty is the in-bond cargo[20] system that manages importer goods in transit and is virtually outside the system of U.S. government security controls.[21] A feature of in-bond cargo is that these shipments whose final destination is not in the United States escape rigorous reporting requirements. By simply transiting U.S. territory they are not subject to the same laws as imported cargo. These cargos are not technically (or administratively) in the United States even though they are physically being warehoused and transshipped while there. Leakage of goods and material into the U.S. commercial stream has been estimated as being over a billion dollars annually. According to the Government Accountability Office, Customs Border Protection's (CBP) tracking on in-bond cargo is a "persistent weakness."[22] Aside from not knowing the exact contents of an in-bond container, CBP officials are unable to guarantee if a shipment designated for export has, in fact, wrongfully entered the U.S. market. Hence, the sum of these facts and conclusions is that the threat is not from the containers, but rather from not knowing what's inside them. This, most simply stated, is the problem.

TARGETING, SCREENING, SCANNING, AND INSPECTING

Because of their commoditization and the defects in audit management, shipping containers are an obvious method for inserting WMDs into the global supply chain and/or any targeted territory. Prior to 9/11, approximately 2 percent of containers shipped to the United States were physically in-spected[23] (complete unloading and reloading of container vans). That per-centage has been increased to merely 5–7 percent by most estimates. The fears, however, that an inspection rate above 5 percent would bring global commerce to a halt are expressed frequently.

Following the 9/11 attacks, the U.S. Congress proposed a bill mandating the inspection of all inbound containers on to U.S. territory. An impracticable legislation, rather than offer a solution, only revealed the misconceptions about the commercial infrastructure and our over-dependence on complex transportation, communication, and utility networks. Such measures would result in not only the total disruption of the U.S. national supply chain, but could create global gridlock as well. As an illustration of the futility of such a plan imagine all 18,000 containers, which daily enter the California ports of Los Angeles and Long Beach, being off-loaded and examined by five cargo inspectors then reloaded. The estimate man hours required to perform the task is 270,000. By 300 percent, that number far exceeds the current level of customs inspection manpower that exists nationwide.[24] As mentioned above, according to most data the inspection rate of containers at U.S. ports, on average, is 5.4 percent.[25] (In the months following the September 11, 2001 attacks, inspection rates may have been as high as 10 percent with the higher rate attributed to cargos of Canadian goods. The threat that terrorists would use a U.S.-Canada border crossing to smuggle in WMDs kept those ports at a higher state of alert.)[26] Higher rates of inspection would have the effect of closing most U.S. container ports because of a lack of surge capacity at other sites. A closure of port facilities for even a modest span of time would result in a loss of billions of dollars to the economy—as the lock-out at the Port of Los Angeles/Long Beach demonstrated in 2002. Because of the futility and disruption that high inspection rates would create, alternative security meas-ures had to be adapted to match and counter the specific terrorist methods of attack, the severity of the risk, and an estimation of acceptable loss.

As a consequence of these pressures, new security procedures resulted. Rather than physical inspection, scanning or non-intrusive inspection using sensor and imaging technology is used effectively at many world ports. Car-go is pulled aside randomly or because of its suspicious nature. The container then passes under the detection tower or arm of a mobile non-intrusive in-spection vehicle (NII). These vehicles are also known as Vehicle and Cargo Inspection System (VACIS) and use gamma detectors to spot anomalies. After conferring with lab analysis, suspect containers are pulled and sent to on-site container evaluation facilities (CES) for full vanning and de-vanning inspection.

The legislation, known as Public Law No. 110-53, Implementing Recom-mendation of the 9/11 Commission Act (2007), is a voluntary program for putting into action private-sector preparedness standards. The legislation also

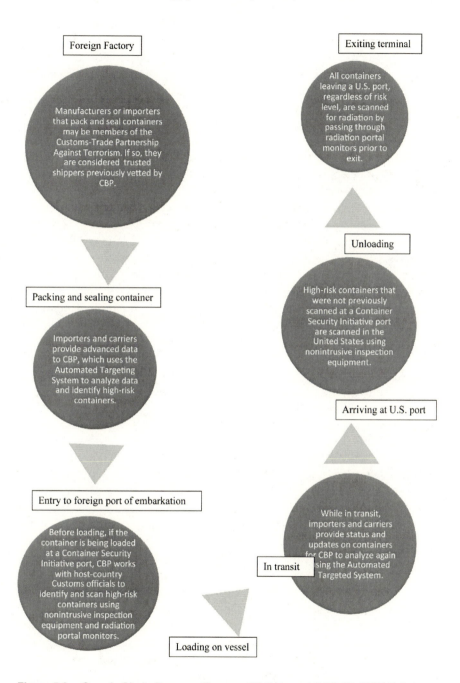

Figure 5.3. Supply Chain Process *(Source: GAO Report GAO-12-422T, February 7, 2012)*

had a five-year horizon for DHS putting in place a system that would scan all containers for nuclear devices. The law would require six hundred ports around the world to scan containers bound for the United States. Over 1,400 radiation portal monitors (RPM) have been deployed thus far. Determined, as its proponents may appear to be, the legislation has raised protests from such trading partners as the European Union, Singapore, and political blocs within India. The outcry and concerns range from it being an unnecessary expense and impediment to trade, to alarm over a perceived attempt by the United States to impose its hegemony.[27,28] Experts also warn that such factors as the probability of detection, the nuisance of false alarms, the technology's risk of being defeated or compromised, costs, and unforeseen conditions may only lead to system failure. Both Michael Chertoff and Janet Napolitano declared the program unnecessary. They contend that 100 percent scanning is far too time consuming.

To date, the feasibility of 100 percent scanning is largely unproven. According to a GAO 2012 document, the program known as the Safe Freight Initiative (SFI) experienced safety and logistical problems. At the pilot ports Qasim, Pakistan, Puerto Cortes, Honduras, and Southampton, UK poor image quality and equipment breakdowns also contributed to frustrations.[29] SFI's purpose was to determine the feasibility of 100 percent scanning of U.S. inbound container traffic. However, as CBP officials upgraded the program with new technology and expanded the list of pilot ports to include Hong Kong, Busan, and Salalah, results concerning the outlook for the goal of complete scanning of inbound container traffic were dismaying. At these larger ports with higher trans-shipment volumes, the program participants complained that costs rose and port efficiencies declined.

Others argue that these types of equipment deployment recommendations are often vendor driven.[30] Without the benchmark of standards and best practices codes, momentum usually defaults to the device or scheme by the company with the most effective marketing strategy or greater sales organization. As a sole solution, strong arguments against higher scanning rates are valid. Logistics and security experts even contend that 100 percent scanning may even be inconsistent with risk-based strategies, which are the basis of the layered security approach. As part of a larger answer to the problem, the option may remain on the table. The ability to know what is in a container at any given moment is the Holy Grail of the maritime security issue. Any aid that increases visibility into the movement of goods through the supply chain is another weapon. Layered defenses that employ several tiers of protection and methodology are the preferred strategy. These options not only exist but also are often the standard practice.

As part of a layered defense, as well as an alternative to a dependence upon 100 percent scanning, is advanced research in data analysis—screening (logic-based methodology).[31] Screening uses analytic tools and algorithm theory methodology. Screening and scanning are conjoint operations to identify potential high-risk cargo and other forms of contraband. They limit the imposition of downtime from unnecessary inspection and lubricate the movement of trade. These methods have already been deployed worldwide and are in constant development for enhancement. This technology not only isolates high-risk containers, but also identifies changes in patterns of data, and creates risk-scoring methods to aid intelligence gathering as well as cargo screening methodology. Such methods are less costly and offer a less intrusive means to track the movement of goods while less onerous than the diplomatic complications of security pacts and international agreements. Unfortunately, federal budgetary pressures are threatening the funding of research in this area at many universities, as is the case of numerous current grant-dependent programs.

TRUSTED SHIPPERS AND LAYERED DEFENSES

Trust is the seminal element underlying several programs designed to address the new security challenges. Fortunately, in maritime trade much of this trust is already in place due to a shipping industry with a history of well-established firms and relationships among companies, owners, and operators. These principal players in maritime trade are: "Well known and established companies that operate as members of conferences in the liner trade—cartels that operate as common carriers on fixed routes and schedules."[32] Seventy percent of the containers shipped to the United States come through only four major port operators: P&O Ports, PSA Corporation, Maersk-Sealand, and Hutchison Port Holdings. However, no matter how familiar these entities are with one another, the security loop can never completely close unless the system reconfigures its constellation of participants, jurisdictional protocols, nodes, linkages, security, and legal codes.

The Customs-Trade Partnership Against Terrorism (C-TPAT) program was an attempt to tighten the trade network through the concept adaptation of the trusted shipper. It hinges its success on the notion that the trusted shipper will act in the best interests of itself and a secure global supply chain. As compliant traders, the private-sector actors will theoretically build an efficient supply chain to better secure and manage private and public infrastructure assets in return for the privileges and benefits. The notion of the trusted shipper also posits the idea that security can be achieved if its requirements create strong incentives for those who adopt such measures and strong disincentives for those who do not.

The C-TPAT program came into existence in November 2001 to complement other programs within Customs Border Protection's layered approach to maritime security. It was formalized into law in October 2006 with the passage of the Safe Port Act. Initially, it was a response to the events of 9/11 by government and the private sector in an attempt to rebound from the catastrophe. The essential features of the C-TPAT program are that it is voluntary and the private companies who elect to commit to improving the security of their supply chain will, in return, receive valuable commercial benefits. The foundation of the program is an honor system. Private-sector firms agree to participate by adopting a minimum standard of security measures. C-TPAT, in turn, offers certification status. The program has no regulatory authority and, therefore, responsibility by members to maintain standards is self-regulating.

This same concept has expanded through CBP to the World Customs Organization (WCO) as a capacity-building effort. The result is the program known as the SAFE Framework. SAFE is a set of broad security standards set forth by the WCO that attempts to provide a baseline of technical guidance for enhancing security and facilitating trade. The WCO established the Framework of Standards to Secure and Facilitate Global Trade (SAFE Framework) to effectively extend C-TPAT beyond the sphere of U.S. bound trade. In 2005 the initiative was adopted by the WCO and in 2006 the terms and conditions of an Authorized Economic Operator (AEO) status were put into document form. For firms who are involved in international trade, AEO is the corresponding designation to C-TPAT certification. C-TPAT certification automatically affords the holder AEO status. One of the primary objectives of SAFE is to foster closer cooperation among national and regional customs administrations by integrating supply chain management of transport nodes.

Generally, a security conscious shipper has already implemented many of the practices C-TPAT and SAFE recommend. At most, by enrolling in the program and agreeing to C-TPAT security measures and standards, the benefits companies receive include the likelihood a participating member's shipments will undergo less scrutiny and, hence, the reduction of inspection time will result in fewer delays and faster time to destinations. Optimally, the framers of the program aim to provide an additional security layer as it creates a global "fast lane" for its members. However, due to earlier manpower shortages and lack of coordination, the program's certification and validation process was rather lax. Often membership depended upon a firm's financial condition. A record of a legitimate commercial history, however, may not be an indicator of future intent or circumstances. Terrorist groups have used shipping vessels and fleets as part of their logistical operations. A legitimate maritime commercial service would be a deadly cover for any group seeking to launch a well-coordinated and devastating attack.

This last issue has an unsettling and ironic twist. C-TPAT, by its own unintended design, may offer terrorists the very access they seek to breach the system and inflict immeasurable economic loss and chaos. Enjoying the benefits of being C-TPAT certified means negligible or no inspection time. Hence, C-TPAT members become targets of terrorists, precisely because of the logic of CBP's own targeting system. The same automated risk assessment mechanisms that make the multi-layered defense a sound strategy against an illegal incursion also make it an instrument for planning and conducting a terrorist event. Finding a disgruntled or willing worker within a trusted shippers' disparate and complex web of interlocking supply chain networks for the purpose of infiltration is not a remote possibility.

These flaws aside, to appreciate the entire supply chain defense structure one needs to understand the U.S. government's layered approach to security and the way in which the programs interact and nest within the filtering apparatus. The U.S. government's supply chain security program does not exist in isolation. It is systemic and lies within a larger defense strategy that enlists the cooperation of members in the private-sector trade community domestically and abroad. The program works in concert with other CBP programs to achieve these twin goals of security against attacks and frictionless trade of foreign shipments onto the territory of the United States. Under CBP's management, for instance, is another program— the Container Security Initiative (CSI). CSI is a risk-based program designed to increase the security of containers shipped to the United States from around the world. CSI deploys a system of enhanced and advanced technology and intelligence-gathering tools for converting information into, what it hopes will be, actionable analysis. At the same time, the program's objective is to facilitate growth and development within the international trade community through bilateral arrangements.

Through this program, the largest world ports are requested to host CSI teams of customs agents. These multi-disciplinary units from within Customs and Border Protection and Immigration and Customs Enforcement agencies identify and inspect high-risk containers bound for the United States before they are loaded onto vessels. A CSI team generally consists of three specialist categories: targeters, intelligence analysts, and special agents. The program involves bilateral cooperation with foreign governments by sharing intelligence, and heightens counterterrorism preparedness across international borders through collaborative involvement. However, much of the program's success depends upon reliable intelligence and efficient staffing balances across CSI ports.[33] Diplomatic considerations are critical and, at times, are out of CSI's control.[34] Local government officials can deny inspection if, after review, they feel further diligence is unwarranted. In such a case, a CSI's recourse is to place a domestic hold on the cargo. When the shipment eventually arrives at its U.S. destination, it will be subject to inspection by U.S. authorities.

In addition to information offered by foreign intelligence sources, the CSI program relies much more heavily on data from another Department of

Homeland Security, risk-based program. The National Targeting Center's Automated Targeting System (ATS) employs a computer model to review and evaluate documentation on all containers scheduled to arrive in the United States. Using manifest data, historical patterns, and intelligence reports, ATS assigns risk levels to cargos. Depending upon the resultant scores, containers may be selected for further document review and possible inspection.

The National Targeting Center also receives data from selected ports, which are participants in the Secure Freight Initiative, mentioned above. SFI, in addition to being a program to test the feasibility of 100 percent scanning for radioactive material, is also a tool for data-gathering and assigning risk factors. Using optical scanning technology procedures for possible radioactive contents, SFI combines this information to identify and classify containers according to destination. The results of record reconciliations, non-intrusive radiographic imaging, and passive radiation detection equipment readings are analyzed and cross-referenced with manifest submissions to determine a risk assessment. If there were need for further scrutiny, CBP proceeds in observance of established protocols of the host country.[35] However, the variance of host nation examination practices, performance measures, resource constraints, technological imitations, and the physical features of foreign ports have created serious obstacles for SFI.[36] As of 2013 the SFI program has shriveled to a single port and plans to continue with the cost/benefit and feasibility study have halted due to a lack of funding.

Lastly, the SAFE Port Act of 2006 requires that importers file ten additional data elements, electronically, to U.S. authorities. The 10 Plus 2 Program, also known as the "24 hour rule," means that importers must submit their data no less than twenty-four hours prior to the lading of containers from the port of exit.

The entire body of programs, initiatives, protocols, and networks is an attempt to create a single organic security "ecosystem" around the maritime supply chain. It does not, however, include inland container traffic or account for the system of import controls of other agencies, such as the Department of Agriculture, Food and Drug Administration, Environmental Protection Agency, etc.[37]

Manpower issues, technical standards for equipment, incomplete (but improving) counterterrorism intelligence, and the monitoring of host government operations have created obstacles.[38,39] However, despite these difficulties, many regard the approach as a major step. Programs such as C-TPAT, CSI, ATS, and SFI, according to some experts, may be the DNA material that allows us to decode the enigma surrounding the frictionless trade versus security dilemma.

Despite what seems to be an exhaustive effort to use information technology and exchange to create a seamless defense shielding, a controversy surrounding these programs concerns several main premises. The essential features of the C-TPAT program are that it is voluntary. Without any regulatory authority, the responsibility and decision to participate rest with the private concern and the commitment is non-enforceable. That decision is made by a host of firms spanning the globe and depends upon financial, commercial, political, and cultural factors.

Additionally, the program is still riddled with inherent flaws. Its current risk management system relies on a company's past experience as an indicator of its current assessment as a "trusted shipper." As a result, screening procedures rely upon "financial soundness" and "business references" to determine a level of security risk.[40] The relevance and effectiveness of this information in predicting, identifying, and interdicting a furious terrorist attack is untested, and hence, unknown. Furthermore, because past experience is the main component of the risk assessment framework, the system is more suited to interdict against conventional criminal activity than a one-time terrorist event. The differences in motivation and modus operandi between a criminal who is intent on escape and a committed terrorist, who is not, may be very consequential in the attempt to anticipate and prevent an event.

In various event scenarios being posed, a terrorist group successfully infiltrates the global supply chain despite the security filters of present state and regime programs, initiatives, technological solutions, and best practices codes and standards. A sole disgruntled, sympathetic, or financially distressed truck driver can neutralize the entire defense plan. Anyone allowing access to a shipment of goods at its point of origin, its production site, can, potentially, put world trade in peril. In 2006 a written testimony by Jeane J. Kirkpatrick and Stephen E. Flynn of the Council on Foreign Relations, describe how a WMD may be placed inside a shipment of consumer products originating in Indonesia and destined for Chicago.[41] In their scenario, the lethal shipment is loaded from a costal feeder ship to an inter-Asian vessel, and finally goes aboard a super-container bound for the U.S. West Coast. One tragedy is, because the product name is from a trusted C-TPAT member, the cargo is never inspected. Rather, it is waived through. Because it is C-TPAT certified, the defense mechanism CSI was conceived to provide would be disarmed. Due to its trusted shipper status, it would not be identified for inspection or special screening by the CSI team of inspectors at any of the ports. Radiation detection devices may also be of no use if the plotters shielded the weapon with a lead packaging.

There are currently fifty-eight foreign ports participating in CSI, accounting for 85 percent of container traffic bound for the United States.

Figure 5.4. Container Security Initiative Ports *(Source: Department of Homeland Security – Customs Border Protection)*

CALCULATING THE DANGERS AND THE RISK

The earlier reports of al Qaeda controlling a fleet of 15–18 bulk and general cargo vessels underscore the need for serious reevaluation of the present supply chain system and less lax attitudes toward transparency it breeds.[42] Vessels such as these have been used for revenue support and to assist in terrorist and other criminal groups' logistical activity. It is obvious that these ships would have utility in paramilitary operations and suicide missions. The statements that emerged from al Qaeda sources trumpeting intentions "to inflict massive economic losses on the United States and its allies,"[43] caused the Paris-based OECD to link these remarks to real-world circumstances. According to a 2003 report, "any important breakdown in the maritime transport system would fundamentally cripple the world economy."[44] A recent assessment report by the Council on Foreign Relations concurs. It is not only the assailability of the system, but also the frailty, which is an issue. Our dependency on the ceaseless flow of trade allows little tolerance for disruption. At the ports, as with most of our public or commercial infrastructure and healthcare system, there is little capacity for surge. Bottlenecks or breakdowns can quickly evolve into panic, particularly if terrorism is suspected. A paper published by the Council on Foreign Relations remarks:

> Transportation conveyances carrying hazardous cargoes potentially can be used both as weapons and a weapon delivery system, gathering death and destruction while simultaneously generating cascading economic consequences. For instance, should a cargo container deliver a smuggled radiation dispersal device ("dirty bomb") into the heart of a U.S. city and be detonated,

Customs Trade Partnership Against Terrorism	Cooperative security agreement between the US government and the private sector that requires businesses to establish security guidelines for member organizations and commercial partners. Participants receive preferential treatment and benefits in return. The WCO's SAFE Framework recognizes C-TPAT certification.
Container Security Initiative	A working network of bilateral agreements between the US and foreign governments to prescreen cargo prior to shipment bound for US territory. Using risk-based computer models, intelligence sources, and commercial history, suspected cargo is identified and targeted for possible detainment and inspection.
Secure Freight Initiative	At six participating foreign ports, optical scanning technology, non-intrusive radioactive imaging, and passive radiation detection equipment scan and identify cargo containers for anomalies regarding documentation records and radiation readings.
The 10 Plus 2 Program	A requirement of the SAFE Port Act 2006 that US importers submit information to customs authorities, at least, 24 hours prior to lading at the port of exit.

Table 5.1. The Layered Approach to Maritime Security

other cities would become alarmed that the trucks, trains, and ships within their jurisdiction would pose a similar risk. The process of stopping and examining the hundreds and thousands of containers located within the United States on any given day would quickly generate gridlock throughout the global inter-modal transportation system, effectively severing the logistical lifelines for manufacturers and retailers worldwide.[45]

The Volpe Center of the Department of Transportation warns that a 10–20 kiloton bomb detonated in a shipping container would wreak somewhere between $100 and $200 billion in disrupted trade. Property loss could be as high as $500 billion. The loss of life could equal fifty thousand or as high as one million. The study goes on to say that, although difficult to estimate, long-term economic effects would be "substantially higher."[46] Stephen Flynn, former President of the Center for National Policy, predicts that even if the loss of life were to be quantitatively modest, the economic impact would force a global recession. Flynn bases his projections on the ensuing chaos and the systems lack of resiliency. Resiliency refers to the system's ability to resume operations near or at the same level of efficiency after a significant event as it did prior to the disruption. According to Flynn the system's fault tolerance is shamefully low. If he is correct, there is no effective way of isolating the impact of a significant event and preventing an aftershock from reverberating throughout the entire supply chain. The effect on global trade, therefore, would be disabling. The capacity of the rest of the system to absorb the surge is unknown, however, estimates assume a cessation of U.S. trade for merely three weeks would have dire global consequences.[47] It is also quite reasonable to assume that citizen confidence in government could be at a crisis—as was the case in Spain in 2004 when the Madrid train bombing forced a turnover of regimes in the subsequent elections.

The bombing incident in Madrid in 2004 was placed at 212 million euros in direct economic loss.[48] The tourism industry suffered only a short-term loss and recovered relatively quickly.[49] However, although there was only a .03 percent decline in Spain's GDP for the year, the incident's impact on Spanish elections was significant. The incumbent party was removed from power and the opposition, whose political stance with the United States was less approving, took its place. Thus, there is reasonable evidence to suggest tremendous pressure might be put upon federal and local officials to demand either much higher inspection rates on cargo, if not a complete shutdown of trade movement through their ports—or face election consequences.

As a way of addressing this threat and demonstrating the disruption potential, The Conference Board and the consultant firm Booz Allen Hamilton conducted a "Port Security War Game" on October 2–3, 2002, in Washington, DC. At that time, the primary purpose of the exercise was to identify ways government and the private sector might improve coordination of activity, not only on a short-term basis but in the long-term, strategic view as well. Although the financial estimates and response calculations are a bit dated, the basic systemic problems remain relevant.

In addressing these questions, participants faced the dilemma of inherent tensions. Competing choices orbited around the options of:

1. Emergency security measures versus their economic impact
2. Short-term solutions versus long-term policies and
3. Homeland security versus trade policy and its implications for foreign policy.

The co-sponsors' aim was also to provide senior policy makers from government and the private sector an assessment of the United States' susceptibility to attack, and what steps might be taken to build system resiliency. CEOs and senior executives from transportation carriers, technology firms, industry associations, manufacturing and distribution industries participated in the event. Also invited were senior representatives from U.S. Customs, U.S. Coast Guard, Department of Defense, Department of Transportation, Transportation Security Administration, Office of Homeland Security, intelligence agencies, and port authorities.

The war game scenario hypothesizes a crude nuclear device is loaded into a container and legitimately enters the global transportation chain. As participants devised a response, four key questions undergo examination: What are the systematic threats to port infrastructure? How can a transparent supply chain operate efficiently? How can government coordinate its efforts with the private sector and on an interagency basis to thwart and respond to such attacks? What are the short-term "cascading" effects on the supply chain and the economy?[50]

The scenario opens with the accidental discovery at the port of Los Angeles of an improvised nuclear device, or "dirty bomb." This device is a combination of radioactive material and conventional explosives. Such a weapon, when detonated, could disperse a cloud contaminating an area of 1 mile or the equivalent of sixty city blocks. The bomb possibly links to a global positioning satellite for detonation purposes and enters the Port of Los Angeles in one of the thousands of containers, which the terminal handles daily. According to U.S. Customs and Border Protection, nearly sixty-five thousand such truck, rail, and sea containers are processed each day.[51] The device's journey may have begun half a world away. The smugglers of the lethal material probably traveled along the established routes of drug traffickers from Asia to Europe before arriving in North America. An entrenched transport infrastructure operating alongside legitimate commerce has been serving the needs of drug trafficking, trade in contraband material, and illegal financial flow for years.

As authorities wrestle with the heightened security alert, port security personnel apprehend three suspected terrorists in Savannah. The situation now attains a new level of complexity as the possibility of a plot to attack multiple targets in the transportation system unfolds. While officials try to assuage public fear, a second bomb is detected in Minneapolis. Over a three-week period the public and private sector introduce response actions and controls. All ports of entry and border crossings are closed. Backlogged ships not targeted for inspection are diverted to Canada and Mexico. With precaution, after assuming that a catastrophe has been averted, ports are reopened on a 24/7 basis on the twelfth day of the crisis. Normal operations finally resume by day nineteen, but not before gas prices skyrocket, the Dow plunges by 500 points, and severe shortages and plant closures occur. However, while all prepare for the worst and hope for the best, the sophistication and intricacy of the plotters' highly coordinated plan fully unfolds. On day twenty a container entering the United States through the Port of NY/NJ explodes on a railcar in downtown Chicago. All major indices plunge, Wall Street suspends trading, and the earnings of half the Fortune 500 firms are in doubt.

The sponsors of the study calculate a closure of two ports for three days and a total shutdown of all U.S. ports for an additional nine days would require three months to clear the backlog. The cost to the economy due to spoilage, manufacturing cessation, and the loss of sales and contracts would be in the vicinity of $58 billion (many experts familiar with this exercise and this estimate believe, even at that time, the numbers to be highly, and even unreasonably, conservative).

Adding to this somber scenario, no public studies or data are known, which can identify the surge capacities of the nations' ports should a closing of one or more ports force cargo to divert to alternative locations. The questions as to the manpower availability and the volume capacity at ports and at inter-modal connections are unanswered. The U.S. government has no present group in place or intention of gathering such data. It publicly takes the position that it will rely upon relevant information supplied to it by the private sector.[52]

Additionally, organizers and participants acknowledged that while various powers had the unilateral authority to declare facilities and services closed down, there is no mechanism in place to coordinate the restoration of these offices, either operationally or legally. Because these facilities are in

Figure 5.5. War Game—Economic Impact *(Source: Booz Allen Hamilton)*

private ownership, the issues as to which state authority or corporate concern has jurisdiction and responsibility over such matters becomes Byzantine at best. The question has caused some to reason aloud about our present notions about federalism, at least in the context of national security.

In 2004 an under-publicized port security event at the port of Boston had municipal and state authorities overriding decisions at the federal level. Concerns about the risk of LNG (liquefied natural gas) tankers entering the port had officials on opposing sides. Ultimately, a decision by the mayor of Boston and the governor of Massachusetts to temporarily bar the ships from entering the port held against federal assurances.[53] These incidents call into question the effectiveness of a national response plan.

Although its findings did not reflect the recent implementation of long term, counter-terrorism measures, the "war game" report suggested that traditional benefit-cost analysis regarding the introduction of counter measures might be useless, due to the range of unknown variables. Those unknown variables include the psychological impact on the economy and the public, which may well be immeasurable. Their figures were also confined to the U.S. economy. The data does not reflect possible disruption of world trade and the potential deleterious effect on the global economy, which, as mentioned above, has become increasingly interdependent over the past decades.

STRONG MARKETS AND WEAK SECURITY

These conclusions only help drive the fact that an open, high-volume maritime supply chain makes the system extremely susceptible to attack. The results of such an attack could cripple world trade and devastate the foundation of the global economy. The very same forces that have accounted for unprecedented prosperity have also harbored the seeds of the global economy's potential ruin. At the height of commerce's effort to establish international linkages, a system of freely flowing trade, and a business model that accounted for minimal inventories—there also exists the potential for a single disaster to force an entire paradigm shift and to throw the order into chaos.

The strength of the maritime supply chain was now its Achilles heel. The diversity and mass of its workforce, the vastness of its reach and range of goods, and the host of intermediaries involved in the process made controls virtually impossible. Compounding conditions was the way the system turned a blind eye toward documentation requirements. Ownership, destination, and product description information were as vague and lax as license and personnel identification checks. According to the authors of a report in 2006 by the RAND Corporation's Center for Terrorism Risk Management Policy:

The effectiveness of point-of-origin inspections for containerized freight is questionable. Many littoral states fail to vet stevedores, do not require that truck drivers present valid identification before entering the port, and overlook the need to ensure that an accurate manifest accompany all cargo. Standards for inspecting containers at originating ports do not exist. [54]

Standards for securing containers evidently do not exist either. The choice of product type, sophistication, and effectiveness of cargo seals is driven by cost. Tamper-resistant and tamper-evident seals cost several dollars. Those with GPS transponders or radio frequency identification (RFID) may be several hundred. Ones costing only a few cents can be easily defeated with crude instruments and, unfortunately, are the most popular. These simple "bolts" offer scant protection and can be removed and reattached quickly. It takes a highly trained eye with a reasonable cause, based on suspicion or ex ante to detect whether a container has been compromised. Technology of container seals continues to undergo testing in both lab and field environments. [55] The CBP recognized how container seals represent a breach in the supply chain integrity and ordered several studies. Yet performance standards have not been set. Complicating the implementation of standards includes the challenge of industry partners who claim to be overburdened by current security mandates. Without a consistent security/technology infrastructure the systems problems and soundness may remain open.

In the RAND report the authors also point out "The vulnerabilities extend to the level of the package." The Trans-International Routier (TIR) haulage system is a universally recognized arrangement for transporting, loading, and unloading merchandize between the warehouse and the port facility. The TIR logo indicates that the package has been properly inspected and sealed by the legitimate authorities. Any container bearing the TIR stamp is exempt from inspection. It is a way to designate a cargo as being sent from a trusted shipper. It is also an example of the intrinsic weaknesses that a program might involuntarily harbor. If a terrorist were to compromise the system at any point, by force, through bribery, or forgery, the TIR logo becomes the lethal package's free pass into the maritime supply chain. Because the package is "trusted" no further scrutiny is required.

The report goes on to anonymously quote a consultant from Control Risks Group who confides that security practices at the port of Rotterdam, one of the world's largest ports, remain "weak, constituting not much more than a tick in the box exercise." It adds that many nations do not audit security measures, which have been enacted by law. This is despite the number of sweeping and well-touted programs and mutual agreements signed and made into law.

Another way for terrorists to fall between the system's cracks is the manner and lenience that commercial sailors enjoy when entering a country while moving about the world. Illegal immigrants are aware of the lax procedures reserved for commercial fleet members, and often pose as seamen in order to bypass the more stringent controls applied to other types of passengers.[56] Ports of call are often drop-off or pick-up terminals for "temporary seamen" wishing to navigate the world as persons seeking a better life or out to fulfill more sinister missions. Adding to the systemic susceptibility and tension was the theft of 3,000 blank UK passports in 2008. Authorities also report that between 1990 and 2002 nearly 20,000 Belgium passports disappeared.[57]

The ease by which the maritime transport system can be compromised was demonstrated in 2001, a month following the 9/11 attacks. Through happenstance, a suspected terrorist was discovered in the port of Gioia, Italy. Port workers intercepted the stowaway while he was attempting to widen the ventilation holes of the cargo container in which he had been traveling. His accommodations included a bed, toilet, heater, and water supply. Among his belongings were a cell phone, laptop computer, airport security passes, and a mechanic's certificate valid at JFK, O'Hare, L.A. International, and Newark airports.

His container was loaded onto a vessel in Port Said, Egypt and scheduled to be trans-shipped to Rotterdam before reaching its final destination in Canada. Unfortunately, the chances of collecting further information about his intentions or connection with other individuals or organizations were lost when he disappeared following his arraignment.

It is obvious that the international trading community needs to take measures to amend the flaws in the system. The vulnerabilities are neither a secret to them, nor to the adversary who exploits them. The opportunity for attack is ever-present. A supply chain that is only 80 percent secure is still fatally vulnerable and, therefore, the maritime supply chain harbors the seeds of its disruption. However, those elements can be rooted out or neutralized with prudent policies and the admittance that something is wrong and requires study and service. An awareness of the problems exists. Lloyd's of London's Rupert Herbert-Burns makes the following admission:

> The combination of the enormous scope and "room for maneuver" offered by the physical and geographical realities of the [earth's] maritime environment . . . presents a sobering and uncomfortable reality . . . [W]hat compounds this reality further is that the commercial milieu that simultaneously affords . . . the ability to deploy, finance operations, tactical concealment, logistical fluidity and wealth of targets of opportunity—the commercial maritime industry—is itself numerically vast, complex, deliberately opaque and in a perpetual state of flux.[58]

Admitting something is wrong is always a first step. Responding to conditions is the true challenge. Currently, analysts, stakeholders, and policy makers are in the midst of both processes. RAND Corporation made public a study referenced above. It evaluates the risk associated with maritime terrorism. As a result of integrating the level of threat, degree of vulnerability, and the potential for consequence, Michael D. Greenberg, Peter Chalk, Henry H. Willis, Ivan Khilko, and David S. Ortiz of RAND have arranged a table for qualitatively assessing risk according to event scenarios. Their conclusions are that the threat from container shipping is equivalent among the various scenarios.

The tradeoff between the significance of the event and the skills and expertise required in order to have a reasonable chance of succeeding, render risk as somewhat uniform. The exception, according to the report, is a nuclear detonation. Because such an attempt would require a relatively sophisticated level of planning, expertise, and logistics system for support, a nuclear detonation represents a lower threat. However, the consequences would be devastating if successful. Therefore, in the view of terrorists, the desirability of these consequences may inflame their passion to launch an attack and assume the risk. The difficulties in projecting an accurate reckoning when measuring risk under this sort of analysis are apparent. Without precedent or quantitative historical data, guidance for establishing policy and even creating measurement tools remain dependent upon heuristic conjecture.

The following page is a re-illustration of the RAND model. It provides a sketch of the consequences, which may result from the six most foreseen scenarios. As a quick reference, the tables provide a picture of both immediate and long-term effects. Obviously, the farther in the future this qualitative analysis extends, the less its accuracy.

Maritime Terrorism Scenario	Potential Human Consequences	Potential Economic Consequences	Potential Intangible Consequences
Sink or disable a ship in a channel or a port	Tens of injuries and deaths of the crew	Tens of mm USD in life and injury compensa-tion, repair and replace vessel Hundreds of mm USD in lost cargo Billions of USD in short term business disrupt-ion, augmented security procedures	Loss of human capital, changes in consumer patterns of consumption
Hijack ship and use to destroy infrastructure	Hundreds of injuries and deaths of the crew, several hundred civilian casualties	Tens of mm USD in repair and replace vessel Tens of mm USD in damaged infrastructure Hundreds of mm USD in life and injury compensation	Loss of human capital, changes in consumer patterns of consumption
Using a shipping container as a delivery device for a conventional bomb	Several hundred injuries and deaths	Millions of USD in damaged infrastructure Millions of USD in destroyed property Hundreds of mm USD in life and injury compensation Billion of USD in short term business disruptions Billions of USD in augmented security procedures	Loss of human capital
Using a shipping container as a delivery device for a radiological dispersion device	Tens to hundreds of injuries and deaths	Hundreds of thousands USD in contaminated or damaged infrastructure Millions of USD in contaminated or damaged property Hundreds of mm USD in life and injury compensation Billions of USD in augmented security procedures Tens of Billions of USD in long-term macro economic effects	Loss of human capital, changes in consumer patterns of consumption, political consequences

Table 5.2. Potential Consequences of Terrorist Attacks, Scenarios on Container Shipping

The above assumptions remind us that the threat from a terrorist attack on the supply chain, particularly the seaborne component, is more than theoretical. From the standpoint of terrorists, the container system's relative openness, accessibility, and potential for devastating impact on global markets makes it an attractive political and economic target. Its function as a conduit for the movement of weapons and personnel gives it another appeal. While the system continues to remain open and anarchic, these features persist. Protecting the container network is difficult and expensive. For these reasons, security approaches rely on layered defense and consequence management. Legitimate stakeholders can organize to meet the challenge of the threat by relying on combinations of sensor technology, tracking software, counterterrorism operations, enhanced intelligence techniques, research in algorithmic theory, visual analytics, data exploitation and game theory methodology, etc. The force it takes to mobilize the government and private stakeholders into decisive action under some unity of command and to demand uniform standards, however, has yet to occur. Hopefully, that decisive action will not be the result of a successful act of terrorism.

NOTES

1. James M. Loy and Robert G. Ross, "Global Trade: America's Achilles Heel," in *Defense Horizons*, Center for Technology and National Security Policy, National Defense University, February, 2002.

2. Stephen, E. Flynn and Jeane J. Kirkpatrick, "The Limitations of the Current Cargo Container Targeting," Written Testimony before a hearing of the subcommittee on Oversight and Investigations, Committee on Energy and Commerce U.S. House of Representatives.

3. *Ibid.*

4. L. Blumenthal, "Funding Appropriation for U.S. Seaports," CREATE Report under FEMA Grant-EMW, 2004-GR-0112 (5 August 2005), p. 12.

5. Flynn.

6. Maritime Transport Committee, Organization for Economic Cooperation and Development (OECD) Directorate for Science, Technology, and Industry, *Security for Maritime Transport: Risk Factors and Economic Impact* (Paris: OECD, July 2003).

7. Marc Levinson, *The Box: How the Shipping Container Made the World Smaller and the World Economy Bigger* (Princeton University Press, 2006), p. 99.

8. Stephen L. Caldwell, "Supply Chain Security: Container Security Programs have matured, but Uncertainty Persists over the Future of 100 Percent Scanning" (GAO Testimony before the Subcommittee on Border and Maritime Security, Committee on Homeland Security, House of Representatives, GAO-12-422T, February 2012), p. 1.

9. Levinson, p. 10.

10. *Ibid.*, p. 11.

11. John, R. Harrald, "Sea Trade and Security: An Assessment of the Post-9/11 Reaction," *Journal of International Affairs*, Fall 2005, Vol. 59, Iss. 1.

12. "Shipping Container Security," HotQuant.com, posted February15, 2003.

13. *Op. cit.*

14. *Ibid.*

15. Levinson, p. 278.

16. *Ibid.*

17. *Ibid.*, p. 256.

18. *Ibid.*, p. 7.

19. Stephen Flynn, "Why America Is Still An Easy Target," *Time, New York* (26 July 2004), Vol. 164, Iss 4.

20. In-bond refers to merchandise that has not yet officially entered into U.S. commerce and is covered by a bond agreement whose beneficiary is the U.S. Government. Should the importer or shipping agent, that includes carriers and customs brokers, not meet any legal or regulatory obligation, CBP has the right and charge to seek recovery against the bond.

21. Robert Strayer, lawyer and legislative assistant to U.S. Senator Susan Collins, interview (May 2007).

22. Loren Yager, "International Trade: Persistent Weakness in the In-Bond Cargo System Impede Customs and Border Protection's Ability to Address Revenue, Trade, and Security Concerns," GAO Report to the Committee on Finance, U.S. Senate, GAO-07-561 (April 2007).

23. Harrald.

24. Flynn, *America the Vulnerable* (Harper Collins, New York, 2004) p. 87.

25. Michael C. Mullen, Director, Office of Trade Relations U.S. Customs and Border Protection, presentation in Washington DC, Trade Symposium 2005 (13 January 2005).

26. Greg Seigle, "Transportation Official Says Strike Would Ripple Across Globe," www.GovExec.com (posted 2/27/02).

27. "A Case for 100-Percent Scanning: Not Proven," *Homeland Defense Journal*, (November 2007).

28. "Are US Security Measures Going Too Far?" in SITPRO Ltd., online journal, London, see http://www.sitpro.org.uk/news/sn200709.pdf.

29. Caldwell, p. 16.

30. Charles D. Massey, "Smart Containers May Not Be So Smart," *Homeland Defense Journal* (November 2007).

31. Logic-based technology is also useful in identifying malware, which can disrupt and disable cyber networks. The same algorithmic principles apply. Software programs track container and network traffic to determine the risk of suspicious "items" based on such factors as their point of origins and specific paths. In the case of cargo screening the software also considers the position of each container during transport.

32. John R. Harrald, Hugh W. Stephens, Johann Rene vanDorp, "A framework for Sustainable Port Security," *Journal of Homeland Security and Emergency Management* (Vol. 1, Iss. 2, 2004), p. 3.

33. Richard M. Stana, "Key Cargo Security Programs Can Be Improved," Government Accountability Office, GAO-05-466T (May 2005), p. 20.

34. *Ibid.*

35. "Secure Freight Initiative, Vision and Operations Overview," see http://www.dhs.gov/xnews/releases/.

36. Stephen L. Caldwell, Maritime Security: Progress And Challenges 10 Years After The Maritime Transportation Security Act, Testimony before the Subcommittee on Coast Guard and Maritime Transportation Committee on Transportation and Infrastructure, (September 11, 2012), p. 46

37. William McLaury Executive Director U.S. Supply Chain Management & Elizabeth Foster, Manager International Trade, Novartis Pharmaceuticals, Corporation, interview, (November 2007).

38. "Maritime Security: The SAFE Port Act: Status and Implementation One Year Later," Testimony before the Subcommittee on Border, Maritime, and Global Counterterrorism; Committee on Homeland Security; House of Representatives, October 30, 2007, p. 32.

39. Flynn, Stephen, "Port Security Is Still a House of Cards," *Far Eastern Economic Review*, Hong Kong, Jan/Feb 2006, Vol. 169, Iss. 1.

40. Customs-Trade Partnership Against Terrorism: Cost/Benefit Survey, Center for Survey Research, University of Virginia, August 2007, p. 26.

41. Jeane Fitzpatrick and Stephen E Flynn (written testimony before Subcommittee on Investigations on Homeland Security and Governmental Affairs, U.S. Senate, March 28, 2006).

42. Crist, p. 12.

43. *Ibid.*, p. 16.

44. *Ibid.*, as cited by Reyes, Brian in "Open to Attack," *Lloyd's List, Lloyd's List International* (July 23, 2003).

45. Stephen E. Flynn, and Daniel B. Prieto, "Neglected Defense: Mobilizing the Private Sector to Support Homeland Security," Council on Foreign Relations (March 2006), p. 28.

46. C. Clark, Abt, The Economic Impact of Terrorist Attacks on Freight Transport Systems in an Age of Seaport Vulnerability, U.S. DOT/RSPA/Volpe Report DTRS57-03-P-80130 (Cambridge, MA), 2003, in Harrald.

47. *Ibid.*, p. 4.

48. F. Reinares, "Survival," Taylor & Francis, Vol. 52, no. 2 (April–May 2010), p. 83.

49. "Home-grown terrorism: What does it mean for business?" www.Lloyds.com, December 2007.

50. Mark Gerencser, Jim Weinberg, Don Vincent, "Port Security War Game: Implications for U.S. Supply Chains" (2003). Booz Allen Hamilton, Inc.

51. "A Day in the Life of CBP." www.cbp.gov/xp/cgov/toolbox/about/accomplish/day.

52. Kevin Dale, Capt., U.S.C.G., Retired, Joint Planning and Requirements Staff, remarks given in Washington. DC, Trade Symposium 2004 (January 14, 2005).

53. *Ibid.*

54. Michael D. Greenberg, *et al.*, "Maritime Terrorism: Risk and Liability," Center for Terrorism Risk Management Policy, RAND Corp. Santa Monica, CA (2006), p. 117.

55. Caldwell, p. 9.

56. Greenberg, p. 115.

57. Patrice Poltzer, "Thousand of UK Passports Stolen, *Time Magazine* (29 July 2008).

58. Rupert Herbert-Burns, "Terrorism in the Early 21st Century Maritime Domain," in Greenberg.

Chapter Six

The Gatekeeper's Challenge

... an opening at any point in the network compromises the entire network.
—Organization for Economic and Cooperative Development Report, 2003

Following September 11, 2001, the vulnerabilities of maritime trade became visible and unacceptable. The challenge is to not only make the system less vulnerable, but also more resilient. While this is being done, planners want to avoid sacrificing the gains global commerce has made, and perhaps even provide an opportunity to exceed those marks. The growth anticipated for containerized trade, it would seem, demands higher standards of security and resiliency. Asymmetrical war alters the battlefield of national defense and business competition. Some of the defenses are in place but are in need of renovation. Perhaps not all the walls and gates need to be torn down. Some will have to be made surer and others rebuilt.

Since its earliest beginning as a nation America's grand strategy, as put forth by Washington and Hamilton, was "to preserve the incomparable blessing of her insulation from Europe's broils through a foreign policy of neutrality and a naval strategy of coastal and commercial defense."[1] The emphasis the founders placed on America's early maritime capability and the young nation's dependency on a naval force for national defense is expressed by Article I, Section 8 of the U.S. Constitution, which grants to Congress the power "To raise and support Armies, but no Appropriation of Money to that Use shall be for a longer Term than two Years," and the power "To provide and maintain a Navy," on the other hand, was without time restriction. Historian Walter McDougall writes: "the original U.S. strategy was also maritime for reasons of political culture." In many regards the culture has not changed. The role of maritime supremacy is principal to the U.S. defense strategy. The United States considers its shores inviolate. However, ports are vulnerable.

The range of potential assailants is, obviously, not restricted to European powers or any other state actors. Terrorists, criminals, and disgruntled employees have incentive and ability to collude, plot, execute, and, for varying reasons, benefit from an attack. The identity of the adversary is indefinite, but their threat can be sensed as financial and political tensions mount at home and around the world.

AN OPAQUE AND EXPANDING RISK ENVIRONMENT

Transparency into the supply chain and the movement of its cargo is the key to security. Unfortunately, to date, the capabilities and efforts to open the record system to scrutiny is still a struggle. This is partly because prior to 9/11 security control inferred large productivity losses. Electronic manifest handling is a recent operational integrant. Logic-based methodology screening, used in such programs as the Automated Targeting System, is also relatively new (originally developed to assess cargo, ATS has undergone controversy for DHS's intentions to apply the system in profiling individuals as high-risk terrorist suspects). By earlier modes of thinking, the weight and volume of paper documentation, increasing competition, and rising expectations of consumers excluded the notion of security as part of the same discussion as efficiency. As reported by the OECD, "not only does perfect transparency not exist, but in fact anonymity seems to be the rule rather than the exception, and not only is it permitted, but in many cases positively encouraged."[2] The ability of authorities to know that the goods that flow through the global supply chain are legitimate is critical. Also, being assured that the vessels that transport these cargos are legally operated and their crews do not harbor criminals or terrorists are, naturally and equally, of fundamental importance. A part of the systems deficiencies are also sub-standard maintenance practices and a disregard for accepted codes of operation.[3] Therefore, physical security checks and workers' identification verification systems need to be standardized and broadly operational. In a nod toward this concern, the DHS created the Internet-based E-Verify program. This system assures a prospective employee's legal right to work in the United States and has a current database of over seventeen million entries. Participation is mostly voluntary and free to the user. It links to the Department of Immigration's database and offers access to eighty million records current, yet the program's aims concern work eligibility rather than security and insider threats.

The race for efficiency in the irregular and unsystematic designing of the global trading system has had its price. However, the post-9/11 reality may have changed the lack of serious consideration given security. Research in homeland security tries to uncover ways of not only securing the supply chain, but in doing so, not sacrifice the efficiencies that technology, innovation, and hard work have gained for global commerce. Transparency is a virtue that can aid both security and asset management.

However, until port operators find a way of confirming what is claimed as being the contents of any box is indeed, actually the same item as was lade and stowed, the system remains perilously unsecured. While we wait for that time, the words of John Meredith, Managing Director of Hutchinson Port Holdings, are an unsettling caveat: "there is no doubt that containers are going to be exploited as a poor man's missile. The question is when, not if."[4] Although many would view this statement as alarmist, its warning should not go unheeded. As a GAO report notes, "the likelihood of terrorists smuggling a WMD in the United States in cargo containers is low [according to the Department of Homeland Security], the nation's vulnerability to this activity and the consequences of such an attack—such as billions of losses in U.S. revenue and halts in manufacturing production—are potentially high."[5]

While the ongoing debate about security of maritime trade resumes, other pressures are mounting. Bottlenecks over the world are forming as a result of the increase in containerized trade. In many ports freight transport infrastructure is reaching maximum capacity. Already container volume is outgrowing the current facility apparatus in place to service it. According to the International Chamber of Commerce's Commission on Transport and Logistics, transpacific cargo will grow by an estimated rate of 10–12 percent. Russia's container traffic has been steadily growing by 15–20 percent a year, and the volume of trade between China and its partners are on a course for further expansion.[6] The explosion of the economies in Asia is further contributing to the challenge. The economic growth in the region has ratcheted up world commerce precipitously. Figures indicate that the economic development in these countries and in other parts of the world have allowed those economies to capture a larger proportion of container throughput in global trade than developed countries by 70 percent. The growth rate in these countries averages out to over 10 percent based upon 2006 estimates.[7]

By the time of the September 11 attacks, the United Nations Conference on Trade and Development (UNCTAD) estimated 5.8 billion tons of goods, hulled by 46,000 vessels, passed through 4,000 ports in 2001. The volume of trade increased by nearly 40 percent between the years 1995 and 2001 alone.[8] As earlier noted, approximately 15 million shipping containers are in circulation.

Annually, the world's seaports record and process between 200 and 300 million containers at each depot as this fleet of boxes crisscross the globe and are repeatedly stuffed, unloaded, and transshipped over a vast network.[9] These pressures make the task of securing the system against disruption extremely daunting. There is no indication of any abatement of high-volume,

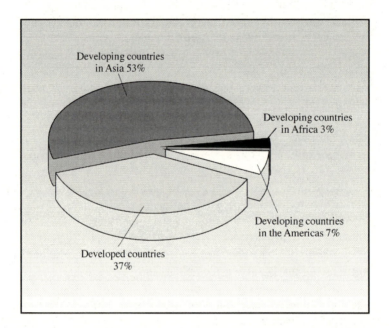

Figure 6.1.   Regional Breakdown of Container Throughput for 2005 *(Source: Review Of Maritime UN Transport 2012, Report by the UNCTAD secretariat. United Nations, New York and Geneva, 2012)*

freely flowing trade. Despite the current economic downturn, the state of urgency has been present for a while and the threat is long term.

In the United States the statistics are no less consequential as it becomes a nation increasingly more dependent on imports. The numbers of inbound traffic break out in the following manner: over 7,500 ships make 51,000 calls at 361 U.S. ports. Over 7 million containers (17,000 per day)[10] are handled and 2 percent to 7 percent currently inspected. In 2004 the U.S. Customs and Border Protection Agency estimated an import value of $1.365 trillion.[11] As of 2012, the US Census Bureau reported a value of over $2.7 trillion[12]. (As reported above) the U.S. Commerce Department anticipates the number of cargo containers to increase to 30 million over the next twenty years.[13]

These figures and events reflect a transport system that is expanding quickly and becoming more complex. At the same time, it depends upon predictable and robust competencies to propel world trade. These efficiencies of seamless conveyance are elemental to the functioning of the supply chain system and, integrally, the global economy. Simultaneously, the global supply chain is a system that is vulnerable from a range of possibilities. Those vulnerabilities span an array of corruption, from documentary fraud and illicit money raising operations to physical violation and attack. The system has already been the target of pirates and criminal organizations, which regularly traffic in contraband materials, weapons, illegal drugs, and bulk quantities of dangerous material. Due largely to the existence of opaque ownership and disclosure requirements, terrorists and criminals have the logistics to move material, funds, and human beings freely around the globe while using legitimate commercial operations as a front for their motives and activity. The opportunity for crime, sabotage, and to create chaos flows throughout the entire security framework.

CRIMINALS, TERRORISTS, AND PIRATES

As summarized in the earlier chapter, even if criminals and terrorists do not share the same motives, their methods can be identical. Unlike terrorist groups, criminal organizations do not seek to overthrow or destabilize the state. They do contest the state's claim in matters of its monopoly over force and law. Not unlike terrorists, however, these organizations offer an alternative system of justice. In addition to justice, what crime can offer marginalized communities, which terrorists do not, is security and commerce. Traditionally, all criminal behavior is not considered terrorism, whereas contrastingly, all terrorism is criminal. The new void left by failed states may have changed the calculus. A system for abuse by criminal and terrorist elements exists where the state security apparatus and infrastructure have malfunctioned or have been destroyed. Both terrorist and transnational criminal organizations inhabit this realm between the state and the rising hostility and counter-movement to cultural and economic globalization. Such societies of marginalized populations offer both market opportunities and labor pools for recruitment. These spaces become contested and inhabited by congeries of "intelligence services, organized crime, terrorist groups, the arms trade, money-laundering banks, hermetic religious cults, and secret societies."[14] It is a realm of simultaneously, cooperative and conflictual relationships that blur "the lines between the legal and illegal."[15] It is also a place ripe for economic and political exploitation.

Outlaw organizations are at a rare advantage in these environments. They come by this advantage by embracing the logic of the market on one hand, and on the other hand, exploiting the democratic deficit in government and corruptive influences of civil society. Under these conditions obstacles severely hamper state law enforcement organs and their sanctioned agencies to form and coordinate countermeasures against crime. Hence, transnational crime and international terrorism finds a convenient place between the forces of globalization and counter-globalization to exploit its advantages and the diverse range of options. The maritime trade system, with its complex interdependent operations, layers of jurisdictional overlap, uncoordinated or nonexistent codes for information sharing and record maintenance, mass quantities of goods, centralized location of ports, and sheer vastness, make it an obvious target for corruption, plunder, and attack.

This problem is particularly acute in the Asian-Pacific region where there has been growing evidence that piracy is tied to international crime organizations.[16] Well-financed criminal syndicates with connections in Hong Kong, Indonesia, and China run many pirating operations. In 2004 Foreign Affairs reported that pirate gangs are actually part of organized syndicates that recruit thugs, corrupt officials, port workers, and work through businessmen to dispose of goods.[17] The same report discusses how attacks have tripled since the mid-1990s despite the fact many incidents go unreported in order for operators to avoid higher insurance rates. Nevertheless, it is a reality of today's maritime sea trade that is difficult to ignore, particularly, since the same report claims that the motives of crime and terrorism, once separate, are beginning to converge.

> Most disturbingly, the scourges of piracy and terrorism are increasingly intertwined: piracy on the high seas is becoming a key tactic of terrorist groups. Unlike the pirates of old, whose sole objective was quick commercial gain, many of today's pirates are maritime terrorists with an ideological bent and a broad political agenda.[18]

Most piracy occurs within the jurisdiction of states rather than on the high seas. Pirate gangs with a base in a courtesan or sympathetic state will seek out ships under the flag of another nation. Knowing that naval vessels are generally forbidden from crossing national boundaries, these criminals take care to plan attacks on targets of foreign countries in the territorial waters of a third country. Disposal of the seized goods finally occurs in the jurisdiction of a fourth state. The chaos inhibits national law enforcement agencies from disrupting criminal activities. According to the International Chamber of Commerce, ongoing maritime territorial disputes, particularly in Asia, contribute to instability over issues of sovereignty and adherence to international norms. The problems not only impede efforts to combat piracy and drug trafficking, but also cooperation in maritime safety, pollution, and search and rescue.[19]

As part of this global web of outlawed activity, pirates have long been, routinely and expansively, taking advantage of the high velocity of trade and the system's porous security sheathing. The Piracy Reporting Centre of the International Chamber of Commerce monitors such activity and reports that piracy has been a highly lucrative venture for well-organized gangs.[20] Aside from confiscating onboard cash and selling the cargo for considerable profit ($1 million USD for an oil tanker, for example), pirates can use the hijacked vessel as a source of steady revenue. "Ghost ships" can be repainted, renamed, and placed back in operation as re-registered commercial vessels. Legitimate shippers, unknowingly, may contract these vessels. Their cargoes are then diverted and resold as the cycle of criminality repeats.

Unresolved maritime and territorial claims have often been in the servanthood of illegal activity. There are many examples of how this exploitation benefited crime and can be seen in the way smugglers, crime organizations, and cargo thieves have been manipulating the maritime trade systems' vulnerabilities for years. Before the world became aware of the international reach and threat from terrorist groups, criminals were profiting from the system's openness and fluidity. Worldwide, cargo theft is estimated to equal between \$30 billion to \$50 billion per year.[21] Piracy, alone, is accountable for \$16 billion.[22] U.S. Customs and Border Protection, on average per day, claims it seizes 2,313 pounds of narcotics in 131 narcotic seizures at ports of entry and another 3,634 pounds of narcotics in 24 seizures between ports of entry.[23] Additionally, hazardous material cargos routinely pass through ports with assistance of corrupt shippers, carriers and/or conspiratorial employees of ports and transport companies. Although some expert views contrast with the 2004 Foreign Affairs report by pointing to the fact that there is only scant evidence that terrorist and pirate syndicates are collaborating, it is reasonable to assume that terrorists have access and knowledge of these practices and can use them to suit their own designs.

THE EXPLOSION OF TRADE AND TRANSPARENCY DEFICIT

As the Booz Allen Hamilton–Conference Board exercise demonstrates, the concern is that while waiting for the moment to strike, a terrorist group could place a container armed with an IND (and/or personnel) within the maritime transport system. The container would be virtually invisible as it moved about unbounded in a complex web of ports, inter-modal transport systems, and a network of tens of thousands of entry points. The lethal shipment becomes part of a global logistics chain that is populated with numerous junctions and whose security standards vary widely and lack any uniformity in operating systems or legal framework. The level of security is nearly as diverse as the range of network nodes. No worldwide security framework exists today that can capture all the constituent parts of the supply chain and provide order to the complex and competing demands of its stakeholders.[24] One of the greatest challenges in addressing security concerns of maritime containerized transport is the lack of uniform system controls.[25] Transparency of the movement of containers around the world is weak, and manifest records are typically vague and corruptible.

Because of these security limitations, numerous terrorist groups have recognized the advantage of being maritime capable. According to the 2006

RAND report, several organizations have adopted seaborne tactics as part of their logistical plan. A partial list includes the following:

- **Al Qaeda:** "The Base"—an Islamic militant terrorist organization founded in 1988 who claimed credit for the World Trade Center tragedy. Its demands are the end of foreign influence in Muslim countries. Reportedly responsible for the bombing of the USS *Cole* and the M/V *Limburg*. Abdel Rahim al-Nashiri is believed to be the chief maritime planner.[26] Known as the "Prince of the Sea," he was reasoned to be the lead planner of attacks on Western shipping interests around the Straights of Gibraltar. A current detainee at Quantanamo, he is also the subject of investigations into allegations that the Bush administration sanctioned the use of torture. Various sources, which include Lloyd's of London and Norwegian intelligence, have claimed that the group had between fifteen and twenty-three vessels. Although material evidence has yet to be uncovered, they corroborated with several other periodic reports.[27]
- **Al Gama'a al-Islamiyya:** "The Islamic Group," a militant Egyptian movement dedicated to the overthrow of the Egyptian government. Credited with carrying out strikes against passenger ships.
- **Abu Sayyaf Group:** a radical Islamic group operating in the Philippines. Its members are believed to have participated in the conflict against the Soviets in Afghanistan. They are responsible for launching an attack on passenger ships in the southern Philippines, including an incident where as many as 116 civilians died.
- **Chechen Rebels** have been responsible for various attacks on passenger ships in the area of the Bosporus Straight. Their long-standing struggle against Moscow has been marked by extreme brutality. They have arrant ties with criminal elements throughout the scattered Chechen diaspora in Russia, Turkey, and other parts of the former Soviet Union and Europe.
- **GAM:** "Free Aceh Movement" was a separatist group, which had been battling the Indonesian government since the mid-1970s. Now officially inactive, they were particularly active along the Straight of Malacca and engage in hijacking and smuggling, usually preying upon smaller seacraft.
- **Jamaat al-Tawhid wa'l-jihad:** "Unity and Jihad Group" notorious for suicide bombing attacks and televised beheadings. Led by the assassinated Abu Musab al-Zarqawi, the group is known for leading attacks against U.S. forces in Iraq and oil facilities.
- **Lebanese Hezbollah:** "Party of Allah" is a paramilitary organization adhering to the Shi'a ideology of the Ayatollah Khomeini. They emerged during the Lebanese civil war in the early 1980s and are reported to have received seaborne training for the purpose of moving weapons, personnel, and material.

- **LTTE:** Liberation Tigers of Tamil Eelam is a militant secessionist group that has waged a violent war against the Sri Lankan government for decades. They were reputed to have the most effective maritime assault capabilities of any sub-state organization.[28] This arm of operations went by the name of "the Sea Tigers." In 2009 the Sri Lankan government claimed victory over the separatist group, however, remnants of the resistance survive and continue to defy authority.
- **Palestine Organizations:** Hamas, Palestinian Islamic Jihad (PIJ), the Popular Front for the Liberation of Palestine-General Command (PFLP-GC), and the Democratic Front for the Liberation of Palestine (DFLP) all are reported to have had or maintain seaborne capabilities.
- **PIRA:** "Provisional Irish Republican Army," a splinter group of the Irish Republican Army has been moving and supplying weapons and related materiel through the use of commercial shipping since the 1980s. Cargo included light weapons, rocket-propelled grenades, detonators, surface-to-air missiles, SEMTEX-H explosives, and fuses.[29]

As in the above example, war game scenarios designed to test countermeasures suggest a weapon of mass destruction could penetrate U.S. territory by entering the global transportation chain legally or illegally. This would be accomplished by one of two means. The first approach might be a simple hijacking. With hundreds of workers having physical access to a container while it's in transit or in a port area, terrorists could easily arrange to infiltrate a legitimate cargo consignment with a deadly device.

A second option would be to use a legitimate trading identity to transport a WMD. Option number two is what is commonly referred to as a "Trojan horse" scenario. Against a hijacking, the security onus resides primarily with the transport authorities, which must protect the physical integrity of the containers as they move across the supply chain. In the case of the "Trojan horse" scenario, however, these measures must also combine with information sharing efforts by customs and law enforcement agencies. The aforementioned use of tracking software, logic-based methodology, and programs such as C-TPAT, SAFE Framework, CSI, et al., are effective. However, if a compromised container enters the supply chain through a trusted shipper, the odds of detection become adverse. With 100 percent scanning technology uneconomically feasible and not yet deployable, a combination of broad breadth screening, selected scanning, and some low-rate inspection may be adequate in thwarting an attack.[30,31] Unfortunately, many shipments avoid inspection through the Trans-International Routier haulage system and due to porous In-bond security controls mentioned above. Also, participation in various counterterrorism programs, such as the ones discussed above, exempt cargo from inspection.

Worldwide, maritime shipping is an industry of 8 to 10 million people working for as many as 40,000 freight forwarders and buying agents. An extremely diverse international labor force provides the pool of employees. Over 1,370,000 seafarers staff the international merchant fleet. This vast labor force moves freely around the globe with relatively liberal travel rights and minimal identification documents. Making matters worse, the black market is a source for falsified seafarer certificates and identity documents.[32] A typical journey taken by the shipment hypothesized in the 2002 war game scenario would have involved as many as twenty-five different players, thirty to forty documents (on average, a large container vessel tracks 100,000 documents[33]), several different modes of transportation, and passed through fifteen or more different locations.[34] The actors involved in the movement of goods through the maritime transportation chain include an international cast of regulatory agencies, liability regimes, operators of various transportation modes, port authorities, freight integrators, and legal frameworks. Interaction is complex and unsystematic. The laconism of a 2008 GAO report expresses the concern and apprehension that these circumstances create: "Every time responsibility for cargo in containers changes hands along the supply chain there is potential for a security breach."[35]

The scope of the risk and the range of potential adversaries are troublesome. The needed balance between efficiency benefits of deregulated trade and security imperatives has yet been struck. A piecemeal approach of cooperative arrangements between private operators and public regulators is what efforts have offered up thus far. This patchwork of security programs and initiatives characterizes the configuration of the international maritime transport network. The systemic deficiencies are obvious. Policies become subject to domestic and established interests. Multilateral approaches and efforts are undercut. Resultant gaps in the global security shielding emerge and circumstances can become more exigent as these conditions persist. The restatement of the OECD report on maritime security not only merits a visit but also seems an ominous complement to the above GAO report assertion—*an opening at any point in the network compromises the entire network.* These two official observations attest to the fact that, although the range of methods for infiltrating the supply chain system may be limited, as contended by the RAND report, the number of opportunities for success is, unfortunately, high.

As mentioned above, no single authority exists to oversee the through-put of containers over the network of an intersecting and interlocking supply chain. The chaos that results from this deficit in uniformity, transparency, and governance has been described as "the gatekeeper challenge." The challenge bubbles to the surface in the form of jurisdictional overlap, duplication, lack of coordination, opaque contours of authority, and ever-occurring turf battles.

Country	Number of officers supplied	Percentage of world market share officers	Country	Number of ratings supplied	Percentage of world market share ratings
Philippines	57,688	9.2	China	90,296	12.1
China	51,511	8.3	Indonesia	61,821	8.3
India	46,497	7.5	Turkey	51.009	6.8
Turkey	36,734	5.9	Russia	40,000	5.4
Ukraine	27,172	4.4	Malaysia	28,687	3.8
Russia	25,000	4.0	Philippines	23,492	3.1
United States	21,810	3.5	Bulgaria	22,379	3.0
Japan	21,297	3.4	Myanmar	20,145	2.7
Romania	18,575	3.0	Sri Lanka	19,511	2.6
Poland	17,923	2.9	United States	16,644	2.2
Norway	16,082	2.6	India	16,176	2.2
Indonesia	15,906	2.5	Honduras	15,341	2.1
United Kingdom	15.188	2.4	Cambodia	12,004	1.6
Canada	13,994	2.2	Viet Nam	11,438	1.5
Croatia	11,704	1.9	Italy	11,390	1.5
Myanmar	10,950	1.8	Ukraine	11,000	1.5
Bulgaria	10,890	1.7	Pakistan	9,327	1.2
Viet Nam	10,738	1.7	France	9,316	1.2
Greece	9,993	1.6	Egypt	9,000	1.2
Republic of Korea	9,890	1.6	United Kingdom	8,990	1.2
World	624,062	100.0	World	747,306	100.0

Table 6.1. The 20 Biggest Suppliers of Officers and Ratings in 2010

While these problems abide, containerized seaborne trade is growing steadily. In 2006, world GDP grew by 4.0 percent. During the same year the volume of global merchandise trade increased by 8.0 percent.[36] Echoing these numbers, the world container fleet grew by 7.8 percent in 2006, and port throughput expanded by 13.4 percent.[37] Strong performance from transition economies (mostly China and Russia) and developing countries in Asia, Africa, and South America contributed to the total estimate and probably has altered the pattern of trade for the future—regardless of economic cycles. This data is a further expression of the expansion and deepening of the economic integration brought about by economic globalization. In addition to the competitive imperative of organizations to diversify supply sources, these increases also reflect an intensification of South-South trade.[38] Using 2006 as a historical marker, 30,686 billion ton-miles of seaborne trade were recorded that year representing an annual increase of 5.5 percent. Of the goods processed by developing countries, 61.1 percent were loaded and 41.4 percent were unloaded, reflecting some equilibrium in the developing world's trade balance.[39]

Seaborne trade anticipates continued growth. As it expands, the security versus frictionless trade dilemma compounds. A modern supply chain must be a low-cost and efficient form of conveyance. To achieve this, the private sector worked to harmonize different transportation modes. These same design features and principles that create an efficient supply chain can be applied to security interoperability and effectiveness. In its haste to react to the catastrophe in 2001, unfortunately, the U.S. government initially responded with measures conceived to address the public outrage, more than provide a long overdue solution to a serious problem. Some of that mindset persists today and is always a threat to resurface in the event of catastrophe.

For terrorists, a shipping container is still an attractive method of smuggling a WMD. The sheer number of containers that circle the planet with a minimum of inspection and high volume of cargo make these transportation

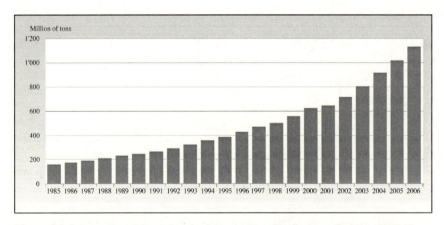

Figure 6.2. International Containerized Trade Growth *(Source: Review Of Maritime UN Transport 2012, Report by the UNCTAD secretariat. United Nations, New York and Geneva, 2012)*

commodities tempting tactical devices. Once a container has been compromised with a weapon, the device may as well be invisible once it enters the trade stream. As it moves along the trade corridors a lethal cargo becomes hidden within the millions of containers with their mass consignments of goods. A closed circuit of data, which identifies, verifies, tracks, and communicates information about the contents of a shipment from its point of origin to its final destination, can be the best solution. Fortunately, however, it is not necessarily the only one. The combination of screening with logic-based software, non-intrusive scanning of selected cargo, and minimal physical inspections has been thus far a success. As for the future, the global security regime will rely on these methods, but also will have to adapt to a vaster supply chain, a network of more participants, greater volumes of cargo, and, perhaps, more political instability.

Furthermore, the present port security framework needs to extend deeper ashore and farther out to sea.[40] To be more reliable and less vulnerable the new security schema demands the involvement of manufacturers, intermediaries, and resellers. As legitimate commerce attempts to harness all the elements, the task will only emphasize more the complexity of the problem. Coordinating the disparate private and public entities, which form the maritime supply chain and, who, for years have been operating on the premise that speed and efficiency override security, is an Augean feat. Satisfying security imperatives while understanding and minimizing any adverse economic effects of security intervention is as much an exhortation as it is a delicate balancing act.

CONCLUSION

The threat presented by transnational crime groups and terrorist organizations, either converged or acting independently, is a redoubtable challenge. Exploitation of the fragmented state of jurisdictional authority has been a practiced art of criminals and terrorists. With the volume of trade increasing precipitously and the range of territorial claims expanding as well, there seems to be little outlook for the abatement of these tensions; particularly, as drug trafficking becomes more profitable and the underground trade routes become more durable. During the height of the Cold War, 140 states were accorded formal sovereignty in the 1960s.[41] The inability of many of these countries to establish themselves as viable nations has consequences in the post-Cold War era. Today, these failed states are susceptible to the abuse of power from within and criminal elements from outside their borders. A typical stance of political leaders in these countries is to assign and demand a greater recognition for sovereign rights than for democratic and human rights.[42] Capitalizing on the official sanctity of borders, ethnic tensions, and the mass movements of refugees that result from weak governance, criminals and terrorists find the opportunities they seek to move assets, form underground communication links, and recruit members and accomplices. They conduct their business with impunity while legitimate actors are hindered by the rules of engagement dictated by the interstate system of protocol and jurisdictional law.

These conditions lend themselves to a global maritime trade system that serves illicit activity as much as it serves legitimate players. An open trading system is essential to national security policies as it is to those who seek to undermine legitimate interests. The growth of Asian and Pacific economies will only compound these problems. Since interior land transport has not kept pace with the economic expansion in these regions, more traffic is relegated to sea. Shipping along the Asian Pacific is densely concentrated along the coasts and through straights before letting out to open ocean transit.[43] A denser, less insulated web of commerce allows for more leakage between legitimate and illegitimate actors and cargo. These trends culminate with a scenario, which is ripe with opportunity for both sides of the law.

To restate the chapter's premise: the uniformity, velocity, and anonymity of containerized traffic offer terrorists ample opportunity to inflict catastrophic damage to the commercial infrastructure. As mentioned above, an escalation of the security risk may abide more subtly and arrantly in a global systemic host. The trend of territorial "unbundling" or "de-bordering,"[44] has not only made borders more porous, but also raised questions concerning governance. Hastening these developments and compounding the pressure on the system of commerce, security, and law is the overall impact of technology. What results is a gradual transformation of the modern nation, function, province, and effectiveness of international borders. The system that drives global commerce was conceived to accommodate the voluminous transfer of financial flows, trade in goods, and "just-in-time" manufacturing processes—but not security. In fact, most conventional thinking dictates that security and anticrime strictures only serve to undermine market liberalization.

With 80 percent to 90 percent of world trade being seaborne[45,46] the maritime trade transport system remains a major integrant of the global economy and source of concern. How security interventions might work to neutralize our vulnerabilities in maritime trade is only part of the problem. How it accomplishes this feat while (1) enabling commerce, (2) making security economically and financially less burdensome at the enterprise level, and (3) folding these elements into an integrated global security regime is the other part.

Finally, maintaining the faith in the democratic principles of commerce is at the center of the gatekeepers' challenge and core of the new security dilemma. Companies that invest in their own security infrastructure contribute to the integrity of the entire global system. Therefore, they should not be penalized competitively because of consequential financial disadvantages or by the damaging disclosure of sensitive market intelligence. To help ease these circumstances and concerns government involvement may be necessary. Economic and tax incentives, guarantees, and a revision of existing legislation are on the table for consideration. Most important, it will require a public/private partnership that seeks to keep the supply chain open and transparent, and, at the same time keeps the commercial playing field level.

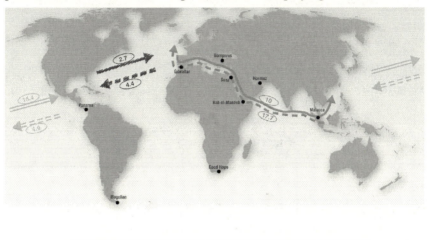

Map 6.1. Major Trade Routes, Container Traffic—2007 *(Source: Review Of Maritime UN Transport 2008, Report by the UNCTAD secretariat. United Nations, New York and Geneva, 2008)*

NOTES

1.   Walter A. McDougall, "History And Strategies: Grand, Maritime, And American," *The Telegram*, Foreign Policy Research Institute (October 2011).

2.   William Langwiesche, "The Outlaw Sea: A World of Freedom, Chaos, and Crime," North Point Press, New York (2005), p. 256.

3.   *Ibid.*

4.   Stephen Flynn "Why America Is Still An Easy Target," *Time* (26 July 2004): Vol. 164, Iss. 4.

5.   Stephen L. Caldwell, "Supply Chain Security: Container Security Programs have matured, but Uncertainty Persists over the Future of 100 Percent Scanning," (GAO Testimony before the Subcommittee on Border and Maritime Security, Committee on Homeland Security, House of Representatives, GAO-12-422T, p. 1.

6.   see International Chamber of Commerce website, www.iccwbo.org/policy/transport/icccijd/index.html.

7.   UNCTAD, "Review of Maritime Transport," 2007, p 89.

8.   *Op cit.*, p. 7.

9.   David J. Closs, Edmund McGarrell, "Enhancing Security Throughout the Supply Chain," IBM Center for Business of Government (April 2004).

10. Hau L. Lee, and S. Wang, "Higher Supply Chain Security with Lower Cost: Lessons from Total Quality Management," *Int. Journal of Production Economics*, Vol. 96, no. 3 (June 2005), p. 289–300.

11. *Import Trade Trends*, U.S. Customs and Border Protection, July 2004.

12. http://www.census.gov/foreign-trade/Press-Release/2012pr/final_revisions/exh1.pdf

13. "Shipping Container Security," HotQuant.com, posted 2/15/03.

14. James, H Mittelman, *The Globalization Syndrome* (Princeton University Press, 2000), p. 206.

15. *Ibid.*

16. International Chamber of Commerce see www.pacom.mil/publications/apu02/s04ship7.pdf.

17. Gal Luft, Anne Korin, "Terrorism Goes to Sea" *Foreign Affairs* (Nov/Dec 2004) Vol. 83, Issue 6.

18. *Ibid.*

19. International Chamber of Commerce.

20. Philippe Crist, "Security in Maritime Transport: Risk Factors and Economic Impact," (Prepared for the Organization for Economic Cooperation and Development, 2003) as cited by Reyes, Brian in "Open to Attack," *Lloyd's List, Lloyd's List International* (23 July 2003), p. 12.

21. *Ibid.*

22. Luft.

23. "A Day in the Life of CBP," www.cbp.gov/xp/cgov/toolbox/about/accomplish/day.

24. UNCTAD, *Maritime Security: Elements of an Analytical Framework for Compliance Measurement and Risk Assessment*, UN: Geneva and New York (2006).

25. "Report on Container Transport Security Across Modes" (Prepared for the Organization for Economic Cooperation and Development, 2004), p. 5.

26. Bronson Percival, *Indonesia and the United States: Shared Interests in Maritime Security*, Washington, DC: United States—Indonesia Society (June 2005), in Greenberg, p. 26.

27. Michael D. Greenberg, *et al.*, "Maritime Terrorism: Risk and Liability," Center for Terrorism Risk Management Policy, RAND Corp. Santa Monica, CA (2006), p. 26.

28. *Ibid.*

29. Peter Chalk, *West European Terrorism and Counter-Terrorism: The Evolving Dynamic* (New York, St. Martin's Press, 1996) in Greenberg.

30. "Report on Container Transport Security Across Modes," Prepared for the Organization for Economic Cooperation and Development (2004), p. 2.

31. Flynn, *America the Vulnerable,* p. 88.

32. BIMCO/ISF Manpower Update Report as cited by Crist.

33. Unisys Corporation, "Your New World: A Visual Guide to Global Commerce," presentation in New York (October 2004).

34. Bryan Reyes, *Lloyd's List, Lloyd's List International* (23 July 2003).

35. Stephen Caldwell, "Supply Chain Security—U.S. Customs and Border Protection Has Enhanced Its Partnership with Import Trade Sectors, but Challenges Remain in Verifying Security Practices," GOA Report to Congressional Requesters, GAO-08-240 (April 2008).

36. UNCTAD, 2006.

37. *Ibid.*

38. *Ibid.*

39. *Ibid.*

40. John R. Harrald, Hugh W. Stephens, Johann Rene vanDorp, "A framework for Sustainable Port Security," *Journal of Homeland Security and Emergency Management* (2004, Vol. 1, Issue 2), p. 2–3,

41. Stremlau, John, People in Peril: Human Rights, Humanitarian Action, and Preventing Deadly Conflict, see http://www.wilsoncenter.org/subsites/ccpdc/frpub.htm,

42. *Ibid.*

43. International Chamber of Commerce, see www.pacom.mil/publications/apu02/s04ship7.pdf.

44. *Import Trade Trends*, U.S. Customs and Border Protection (July 2004), p. 80–84.

45. Philippe Crist, "Security in Maritime Transport: Risk Factors and Economic Impact," Prepared for the Organization for Economic Cooperation and Development, 2003, p. 7.

46. Flynn, *America the Vulnerable,* p 84.

Chapter Seven

The Cyber War: New Battlefronts, Old and New Enemies

The Internet is a critical infrastructure necessary to the functioning of commerce government and personal communication and national security. The system is not secure.
—Intelligence and National Security Alliance report, November 2009

In a statement for a 2002 report prepared by the Center for Strategic and International Studies (CSIS), Jim Lewis, the widely respected cyber expert and former official with the Department of State and the Department of Commerce comments:

> The idea that hackers are going to bring the nation to its knees is too far-fetched a scenario to be taken seriously. Nations are more robust than the early analysts of cyberterrorism and cyber warfare gave them credit for. Infrastructure systems [are] more flexible and responsive in restoring service than the early analysts realized, in part because they have to deal with failure on a routine basis. [1]

Six years later, in its 2008 report, "Securing Cyberspace for the 44th Presidency," the same CSIS concluded:

> Cybersecurity is among the most serious economic and national security challenges we face in the twenty-first century. Our investigations and interviews for this report made it clear we are in a long-term struggle with criminals, foreign intelligence agencies, militaries, and others with whom we are intimately and unavoidably connected through a global digital network; and this struggle does more real damage every day to the economic health and national security of the United States than any other threat. As one general put it in his briefing to us: *In cyberspace, the war has begun.*

Interestingly, the project director for the 2008 report was, again, Jim Lewis. The contrast of analysis is not only striking for its reversal of positions, but also in its tone. The 2008 report called for a profound reorganization of our national defenses that embraces a spirit of partnership between the U.S. government, its allies, and the private sector. It also urges a break with the past on issues of deregulation, security classification, and the call for leadership in order to drive forward a comprehensive cybersecurity strategy. The authors also concede that the information age has forced the U.S. security establishment to rethink how federal government operates across boundaries within and outside itself.[2]

How such previous attitudes could have been overturned so radically in a relatively brief span of time infers more about the dynamic of the information-communication technology (ICT) revolution rather than what it might suggest about contradictory statements or the quality of the analysis. At the times when he spoke, both statements by Jim Lewis were probably correct. Between 2002 and 2008 the pace of technology and the rate of growth and expansion of critical infrastructures have intensified society's use and dependency upon ICT. In the United States, over 95 percent of computers and networks are non-government. Commercial trade, financial institutions, energy providers, the transportation industry, etc., rely on networks to meet consumer demands, and the dependency is growing. As end users, the public depends on these networks to provide an expected level of quality of life.

CYBERSPACE

What, then, is cyberspace? Metaphorically, it is the realm of human community linked by computer transactions. Physically, it is the hardware, software, and transport elements that equate to the network architectures through which energy passes delivering information. However, less specific or technical—but as unerring, is the definition by the science-fiction novelist William Gibson who first introduced the term. In his 1984 book, *Neuromancer*, he expresses cyberspace as a "consensual hallucination . . . a graphic representation of data abstracted from the banks of every computer in the human system." Although both definitions can be considered true, for the purposes of this analysis the definition offered by the U.S. Joint Chiefs of Staff is the most appropriate for the following discussion:

> A domain characterized by the use of electronics and the electromagnetic spectrum[3] to store, modify, and exchange data via networked systems and associated physical infrastructure.[4]

This strategic definition, rather than Gibson's "hallucination," allows us to discuss cyberspace and attendant concepts with the same terms that we use to understand and express our notions about the oceans, the ecosystem, outer space, or other frontiers of human endeavor where serious challenges co-exist alongside opportunities for cooperation. However, to have a basic grasp of those concepts and terms, we need to devote some time and explanation to clarifying the elements and scientific principles that make possible an appreciation of the organism that is the current information/communication system. Also, such familiarity with a few specifics gives us a sense of the system's fragility and our own national vulnerability.

An understanding of cyberspace begins with an understanding of tele-communications. In cyberspace circuits, or routes, travel of information can be physical (copper wiring, optical cable) or radiation based (microwave, WiFi). Vulnerability to attack is a feature of the transmission medium. Physical connections are subject to tapping and severed connections. Radiation-based connections can be disrupted from broadcasted electro-magnetic signals. Walter Morris, Computing Manager at Rutgers University, offers a wide-angle perspective on the domain of telecommunications by simply saying:

> While cyberspace refers to a non-physical abstraction, it is achieved using computers networked via various means of communication. Information is exchanged between the nodes on a network in numerous ways, some physically connected and some using various radio transmitters/receivers.

Whether physically connected or radio transmitted, the integrity and security of these circuits are vested in the communication system's ability to redirect traffic to alternative pathways in the event of circuit failure. Whether a copper-based, wireless, or optical data transport environment, a network is resilient to outside physical attack and disruption due to this fundamental element—redundancy. A simple but significant feature, redundancy merely refers to the multiple paths by which information flows. As stated above, those multiple pathways can be copper wiring, radio frequency, or optical fiber. As long as communication flow has a reliable and alternate (redundant) route, the circulation of information continues as a matter of routine.

The material elements of these paths made little difference in the original scheme. The ability to withstand an intentional or natural onslaught and maintain operational stability by diverting a signal to an alternative routing system was the only concern in the early design, and is still the major concern today. What has changed is the growth of these networks, the volume of information transmitted, the threat vector, and the struggle to adapt to a new and perilous environment. These changes arose from the natural and irresistible forces of technological development and advancement.

Once optical cable made possible the transport of high volumes of data at the speed of light, the growth in optical fiber networks over copper cable systems surged robustly and irreversibly. The changeover in technology set loose immense growth in the capacity and efficiency of I/C networks. It also unleashed a dependence on electronic networks, which is nothing less than a systemic addiction. Although optical fiber cannot yet replace copper in every instance, its impact on telecommunications has been momentous and incontrovertible. In a frequently used metaphor, wavelengths of light are the traffic lanes, by which information travels along the information highway. When lanes become inaccessible or overburdened with data, the system uses alternative routes by switching lanes or adding more. Adding more lanes, or in other words, widening the bandwidth was the solution and one of the drivers of investment craze of the late 1990s. It, also, may have been a contributing factor to the over-investment and eventual implosion of the telecommunication industry.

What exactly, then, is it that streams along the information highway? In most transport forms, electronic messages are disaggregated into bits of data at the origin point—contained and sent in the form of small packets that have routing information in what is called a packet header. Routers along the network read the packet headers and relay the packets toward their destination. At the destination point the data is reassembled as packets arrive to form the original message. A breakdown or interruption of transmission any place along the network will not cause a system failure. The data packets will simply be rerouted. Unless messages are encrypted or transmitted over virtual private networks (VPNs), information flows according to this mode of transport. The system's openness contributes to this resiliency as well as its vulnerability. VPNs are often considered more secure. However, as opposed to a packet routing system, they are more subject to insider threat. If a message is intercepted at a point within a VPN or an encryption decoded before it reaches its destination, the message can be revealed and security is compromised.

The data packet system relies upon standardized communication protocols to assure operation and control. The Transmission Control Protocol/ Internet Protocol (TCP/IP) is the common set of protocols (the rules governing the transmission of data between devices) invented in the early stages of development, and used today to form the global system of interconnected networks. It is the military grade protocol suite that transports packets of information between devices and throughout the network as it verifies correct delivery between servers. By reading the IP header, a routing device can determine the source and destination of each packet. The critical information in the IP header allows the transport layer of the TCP/IP, or "protocol stack" to operate across networks. The IP header is simply a string of numbers that machines, such as routers, read to direct packets toward their destinations and, hence, form connections. At the receiving end, the header carries information that also instructs the destination computer how to recreate the message from the incoming packet data.

These strings of numbers, by which machines communicate, are translated into letters by the Domain Name System (DNS) for easier understanding by humans. Therefore, rather than having to type 66.249.90.104 when accessing a search engine, you can enter the more user friendly Uniform Resource Locator (URL): "google.com." Thirteen root servers house the DNS databases, which facilitate translation between IPs and URLs. The former U.S. Department of Commerce agency, Internet Corporation for Assigned Names and Numbers (ICANN), allocates top-level designations such as com, org, edu, gov, mil, and so on, and maintains and updates the data. ICANN is now a private entity, and as a result of international pressure, has facilitated the movement from a less English-centric system of domain naming to accommodate other languages. The policy shift was a modest signal of progress away from a U.S.-dominated Internet toward a spirit of international cooperation and a more global public good.

THE INCEPTION OF CYBERSPACE

In 1968 the Advanced Research Projects Agency (ARPA), which later became the Defense Advanced Research Projects Agency (DARPA), began work on what would later become the modern-day Internet. The project's goal was to invent a communications network, which could sustain physical attacks and survive malfunctions occurring at other points along the system. ARPAnet, as it was called, required a minimum level of security because the number of users was, initially small, trusted, and known to one another. Shortly after the inception of ARPAnet, the National Science Foundation (NSF) realized the potential impact this technology could have on university research. Unfortunately, to have access to ARPAnet an institution had to have a research contract with the Department of Defense. The disadvantage of having no contractual relationship with DoD put many universities outside the circle, or circuit, of research and information sharing. Under such conditions the full potential of these new skills and equipment would not be met.

In order to provide an apparatus to keep pace with the technology, the NSF created a successor system called NSFNET. NSFNET linked to ARPAnet with a backbone network, which employed TCP/IP. From the start NSFNET was an instantaneous success and, within a short time, became overloaded. The NSF realized it could not continue financing the build out indefinitely and, therefore, set plans for its commercialization.[5] By the 1990s companies called Internet Services Provider (ISPs) overtook an Internet, which previously had been dominated by government, university, and industrial researchers. These ISPs competed in regional areas based upon price and quality of service, and in the process signed up millions of customers. As Andrew Tannenbaum remarks in his seminal work, *Computer Networks*:

> Many people like to criticize the Federal Government for not being innovative, but in the area of networking, it was the DoD and the NSF that created the infrastructure that formed the basis of the Internet and then handed it over to industry to operate.[6]

As business assumed the role of driving force behind the design and direction of the Internet's future, security became, and persists, as an obstruction to commerce. The reigning wisdom affirmed that security creates friction to not only trade, but also communication. While the modern Internet grew beyond its original, conceptual boundaries, features to enhance consumer demand were added. Internet service providers realized the benefit of the capability to have voice communication or Voice over Internet Protocol (VoIP). This feature made it increasingly dependent upon the Public Telecommunications Network (PTN). The expanding interdependency between PTN and the Internet further elevates the risk of infrastructure vulnerability.[7] Since PTN has become more software driven, the reliance on computer networks has intensified. Increased usage demanded a need for larger scale of operations and resulted in the creation of more access points. Security concerns fell further to the wayside.

At its inception as a U.S. military project the Internet's security concerns were minimal. It was an open system because it was closed to others outside its small circle of users with authorized access to specific government-owned and sponsored large mainframe computers. Due to the government's original intention to keep the function and system limited and proprietary, much of the security issues faced today are inherited traits of a previous generation of development.

Currently the Defense Department alone has over 15,000 computer networks and seven million computers and other network devices. DoD withstands more than three million log-ons each day.[8] For the above reasons TCP/IP, which lacks even base security controls, is perilously outdated.[9] It is from this design of over thirty-five years ago that the current network of connection support between autonomous systems and domain name services depends. Therefore, the Internet is inadequately secure by these current communication protocols. Despite good intentions, in the haste to maximize its utility the original designers sacrificed resiliency and imperiled the stability of the many networks, upon which commerce, government, and the routines of daily life so dearly depend. As if conceding these points, among its defensive strategy recommendations, the National Research Council goes as far as to urge: "Minimal exposure to the Internet, which is inherently insecure."[10] As a result of several top-level meetings (and, perhaps, in response to the

NRC's recommendation) the Bush White House launched its National Cybersecurity Initiative (NCSI) during the waning days of its administration. The "cyber-initiative" included a dramatic rescaling of the points at which federal networks connect with the Internet. The Office of Management and Budget set a limitation of fifty "points of presence" by June 2008. However, in March 2008, then Homeland Security Secretary Michael Chertoff remarked, "we have no final number yet," with respect to a survey of all "points of presence."[11] According to Bruce McConnell, former chief of information technology and policy at the Office of Management and Budget, "Trying to catalog where things are so you can turn them off is a daunting task in and of itself."[12]

In the view of the above assessments, the present security challenges are unmet. No longer a closed research project, but rather a global public good, the architecture suffers from a host of vulnerabilities. A report released on May 29, 2009 by the Acting Senior Director for Cyberspace assessed the information and communication infrastructure as thus:

> Without major advances in the security of these systems or significant change in how they are constructed or operated, it is doubtful that the United States can protect itself from the growing threat of cybercrime and state-sponsored intrusions and operations. Our digital infrastructure has already suffered intrusions that have allowed criminals to steal hundreds of millions of dollars and nation-states and other entities to steal intellectual property and sensitive military information. Other intrusions threaten to damage portions of our critical infrastructure. These and other risks have the potential to undermine the Nation's confidence in the information systems that underlie our economic and national security interests.[13]

In the absence of a major upgrade in system security the approach to security has been a "patchwork of niche products and work-arounds."[14] Such methods are responsible for many analysts claiming that security will always be a step behind attackers.[15] As Melissa Hathaway, lead member of the team that prepared the 60-Day Cyberspace Policy Review for President Obama, stated:

> ... our technical defenses have not kept pace with the threat, and it remains easier today—and I suspect for some time to come—for our adversaries to create an offense than for us to create a defense.

As a result of the 2008 report, the April 2009 Cyberspace Policy Review Report and others called for a national comprehensive strategy that includes codes and best practices standards. In the long run, until these situations are addressed, the conclusions, doubts, and fears expressed above will remain.

Unfortunately, the barriers to amending the prevailing security environment are severely challenging to national governments and international

Component	Definition
Backbone	Principal data routes between strategically interconnected networks
ATM Switch	Asynchronous Transfer Mode is a dedicated switching technology that transmits digital data over a physical medium
Router	A device that forwards data packets by reading address information
Amplifier	Sometimes known as a repeater, it boosts signal strength to overcome attenuation between nodes
Server Farm	A group of computers housed in a single facility and can involve dozens or even thousands of rack mounted servers
CO-LO	Co-location is a physical facility that houses network hardware equipment and offers security and multiple connection feeds
VoIP	Voice over Internet Protocol is the method for taking analog signals and turning them into digital data that can be transmitted over the Internet
PoP	Point of Presence is the juncture where signals transfer from the telephone system to the ISP network, become digital and are packet switched
NAP	Network Access Points are major switching facilities that tie Internet access providers together in peering arrangements. Originally, NAPs were the key components in the transition of the Internet from a government project to a commercial utility
ISP	Internet Service Provider is a company that provides Internet service
WAN	Wide Area Network interconnects computers over a wide area and requires higher data transfer rates than a LAN
LAN	Local Area Network interconnect computers over a limited area such as a home, school, office building, etc
SAN	Storage Area Network is a type of LAN designed to handle large data transfers in support of data storage a retrieval

Figure 7.1.   Internet Architecture *(Source: Computer Networks, Prentice Hall, 2003)*

commerce. The private sector primarily owns the electronic infrastructure, making security a business decision. In order to meet the demands of global commerce, corporate strategists are forced to favor their revenue-generating units over investment in security. According to Tom Kellermann, a member of President Obama's Commission on Cybersecurity, only 6 percent of corporate IT budgets go toward cybersecurity.[16] As long as the threat of catastrophe remains only an abstract fear, corporate boards will continue to view their responsibilities as vested in creating and accumulating assets, while leaving to subordinates the job of protecting those assets.

Equally unfortunate is that the public sector often takes its cues from the private sector. Deregulation of the telecommunications industry by obliging legislation and government agencies has over time helped to accelerate the growth of the Internet. Subsequently, the increase in the number of networks and access points only increases the opportunity and odds for an attack. This lack of regulatory oversight has had its impact on security. The lack of benchmarks to uphold security standards and the failure to create any incentives for industry to seriously self-regulate has consequences for national security for any country. With only market incentive to drive the demand for improved and secure protocols, even existing methods and approaches to network security, although well known, are foregone.[17] New technologies that would create a more robust security network are, to the lament of many, underdeveloped. Rather than a distributed security dynamic, the current system is an assembly of off-the-shelf components in practice to maximize existing capacity.[18] Hence, partly because of over-dependence in market forces, the current system is left open and dangerously at risk. This benign neglect could, at some future point, be a root cause of a national catastrophe. Writing in 2006, Dan Verton remarked in *Black Ice: The Invisible Threat of Cyber-Terrorism*:

> . . . the concept of allowing market forces to dictate security requirements remains the centerpiece of the [G.W. Bush] administration's policy on cybersecurity . . . government regulation of the Internet and software security requirements is out of the question.[19]

The author presses the point to suggest that such approaches to national security by the Bush administration nearly abdicated any role it had for this responsibility.[20] The continuing competitive pressure of the free market economy has forced the world systems of communication and transport to outgrow the apparatus of international laws, codes, and commercial best practices standards. These factors facilitated trade in the industrial age. However, in the information age, the clash of modern technology, economic imperative, and the current structure of interstate relations is a significant hindrance to reform. Despite the complexity of the threat and the problems that a vulnerable ICT infrastructure present, a security regime at any level will not have consensus support if, at the same time, it does not enable business. The policy dilemma is how to assure that information is secure and commerce is not compromised.

Cyberspace today, as with the global supply chain, bears a set of formidable traits: enormity of size, opaqueness, complexity, and hence—vulnerability. It is another anarchic realm where states sometimes view cooperation as contrary to national interest. Global corporations can simultaneously be victims and unsuspecting abettors of crime. It is also an environment where the definition of what constitutes illegal activity, acts of war, and ownership of property rights and accountability remain obscure. Furthermore, in addition to these conditions is the complexity of a struggle with "intimate and unavoidable" adversaries noted in the CSIS's report. Adversaries in this case can be state and non-state actors, previous foes or traditional allies. The world has changed dramatically since the inception of the Internet with the advancements in technology. The upgrade in architecture, security, and policy should also reflect the change in culture and the new nature of competition.

THE MILITARIZATION OF CYBERSPACE

From its beginnings as a closed military project cyberspace has undergone several generations of evolution. With the commercialization of the Internet in the early 1990s, the increase in efficiency, reduction of cost, ease of access, and inherent insecurity has shaped policy, commerce, and the attendant issues of national defense and global competition. Today, it seems ironic that as the Internet expands to become a vast public good the world may face the prospect of another re-militarization. However, in this scenario the reality is far more threatening and the consequences far less fathomable. As national borders become blurred by the imperatives of global commerce and manipulated by the lure of transnational crime, so do the roles of state and non-state actors become complex and transformative. The transformation may well determine the assessment of power alignments, rules of governance, and the separation of human, sovereign, and individual rights of privacy.

Despite the hope that many had that the information age would bring with it new accesses to empowerment and a spirit of democracy, the trend is that these hopes may give way to a revived and ominous era of competition between states. Signaling these developments, in November 2008, the U.S.-China Economic and Security Review Commission made the following recommendation to the U.S. Congress: "The Commission recommends that Congress urge the Administration to engage in consultations with its allies on an alliance based approach to dealing with cyber attacks originating in China."[21]

The study further asserts that Chinese military planners believe the United States is waging a cyber-based war on their nation, and, therefore, in order to protect their intelligence and infrastructure assets China must develop its own capabilities. These "capabilities" will not only allow China to defend its own exploitable weakness, but also wreak havoc upon the U.S. system, which they believe is extremely vulnerable because of its dependency on information technology. Additionally, the authors maintain that part of China's strategy is the contention that preemption is key to the success in an outbreak of hostilities, either conventionally or with respect to cyber operations.[22] However, in a report compiled by Chatham House, the assessment is that China's primary focus has been in preparation for counterstrike capabilities, rather than a first strike maneuver. Yet, the same report goes on to say:

> In order to offset its conventional weakness the PRC is transforming its armed forces from a mechanized to an "information" force and have stated they intend to use information "as a tool of war or as a way to achieve victory without war."[23]

In the post-Cold War era of conflict, cyber capability is a vital asymmetric competency that allows a less armed opponent to engage a stronger military foe effectively and successfully. The ability to disrupt, delay, or obfuscate conventional operations affords those with limited military power a menacing defensive and offensive advantage. Without the release of a single missile, bomb, or loss of life, a superior military power could be completely paralyzed. The dependence on inter-locking networks for commerce, financial services, communications, utility grids, and government and military logistical needs leaves the United States, in particular, a nation at risk. Whether they are private-sector networks, unclassified government archives, or classified and secure systems—all are vulnerable to varying degrees. Furthermore, as the general interviewed in the 2008 CSIS report asserts: *the war has begun.*

Beginning in 2003, investigators believe that cyber attacks originating in China have systematically and routinely been launched against government targets in the United States. This massive cyber-espionage operation, codename "Titan Rain," is the archetype of post-modern warfare. The operation illustrates not only the paradigm shift of technology and strategy for the extended future, but also the potential for changes in power alignments and the notion of governance. More immediately, Operation Titan Rain reflects an inadequacy by the country's current defense structure to assess and respond effectively and even legally to such attacks. The assault calls into question issues over jurisdictional responsibilities, rights of privacy, and the roles of nation states and the private sector over accountability for security.

According to a 2005 *Time* article, a mid-level systems analyst first uncovered Titan Rain while doing volunteer work for military intelligence.[24] Initially lauded by his government handlers for his work in discovering the intrusion, Sean Carpenter subsequently lost his security clearance and was fired from his job with Sandia Corporation. His offenses were the inappropriate use of company information and violating U.S. law by breaking into a foreign nation's computer system. Prior to his legal problems, Carpenter donated months of his time and energy to helping the Department of Defense and the FBI track down the source of these electronic intrusions. His investigation led to the conclusion that information systems had been compromised from numerous U.S. government agencies, including the United States Air Force, NASA, Redstone Arsenal military base, and also the World Bank. He believes the operations originated from Guangdong Province in China, and the information was warehoused somewhere in South Korea before finding its way back to Guangdong. Expert estimates claim that as much as twenty terabytes of information, or twice the print collection of the Library of Congress, was gathered.[25] Adding to his sense of betrayal by government authorities and company officials, Carpenter was dismayed that the investigative tools he acquired are not being used. After months of work he angers at the thought that no one "... asked for the passwords or other tools that could enable them to pick up the investigative trail at the Guangdong router."[26] Thus, the Carpenter case is a telling account on the state of our national vulnerability and the inadequacy of the legal system to prosecute justly in cases involving cyber crime and espionage. The electronic information age has, in some ways, surpassed its users. Its surge is revealing fractures in the structures of national defense and exposing flaws in the courts. Unless institutions adjust, the pace of technology will surely apply more stress as time advances.

According to the 2008 Commission Report to Congress, there may be as many as 250 hacker groups operating in China with either government support or "encouragement."[27] These individuals are often trained at Chinese military academies in cyber operations and the transference of such skills to the arena of cyber war is seamless. As Robert Keohane and Joseph Nye have noted above, the environment of competition wrought by globalization has transformed and redefined military tactics. In their assessment it is not, necessarily, by design that "the asymmetry of global military power and the inter-connections among networks [has raised] new options for warfare." Yet, neither is it by mere random choice that they cite the Chinese in their examples as major players in the information war. The distrust from past conflict still lingers in the post-Cold War era of competition. Exacerbated by previous rivalries, today's thickening arena of increasingly intensive and extensive web of international relations makes the combination of terrorism, drug trafficking, environmental degradation, and computer virus propagation attractive as well as cost effective and militarily potent.

In a conflict of such asymmetric weaponry the advantages of a cyber-strike are multiple and varied. First, they can be launched instantaneously. A

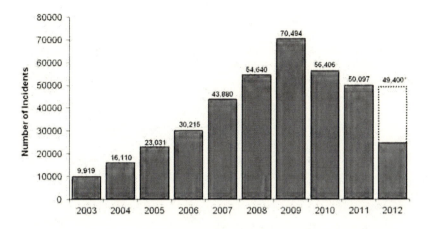

Figure 7.2.   U.S. Department of Defense reported incidents of malicious cyber activity, 2003-2011, with projected numbers for 2012 *(Source: U.S.-China Economic and Security Review Commission, USCC 2012 Annual Report, November 2012)*

target would have little or no time frame to prepare in defending itself. A second feature of an attack is the inability to establish attribution. Attribution, or the identification of the source of a cyber attack, is an issue of serious concern. Cyber attacks not only move at the speed of light, they occur in layers and travel along tortuously indirect paths toward their objective. Since the current communication protocols lack the sophistication of the evolving array of hacking tools, it has become an increasing struggle for legitimate users to attribute incursions to a guilty source or point of origination. Therefore, by their nature, cyber attacks make it difficult for their victims to identify the enemy and, hence, retaliate appropriately. Furthermore, industrial nations are highly computer and network-dependent, while non-industrial states are not. The lack of technology dependence has an intrinsic immunity from cyber war. In the case of non-state actors this immunity is not only more innate to these attackers, it makes attribution and retaliation against them more difficult.

Finally, despite the absence of violence, cyber war can have the same destructive power as conventional warfare. Physical force, or a kinetic attack, aims to destroy an enemy's ability to wage war. Disabling a power grid, food supply, or any combination of elements of critical infrastructure can net the same result. Gen. James Cartwright, Vice Chairman of the Joint Chiefs of Staff claims that the consequences of a cyber attack could "… be in the magnitude of a weapon of mass destruction."[28] Secretary of Defense Leon

Panetta used a stark analogy to describe potential consequences when he said in October 2012:

> The collective result of these kinds of attack could be a cyber Pearl Harbor; an attack that would cause physical destruction and the loss of life. In fact, it would paralyze and shock the nation. And create a new, profound sense of vulnerability.

Yet, these acts of aggression are without a multilateral consensus on whether they legally constitute acts of war.[29] In truth, there is no universally agreed definition on what constitutes a cyber attack, according to William J. Lynn, Deputy Secretary of Defense.[30] The problem inhibits our ability to respond, reorganize our defense community, set standards, design and coordinate effective global cybersecurity policy, or fairly judge and discharge Sean Carpenter of his legal circumstances.

In the debate over the direction of U.S. defense policy, this asymmetric feature of cyber war is a compelling element. The strategic advantages once held by hegemonic powers in the interstate system are neutralized in the information age. The cost of "militarizing" cyberspace is low, and the material resources are widely available. Therefore, the price of entry for less developed states and violent non-state actors is no longer an obstacle. Consequences of this paradigm shift in warfare are the proliferation of cyber warfare programs and development of nontraditional alliances between state and non-state actors, criminal gangs, and terrorist organizations.[31] In this environment jurisdictional divides become meaningless to aggressors and create barriers for guardians of infrastructure assets and prosecutors of cyber crime. Furthermore, international codes of justice and best practices standards are unenforceable, and the attempts to establish order is uncoordinated and, at times, insincere. As stated above, similar to the international supply chain, the system is plagued by its utter vastness and often intended opaqueness. A colleague has described cyberspace as: "an electromagnetic wilderness."[32] The authors of the CSIS report refer to it as

> ... part town square (where people engage in politics and speech), part Main Street (where people shop), part dark alleys (where crime occurs), part secret corridors (where spies engage in economic and military espionage), and part battlefield.[33]

Moreover, the technological threat vector posed by cyber war is metamorphic and tightly interlinked with the global economy. Adding to the dilemma is the fact that the defense network in place to protect commerce and civil society is rooted in an interstate system encumbered by layers of formal protocol. Claims of national interest, state sovereignty rights, and political parochialism are the conditions of a former epoch and the mortmain, which hangs malignantly over the effort to adapt and meet the challenges of the new reality. Therefore, the conquest of this "wilderness" will require reorganizing society through policies that are more multilateral and which can offer incentive for collaboration on a much grander scale. Otherwise, the alternative may be a partial return to Cold War power alignments and struggles with the addition of a cast of actors that include corrupt regimes, technologically sophisticated terrorists, and criminal organizations.

A RETURN TO THE COLD WAR

In the case of China, many analysts fear its leaders not only view cyber warfare as central to the overhaul of the national military, but also an important pathway toward economic development.[34] Aware of their comparative economic and military inferiority versus the United States, the People's Republic of China (PRC) seeks to neutralize their disadvantages. By maximizing new realisms posited by the asymmetric environment of the information age, China hopes it can level the playing field.[35] A coeval of information technology has been the Revolution in Military Affairs (RMA). As discussed in chapter 2, RMA is the application of IT to military purposes. The everexpanding application of ICT and the rise of dual use technology have created a mesh of opportunities and risks ripe for exploitation. Since the end of the Cold War there has been a feverish effort by the American military to adapt its forces to the emerging paradigm. The effort has also been met by less powerful states and non-state actors, which recognize the relative competitive gains they can achieve militarily against traditional superior powers.[36] As expressed by the Chinese word for *crisis*, the confluence of these trends has offered up a convergence of opportunity and danger for China and its perceived rivals. It is a crisis that the PRC hopes to exploit against its adversaries on the one hand, and on the other hand, deflect as it seeks to defend its national interests.

According to Michael Pillsbury of the National Institute of Strategic Studies, China's own efforts to compete in RMA has resulted in projects known as *shashoujian* (assassin's mace). Having the project code number 998, *shashoujian* is believed to be a response to America's continued efforts in RMA and an important instrument in countering U.S. hegemony in regional and global affairs.[37] Metaphorically, the term broadly refers to any action, technique, configuration of power, or technology deployed to overcome and reverse the tide of battle. The concept has been part of the discourse on military policy in China since at least 2000.[38] In 1999 PRC President Jiang Zemin, a former Chairman of the Central Military Commission, declared:

> We should set great store by stepping up high technology innovation for national defense purposes and by developing technology useable for both mili-

tary and civil purposes as well, and we should also master several *shashoujian* for safeguarding our national sovereignty and security as soon as possible. [39]

Compensating for its relative late arrival to cyber warfare, China attempts to gain parity with the United States and Russia through projects such as *shashoujian*. For many in the military establishment, the inspiration for these efforts has origins in a Chinese proverb: "kill with a borrowed sword." The expression bespeaks of China's military policies that seek to overcome technological deficiencies with superior strategies. [40] "If you are limited in your strength, then borrow the strength of your enemy." So said Sun Zi, the legendary second-century BCE military strategist and traditionally recognized author of *The Art of War*. By taking the advice from an ancient text, China has girt itself to vigorously compete in the cyber conflict. As part of this strategy, the People's Liberation Army (PLA) has been establishing and cultivating relationships with patriotic hackers. "Hacktivism," or the combination of political activism and computer hacking, has evolved into a new phenomenon—state hacktivism. State hacktivism involves patriotic hackers who are motivated for nationalistic reasons, and operate in the service of their countries. In this practice area, China is particularly expert in organization and recruitment. The government sponsored Network Crack Program Hacker (NCPH), identifies proficient groups of hackers through competitions. Those selected receive monthly stipends from the PLA. According to Panayotis Yannakogeorgos of the U.S. Air Force Air Command and Staff College, they are recruited to not only ply their craft on foreign targets, but also to teach army cadets the tactics and tools for conducting cyber war. Joel Brenner, a former senior government counterintelligence official whose past posts include inspector general for the National Security Agency and chief executive of the Office of the Directorate of National Intelligence remarks about China's cyber threat:

> Some [attacks], we have high confidence, are coming from government-sponsored sites. The Chinese operate both through government agencies, as we do, but they also operate through sponsoring other organizations that are engaging in this kind of international hacking, whether or not under specific direction. It's a kind of cyber-militia. . . . It's coming in volumes that are just staggering." [41]

Not only as political rivals, but also as business partners, China has capitalized on the "borrowed sword" to breach security defenses and to make gains in the struggle over cyberspace. American and non-U.S.-based ICT firms are often unwitting hosts of the strategy. [42] Competitive pressures force U.S. companies to rely on China's outsourced production facilities to assemble and manufacture products. Because of the efficiencies of the extended enterprise, the attractive pricing of products from developing countries and transition economies, and the dynamic of the global marketplace, Western companies are irresistibly lured into commercial alliances with non-Western partners. These joint venture arrangements are openings for a hostile player to implant viruses, malware, Trojan horses, and backdoors into equipment for proprietary civilian and military use. Once commercially available, the corrupted technology and component parts can infest systems anywhere in the world. Electronic chip and systems manufacturing, enterprise software, production facilities, and control systems are all vulnerable.

The subversion of information systems is subtle, mostly impossible to detect, and potentially ruinous. The disabling of the U.S. Pacific Command Headquarters has been attributed to the use of a malicious code produced in China.[43] According to some reports, a State Department official released a Trojan horse by opening an e-mail. This allowed a hacker covert access and denied PAC Command Internet use.

Through these same methods, Chinese hackers have also been credited with electronic intrusions against the State Department and the departments of Defense, Energy, Agriculture, Treasury, and Health and Human Services. For obvious reasons, the Pentagon and its sprawl of private contractors are particularly targeted. Boeing, Raytheon, General Dynamics, General Electric, and Lockheed Martin have all experienced attacks from cyber spies looking for sensitive information.[44]

Source codes, or the software programming instructions, are particularly appealing targets. The ability to copy or corrupt these millions of lines of instruction gives hackers the capability of tunneling into information systems around the world. Once the information is accessed, there is little to prevent someone from stealing intellectual property and inserting their own code. According to Google, this is precisely what has occurred not only to them, but to at least thirty other California-based companies.[45] In addition, over the past several years, counterfeit Cisco routers have surfaced. Their intrusion creates the fear that implanted software could give foreign or other unauthorized agents the capability to tap into networks with the same ease as law enforcement agencies.[46] As required of network hardware manufacturers by law, Cisco Systems produces according to specifications that allow the U.S. government wiretapping capability for investigative purposes. In such a case, a corrupted router "could provide the perfect over-the-shoulder view of everything coming out of a network" according to Jeff Moss, a security expert with the Homeland Security Advisory Council.[47]

From a military standpoint, these capabilities can expose a nation to a new scope and dimension of threat. Quoting the commander of the Air Force Cyber Command: "You don't need an army, a navy, an Air Force to beat the U.S., you can be a peer force for the price of the PC on my desk."[48] What can and, perhaps, has resulted is an "Internet too unwieldy to be tamed."[49] What may have also been unleashed is "espionage on a massive scale," says Paul

Kurtz, a security consult.[50] In support of these statements, current estimates claim Department of Defense computers undergo millions of scans on a daily basis along with thousands of potentially damaging probes.[51]

Although China is often cited as the greatest cyber menace to the United States, Russia's military programs and adventures in cyberspace may have been the most conspicuous. The end of the Cold War, the restructuring of power alignments, and the passing of the USSR has not dismantled Russia's technological/industrial base or diminished its capability. The Russian assault on Estonia's e-government operations and electronic incursions into Georgia was early evidence of Russia's prowess and intent. It was also an indication that the cyber world was becoming militarized and the fears of military experts were, perhaps, well founded.

During protests and retaliation for the removal of a statue at a Soviet-era war memorial in Tallinn in 2007, not only were Estonian government ministry websites taken out, but those of political parties, news agencies, banks, and telecommunication companies were also disabled.[52] A minister of defense in this nation of 1.3 million reportedly admitted to Gen. William Lord, Chief Information Officer for the Air Force, that "one million computers" attacked his country.[53] The electronic offensive by Russia raised alarms and cut at the core of the NATO alliance. Cries of concern about issues of collective self-defense rose to the surface and almost as quickly became muted because of a lack of definition, precedent, framework for resolution, and any clear policy guidance on an appropriate response. At the time there were also bitter disputes between Russia and former Soviet republics and Eastern satellite states, which added to the tension. This electronic incursion may have been an act of frustration, or a signal to its rivals that Russia was prepared to open a new field of conflict to protect its interests or press its grievances. Prospects for how policy could be set to attend to future state sponsored incursions were faint, if not dark. As officials struggled to make public statements and offer assurances that the situation would be seriously addressed, the system of state relations was experiencing a new strain of "machtpolitik" that, in effect, stifled these policy makers and frustrated their efforts to act.

The year following the strike on Estonia, Russia combined military operations with a cyber attack against the Georgian government. Through a cyber-criminal organization known as the Russian Business Network, an electronic assault on government websites crippled Georgia's public information infrastructure.[54] Unlike the Estonian event, these attacks were coordinated with an armed invasion force. However, it was not the first time Russia employed cyber technology alongside military action. In 2002 a similarly orchestrated attack of armed kinetic force and an electronic incursion against servers occurred in Chechnya. As in the case of China, the Russian government has officially disavowed connection with any cyber offensive by itself or others working on its behalf.

Because of the United States' lead in the information war, Russia's anxiety over the competition in cyberspace arouses the same tensions, as had the Cold War period. The technology gap, national paranoia, recurring xenophobia, and a history of distrust have helped shape an emerging Russian worldview with roots in an old fortress state mindset. Foreign affairs correspondent James Adams writes:

> [Russian military officials] want to transmit a common message that Russia is a nation at war. It is an information war that the country is losing at home and abroad, and the current technology gap is comparable to the perceived missile gap of the 1950s that did so much to fuel the Cold War. This time, the race is not for space, but cyber space. And all the Russians are angry that America appears to be winning the war and that victory appears more assured every day. [55]

Therefore, Russia is considering building its own Internet in order to de-link from the present system. The Internet, which the United States designed, developed, and now controls 80 percent of its infrastructure, has become a security risk for Russia's national defense and strategic interests.

It is not only traditional rivals for which the United States has concern. Allies, as well, constitute the growing cyber threat vector. According to the *National Intelligence Estimate* of January 2013, Israel and France are among the most aggressive in cyber espionage. Advanced persistent threat (APT) attacks from these countries against the United States may "pale in comparison to China's effort" and are mostly economically motivated. [56] However, the electronic intrusions are serious and call attention to the nature of the competition and its overlap of politics and economics.

While the United States may be the most targeted country of cyber attacks, it is often accused of being the most active. In the application and art of cyber warfare many countries regard the United States as their primary menace. Bruce Newsome, former RAND analyst and lecturer at the University of California, Berkeley, cites the Office of the National Counterintelligence Executive, admitting that "In 2010, the German government assessed the US and France as Germany's primary economic espionage threats 'among friends.' In 2011, France's Central Directorate for Domestic Intelligence described the US and China as the leading 'hackers' of French businesses." [57] The United States has also been accused of cyber attacks on an array of foreign countries that range from Russia, China, North Korea, Iran, and Syria, to Hungary, Canada, and Australia.

Efforts at international conferences and summits to establish accords and norms for the regulation of cyberspace have become tug-of-wars between the United States and Russia. Under dispute are not only the language of laws, but also the fundamental nature of their purpose. The United States, naturally, opposes restrictions in a sphere of activity where it holds a compelling advantage. On the other hand, under-advantaged states push for a more regulated environment in order to lessen their vulnerability and exposure to cyber risks. In much the same way local industry might seek economic protection from its government against foreign competition with competitive advantages, Russia pushes hard in these negotiations for regulatory control. This tactic is usually regarded by the United States as an attempted "protectionist policy" that allows Russia to buy time while it works to narrow the technology gap and level the playing field.[58]

Some analysts believe, however, that this kind of shortsightedness by the United States may lead to an Information Age weapons race.[59] Other experts have already warned that "major governments are reaching the point of no return in heading off a cyber-war arms race."[60] The weapons in this conflict fall into six basic categories. They include the following:

- **Logic bombs** are internal pieces of code, which activate upon a specific time and date, or triggered by an event. Logic bombs can spread and spawn by a *Trojan horse* (see below). Once embedded within a system they damage circuitry or cripple operations at critical points and times.
- **Trojan Horses** are malicious programs that mask their true function by appearing legitimate or useful. They may spread through logic bombs and by *worms* (see below). Their purpose is to grant unauthorized access for hackers into systems for either stealing data or to inflict damage.
- **Worms** go from computer to computer implementing malicious programs. During transmission, they may spawn additional malware. Unlike a *virus* (see below), they do not need to attach themselves to an existing program. They are stand-alone programs, which can disrupt networks by simply occupying data space and overloading systems.
- **Viruses** are the most common category of malware. Unlike *bacteria* (see below), they carry malicious code. Viruses can only attack programs or data by attaching themselves to a program in order to replicate themselves. A virus passes through dormant and triggering phases before performing its function. During its function, or execution phase, results range from benign defacement to total system ruin.
- **Bacteria** do not carry malicious code. Bacteria replicate and damage device storage reserves by overloading disks and memory capacity. Commonly, bacteria cause Distributive Denial of Service (DDoS) attacks by consuming large volumes of system resource.

Outside these definitions are two cyber weapons worth noting because of the seriousness and scale of their attacks and potential for network contamination:

- **Botnets** are an array of computers which run applications controlled by their owners that spy and disable networks and websites.
- **Microwave** radiation devices burn out computer circuits from miles away.

In this intensifying high stakes game, there is also the belief that Russia is secretly enlisting China in support of its efforts to shape international policy on arms control treaties in cyberspace.[61] Whichever side prevails, the possibility to wreak havoc and plunge the world into a new epoch of confrontation is not only real, but may already be upon us.

In December 2009 a turning point in negotiations over the militarization of cyberspace could have been reached. During this period, talks began between the United States and Russia regarding the possibility of international treaties to address the challenges posed by cyber warfare. Despite many contentious items, a common ground may be in the United States' interest to control Internet crime versus Russia's apprehension over cyber weapons development and proliferation.[62] Nevertheless, for now and the foreseeable future there are no rules in cyberspace or standards of behavior on which all major rivals can agree.

The parallels to the old order appear striking. Yet, at the same time, the configuration of power alliances would be a stark break with the past. According to a 2009 report commissioned by McAfee, Inc., criminal organizations are becoming more motivated by nationalistic pride rather than mere monetary gain. A prime example is Russia. The authors of the report cite McAfee's own Vice President of Threat Research, Dmitri Alperovitch, who maintains that a righteous attitude toward the West is propelling much cyber crime. An indication of these moral postures is found in a warning posted on an online forum.

> We will recreate historical fairness. We will bring the USA down to a level of 1928–33.[63]

Spheres of influence would not be geopolitical but "virtual-political." Rather than bound by territorial jurisdictions and state borders, hegemons and their satellites would be linked by electronic connections. Whether associated by cultural and traditional ties, or motivated by unadorned, economic self-interest, the new order would be a constellation of states, corporations, terrorists, criminals, and social activists. Within this arrangement, it would be difficult for any single participant to have a monopoly on violence or arms control. Determining the extent and impact of the anarchy is impossible to suppose.

NOTES

1. "Cyberterrorism: How Real Is the Threat," United States Institute of Peace, (December 2004).

2. "Securing Cyberspace for the 44th Presidency," Center for Strategic and International Studies Commission Report, Washington (December 2008), p. 78.

3. What is known as the electromagnetic spectrum is the combination of electric and magnetic fields. The reciprocal relationship between electricity and magnetism form the medium. When these forces are unified mathematically they create electromagnetic (EM) waves of radio and light. The oscillation of atomic interaction determines wave frequencies, which govern over such properties as visibility, energy, and can create the separate pathways, or wavelengths, along which information streams.

4. Panayotis Yannakogeorgos, Technologies of Militarization and Security in Cyberspace, doctoral dissertation, Rutgers University (April 2009), p. 28.

5. Andrew Tannenbaum, Computer Networks (Prentice Hall PTR, Upper Saddle River, NJ, fourth edition, 2003), p. 56–58.

6. *Ibid.*, p. 56.

7. Hedieh Nasheri, *Economic Espionage and Industrial Spying* (Cambridge University Press, 2005), p. 98.

8. William Lynn, Deputy Secretary of Defense, in "U.S. Creates Military Cyber Command to Defend Computer Networks," *Global Security* (15 June 2009).

9. Bill Hancock, "How to Stop Talking About—And Start Fixing Cyber Security Problems," *Cutter IT Journal* (May 2006), in Yannakogeorgos, p. 212.

10. Making the Nation Safer: The Role of Science and Technology in Countering Terrorism, National Research Council of the National Academies (The National Academies Press, Washington, DC, 2002), p.150.

11. Shane Harris, "China's Cyber Militia" in *National Journal Magazine* (31 May 2008), http://www.nationaljournal.com/njmagazine/cs_20080531_6948.php.

12. *Ibid.*

13. "Assuring and Trusted and Resilient Information and Communication Infrastructure" *Cyberspace Policy Review* (April 2009).

14. "Securing Cyberspace for the 44th Presidency," Center for Strategic and International Studies Commission Report, Washington (December 2008), p. 58.

15. Hedieh Nasheri, *Economic Espionage and Industrial Spying* (Cambridge University Press, 2005), p. 51.

16. Thomas Kellermann, interview with Bloomberg News (8 March 2011), http://www.bloomberg.com/news/2011-03-08/kellermann-says-cyber-foes-threaten-u-s-economy-video.html.

17. Making the Nation Safer, p. 145.

18. *Ibid.*, p. 141, 152.

19. Dan Verton, *Black Ice: The Invisible Threat of Cyber-Terrorism* (McGraw-Hill, Emeryville, CA, 2006), p. 25.

20. Panayotis Yannakogeorgos, Promises and Pitfalls of the National Strategy to Secure Cyberspace, Division of Global Affairs, Rutgers University (2009), p. 9–10.

21. 2008 Report to Congress of the U.S.-China Economic and Security Commission, p. 168.

22. *Ibid.*, p. 166.

23. Paul Cornish, *et al.*, "On Cyber War," Chatham House Report (November 2010), p. 6.

24. Nathan Thornburgh, "The Invasion of the Chinese Cyberspies" *"Time.Com,"* 25 August 2005.

25. Jason Schifman, "The Need for a Strategic Approach to Cybersecurity," work in progress, University of Pennsylvania, April 2009, quoting Major General William Lord in "Air Force and the Cyberspace Mission Defending the Air Force's Computer Network in the Future," Center for Strategy and Technology, December 2007.

26. Thornburg.

27. 2008 Report to Congress of the U.S.-China Economic and Security Commission, p. 164.

28. Harris.

29. *Op. cit.*

30. Edward Turzanski, Lawrence Husick, "Why 'Cyber Pearl Harbor' Won't Be Like Pearl Harbor," presentation to the Foreign Policy Research Institute, October 12, 2012.

31. Panayotis Yannakogeorgos, "Technologies of Militarization and Security in Cyberspace" (doctoral dissertation, Rutgers University, April 2009), p. 14.

32. *Ibid.*, p. 1.

33. "Securing Cyberspace for the 44th Presidency," Center for Strategic and International Studies Commission Report, Washington, December 2008.

34. Schifman, p. 12–14.

35. Alaster Iain Johnston, "Toward Contextualizing the Concept of a *Shashoujian* (Assassin's Mace), Harvard University Government Department, August 2002, p. 27.

36. Mary Kaldor, *Beyond Militarism, Arms Races, and Arms Control*, essay prepared for the Nobel Peace Prize Centennial Symposium, December 2001.

37. *Ibid.*

38. Michael Pillsbury, "China's Military Strategy Toward the U.S.: A View from Open Sources," *U.S.-China Economic and Security Review Commission*, November 2001.

39. Johnston, p. 325.

40. Timothy L Thomas, "China's Electronic Strategies," in *Military Review*, May-June 2001.

41. Harris.

42. Yannakogeorgos, p. 72–73.

43. Barrington M. Barret, "Information Warfare: China's response to U.S. Technological Advantages," *International Journal of Intelligence and CounterIntelligence*, 18, November 4, 2005.

44. These threats not only originate from China. The rise of new centers of design and production across the globe has created new opportunities for hardware and software manipulations by state and non-state actors.

45. John Markoff and Ashlee Vance, "Fearing Hackers Who Leave No Trace," *New York Times*, January 20, 2010.

46. *Ibid.*

47. *Ibid.*

48. William T. Lord in "The New E-spionage Threat," *Businessweek*, April 2008.

49. Brian Grow, Keith Epstein, Chi-Chu Tschang, "The New E-spionage Threat," *Businessweek*, April 2008.

50. *Ibid.*

51. William Lynn, Deputy Secretary of Defense, in "U.S. Creates Military Cyber Command to Defend Computer Networks," *Global Security*, 15 June 2009.

52. "Russia Accused of Unleashing Cyberwar to Disable Estonia," *Guardian*, 17 May 2007.

53. Harris.

54. "Georgia's State Computers Hit by Cyber Attack," *The Wall Street Journal*, 12 August 2008.

55. James Adams, "The New Arms Race," in the Next War: Computers are the Weapons and the Frontline Is Everywhere," Hutchenson, 1998 in Yannakogeorgos.

56. Ellen Nakashima, "U.S. said to be target of massive cyber-espionage campaign," *The Washington Post*, February 10, 2013.

57. Bruce Newsome and Jack Jarmon, *A Practical Introduction to Homeland Security, National Security, and Emergency Management* (forthcoming).

58. Adams in Yannakogeorgos.

59. Timothy Thomas, "Russian View of Information Based Warfare, *Airpower Journal*, 1996, in Yannakogeorgos.

60. *Ibid.*

61. John Markoff, Andrew E. Kramer, "U.S. and Russia Differ on Treaty for Cyberspace," *New York Times*, 28 June 2009.

62. John Markoff, and Andrew Kramer, "In Shift, U.S. Talks to Russia on Internet Security," *New York Times*, 13 December 2009.

63. "Virtual Criminality Report 2009," Commissioned by McAfee, Inc., prepared by Paul Kurtz, Good Harbor Consulting, 2009, p. 12.

Chapter Eight

Cyber Guerilla War

... anyone can go to a criminal gang and rent a botnet. We've reached a point where you only need money to cause disruption, not know-how.
—2009 McAfee, Inc. Report

NET WAR AND NET WARRIORS

Cyberspace infrastructure is the critical underpinning of the global economy and, therefore, its integrity is essential to national security, public safety, and modern civic intercourse. The hyper-interconnection, which evolved parallel with globalization, expanded opportunities for all. Whether those opportunities are used as a way for people to improve their lot, or destroy the quality of life of others is beyond its original design and control.

The asymmetry of today's warfare and the accessibility, anonymity, and ubiquity of the Internet has created opportunities for transnational crime organizations and international terrorism to plunder and recruit. Like state-sponsored programs, these non-state actors have the capability to disrupt utility grids, telecommunications networks, defraud businesses and financial institutions, and disable and compromise government sites. Examples include:

- In 1995 the successful intrusion into U.S. Government files and downloading of sensitive information concerning North Korea's ballistic weapons research. The culprit was a sixteen-year-old British student. [1]
- 1999—the "Melissa" computer virus, which caused over $80 million in damages to personal computers, business, and government networks by infecting e-mail gateways and clogging systems. [2]

- An attempt to divert $400 million of EU funds from regional development projects in 2000. The funds were to be laundered through various online components of major money center banks, including the Vatican bank. Interdiction occurred only due to the misgivings of a coconspirator who, eventually, turned informant.[3]
- The financial support of the 2002 bombings in Bali, which police claim were provided by funds obtained through online credit card fraud.[4]
- A Russian-based hacking operation, which involved fraud and extortion in 2003. Aggregate losses amounted to approximately $25 million.[5]
- The 2004 investigation and termination of a criminal organization that involved 4,000 members engaged in stolen identities and credit card information. Known as "Operation Firewall," this Secret Service exercise culminated in the elimination of a major hub for online identity theft.[6]
- The 2005 conviction of a Massachusetts juvenile responsible for the theft of personal information and initiating panic with bomb threats. The convicted hacked into Internet and telephone service providers over a fifteen-month period before being apprehended.[7]
- In May 2006, the Department of State believed its networks were hacked by unknown foreign intruders resulting in the download of terabytes of information.[8]
- May 2006, a public statement by a senior Air Force Officer reveals that "China has downloaded 10 to 20 terabytes of data from NIPRNet."[9]
- NASA blocks e-mail prior to shuttle launches fearing harmful attachments in December 2006. At the same time *Business Week* reported that unknown foreign agents had obtained the plans for the latest space launch vehicles.[10]
- The Bureau of Industrial Security, which reviews high-tech exports at the Department of Commerce, had its networks hacked by foreign intruders and forced off-line for several months in April 2007.[11]
- In May 2007 "the National Defense University had to take its e-mail systems offline because of hacks by unknown foreign intruders that let spyware into the system."[12]
- Reportedly, in August 2007 the British Security Service, the French Prime Minister's Office, and the Office of German Chancellor Merkel complained to the PRC about electronic intrusions.[13]
- A compromise of a major U.S. retailer's database that resulted in the loss of information of 45 million credit and debit card accounts in 2007.[14]
- Databases of the Republican and Democratic presidential campaigns were hacked into by unknown foreign sources over the summer of 2008.[15]
- In November 2008 classified networks at the DoD and CENTCOM were hacked and disabled for several days before the systems could be restored.[16]

- The corruption of 130 ATM machines that produced fraudulent transactions in forty cities in 2008.[17]
- The estimated losses of $1 trillion due to intellectual property theft in 2008.[18]
- The appearance of the "confiker" virus/botnet in 2008.
- January 2009—Israeli's Internet infrastructure was paralyzed during that country's military offensive in the Gaza Strip. The attack, which concentrated on government websites, was launch from within the former Soviet Union and financially supported by Hamas or Hezbollah, officials believe.[19]
- February 2009—French combat aircraft were grounded following the infection of databases by a computer virus known as "conflicter."[20]
- March 2009—Canadian researchers uncover a computer espionage system implanted in government networks of 103 nations. The researchers attribute the effort to China.[21]
- March 2009—on a file sharing network in Iran, the plans for the new presidential helicopter, Marine 1, are discovered.[22]
- May 2009—unknown hackers gain access to the data in the Homeland Security Information Network (HSIN) collecting data on federal, state, and local employees and contractors.[23]
- June 2009—the Applied Physics Laboratory of Johns Hopkins University had its networks penetrated and eventually forced to go off-line.[24]
- June 2009—Wolfgang Schaeuble, German Interior Minister, noted in a security report that China and Russia have been increasing espionage efforts and cyber attacks on German firms.[25]
- Critical infrastructure attacks on targets in the United States and overseas leading to outages at electrical power stations in multiple locations and cities.[26]
- The FBI claims that al Qaeda terrorist cells rely on stolen credit card information as financial support.[27]
- The CIA identification of at least two known terrorist organizations with the capability and intent to launch cyber attacks on the U.S. infrastructure.[28]
- Due to cyber attacks, an estimated annual direct loss of $67.2 billion for U.S. organizations according to 2005 figures[29] and a revised figure of over $1 trillion worldwide for 2008.[30]
- Stuxnet worm 2009–2011.
- The estimation that China hacked 15 percent of all Internet traffic in 2010.[31]

Despite the volume of evidence to support justification for alarm, data on these assaults do not reflect the true scale of the problem. Public records are not only inaccurate due to detection issues, but often times by sheer intent.

Reports are obviously lacking when victims are unaware of electronic intrusions. Frequently, because of manpower and technical skills deficit, cybercrime goes on unmasked and with no ill consequences for the perpetrator. However, when cyber crimes do surface there are incentives for the injured party to keep these accounts out of the public realm. The consequences for a victimized organization can be dismaying. The fear of negative publicity is always a concern for private-sector enterprises as well as public offices and organizations. In the case of a security breach of a business firm, the instance can open an organization to lawsuit and adverse market impact. Studies at Georgia Tech reveal that firms that experience an interruption of operations will suffer an attendant decline in stock value. Furthermore, depending upon the duration of downtime, recovery can extend over several business quarters. This is particularly true if it involves a financial institution.

Public disclosure of security failure can also be a signal to attackers that vulnerabilities exist and an organization may be ripe for exploitation. With these circumstances also come fears of job loss and the demise of reputations. In weighing the costs and impact of reporting such incidents, it is easy to understand why many organizations opt to remain silent about their situation rather than draw public attention. Additionally, the allocation of time and resources, as well as the poor record of prosecution create further disincentive to report such offenses. The era of cyber crime has created a new set of legal problems and issues. Theft infers possession, which is a difficult, delicate, and more complicated argument when the property is intellectual rather than tangible. Furthermore, the information disclosed during the process of cross-examination can run the risk of being as damaging to the plaintiff's self-interest as the original crime.

Regardless of the reticence to admit to these victimizations, the economic loss to business and the consumer is still staggering. According to the GAO 2007 report, the direct losses due to computer crime, without an estimation of related costs, are $67 billion. Identity theft via electronic means amounts to over $56 billion. Worldwide, over $100 billion in losses from spam alone annually occurs. Spamming is more than a simple nuisance. Not only a malicious way to clog a system, spam can act as a carrier for malware and a host of other cyber threats.[32] Since the publication of this report, Verizon puts the total cost to U.S. business due to industrial espionage at $250 billion.[33] Dan Dunkel, a cybersecurity consultant says:

> With tremendous technical advantages come potentially devastating risks. As digital citizens we lack a fundamental "open" dialogue to confront the obvious trends in international cyber crime, or to address the complex technical, business and legal issues that will ultimately better secure cyberspace. We need to make cyber crime and security an international priority.[34]

As stated above, these numbers not only reflect an unknown percentage of unreported and under-reported incidents, they also represent a statistic, which continues to rise. The cybersecurity threat is outpacing attempts at a solution. It hovers over the national, organizational, and individual levels. Now a Senior Advisor at the Belfer Center at the John F. Kennedy School of Government at Harvard, Melissa Hathaway writes:

> I believe that we are at a strategic inflection point—and we must band together to understand the situation and ascertain the full extent of the vulnerabilities and interdependencies of this information and communications infrastructure that we depend upon. As I reflect upon the situation, one of the key recurring questions is whether we really understand the intersections of our critical assets and the networks and how we as entities interface with the communications infrastructure and the energy grid and other critical services that are provided on the backbone of interdependent networks. [35]

An understanding of cyberspace infrastructure is not complete without an understanding of its fragility and our vulnerability should it fail. Table 8.1 on the following page represents the various technique categories of cyber crime and a brief description of their methods and harmful effects.

VULNERABILITIES AND CRITICAL INFRASTRUCTURE

Perhaps one of the primary roots of U.S. vulnerability is SCADA, supervisory control and data acquisition systems. SCADA systems are computer systems, which automate, monitor, moderate, and control industrial plant functions and critical infrastructure. The technology is ubiquitous. The power grid is particularly dependent upon SCADA. As with the original Internet, these systems were designed with little attention to security. Data is sent "in the clear," or over open pathways that rely on the Internet and often require no authentication. [36] Furthermore, for economic reasons and owing to an enduring spirit and environment of deregulation, SCADA systems increasingly depend upon commercial off-the-shelf (COTS) components as security patches and to optimize existing capacity. [37,38]

The use of COTS as security countermeasures may not only be perilous, but also impractical according to at least one independent analysis. A study by the University of California, Berkeley, and Carnegie Mellon University asserts that patching and frequent updates may be unfeasible for control systems in certain instances. Upgrades sometimes take months of advance planning and require suspension of operations. Therefore, the justification for installing security patches may be negated by economic considerations or market demands. These patch updates may also violate manufacturer certification under certain conditions and open the operator up to litigation. [39] Many

TYPE	DESCRIPTION
Spamming	Sending unsolicited commercial e-mail, which also is sometimes used as a delivery platform for malware
Phishing	The use of spam or pop-up messages to deceive people into disclosing sensitive information. Internet scammers use e-mail to "phish" for information such as social security numbers, passwords, financial account data
Spoofing	Creating a fraudulent website that mimics a legitimate website in order to hide the origin of the spoofer's e-mail
Pharming	A method used by phishers to deceive users into believing they are communicating with a legitimate website. By exploiting software vulnerabilities pharmers can redirect unwitting users to fraudulent websites despite typing in legitimate addresses
Denial of service attack	Disabling a computer system by taking up a shared resource leaving none of the resource available for legitimate users
Distributed denial of service	A variant of a denial of service attack that uses a coordinated attack from a distributed system of computers rather than a single source
Viruses	A program that infects computer files and interferes with operations by inserting itself. Viruses are designed to spread from one computer to another when loaded by attachments (see Chapter 7)
Trojan horse	A computer program that conceals harmful code (see Chapter 7)
Worm	An independent computer program that reproduces by copying itself from one system to another across a network. Worms, unlike viruses, do not require human involvement to propagate (see Chapter 7)
Malware	Malicious software that executes harmful or disruptive operations. Often viruses, worms, or spyware masquerade as useful programs to deceive users into activating them (see Chapter 7)
Spyware	Malware installed without the user's knowledge to covertly track and/or transmit data to an unauthorized third party
Botnet	"bots" (short for robots) are programs installed covertly in targeted systems and allow unauthorized users to remotely control computers. Botnets are networks of remotely controlled computer systems (see Chapter 7)

Table 8.1. Techniques Used to Commit Cybercrimes

industrial controllers and SCADA systems must be replaced entirely and run the risk of hardware being compromised.[40] These concerns, combination of control systems' vital role in critical infrastructure operations, and the general awareness of the lack of security used in their design and support, make

SCADA systems attractive targets for malicious hackers, criminals, or potential terrorist agents.

Networks with proprietary protocols, which control plant, energy, and transportation operations are often physically separate from the networks used for communication and such activity as Web surfing and document sharing. However, although most critical infrastructure runs on two or more separate networks in order to shelter the system from inadvertent virus contagion or electronic attack—this, unfortunately, is not sufficient. These proprietary protocols provide an additional failsafe because they, supposedly, are familiar to only a few expert programmers. Yet, a discouraging assessment to these reassurances is the warning by various system consultants who claim that there is Web-based translation software that can convert proprietary protocols into other computing languages.[41] Such hacker tools are widely accessible and when deployed can offset the advantage of running separate networks.

Additionally, SCADA not only manages the soft elements of the network, which are associated with disruption issues, but physical elements fall under these systems' controls as well. Therefore, physical damage may result in the destruction of infrastructure. The long-term consequences are networks, which have to be rebuilt, and their components must be remanufactured from scratch.[42] The fragility of the entire system is further compounded by the ironies of an open Internet. According to the National Research Council's Committee on Science and Technology for Countering Terrorism, these vulnerabilities are widely known and details on system exposure are accessible to all on the World Wide Web. In the committee's 2002 report, it states:

> Product data and educational videotapes from engineering associations can be used to familiarize potential attackers with the basics of the grid and specific elements. Information obtained through semi-automated reconnaissance to probe and scan the networks of a variety of power suppliers could provide terrorists with detailed information about the internals of the SCADA network, down to the level of specific makes and models of equipment used and version releases of corresponding software. And more inside information could be obtained from sympathetic engineers and operators.[43]

Stephen Flynn, in his 2007 book, *The Edge of Disaster*, reveals in one example how precariously tethered national security is to the national power grid. He cites a 2006 report by Siobhan Gorman of the *Baltimore Sun*. In the report the NSA feared the installation of two supercomputers would overload an already extended power grid. Under such stressed conditions the agency concluded that the longest period of time the electrical infrastructure could forestall a collapse of the system was two years. In the event of a meltdown, it would take between eighteen to thirty months to design and procure equipment, obtain permits, and build a new power station. In the interim, the

NSA's ability to process its work and operate normally would be severely hampered.[44]

The U.S. electrical power grid, according to Gilbert Bindewald of the Department of Energy's Office of Electricity Delivery and Energy Reliability, "was never holistically designed," and "developed incrementally in response to local load growth."[45] The result is a service environment of constant change and uncertainty. The system's complexity, decentralized flow control, and fluctuating dynamic of consumer usage contribute additional challenges to security. A sudden drop in voltage, either because of uncontrolled demand or the result of false information inserted into SCADA could cause collapse.

There are many examples where the manipulation of the computer code could have a devastating effect on critical infrastructure. According to Bindewald, "electricity [is] the ultimate just-in-time production process."[46] The absence of flow control, and the lack of any large-scale storage capacity make the electric power grid unique and vulnerable. The same features that propel and permeate commercial life are the symptoms of a deficient immunity to a cyber attack.

Today the power grid is decentralized, aging, susceptible to blackouts, reliant on SCADA, and under increasing demand due to the expanding digital economy.[47] Only by making the grid "smarter" or by changing the supply mix (using alternative energy sources) can the power infrastructure and daily routines be made more secure. However, these are mostly longer-term solutions, and the vulnerabilities discussed above represent prevailing conditions. In the meantime, network-based attacks exploit system flaws and unpatched systems. Once the attacker establishes a foothold on a system in the target network, further exploitation can take place by which the attacker can expand his control over command and control systems and affect operations. Once inside a system, detection tools for finding hacker malware exist. However, the challenge to stay apace of the evolution of hacking techniques with detection software is daunting.[48]

Already, there have been several reports involving major power outages by Internet-enabled intrusions.[49, 50] Many are instances in places other than the United States. However, the August 15, 2003 power blackouts, which occurred in the northeast United States, have opened up a national discussion about the grid's vulnerability to hacker activity. In the intelligence community, speculation persists that the outage can be attributed to China or agents working in collaboration with the PLA. The 2003 outage affected fifty million people in three states, including Canada. It covered a 9,300 square-mile area and had an estimated economic toll of between $6–$10 billion.[51] The cause of the power failure has, arguably, never been fully understood. However, many of those in the counterintelligence community believe the PLA gained access to one of the networks that controlled electric power systems. The result was the greatest blackout in North American history. [52]

Officially, no involvement by a foreign government or national has been cited. Rather, "overgrown trees," which came into contact with high voltage lines are credited with the failure of more than 100 power plants in Michigan, Ohio, New York, and north of the border. A widespread computer virus supposedly put the system over the edge by disrupting the communication lines used to manage the power grid. [53] Whether an ill-timed event or an event by design, the outage forced one industry analyst to assess "that security for the nation's electronic infrastructures remains intolerably weak" and to also emphasize that incident confirms "that government and company officials haven't sufficiently acknowledged these vulnerabilities." [54]

Another outage in 2008 also raised speculation of hacker intrusion originating from China. A power failure cut off three million customers of Florida Power & Light along the state's east coast. The company blamed "human error" for the disruption. However, there are some inside government and industry who maintain that hackers inside China have devoted considerable resources to mapping and analyzing the U.S. critical infrastructure, and by mistake or with intention, may have set off the incident.

As discussed, the Chinese are not alone in their quest for advantage in cyberspace. In fact, it was also reported that computer intrusions penetrated European utilities in 2006, and that assaults similar to these might have a history as far back as the Cold War. According to a press report in 2004, a portion of the Siberian pipeline exploded in 1982 with the use of a logic bomb. [55] Today, the field is populated with many competitors and combatants. The warfare is asymmetrical, unpredictable, and absent of any conventional wisdom—yet, the questions of all industrial societies are always the same: Who is the enemy? What are their intent and objectives? How do we maintain our security while enabling our work and protecting a way of life?

In summary, cyberspace has become the new battlefield because it is the core of critical infrastructure and industrial control systems. Although this has been the situation for decades, attacks have been randomly confirmed, and many more have gone unreported or undetected. Sources of attacks are myriad. Cyber criminals, disgruntled employees, terrorists, activists, organized crime, and state actors all have their own resources and motivations. Meeting the challenges of these security threats is achieved through prevention, detection, recovery, resilience, and eventually—deterrence. However, the war is asymmetrical and, at present, the technological advantage is with the attacker.

This is partly due to the fact the range of possible targets is almost endless. In the United States it is also due to the obsolescence of the overall infrastructure and an early insouciant attitude toward security. A third frustration is the fact that the action/reaction cycle to the threat is so sudden that the very innovation used to address the original vulnerability can create further instability. Countermeasures often do not result without a perceived need. Until the "zero-day" event (the moment when a cyber weapon activates and becomes operational) anti-viruses and counterweapons and tools are often unavailable. Offensive action is easier, cheaper, and quicker than it is for defensive action.[56]

Overall, the cybersecurity threat is outpacing attempts at a solution. It should be noted that those who monitor these developments estimated that 45 percent of the malware at large in the world in 2011 was released in 2010. They further maintain that the emission rate in 2011 would be even greater.[57] As of 2012, the same sources claim "there are over sixty-eight million unique malware signatures known, and new malware is being seen at a rate of one every eight seconds."[58]

The most publicized example of malware was the Stuxnet virus. It was released in 2009 and its notoriety came with the disablement of the Iranian nuclear program at Natanz. Reportedly, it was spread by the unauthorized use of USB sticks and networks. The attack involved four separate exploit codes, one of which may have been purchased from a private source by the U.S. or Israeli government; presumably, the two states attributed with launching the attack.[59] Once activated, Stuxnet caused rotor failure of centrifuge operations forcing centrifuges to dump contents. As the delicate, finely tuned instruments spun uncontrollably, vibrations damaged equipment and approximately 3,700 of the 9,000 centrifuges at the facility were damaged.[60] While this was occurring, the control center was reporting that all systems were operating normally. Most experts believe Stuxnet was a joint project by the U.S. National Security Agency and Israel. The project yielded valuable data and lessons on cyber warfare. Tens of thousands of industrial networks have now been mapped and another tool for data exfiltration has been cast.

Stuxnet is still in circulation. Some fear that clones using Stuxnet codes are appearing and could be combined with botnets to launch future attacks delivering new payloads on other industrial targets. Stuxnet preys on widely used Siemens industrial control software and databases and Vacon and Fararo Paya controllers. Given the pace of the constantly morphing threat vector, the technology is already considered "old," by current standards. It is not irrational to fear that a new generation of the virus may already be in the hands of non-legitimate actors and in development. It is possible that it may even be deployed somewhere and lying inactive as it awaits a reset command. A worm dubbed "Duqu" appeared in 2011. It uses Stuxnet source code and facilitates data discovery and exfiltration operations, according to Lawrence Husick and Edward Turzanski, senior fellows at the Foreign Policy Research Institute. Other examples of malicious software go by the names "shamoon" and "flame" and have the capability to not only disrupt, but also destroy systems. Meanwhile, several U.S. banks, including Capital One,

BB&T, Ally Financial, Bank of America, PNC, JP Morgan, SunTrust, and Regions Bank have been the victims of DDoS attacks. A presumed culprit has been Iran.

In cyberspace we are hyper-connected to a series of networks where lines between private and public security blur. At the same time the linkage in human affairs is organic, as competitive and complementary impulses drive events while we all undertake to ply at our work and live our lives. In common is our need to conduct business, power our households, access financial assets, provide and receive healthcare. Therefore, the security of these networks is central to our way of life. The fragility of these networks and our reliance upon them puts us in a perilous state. We are vulnerable to a host of threats from state and non-state actors, natural disasters, and our own overuse of valuable resources.

The transition from the industrial age to the information age has been disorienting for strategists and policy makers. The imperatives of international trade and commerce have suppressed the calls for investment in security. Economic policies, which require unquestioned faith in the market and posited the belief in privatization programs, while heaping scorn on government and regulatory involvement, may have put the system on to a precarious ledge. What exists is a cybersecurity understructure resembling a Rube Goldfarb contraption of patches and workarounds unsuited to accommodate the traffic demands of SCADA systems and custom large-scale implementations. As Mark Cohn, a thought leader and Vice President of Enterprise Security at Unisys Corporation remarks:

> The marketplace driven interconnectedness that we have been so excited about over the last twenty years combined with orders of magnitude changes in available bandwidth put some of those systems into a mode their designers never envisioned: we can't unravel those trends and backtrack but we did, in fact, know how to build fault tolerant systems that in some cases never failed and could apply the same engineering approaches for a "smart grid" if it were possible to arrange the right political and economic circumstances. [61]

The landscape of town squares, Main Streets, dark alleys, secret corridors, and open battlefields that the CSIS Commission Report described is not a static environment. It is dynamic, and instability is an accepted condition— for now. Many fear that without an open debate, the condition will remain chronic. As the above metaphor infers, cyber conflict ensnarls many actors, on varying levels, and in so many ways. Furthermore, because the target environment is so target rich, the establishment of order may require new partnerships between the public and its government, a rewriting of legal codes, and new mechanisms for mobilizing society.

In addition, a frighteningly, deadly backdrop to the above scenario is the prospect that as sub-state actors are becoming key players, an interstate cyber

Cold War may have already begun. Under the conditions of asymmetrical warfare, nation states and cyber criminal groups can make for natural allies. Cyber war and cyber crime employ the same weapons and require the same skills. However, the skills and weapons may now be for sale. We may be at the onset of an interstate war among past Cold War rivals and, simultaneously, engaged in an asymmetric conflict of non-state players. A cyber expert claims:

> Many of the challenges of cyber war mirror those in cybercrime because nation states and cyber gangs are all playing from the same instruments. For instance, anyone can go to a criminal gang and rent a botnet. We've reached a point where you only need money to cause disruption, not know-how and that is something that needs to be addressed. [62]

Many believe there already exists a thriving black market for malware. In testimony to the Senate Armed Services Committee, the head of DoD's Cyber Command claimed online sources provide hackers and state-sponsored groups the means to acquire weaponized "cyber-tools."[63] Through websites, various legitimate firms, and disreputable entrepreneurs, criminals, terrorists, and hostile states can have the capability to attack advanced systems without having the in-house expertise normally necessary to develop these cyber-weapons. Legally the market for exploits is protected under the freedom of speech. Because these codes have dual use applications as either cyber tools or cyber weapons, determining their lawfulness or criminality is in a continuing state of disagreement among legal experts.

The Comprehensive National Cybersecurity Initiative (CNCI) released by the Obama administration in 2009 attempts to address many of these challenges. The document recognized cybersecurity as "one of the most serious economic and national security challenges we face as a nation." It also admits to the inadequacy of the country in its preparation to counter the threat.[64] In protecting the nation's digital infrastructure, the administration vowed to work with all levels of government and the private sector to promote research and development, education, and awareness to ensure an "organized response" to cyber threats and warfare. Although the document produced some specific directives for securing government enterprise, there is not a matching initiative for the private sector. The fear of regulation and the pressure from many in commerce as well as those in Congress has amounted to a message to the private sector (whether sought or unsought): "you are on your own."

Within this environment, the guerilla combat of the post-Cold War era has been opened to a much larger pool of participants, whose cover is the anonymity and ubiquity of the "net." The general awareness that the critical infrastructure is critically vulnerable is as tempting to prospective attackers as it should be unnerving to its defenders and users. The tension creates a gambit for all international players. For state actors it may become a grand game of "chicken" to see who would launch a first strike. Many experts claim in preparation for that moment, some nation-states have been surveying the landscape to identify vulnerabilities in infrastructure systems of power grids and communication networks. In the words of an expert quoted in the McAfee report, nation-states are, "laying the electronic battlefield and preparing to use it."[65] The Stuxnet experience may be one such salient case.

All the while there has been a lack of public debate and an attendant void of national strategy in the United States. Further hindering the debate is even the lack of a functioning lexicon to express a crime, attack, or a justifiable retaliation in cyberspace. Rules of engagement, established responses, and notions concerning deterrence or collective security are presently moot points, which cannot be resolved until there is a framework for guiding doctrine and action. During this failed process classified information is kept secret, goes unshared, or falls between the cracks. The procedure for laying out a strategy is further stifled by bureaucratic divides and the walls erected among the military, law enforcement, national governments, and global commerce. As this "dialogue of the deaf" persists, the want for action languishes. While much of the discussions go on behind the closed doors of government, the public and the private sector continue to be the target of daily assaults, and will so for the foreseeable future.

Another factor limiting response is a lack of verifiable and quantitative data. Because of the reasons cited above, governments, corporations, and other victims are hesitant to come forth and admit to their victimization. As a result much of the data on cyber crime is merely anecdotal. Anecdotal data can lead to alarmism and encourage military response as the only option. Such action might feed the public's fears and satisfy its rage, but may not be appropriate and almost surely cause greater instability.

On the other hand, calls for consensus building are well worn throughout history. Without the incentive of a mighty stick or irresistible carrot, agreements are seldom achieved and their importunity goes on ignored when demands are based on nothing more than irrepressible optimism about market forces. At present there are no such self-regulating mechanisms or pressures to force stakeholders into a consensus. The to and fro between a Doomsday reckoning and Utopian fantasy appears to represent the state and direction of the discourse. Without some analytical discipline to assess the threat cyber crime and cyberterrorism pose, the best hope for positive steps might be somewhere in between.

CONCLUSION

As to the overall challenges of cyber security, for additional interpretation it might be wise to recall a fictitious dialogue between Socrates and a Greek aristocrat, Meno. Meno poses a question to the philosopher: "How will you look for something when you don't know what it is?" The stated and ensuing exchange is referred to as "Meno's paradox." In the current arena of conflict, solutions are elusive. The competition over political and economic control by state and non-state actors, the expanding web of criminals, terrorists, disgruntled workers, hacktivists, et al., add to global security's version of that paradox. The combatants are indistinct. Their motives are often vague. Demands are rarely offered. The shadowy world of failed states and opaque cyberspace has resulted in changing roles for states, altered the impact of NGOs on civil society, and created new spheres of authority, with which the national security establishment has no history or experience.

As an example, crime and terrorism traditionally abided by separate ontological norms and dwelled in two diverse and lawless realms. However, in today's security environment, these realms are beginning to overlap and the consequences are evolving into a previously unknown blend of potent danger and plight for governments, the private sector, and civil society. What emerges has been called the crime-terrorist nexus and has been quietly expanding for years. As it unfolds, it creates a serious dilemma for security, law enforcement professionals, and their functional responsibilities. Obscured by a complex of motivational factors and a constantly morphing threat vector, this new menace poses a severe challenge to established protocols and approaches to national security.

Even though motives sometimes differ, the *modus operandi* of these sundry actors can be similar if not identical. The intensification of the globalization process and the emergence of cyber crime and warfare have enabled illegal activity—whether motivated by material gain, ideological, or religious incentive. Despite the overwhelming advantage of resources of nation states, law enforcement agencies, and legitimate global commerce and industry, technology equilibrates many players with a level battlefield of accessible and comparative weaponry. Furthermore, transnational crime syndicates and international terrorist organizations often reflect the same efficiencies as multinational corporations due to the similarities of disaggregate organizational structures, agile and decentralized chains of command, and technologically trained "staffs." Moreover, the connection between the criminals and terrorists is more common and apparent as terrorists become more entrepreneurial and resort to self-financing.

The array of failed states, the role of multinational firms, the obsolescence of traditional militaries, the exploitation of jurisdictional divides and legalities, and the opaque circumstances that influence attribution of attack and response are only some of the issues that create and impact this shifting global security paradigm. The result is an opening within the global system for criminals and terrorists to nest, proffer, and are poised to exploit. As law enforcement agencies and national security organs grapple with questions of jurisdiction and mission ownership, a new threat takes shape that does not comfortably conform to previous patterns of activity, analysis, and protocols for response.

Inhibiting the ability to interdict is the lack of experience with this kind of threat, and the paucity of data that could help create predictive modeling methods and tools. These new opponents create a multivariate network of plotters. In some cases, they may be unrelated, stateless, and widespread—and in other cases, not. As a result, Meno's question becomes a troublesome and persistent dilemma for the security and defense communities as a simple, hypothetical query evolves into a somber, global concern.

NOTES

1. Jason Schifman, "The Need for a Strategic Approach to Cybersecurity," work in progress, University of Pennsylvania, April 2009, quoting Major General William Lord in "Air Force and the Cyberspace Mission Defending the Air Force's Computer Network in the Future," Center for Strategy and Technology, December 2007, p. 2.

2. Hedieh Nasheri, *Economic Espionage and Industrial Spying* (Cambridge University Press, 2005), p. 104.

3. Phil Williams, "Organized Crime and Cybercrime, Synergies, Trends, and Responses," in *Global Issues 2001*, U.S. Information Agency.

4. Dave Powner, "Cybercrime—Public and Private entities Face Challenges in Addressing Cyber Threats" (GAO Report to Congressional Requesters, June 2007, GAO-07-705).

5. *Ibid.*

6. *Ibid.*

7. *Ibid.*

8. James Lewis, "List of Significant Cyber Incidents Since 2006," Center for Strategic and International Studies, http://csis.org/publication/23-cyber-events-2006, posted 12 June 2009.

9. *Ibid.*

10. *Ibid.*

11. *Ibid.*

12. *Ibid.*

13. *Ibid.*

14. "Assuring and Trusted and Resilient Information and Communication Infrastructure," *Cyberspace Policy Review* (April 2009).

15. Lewis, *op. cit.*

16. *Ibid.*

17. "Assuring and Trusted and Resilient Information and Communication Infrastructure," *Cyberspace Policy Review*: April 2009.

18. *Ibid.*

19. James Lewis, "List of Significant Cyber Incidents Since 2006," Center for Strategic and International Studies, http://csis.org/publication/23-cyber-events-2006, posted 12 June 2009.

20. *Ibid.*

21. *Ibid.*

22. *Ibid.*

23. *Ibid.*

24. *Ibid.*

25. *Ibid.*

26. *Cyberspace Policy Review.*

27. Powner (June 2007).

28. *Ibid.*

29. *Ibid.*

30. Melissa Hathaway, *Five Myths About Cybersecurity,* Belfer Center for Science and International Affairs, John F. Kennedy School of Government (21 December 2009).

31. Edward Turzanski and Lawrence Husick (2012).

32. Powner GAO.

33. Sean McGurk, Verizon Risk Division, presentation to Department of Transportation, Transportation Research Board (4 December 2012).

34. Dan Dunkel, President, New Era Associates, interview, December 2010.

35. Melissa Hathaway, "Strategic Advantage: Why America should Care About Cybersecurity," Belfer Center for Science and International Affairs, John F. Kennedy School of Government, Harvard University (October, 2009), p. 1.

36. "Making the Nation Safer: The Role of Science and Technology in Countering Terrorism," The Committee on Science and Technology for Countering Terrorism, National Research Council of the National Academies (The National Academies Press, Washington, DC, 2002), p. 140–41.

37. *Ibid.*

38. Schifman.

39. Alvaro A Cardenas, *et al.,* "Challenges for Securing Cyber Physical Systems" (Report prepared by the Department of Electrical Engineering and Computer Sciences, University of California, Berkeley, Department of Civil and Environmental Engineering, University of California, Berkeley, and the Department of Electrical and Computer Engineering, Carnegie Mellon University, 2009).

40. Turzanski, 2012.

41. "If These Networks Get Hacked, Beware,"*BusinessWeek Online*, 17 September 2003.

42. National Research Council of the National Academies, p. 140.

43. *Ibid.*

44. Stephen Flynn, *The Edge of Disaster* (Random House, New York, 2006), p. 83.

45. Bindewald, Gilbert, "Monitoring and Modeling of the Electric Power System," Presentation, 28 October 2009.

46. *Ibid.*

47. Bindewald.

48. "If These Networks Get Hacked, Beware,"*BusinessWeek Online*, 17 September 2003.

49. Hathaway, p. 13.

50. Yannakogeorgos, Panayotis, *Promises and Pitfalls of the National Strategy to Secure Cyberspace*, Division of Global Affairs, Rutgers University, 2009, p. 22–23.

51. Flynn, *The Edge of Disaster*, p. 69.

52. Harris.

53. *Ibid.*

54. *Ibid.*

55. Cardenas.

56. Paul Cornish, *et al.*, "On Cyber War," Chatham House Report, November 2010, p. 28.

57. Lawrence Husick, Senior Fellow at the Foreign Policy Research Institute, presentation on 11 July 2011, Washington DC.

58. Turzanski, 2012.

59. "The Digital Arms Trade," *Economist,* 30 March 2013.

60. *Op cit.*

61. Mark Cohn, Unisys Corporation, correspondence, January 20, 2010.

62. "Virtual Criminality Report 2009," p. 11.

63. *Economist,* 30 March 2013.

64. Comprehensive National Cybersecurity Initiative http://www.whitehouse.gov/cybersecurity/comprehensive-national-cybersecurity-initiative.

65. *Ibid.*, p. 3.

Chapter Nine

Terrorism Versus Crime

... it is not inconceivable that the major global divide will be caused not by competing ideologies, the struggle for power ... but by clashes between states that uphold law and order and those that are dominated by criminal interests and criminal authorities.
      —Phil Williams, Ridgeway Center for International Security Studies

A display of particular brutality occurred in the Mexican town of Uruapan in September 2006. On one night in the central state of Michoacan several gunmen entered a local bar firing their weapons and ordering patrons to the ground. The initial panic intensified into horror as the intruders tossed five severed human heads onto the dance floor and then left with the same gush as when they entered. Represented in the violence was not merely a demonstration of terror tactics by a group of local thugs, but perhaps a foreshadowing of an irreversible paradigm trend taking place on a global scale. Some security experts suggest that this and similar incidents signal a dynamic shift away from past patterns of criminality. They warn that such scenes are harbingers of an impending security challenge, with which we may be poorly prepared to meet. The change they fear is that the lines between criminal and political violence have been blurred and the once separate terrains of crime organizations and terrorist groups may now be colliding.

Authorities claimed the beheadings were linked to "organized crime." The region is known for trafficking in drugs and the extreme violence that accompanies the trade. At the time a government campaign against local crime organizations was being met with violent retaliation in order to pressure authorities into returning to a previous "understanding," which involved widespread government collusion.[1] Newspaper reports stated: "Arrests of major drug cartel leaders have sparked an increasingly brutal and ruthless drug war in Mexico as gangs battle for control of lucrative routes."[2]

Unlike most criminal incidents where perpetrators prefer anonymity, in this case the group committing the violence identified itself. La Familia Michoacana (*the family of the state of Michoacan*) is a designated drug trafficking organization (DTO). Its reputation for the production and distribution of methamphetamine and marijuana is well established, as are its network of corrupt officials and proclivity for the odd publicity stunt. Despite its obvious economic motives and activities in the lucrative drug trade, its stated purpose is to do "the work of God."[3] To emphasize this last point, in addition to the severed heads the armed men left behind a cardboard placard, which read: "The family doesn't kill for money. It doesn't kill for women. It doesn't kill innocent people, only those who deserve to die. Know that this is divine justice."[4] Apparently, the authors of the note felt this act of horror and intimidation was not complete without an ideological annotation.

Similar moral justifications for crime and violence appear in other regions. However, sometimes such proclamations are an extension of ideology, not in afterthought or an assertion of false outrage. A 2010 Congressional Research Service document (International Terrorism and Transnational Crime) reports that validations of crime in the service of ideology have been appearing in public since the 1980s. As a leader of an al Qaeda associated group, Fatah al-Islam explains:

> Stealing money from the infidels, from the usurious banks and the institutions which belong to the infidel regimes and states, is a legal thing which Allah has permitted us to do. This money is being seized from them and instead directed towards jihad.[5]

Abu Bakar Bashir, a spiritual leader of the Southeast Asian Islamic extremist group Jemaah Islamiyah, put it more curtly: "You can take their blood; then why not take their property?"[6] However, theft is not the only form of onslaught. The narcotics trade is viewed as another means to an end. A fatwa issued by Hezbollah assures followers: "If we can not kill them with guns, so we will kill them with drugs." The Taliban has been an active participant in Afghanistan's drug trade for years. One of its members, Khan Mohamed, now serving two life sentences in the United States, viewed selling heroin as a form of jihad: "Whether it is by opium or by shooting, this is our common goal."[7]

How opium is a major source of funding for the Taliban is not only a disturbing example of an unfolding pattern, it may also represent the liminal stages of a dreadful dynamism at loose and gaining global momentum. A 2011 article in *Newsweek* puts the short event chain simply: "Once the crop is in, the guerillas will retrieve their hidden weapons and head for the battlefield."[8] According to the same article, the equivalent of $2,300 would cover the cost of one major ambush attack involving IEDs, RPGs, automatic weapons, and suicide bombers (UN statistics estimate that revenues from illegal drugs in Afghanistan alone exceeds $3 billion annually[9]). Given Pakistan's involvement and proximity to trafficking routes and the pace and lack of transparency of its nuclear weapons program, the situation commands further unease—if not utter alarm. Furthermore, the elimination of Osama bin Laden may have been a necessary signal to the terrorist world, but did little in disrupting these sorts of operations and nothing in assuaging passions.

As tensions and the need for self-financing increase, this blend of *modus operandi* with ideology may be a sign that the motives, tactics, and even the very essence of world crime may be percolating into a new, more lethal concoction and a deviation from past norms. Furthermore, the same mechanisms that promote international trade are facilitators for crime and offer similar inducements for terror.

Access to technological innovation and the formation of global goods and financial markets have enabled international commerce, but have also offered opportunity to criminals and terrorists. Just as global corporations find markets to exploit, take advantage of capital and exchange rate spreads, move funds, and occasionally reorganize—so can transnational crime and terrorism find sources of lucre, move their assets, and mobilize forces, associates, and sympathizers. International businesses recruit worldwide. They take advantage of local laws promoting investment. They seek out tax havens from welcoming governments. In a similar way, the growth of diasporas and the expansion of failed and "courtesan" states are indispensable tools and reliable conveniences for those outside the law. They offer safe havens, labor pools, lucrative markets, and transit terminals. The economic mechanisms they provide create severe disadvantages for legal authorities. The paradigm shift lends itself to a new pragmatism in the criminal world, the logic of which transcends previous conventions and perceptions relative to the practice and analysis of criminal and terrorist activity. The break with the past, to some analysts, is becoming obvious. Meanwhile, the methods we use to analyze crime and terrorism may be turning obsolete. As Erroll Southers of the DHS National Center for Risk and Economic Analysis of Terrorism Events (CREATE) at the University of Southern California explains:

> In our zeal to prepare for and respond to threats or future attacks, the analytical emphasis on technological countermeasures has far outweighed the cultural or "human element." Our research efforts of modeling terrorist networks to illustrate predictable attack path development and enhance intelligence analysis, must also engage the "real world" notions that often realign plots along unexplainable continuums. These examinations should prioritize the understanding of our adversaries' motivation and decision-making processes. This ongoing challenge, accompanied by the lack of a clearly defined national intelligence enterprise embracing our civil liberties, leaves us ill-equipped to appropriately allocate scarce resources, designed to facilitate predictive policing and thwart

future terror attacks. If someone is intent on attacking us, we will dramatically improve our chances to detect or deter them, if we understand why.[10]

Understanding "why" is a new art form in security studies. Traditionally, economic crime and political terrorism were separate domains. Moreover, the dwellers of these realms were usually at opposite ends politically. While terrorists seek the destruction of the state, criminals have a vested interest in the state's survival. Organized crime, typically, has long-term financial interests and in order to allow their parasitic relationship to thrive, a functioning and stable host is essential. Therefore, crime members are often established members and depend upon state institutions and structures to operate, expand, and invest. Crime organizations such as the Japanese Yakuza and the American Cosa Nostra have a disposition toward strong loyalty to the state. As Louise Shelley of the Transnational Crime and Corruption Center explains:

> Longstanding transnational crime groups and their more recently formed counter-parts have a very different relationship with the state and to terrorism. The older crime groups, often in long-established states, have developed along with their states and are dependent on existing institutional and financial structures to move their products and invest their profits. With the exception of Colombia, rarely do large established crime organizations link with terrorist groups, because their long-term financial interests require the preservation of state structures. Through corruption and movement into the lawful economy, these groups minimize the risk of prosecution and therefore do not fear the power of state institutions.[11]

On the other hand, terrorists have no such concern or claim. Historically, and as mentioned above, terrorists challenged the authority of the state and often sought its overthrow. Terrorism worked against the very institutions and structures that were the apparatus of functioning economies and pluralistic governance. Their limited horizons, either economic or political, put them outside any prospect for legal inclusion or illegal collusion with the greater society. Today, however, old maxims and praxis may not apply. A predictable question in the study of the crime-terrorist nexus is: Does an arrangement of shared methods between these collaborators mean a reinterpretation of base motives as well? Or, stated another way: Can terrorism achieve its objectives through crime, as might criminals further their economic interests by politicizing operations? If the answer to these questions is "yes," there is the potential result of crime and terrorism using the same methods and having the same motives to attain their desired goals. The melding of such forces makes a compelling case for the crime-terrorist nexus. Although signs of any formal grand strategy between criminal organizations and terrorists do not yet exist, the increasing rate of opportunity for collaboration offer up a disturbing prospect.

Despite a lack of hard statistical support, there is a growing uneasiness among intelligence and security experts that a potential convergence of criminal and terrorist operations, skills, and motives has been taking form for decades.[12, 13] Mostly, these beliefs are founded upon limited anecdotal evidence. Many officials of various U.S. and foreign law enforcement agencies, intelligence organizations, and academia, yet, support similar conclusions about the crime-terrorist nexus. While it neither has a formal framework for negotiating agreements or disputes, nor a shared history and culture, opportunities for collaboration often abound. The threat from this phenomenon is not always apparent. There is far more overwhelming data on criminals and terrorists' long precedent of fighting among themselves—in addition to their assaults against the legitimate world. Criminal gangs have abiding histories of wars over turfs and regional superiority. Terrorists also compete in political and ideological struggles. The death tolls and stakes have often been high. However, in spite of traditional character and lack of interaction, the debate regarding this new realism between crime and terrorism is taking shape. Regardless of the lack of reliable intelligence, concern by authorities is growing. The true threat comes from a fear of a thickening web of professional criminals, terrorists, activists, and marginalized groups who oppose laws and resort to crime out of hatred, greed, or the necessity to survive. Whether by design or happenstance, the potential perils can be alarming and the security countermeasures are mostly in development.

The nature of this unfolding trend is as complex as it is unpredictable. Formal arrangements between terrorists and nonpolitical criminals are rare but exist. Motivations, operations, and tactics can interact, overlap, and merge depending on the circumstances and actors. These same functional formations can dissever and disappear, only to reconstitute at a later point without either warning or attention. Distinctions are, therefore, blurred and the threat vector is dynamic. Experts offer two tracks as a way to describe the evolution of the crime-terrorist nexus. To many observers it is a matter of whether these organizations are transforming internally or converging to form hybrid groups.[14] Through the transformation process the outlawed group becomes an organization with "in-house" capabilities, which expand their structure and operations in order to accommodate either crime or indiscriminate violence against the state—whichever competency they lack. A slight alternative to this model is the convergence theory. In this latter case an established crime or terrorist organization can ally with a partner who brings into the collaboration the requisite expertise and/or logistical support necessary to make the new entity sufficiently lethal, destructive, and effective in an environment of chaos.[15] These arrangements can be temporary or long term, strategic or tactical. In either instance, the situation for legal society is becoming more perilous. Thomas Sanderson of the Center for Strategic and International Studies claims: "… it is clear this growing threat is complex and increasingly difficult to counter with standard law enforcement and military counter-measures."[16]

Several forces may be impelling the nexus between crime and terrorism. One driver is the need for many terrorist organizations to become self-financing. The successes of the government's efforts to track financial transactions and interdict the flow of funds to these groups have made crime an obvious option. Some analysts claim that many terrorists' sole support comes from their association with organized crime.[17] The lucrative narcotics trade, for instance, is a field of endeavor of seemingly limitless growth. It is constantly attracting new entrants as business expands. The increase in opportunity creates partnerships and rivalries. As a result even well-established criminal groups are under threat from the evolving collection of players as new competitors force their rivals to the fringe.

In general, the loci for interaction between crime and terrorism are mutually convenient and advantageous. Shared spaces include neighborhoods, penal institutions, conflict zones, and failed states.[18] Studies, furthermore, note that wherever there is a low regard for the state, its institutions, or the ruling elite, there is a greater opportunity and motivation for criminals and terrorists to unite.[19] The interactions breed professional and personal familiarity. Meanwhile, the threat to legitimate society is compounded with the changing landscape of crime and terror. The overhanging result is a more populated and complex web of illegal operations, arrangements, and—perhaps—longer term plans.

These "alternative, exploitive forms of financing,"[20] are made more problematic by the dynamism that accompanies globalization—and applies to both crime organizations and transnational terrorism. As crime and terrorism become more globalized, efficiencies evolve. James Mittelman writes that "… what drives organized crime groups increasingly are efforts to exploit the growth mechanisms of globalization."[21] Many terrorists are discovering the same basic *précis* holds true in their field. Hence, terrorists-entrepreneurs do not confine activity to crimes such as illegal arms, narcotics, human trafficking, kidnapping, extortion, fraud, murder for hire, etc. As part of their toolkit, terrorist organizations (as well as with crime syndicates) impute "taxes" for protection, regional safe havens, or use of trafficking routes.[22] They also collect licensing fees from associate groups and enter into partnerships in order to compete in vertical crime markets.[23]

In addition to the "stick" applied by successful national military and law enforcement programs there is also the "carrot" every criminal eyes, which is the prospect of "going legit." This fortunate circumstance for those outside the law may be elusive in established states where opportunities to be a political insider by corrupt means are limited due to the rule of law and the dominance of matured, democratic institutions. However, in the post-Cold War era the ring of failed states bereft of superpower sponsorship offer new opportunities for the criminalization of politics. Gaining political leverage through corruption and/or intimidation in these nations is a natural disposition for many parties in these dire economic environments that now circle the globe. Attaining power via direct political involvement or over lucrative economic sectors can be achieved more quickly with force and violence. To this end, many groups have become what Tamara Makarenko calls "conglomerates of causes."[24] They combine the resources of crime and terror to create an entity, which bears the criminal and political characteristics of both types in a single organization.

FROM CENTRAL ASIA TO THE BALKANS

Tamara Makarenko, an expert on the interplay between crime and terror, describes the relationship between the Albanian mafia and the Kosovo Liberation Army (KLA) as the "most illustrative nexus between a criminal and terrorist group."[25] During the 1990s, together, they held control of the enormous Balkan heroin trafficking routes. (Links to former Mujahedin fighters in Afghanistan by the KLA were known, and Afghanistan was the first to recognize Kosovo's claim of independence.) Personal connections through an original arrangement that provided the KLA with weapons from drug sales formed and still abides. This nexus evolved over time into a complex of operations driven by political and criminal motives. Testifying before the U.S. Congress, Ralf Mutschke, the Assistant Director of Interpol reported:

> Albania organized crime groups are hybrid organizations, often involved both in criminal activity of an organized nature and in political activities, mainly relating to Kosovo. There is evidence that the political and criminal activities are deeply intertwined.[26]

Mutschke further stated that in addition to drug trafficking and money laundering, legitimate fund-raising activities also occur. Before its disbandment in 1999, financing for the KLA came from various sources. Not only through illegal means, but also via loans from Islamic countries and individuals. As an indication of how interlocked and dispersed the fund-raising network is organized, one contribution allegedly included $20 million in largesse from Osama bin Laden.[27] Albanian groups controlled about 40 percent of the heroin trade in Europe according to the report. Along these drug routes they formed networks with Turkish, Bulgarian, Romanian, Italian, Greek, and Central Asian criminal organizations. Their activities forced Mutschke to conclude the "Albanian Republic itself, is definitely a cause of concern to the international community, especially when one takes into account the geopolitical instability in the region . . . the links between drug trafficking and terrorism in Central Asia."[28]

Upon its disbandment, many members of the KLA found themselves part of other armed groups or entered into politics. The contacts formed in earlier years continued, and vague accusations persist that opium cultivation and heroin production resumed in the region. Although the KLA no longer exists, its affiliation with crime demonstrated how deeply relationships might form when conditions align.

Other examples of places where crime and terrorism co-mingle are in Central Asia. A main participant in narco-terrorism is the Islamic Movement of Uzbekistan (IMU). Founded and formerly led by a figure in the Islamic underground movement, Tohir Abdouhalilovitch Yuldeshev, and a former Soviet paratrooper, Jumaboi Ahmadzhanovitch Khojaev, the group is a player in the world of illegal narcotics. Despite it being nearly wiped out by Operation Enduring Freedom, it continues to function thanks to its drug trafficking operations. As with many criminal and militant groups in the region, drug trafficking is an economic lifeline. In the instance of the IMU, the drug trade allows it to prolong its existence without the cadre of leadership and a significant body of rank and file members. According to Phil Williams, ideology unites members with a common cause and a shared enemy.[29] "Being a greedy criminal is not necessarily incompatible with being a committed terrorist or insurgent."[30] This is also the view of other analysts who believe the emotional and psychological sustainability of a jihad combined with the financial support from illegal trafficking in narcotics might even permit the movement to revive and grow.

In the illegal drug trade the greatest profits come from the refinement and distribution of substances, rather than from their production.[31] The raw materials, fixed capital, and labor needed to create product are relatively inexpensive since they are sourced from regions of extreme poverty. It is the transportation costs and the risk of interdiction that drive up the price of illegal drugs. Therefore, the security and integrity of the transportation infrastructure is central to the illegal drug industry and greatly influences pricing. Not coincidentally, the IMU worked to secure and control the transportation and flow of drugs from the region into Russia and Europe.[32] It accomplished this by using terrorist tactics and crime connections.

Prior to its current calling, the IMU was solely bent upon an Islamic revolution to establish Uzbekistan as a Muslim state. IMU's origins spring from this failed effort in the period following the disintegration of the Soviet Union. Undeterred, the group's cry for an Islamic revolution spread beyond Uzbekistan and into Tajikistan. There it was met with a similar lack of success. Nevertheless, the cause attracted followers. Drug trafficking became a way to support the growing movement. With 75 percent of the world's heroin supplied by Afghanistan, trafficking in Central Asia is an irresistible force. A contributing factor in the incentive to enter the drug trade is the low risk of capture and arrest. Opportunities for lawlessness abound and the fear of loss is low where state structures are crippled and authority is weak. In these spaces the interaction of terrorism and crime create a natural momentum through a vicious cycle of cause and effect. The IMU quickly discovered that lucrative trafficking operations fund terrorist activities, which produce regional instability and an environment suited for crime. In an atmosphere of chaos, a well-funded terrorist group can function more freely and less fearfully—as can criminals. As the cycle repeats, the profits and incentives increase.

Meanwhile, IMU's ideological roots remain firm in the minds of most followers. The group's ties to Islamic radicalism run deep. It had comrades among members of the Taliban and al Qaeda. A report claims the IMU may have supplied bin Laden with fissile material for the production of a nuclear improvised explosive device.[33] (If true, the material was most likely acquired through IMU's connections with Russian crime organizations.) Under such circumstances, followers and friends of the IMU see no contradiction between words and deeds. The group's leaders can appeal to recruits and ask for sacrifice while taking the moral high ground against the infidel. Crime, they can claim, is merely a weapon and the victim is only the enemy. Throughout his campaign of violence and crime, Yuldeshev (Khojaev, who later took on the *nom de guerre* Juma Namangani, was reported killed by U.S. air raids) established links with sympathizers in Pakistan, Saudi Arabia, United Arab Emirates, Turkey, Iran, and Chechnya. The organization he helped found has been inching westward as it enters into strategic alliances and collaborates in international activities with Eastern European organized crime groups from former Communist Bloc countries and the republics of the former Soviet Union.

Furthermore, the routes they established can be used to transport arms and personnel in order to either launch an offensive or escape capture. They also provide safe havens for insurgents and warehousing for contraband goods or supplies. More than ninety tons of heroin pass through central Asia every year. Authorities in the region are the most lax on earth in their efforts to control the flow. Illegal profits from the narcotics trade far eclipse the income generated by legitimate business and foreign aid, prompting one analyst to remark that the trafficking in drugs is "corroding society, but it brings stability to it."[34]

The IMU is not the only Islamic organization active in regional drug trade. Hizb-ut-Tahrir (HT) Islamic Party of Liberation is a pan-Islamic movement calling for a Caliphate, which would unite all Muslims under a single state. Founded in East Jerusalem in 1953, it espouses radical political changes to dismantle the state apparatus in countries it regards as "colonists states" or in Muslim countries where "religious despots" govern.[35] HT be-

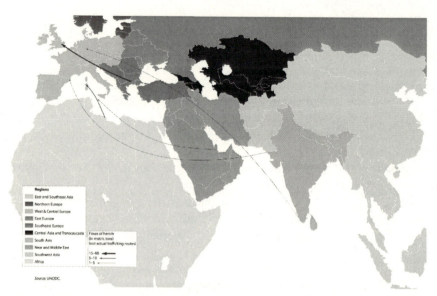

Map 9.1. Heroin Flows to West and Central Europe, 2009 *(Source: UNOCD, World Drug Report 2011 (United Nations Publication, No. E.11.XI.10))*

came active in Central Asia during the mid 1990s and has been a leading Islamic group in the region.[36] It grew rapidly by appealing to the rural poor, but also had the support of backers in Saudi Arabia and Muslim communities in Western Europe. These connections made the HT a formidable force. It claims to be active in over forty countries and its membership is close to one hundred thousand. In addition to a relatively large following, their movements are very difficult to track because of its secretive nature. They apparently use the same route infrastructure as the IMU to move products.

Officially, the HT rejects the use of violence to gain political power in the Muslim world and officially denounces terrorism. However, throughout the party's history members have been known to engage in terrorist activity.[37] Despite its official claims, several alleged assassination attempts against regimes in Uzbekistan and Kyrgyzstan indicated there might be exception cases. The organization operates groups of independent cells. Depending on circumstances, these units may choose to employ violence, crime, or any mixture of methods to achieve perceived immediate or long-term goals. Intelligence and analysis about the future role, intentions, and impact of the HT are only speculative due to its enigmatic nature. However, its recent history has prompted one scholar to describe it as a "conveyor belt for terrorism."[38]

As the crime-terrorist nexus grows it may find in Chechnya an example of collusion between terrorism, economic crime, and the workings of a failed state that exceeds all others. Terrorist links with organized crime are seamless and often bound by kinship. Furthermore, in addition to linkages with other foreign Muslims, Chechens can take advantage of members of diaspora groups, particularly in Russia. Through their network they have successfully marshaled assets from abroad, moved sophisticated war materiel, and organized intelligence-gathering operations. [39]

In the Caucasus region of southern Russia, the relationship between crime, terrorism, economics, and politics is as arrant as it is fluid. The anarchy has not only created more opportunity for crime and terrorism, but meld religious and ethnic cleavages with unlawful trafficking and trade. [40] As with other cases, instability has allowed strong criminal structures to thrive and to extend into the political sphere. Chechen "separatists" engage in such criminal activity as drug trafficking, protection racketeering, extortion, kidnapping, auto theft, arms dealing, counterfeiting, bank fraud, illegal trade in oil, and precious metals to the point where differences between their motives and those of standard criminals are irrelevant. Efforts by Russian law enforcement and security authorities to exploit any differences between Chechen criminal groups and insurgents have yielded no results. [41]

Oil and gas were the major economic influencers in the conflict between Chechnya and Russia. The outbreak of the war disrupted oil trade in Russia with an economic cost of $30 million per day. [42] The breakaway territory had not only become a major pipeline intersection, but a prominent refining center. Since then, a bypass pipeline has been constructed and became operational in 2000, but not before much hard currency was diverted outside Chechnya into overseas accounts. Therefore, Chechen organizations are not only active, but also well financed.

Today, opium may be surpassing oil and natural gas as the most lucrative natural resource from the fields of Central Asia. Experts regard Chechen gangs as one of the most active groups involved in narcotics trafficking in Central Asia, the Caucasus, and many regions within Russia. [43] Chechens have a history of activity in the global narcotics trade, and thanks to connections made through their networks with other crime organizations they have expanded their interest. Their dominant role in the drug trade in Russia also speaks to their ability to access high-ranking government officials through influence. In other parts of the world the material and emotional elements are in place to support a linkage between crime and terror. The combination and course of these events may be setting conditions for further development by opportunists, whether they are terrorists or nonpolitical criminals.

Add to the above criminal interests such examples of "exploitive financing" as counterfeiting, bank fraud, kidnapping, extortion, protection, and all forms of smuggling and stealing and what emerges is a vast web of illicit activity. The convergence of these opportunities, channels, and conditions reflect an era of high risk from criminal and terrorist groups, which can reach into almost every corner of the world. Chechnya is at an intersection of drug traffic between Central Asia and Europe. The Trans-Caucusus, because of its geographic location, well-developed network of collaborators and abettors, and organizational solidarity has the potential to make the region an important fixed point along the crime and terrorism nexus.

Opium and heroin trafficking had long been concentrated along the routes from Afghanistan, to Tajikistan, Uzbekistan, and Kyrgyzstan. Such facilitating factors as a common language, pervious borders, the chaos of regional conflicts, economic instability, and proximity to the source have allowed trade to prosper.[44] Changes in the post-Cold War political map were contributors as well. The breakup of the Soviet Union created the longest border in the world. The Russian-Kazakh border now divides Russia from its former Soviet Socialist Republic and marks an area rife with opportunity for smuggling. To the neighboring south, heroin production represents Afghanistan's largest economic sector. According to the United Nations Office on Drugs and Crime, 6,610 tonnes (metric tons) of opium were produced in Afghanistan in 2006.[45] In some locales along the drug route, nearly 80 percent of the population work for smugglers. Compensation can be ten times greater than official salaries. Those living on the edge of poverty may not only view the temptation of drug trafficking as irresistible, but the option to resist—irrational. The same practicality can apply to law enforcement officials and government authorities whose salaries can be as low as $10–$30 per month.[46]

The demand and unlimited supply of opium make narcotic trafficking a lucrative and irresistible enterprise. Since then, the disintegration of the Soviet Union drug trafficking in Central Asia has grown to startling dimensions. The Northern Route through Central Asia is mostly heroin. The Balkan Route, via a link of seaborne connections, is primarily opium and morphine. Eventually, both streams converge in Russia as well as Western Europe. The drug trade is a primal force in the region. It buttresses organized crime, terrorism, official corruption, and offers economic relief to the populations marginalized by poverty in Central Asia and the Trans-Caucasus. By most accounts, business is good and growing. Simultaneously, the deep roots of radicalism and old hatreds abide from Central Asia to the Balkans. To the north is Russia.

THE RUSSIAN CONNECTION

The security environment and political-economic forces propel the illegal narcotic industry's reach to worldwide proportions. Regional terrorists and their criminal affiliates have extended their supply network well beyond their local provinces. The Golden Crescent, the crossroads of central, south, and western Asia, is the primary area for the illicit production and trans-shipment of opium. Drug trade from this region has not only thrived with the aid of Chechen guerillas, criminal elements, and political cell members, but also the Russian military. Corrupt officials in the Russian army have reportedly provided supply vehicles returning from missions in Central Asia for use as transports for illegal narcotics.[47] A connection point along this route is through Tajikistan. According to a reporter for the Moscow Stringer news agency, Tajik army officers offer Russian weapons to Afghan warlords in exchange for narcotics. The Tajik sell the drugs to the Russian military, which transports the product into Russia.[48] Several military air bases are transit points for the Russian domestic supply chain. Chkalovskiy airfield outside Moscow is the primary one.

The results of these transactions are that cheap and bountiful arsenals of high-quality weapons are put into the hands of outlaws, while the Russian military becomes more deeply involved in the narcotics trade. According to a 1999 report by the Heritage Foundation, officials with the Uzbekistan government alleged Russian military commanders insisted in remaining on in Tajikistan for the purpose of continuing to traffic in drugs. The same report claimed:

> Most worrisome are intelligence reports of the tremendous Russian military air cargo capability being utilized to ship drugs from Southeast Asia and Central Asia to Western Europe and North America.[49]

Once mainly end points, population centers such as St. Petersburg and Moscow are now transit points for the global distribution of narcotics. Therefore, Russia is both a colossal transit depot and an immense market. The backdrop to these events is the conclusion by most investigators that police corruption in Russia is a serious problem at all ranks.[50] Easing drug cargos past controls or blocking criminal cases from going forward are no grave obstacles when both state salaries and the risk of prosecution are extremely low. The vast expanse of Russia's borders, the host of couriers, and the willingness of officials to cooperate make possible a compliant security framework. Furthermore, the relationship between police and crime group members can run deep. These ties may be formed on an individual level and extend back to the time of youth. Nurtured over extended periods and through interaction and common self-interests, kinships emerge that transcend simple monetary rewards for either side.[51] The political and economic transition period of the 1990s created fertile ground where these relationships could form and thrive.

During the privatization period new businesses and reconstituted government agencies staked out areas of the criminal market.[52] No longer a transition state, Russia's social structure has been stabilized since its conversion from Socialism. At the same time, official corruption is tightly entwined with the organs of government and the levers of power. Corruption is an innate substance of the country's DNA system of governance. Corruption and crime are facts and a way of life that is not only allowed to exist and nurtured, but also exported. The upheaval created with the implosion of the USSR echoed beyond Russia's borders. Revolutions in technology and the increasing hyper-connectivity of the global economy are carriers of the reverberation. James O. Finckenauer and Yuri A. Voronin, while at the National Institute of Justice in 2001, assessed conditions:

> In the decade since the collapse of the Soviet Union, the world has become the target of a new global crime threat from criminal organizations and criminal activities that have poured forth from over the borders of Russia and other former Soviet republics such as the Ukraine. The nature and variety of the crimes being committed seems unlimited—drugs, arms trafficking, stolen automobiles, trafficking in women and children, and money laundering are among the most prevalent. The spillover is particularly troubling to Europe (and especially eastern Europe) because of its geological proximity to Russia, and to Israel, because of its large numbers of Russian immigrants. But no area of the world seems immune to this menace, especially not the United States. [53]

The Russian word *Krysha* (roof) became a term for "protection" and a means of extracting revenue. "Protection services" allowed the "police mafia" to claim a piece of the pie in the era of new capitalism, and a grander place for itself in the criminal world. Traditional crime syndicates were forced to compete and many either shared or lost their standing in the new arena. Their displacement was hastened by the rise of the police mafia and gang battles. These gangster wars during the mid-1990s may have claimed thousands of lives. A result of the conflict was a new theater of law enforcement operations in Russia. Criminalized privatization and the commercialization of crime shaped the rising social order and its security framework. The conditions of the prevailing public edifice and the economic opportunities of the illegal narcotics trade were the elements of a perfect storm. Economic gain and social chaos are not only the results, but also the forces perpetuating the onslaught of corruption.

Today's Russian organized crime operations and membership are vast. Its infiltration of government and business seems virtually boundless. The target of its ambition is the world, and its roots extend back over 400 years. [54] The administrative bureaucracy created by tsars set the genetic code for the culture and its current complex relations with the state. The earliest recordings of organized crime in Russia emerge in the 1920s and 1930s from Gulag accounts. The *vori* (thieves) was more than an undiscriminating term for criminals, undesirables, or any *mauvais sujet*. The word referred to a world with its own dress, language, code of behavior, and rudimentary court system. [55] It most likely evolved from the pre-revolutionary criminal *arteli*, and its native territory was the Gulag prison system. It was a fraternity, which lived by strict, self-regulating rules. Steve Handelman, in his 1995 work, *Comrade Criminal,* writes: "No tradition was more compelling than the underworld code."

However, the frailty of the Soviet economy in the 1960s and 1970s and the explosion of economic opportunity and lawlessness in the rubble of the former Soviet structure made many *vori* traditions obsolete (particularly the requirement of lengthy prison sentences as a test of commitment to the code). In the latter half of the twentieth century economic opportunities imposed change upon the original fraternity of thieves and forced traditionalists to fade into the background. Yet, even within this new environment the presence of *vorovskoi mir* (thieves' world) in post-communist Russia "is as impossible to imagine as it is to conceive Russia without winter. The gangster reigning over the former state hotel he had 'privatized' is a symbol of culture that only matches the Russian Orthodox Church in durability and the determined faith of its adherents."[56]

In the 1950s the official numbers of *vori* were becoming faint, only to revive during the 1960s and 1970s.[57] The stagnating Soviet economy was the reason for its resurgence. Bottlenecks abounded and the fiscal cost of the Cold War arms race was taking its toll. An immense industrial-based economy lacked an efficient service sector and was losing ground in its competition with the West. The sclerotic Soviet administrative system, therefore, had to rely on *tolchkatki* (literally, pushers—or brokers) and *vori* services to grease and add support to an apparatus that its economy had outgrown. It was during this time that many experts agree the Russian mafia took shape and formed its present bonds with government and the state bureaucracy.[58] That nexus of officialdom with the underground economy intensified in the 1980s to the 1990s as the post-communist era opened up new commercial opportunities and created the anatomy and face of the present Russian Mafia. New market entrants from within Russia who controlled financial resources and connections in government culled the remnants of the earlier herd and introduced additional criminal mass and energy. Crime syndicates with transnational ties based on ethnic kinships also added to the competition. Its current configuration with its sophistication and transnational character is more potent and menacing today than the previous generations.

To understand the extent and weight of corruption in Russia, it is necessary to be familiar with some recent history. The "classless society" of the former Soviet Union held aside a secret world of privilege for a special caste. The *nomenklatura* referred to the list of Communist Party elites who dominated the center of political life in the USSR. Their numbers approximated 1.5 million and their license to exploit the system was unlimited. It freely plundered its own state. Except for an internal system of punishment and reward, its powers were unchecked. Georgi Arbatov, an official of the Central Committee and himself a former member, wrote about the old polity:

> [It] was organically connected with corruption. . . . An enormous and parasitic *apparat* gives or takes away, permits or prohibits, takes care of everything, can fire anybody, demote anybody, often throws him in prison or, raises him up. And who with such power at his disposal can resist the temptation?[59]

It was also crime at the highest levels of authority. Part of the wealth of the Soviet Union financed clandestine operations for the defense of the state, but also found its way into private offshore accounts of party favorites. Through a network of KGB channels, terrorist groups, foreign communist organizations, commercial covers as well as party member lifestyles were underwritten. In the end, the Union of Soviet Socialist Republics could not support the corruption and inefficiency of the system it fathered. Its collapse set loose a massive economic and political shockwave. Once the rubble had settled, however, amid the ruins the *nomenklatura* stood erect and in position to take advantage of the new order.

Communism had given way to capitalism. The command economy made a torturous journey toward a free market during the transition period, and the party *nomenklatura* discovered "*nomenklatura* capitalism" *en route*. Many post-Soviet "businessmen" expropriated or moved their way into key industries and the embryonic banking sectors.[60] Using the connections it forged with associates abroad and its relationships with the *vori*, *nomenklatura* capitalists became exporters of strategic raw materials, international investors, real estate developers, money launderers, arms dealers, extortionists, and illegitimate owners of legitimate businesses. A frustrated former press secretary for Boris Yeltsin declared in 1992:

> The criminal party has left the stage, but the criminal state has remained. Mafia habits, embezzlement of public funds, and corruption remain the norm of social relations and penetrate the atmosphere in which the country and one of our citizens lives. Our efforts to present [defeat of the *coup*] as a victory for democracy are nothing more than a self-deception. On the whole, Communists were defeated by other Communists.[61]

Pavel Voshchanov, Yeltsin's press secretary who made the above remarks, unfortunately, has his government partly to blame for the situation it found for itself. The early failures of nascent democratic institutions in Russia provided a vacuum that crime was eager to fill. Criminal organizations moved in to not only establish order in accord with their own brand of justice, but also took over other government services such as providing funds for schools and hospital repairs, establishing charities, and offering outlets through public activities.[62] The consequence was a further erosion of confidence in the government and a lenient public attitude toward organized crime.

Today, the lack of political will and government resources to combat organized crime in Russia is also a problem for other legitimate states. Commenting on the state of the world financial system, Mark Cohn of Unisys Corporation offers: "Perhaps, the U.S. banking industry's greatest competition comes from Russian crime syndicates. Both Russian organized crime and foreign intelligence services have very sophisticated collection capabilities."[63] Mr. Cohn adds that not only is money being siphoned off from major U.S. bank accounts, but also these liquid assets are being reinvested in projects around the world. The net effect is that U.S. bankers are cut out of international investment opportunities by competing interests and with the use of their previously owned assets and funds.

Additionally, Russian organized crime's penetration into legitimate commerce makes its network more difficult to dislodge and, perhaps, more problematical to contain. Their political and economic resources give this new strain of corruption a particular potency. According to Finckenauer and Voronin, organized crime in Russia even attempts to take a share of monopolies normally reserved for the state. The regulation of business markets, territorial districting, taxation (protection fees), and tariffs are a few of the areas contested. Hence, the weakened rule of law has created the surge in privatized forms of violence, and an uncontrollable rise in rent seeking. As a result of this relationship, which was formed during the transition from a command economy to a demand economy: "organized crime in Russia evolved to its present ambiguous position of being both in direct collaboration with the state, and at the same time, in conflict with it."[64] The public unrest manifested by anti-Kremlin demonstrations in Moscow in late 2011 is the first meaningful sign of challenge to these forces.

Weber's concept of the state's monopoly over organized violence is eroding in many places in the world. Compelling an opponent to submit to another state's will through force or military means is limited in today's environment of economic globalization. Power politics is more dependent upon economic might. In order to take advantage of the logistical inter-connectivity of the global market and the political constraints of the interstate system—new power alliances are surfacing. In this postmodern era of conflict and competition, the marriage between the government and crime in Russia may, ultimately, be one of convenience. Will the same be so for the collaboration between criminals and terrorists? How Russian organized crime (ROC) chooses to wield its authority and interact with terrorism is a concern worthy of serious attention. Whom it decides are its enemies or its allies will determine its actions—as will its ability to politically withstand public outcry.

There are many actors on this stage and their roles and motivations are unscripted. There is also no grand plan or overarching authority. For the time being in Russia, the purposes of Russian organized crime and its integral relationship with the state appear economic rather than ideological. However, new opportunities for plunder and chaos always arise. Members are continually being added to the network and events occur unrelentingly. Meanwhile, the tensions from a past era still linger and sometimes surface. To assume that the situation will remain static is to assume—wrongly—as the 2011 anticorruption protests can attest.

In the face of these protests, a man who had long been viewed as one of the chief architects of Vladimir Putin's political system resigned his post as Deputy Head of Administration. Vladislav Y. Surkov left office in late 2011 with the following *précis* of his professional achievements:

> I was among the people who helped President Yeltsin realize a peaceful transfer of power. I was among those who helped President Putin stabilize the political system. I was among those who helped President Medvedev liberalize it.[65]

However, when asked directly about the cause of his resignation he replied: "Stabilization devours its young." On the subject of his role in addressing the national dissent and his future, he waxed philosophically, albeit, with a hint of sarcasm: "I am too odious for this brave new world," he rejoined. Meanwhile, the ROC's access to the warehouse of Russia's wealth of raw and strategic materials could endanger our relative peace. One rogue exploit or group of entrepreneurial terrorists, motivated by whatever reason, could reset fears, strategies, and the requirements of the security infrastructure.

THE WESTERN CRIME-TERROR NEXUS

Linked into the Russian/Soviet connection is the Revolutionary Armed Forces of Colombia (FARC). Originally a Marxist-Leninist guerilla organization, it rose in defense of peasants' rights in 1964 and operated as the armed wing of the pro-Soviet Colombian Communist Party.[66] In addition to its connection with Russian organized crime, it also maintains contacts with Ukrainian, Croatian, Jordanian, and other armed groups in various countries from whom it attains weapons and communication equipment.[67] The FARC became a formidable guerilla force by the 1990s. A series of military successes gained it some political victories in the form of territories in 1998, which were ceded to them by the Colombian government (the government later attempted to retake the areas in 2002). With these victories, widespread support of the countryside, and a fighting force of nearly 17,000, FARC created "liberated zones," which it now maintains. These areas eventually became drug-producing regions. The drug trade, ostensibly, financed its cause to continue the Marxist struggle even beyond the end of the Soviet era.

Their Marxist revolution also employed such tactics as kidnapping, robbery, assassination, and the conscription of children.[68] As external aid subsided, the FARC's criminal operations increased. It is designated by the U.S. State Department as a Foreign Terrorist Organization (FTO). Yet, its narcotics operations may have eclipsed its terrorist pursuits.[69] According to the 2010 Congressional Research Service report, it forced farmers to grow coca in its territory, taxed harvesters and buyers of coca paste, collected protection money from laboratory processors, and leased airfields to traffickers.[70] The decline of the Cali and Medellin drug cartels created more opportunity for the FARC. By filling the void left by its rivals, estimates in 2000 suggest the FARC's revenues from illicit narcotics equaled $500 million annually.[71] The gains it made during its political struggle against the government provided their cause with 42,000 square kilometers of land in the Caqueta region. The settlement made the FARC a major player in the cocaine trade. It continues to claim it is a political organization while its interests are increasingly economic. Beyond its borders, the FARC formed trafficking networks with Mexican and Caribbean crime organizations. In exchange for its supplies the organization sometimes receives weapons in addition to cash.

The circuit of farming and harvesting, refinement, distribution, and profit extends into North America and back. The FARC is a model of a group with in-house capabilities, which combines criminal and terrorist resources. It is an example of the crime-terrorist nexus, discussed above, which conforms to the paradigm of a terrorist organization with an internal, institutionalized criminal structure. In addition to the FARCs revenues from the drug trade, its exploits into extortion and kidnapping yield as much profit as narcotics. It has gone as far as to form a special unit devoted to the taking of hostages.[72] The FARC seems to have struck an internal balance between crime and terrorism, and evidently, a Faustian bargain over its ideological purity. It is also not the only crime-terrorist organization in the region.

The National Liberation Army (ELN) has ideological roots similar to the FARC. More skewed toward Maoism and influenced by Cuba rather than the Soviet Union, the object of its wrath is the same—American imperialism. Also similar to the FARC is its history against the Colombian government. The ELN targets foreign businesses, particularly oil operations. Many nonpolitical operations parallel the crimes of its larger brethren organization, i.e., extortion, kidnapping, assassination, etc. Not as popular as the FARC (estimated strength approximated at around 3,000),[73] it reflects the same organizational model. It is a terrorist organization with an institutionalized criminal component actively engaged in the drug trade. In a telling incident regarding the interaction between Colombian crime and terrorist groups, the Medellin cartel allegedly hired the ELN in 1993 to set off a car bomb because the Medellin did not have the capability.[74] Today, the Medellin and Cali cartels are gone. The ELN and the FARC control much of the country-

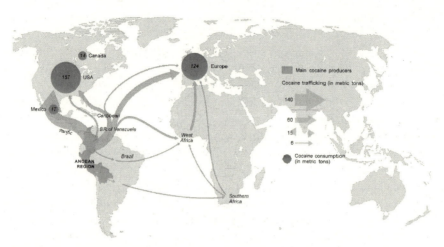

Map 9.2. Main Global Cocaine Flows, 2009 *(Source: UNOCD, World Drug Report 2011 (United Nations Publication, No. E.11.XI.10))*

side. The government struggles to reassert its authority after nearly collapsing a decade ago.

Sendero Luminoso—the Shining Path—is another Maoist-inspired group with Cold War roots and a story of renewal that owes its rejuvenation to illicit drug trafficking.[75,76] Its founder, Abimael Guzman, was a former university professor. Guzman's central thought revolved around a core philosophy, which included a mixture of Marxism, Maoism, and native Indian traditionalism of the Quechua-speaking and mestizo Peruvians.[77] Its methods were ruthless and it support was often forced.[78]

Guzman was captured in 1992 after a decade of terror. He renounced violence the year following his capture. Over five thousand of his followers accepted government amnesty. Over thirty thousand deaths is the estimate of lost lives in the struggle against the government over the people.[79] However, the terror did not end with Guzman's removal. The remnants retreated to the mountains. Their numbers were estimated to be a few hundred, yet the bloodshed persisted. By 2000, after two decades of carnage, the total brutality had claimed 70,000 lives. Today it continues, and cocaine is at the heart of the resurgence of rebel activity. A 2009 *New York Times* article reports:

> [Shining Path] has followed the much larger Colombian rebel group, the FARC, in melding a leftist insurgency with drug running and production. . . . The Shining Path, taking a page from Colombia's rebels, has reinvented itself as an illicit drug enterprise, rebuilding on the profits of Peru's thriving cocaine trade.[80]

The same article describes a criminal enterprise that produced 290 tons of cocaine in 2007 (the latest year of available data). Ninety percent of Peru's coca goes to cocaine production as the Shining Path employs approximately 500 laborers and 350 armed personnel.[81] Shining Path's combatant force is disciplined and well armed with Russian built equipment and transport vehicles. As with their counterparts in Central Asia, discussed above, they use their knowledge of the local terrain to their advantage. Without warning they can attack, dissever, and reform without detection. In their economic pursuits, they operate criminal smuggling businesses, extort taxes and protection fees from farmers, and operate cocaine laboratories. Despite the assertion that their numbers have dwindled significantly since the height of their popularity, Alberto Bolivar, a Senior Fellow at the Foreign Policy Research Institute, cautions:

> There are those who say, 'Why worry about a few hundred fighters in the jungle?' But they easily forget the Shining Path began their armed struggle in 1980 with just a few hundred guys. Two decades later, 70,000 people were dead.[82]

How might their numbers increase? How might the impact of criminal activity influence their recruitment efforts and organizational structure? These questions are pregnant with meaning for not only Peruvian officials, but also global security specialists. In the meantime, the forces of globalization will exert influence on economic and political life, and the nature and course of events. The crime-terrorist nexus might assume various forms and claim to espouse a mixture of ideological and strategic motives. The challenge is to combat an opponent, which is not quite known, and who might be an entity unrecognizable even unto itself.

In the meantime, while once fading Latin American terrorist groups resurge from their Cold War origins, the increasing cooperation between drug traffickers and Middle Eastern terrorists becomes a growing concern. The need for financing and the lure of the drug trade draws organizations such as al Qaeda and Hezbollah to the continent where, alongside the FARC, experts believe they have established training camps, recruiting centers, and networks of mutual assistance.[83] In a 2011 report by the Foreign Policy Research Institute, Vanessa Neumann writes that

> ungoverned areas, primarily in the Amazon regions of Suriname, Guyana, Venezuela, Colombia, Ecuador, Peru, Bolivia, and Brazil, present easily exploitable terrain over which to move people and material. The Free Trade Zones of Iquique, Chile; Maicao, Colombia; and Colon Panama, can generate undetected financial and logistical support for terrorist groups. Colombia, Bolivia, and Peru offer cocaine as a lucrative source of income. In addition, Cuba and Venezuela have cooperative agreement with Syria, Libya, and Iran.[84]

These territories have been a homeland for Egyptians, Syrians, Lebanese, and Palestinian refugees since the 1960s. The Muslim and Arab population in South America attracts Shi'a and Sunni from all corners bringing with them their traditions, businesses, and aspirations, as well as discontents, terrorists, and crime. Furthermore, the confluence of these groups with regional politics and economic life will have serious impact. Increasing official corruption, an expanding drug trade, the potential of the energy sector, and perhaps the influence of events occurring in the Arab world means U.S. policy makers might be wise to prepare for a strategic change in the hemisphere's security environment. In the twemty-first century, the price of poor governance is global. Due to globalization, it can be equally as costly to bear when its source is from abroad as might be the price if allowed to persist at home.

NOTES

1. John Wyler Rollins, Liana Sun, "International Terrorism and Transnational Crime, Security threats, U.S. Policy, and Considerations for Congress," Congressional Research Service, 2010, p. 31.

2. "Human Heads Dumped in Mexican Bar," BBC News, 7 September 2006.

3. *Op. cit.*

4. *Ibid.*

5. *Ibid.*, p. 7.

6. *Ibid.*

7. *Ibid.*

8. *The Taliban After Bin Laden*, "Newsweek" (23 and 30 May 2011), p. 44.

9. Reuters, 11 June 2008, http://www.reuters.com/article/2008/06/11/idUSN11301171.

10. Southers, Erroll—interview, April, 2001.

11. Louise Shelley, The Unholy Trinity: Transnational Crime, Corruption, and Terrorism, *Brown Journal of World Affairs*, 2005 (Winter/Spring 2005).

12. Rollins, p. 1.

13. Thomas M. Sanderson, "Transnational Terror and Organized Crime: Blurring the Lines," *SAIA Review*, vol. XXIV no. 1 (Winter-Spring 2004), p.49.

14. *Ibid.*

15. Peng Wang, "The Crime-Terror Nexus: Transformation, Alliance, Convergence," *Asian Social Science* (Vol. 6, no. 6, June 2010), p. 14.

16. *Ibid.*

17. Louise I. Shelley, *et al.*, "Methods and Motives: Exploring Links between Transnational Organized Crime and International Terrorism," *National Institute of Justice*, Office of Justice Programs, U.S. Department of Justice, June 23, 2005, p. 11.

18. *Ibid.*

19. *Ibid.*

20. Mary Kaldor, "Beyond Militarism, Arms Races, and Arms Control." Talk delivered at the Nobel Peace Prize Centennial Symposium, Oslo, Norway, 6 December 2001.

21. James, H. Mittelman, *The Globalization Syndrome* (Princeton University Press, 2000), p. 208.

22. Rollins, p. 8.

23. Mittelman, p. 213.

24. Tamara Makarenko, "The Crime-Terror Continuum: Tracing the Interplay between the Transnational Organized Crime and Terrorism," *Global Crime*, Vol. 6, No (1 February 2004), p. 136 .

25. *Ibid.*, p. 132.

26. Ralf Mutschke, "The Threat Posed by the Convergence of Organized Crime Drug Trafficking, and Terrorism," Testimony of Assistant Director, Criminal Intelligence Directorate, U.S. Congress, House Judiciary Committee, 106th Cong., 2nd sess. (13 December 2000).

27. Glen E. Curtis, "Involvement of Russian Organized Crime Syndicates, Criminal Elements in the Russian Military, and Regional Terrorists Groups in Narcotics Trafficking in Central Asia, the Caucasus, and Chechnya," Library of Congress, Federal Research Division (October 2002), p. 11.

28. *Ibid.*

29. Luke Falkenberg, "Trafficking Terror Through Tajikistan," *Military Review* (July-August 2013).

30. Phil Williams and Vanda Felbab-Brown, "Drug Trafficking Violence and Instability," U.S. Army War College, Strategic Studies Institute, Carlisle Barracks, PA (April 2012), p. 44.

31. Wang, p. 14.

32. According to a 2002 Library of Congress report, a $50 kilogram of raw opium in Afghanistan brought $10,000 in Moscow. A kilogram of heroin made from that opium cost $200,000 in New York and London. The same report claims the IMU began setting up heroin refining laboratories in Tajikistan in 2001.

33. Mark Burgess, "Islamic Movement of Uzbekistan (IMU)," *Terrorism Project*, Center for Defense Information (posted 25 March 2002), www.cdi.org.

34. UNODC, World Drug Report (2011), p. 53 sic, Luke Falkenberg, "Trafficking Terror through Tajikistan", Military Review, (July-August 2013)

35. Samantha Brietich, Central Asia: Hizb-ut-Tahrir on the Rise (8 August 2008), International Relations and Security Network
http://www.isn.ethz.ch/Digital-Library/Articles/Detail/?lng=en&id=88668.

36. Emmanuel Karagiannis, The new political Islam in central Asia: From radicalism to the ballot box? *The Brown Journal of World Affairs, 19*(1), 71–82 (2012). Retrieved from http://search.proquest.com/docview/1326331342?accountid=13626.

37. Michael Whine, "Is Hizb-ut-Tahrir Changing Strategy or Tactics?" *Center for Eurasian Policy Occasional Research Paper*, series I (Hizb-ut-Tahrir), No. 1.

38. Zeyno Baran, in "Hizb-ut-Tahrir in America," by Shiraz Maher, Hudson Institute, July 15, 2010.

39. Kyle Jarmon, "The Crime-Terrorist Nexus: The Chechen Example," posted April 15, 2010 on www.atlantic-community.org.

40. Mittelman, p. 215.

41. Nabi Abdullaev, "Chechnya's Organized Crime-Rebel Nexus," *International Relations and Security Network*, posted 2 April 2007, www.isn.ethz.ch.

42. John Arquilla and Theodore Karasik, "Chechnya: A Glimpse of Future Conflict?" in *Studies in Conflict and Terrorism*, Vol. 22, p. 224 (19 April 1999), p. 209.

43. Curtis, p. 23.

44. Curtis, pp. 8–9.

45. Sergei V. Golunov, *et al.*, "Drug Trafficking Along the Russian-Kazakh Border," in Russia's Battle with Crime, Corruption, and Terrorism, ed. Robert W. Orttung and Anthony Latta (Routledge, 2008), p. 52.

46. Falkenberg, p. 11.

47. *Ibid.*, p.14.

48. Yuriy Spirin, "Heroin Heroes," report of Stringer News Agency, February 12, 2002.

49. Ariel Cohen, and John, P. Sweeney, *International Crime,* Heritage Foundation (1999), p. 548.

50. Golunov, p. 67.

51. Alexander Salageav, Alexander Shashkin, Alexey Konnov, "One Hand Washes the Other," in Orttung.

52. Curtis, p. 24.

53. James O. Finckenauer, Yuri A. Voronin, "The Threat of Russian Organized Crime, U.S. Department of Justice, Office of Justice Programs" (National Institute of Justice, 2001), p. 1.

54. Finckenauer, p. 4.

55. Federico Varese, *The Russian Mafia: Private Protection in a New Market Economy* (Oxford University Press, 2001), pp. 146–47.

56. Stephen Handelman, *Comrade Criminal* (Yale University Press, 1995), p. 30.

57. *Ibid.*, pp. 167–69.

58. Finckenauer, p. 6.

59. Handelman, p. 98.

60. Finckenauer, p. 20.

61. Handelman., p. 107.

62. Finckenauer p. 24.

63. Mark Cohen, presentation on *Convergent Risks to Business and Government*, University of Pennsylvania symposium (21 April 2010).

64. Finckenauer, p. 6.

65. Ellen Barry, "Architect of Putin's Political System Is Reassigned," *The New York Times*, 27 December 2011.

66. Gus Martin, Understanding Terrorism: Challenges, Perspectives, and Issues (Sage Publications, 2003), p. 145.

67. Rollins, p. 10.

68. Martin, p. 145.

69. Rollins, p. 17.

70. *Ibid.*

71. Makarenko, p. 137.

72. Rollins, p. 18.

73. Martin, p. 145.

74. Markarenko, p. 131.

75. Global Security (posted 2006), http://www.globalsecurity.org/military/world/para/sendero_luminoso.htm.

76. Simon Romero, "Cocaine Trade Helps Rebels Reignite War in Peru," *The New York Times* (17 March 2009).

77. Martin, p. 146.

78. *Ibid.*

79. *Ibid.*

80. Romero.

81. *Ibid.*

82. *Ibid.*

83. Vanessa Neumann, "The New Nexus of Narcoterrorism: Hezzbollah and Venezuela," *Foreign Policy Research Institute* (December 2011).

84. *Ibid.*

Chapter Ten

Building a Global Network

Some of them [Chinese criminal gangs] are good and patriotic.
—Deng Xiaoping, Chairman of the Communist Party of China, 1984

THE TRI-BORDER AREA (TBA)

In the border territories where Argentina, Brazil, and Paraguay intersect is Iguassu Falls. It is a natural wonder of 275 cascades that converge to form a horseshoe out of the landscape and create a splendor that attracts tourists from around the world. The same area offers an even greater allure for terrorists and criminals seeking a haven in which they can conduct business, recruit, raise and launder funds, and plot. Known as simply the Tri-Border Area (TBA), the region's beginnings as a center for lawlessness date to the early 1970s when Brazil and Argentina established a free trade zone to take advantage of the falls' potential as an energy producing facility and tourist attraction. What evolved was a hive of illegal activity for terrorists and criminals whose operations corrupt officials shelter and lubricate. A 2003 Federal Research Division Report of the Library of Congress describes the area as: "In effect, a mutually beneficial nexus among these three actors [official corruption, organized crime, and terrorist groups]." It also adds that: "The TBA serves as a microcosm for examining this relationship."[1] In agreement with the above estimate, a report published by the U.S. Department of Justice reads:

In sum, for the investigator or analyst seeking examples of perfect conditions for such cooperation [between terror and organized crime], the Tri-Border Area is an obvious choice.[2]

187

The area is accessible by sea and has an adequate outlet into the Atlantic large enough to accommodate small and medium cargo vessels. Three population centers serve as hubs. Puerto Iguazu in Argentina, Foz do Iguacu, Brazil, and the Paraguayan city of Ciudad del Este provide the region with modern communication, transportation, and banking services. Porous borders and a network of over a hundred hidden airstrips contribute to the underground infrastructure.[3,4] The area is a melting pot of crime, terrorism, and corruption. Extremists and criminals assemble and collude from all corners of the world. It is a geographical space where transnational crime and terrorism can converge and operate—not only at plying their crafts but also in deploying the machinery of the global economy.[5]

Forty thousand people cross the bridge between Ciudad del Este and Foz do Iguacu, undocumented, unchecked, and on a daily basis. Ciudad del Este teems with over five thousand businesses that are ideal for illegal transactions.[6] With a population of approximately 320,000, the city ranks only behind Hong Kong and Miami in volume of cash transactions. In addition to local and other South American organizations, the TBA includes syndicates and cells from Chile, China, Colombia, Corsica, Ghana, Libya, Ivory Coast, Japan, Korea, Lebanon, Nigeria, Russia, and Taiwan.[7] The range of criminality is the same as elsewhere. The litany of obstacles that effective law en-

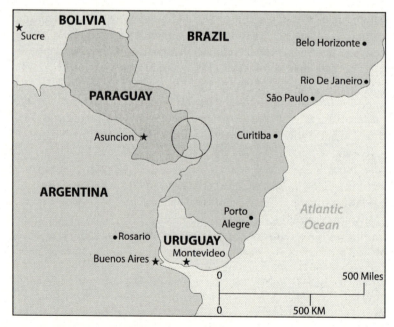

Map 10.1. Tri-Border Area of Argentina, Brazil, and Paraguay *(Source: Library of Congress, Federal Research Division, July 2003)*

forcement faces is also the same: inadequate training, poor equipment, lack of vigorous public support, and low pay, which fosters endemic profiteering by officials. In the TBA the symbiotic relationship among crime, terrorism, and official corruption is one of the most arrant examples of systemic lawlessness on the planet. The degenerate security infrastructure is a magnet for these elements and a locus of human rights violations as well.

The 2003 Federal Research Report claims that Islamic fundamentalist groups in the TBA and other similar places in Latin America send between US$300 million and US$500 million a year in profits to radical groups in the Middle East. The sources of these profits come from illegal drug sales, arms dealing, smuggling, money laundering, and product piracy. The report continues to say that al Qaeda and Hezbollah have had a presence in this "microcosm" for over a decade. They have established networks among the sizable Islamic community and despite the schism between the Sunni and Shi'ite sects the philosophical orientations appear (at least temporarily) to have been put aside for the benefits of a strategic alliance.[8] Al Qaeda's activities also included money laundering, arms, drugs, and even uranium trafficking. Chinese and Russian (Chechen) mafias are involved as associates.[9]

The TBA is host to between 20,000 and 60,000 ethnic Arabs (six million was the estimate total of Muslims living in Latin American cities in 2005[10]). The community's beginnings in South America link to the upheaval of the Lebanese civil war that began in 1975 and continued through 1990.[11] During that time their diaspora grew and took root as the instability in the Middle East forced immigration. Because of the frail security framework, the population soon became susceptible to extortion and their home a sanctuary for extremists.[12] Other Islamic terrorist groups include the Egyptian Al-Jihad, Al-Gama'a al-Islamiyya, and Hamas.

While the TBA remains a destination for fugitives and the address of fronts for raising, laundering, and transmitting funds to extremist causes abroad, Islamic terrorist activities within the TBA seem to be limited to assassinations against those who oppose their interests. In the past several years reports claim the population and incidences of illegal activity are swelling. Many assume Islamic terrorist groups have moved into other regions in Venezuela, Uruguay, and Chile. The increased activity and response to a limited success of law enforcement countermeasures has given reason for some experts to contend that a "second tri-border area" was developing between Brazil, Bolivia, and Peru to alleviate the pressure from security forces and accommodate the overflow from the migration of Muslim communities and the attendant Islamic extremist groups.[13]

Meanwhile, money laundering continues to be a major enterprise among crime-terrorism collaborators. A sum equal to almost 50 percent of Paraguay's gross domestic product—$5 billion—is laundered every year from Ciudad del Este alone.[14] Brazilian officials assert over $6 billion as the total amount of money laundered in the TBA.[15] The sources of these funds come from fraud, tax evasion, trade in contraband, arms and drug trafficking, and overt assaults. The diaspora community from the Middle East is a means for conveyance in the transmittal and remittal of assets to and from Islamic states in Asia and Africa.

Collaboration is not only between Islamic communities but also between mixed ethnic groups with mutual interests. Reports tell of arrangements between Hezbollah, Hong Kong triads, Chechen groups, and Chinese mafia. Furthermore, few members of the non-indigenous communities are legally registered. Their comings and goings can be undetected, and efforts to interdict and extradite are easily thwarted. Corruption in the Immigrations Department is at the source of this serious problem according to ministerial officials.[16] In fact, official corruption is so cemented in the structure, process, and criminal pattern within the TBA, that the Drug Trafficking Investigating Commission of Brazil's Congress concluded that only a complete restructuring and rearming of the police might address the problems. The report also calls for intervention by the military.[17]

As the Lebanese, Irish, Chechen, and scores of other examples can attest, conflict zones not only breed instability and hatred between opposing groups, but can also export tensions and violence to other regions. The past accompanies the migration of diaspora communities as does language, customs, shared narratives, and old enmities. Traditions of criminality and separation of ethnic groups from the larger society also produce patterns for criminal-terrorist behavior.[18] However, the incentive and rationale for a crime-terrorist nexus may exist regardless of national origins or places of citizenship. Conditions for collaboration will survive as long as kindred interests and opportunities abide. As always, where the state and the security infrastructure are weak, crime and terrorism will fill the void. As in the instance of the TBA the de-bordering of crime, identity, and allegiance can converge with commerce to create marriages of convenience.

In one noted case of crime and terrorism "without borders" the investigations surrounding a Hong Kong businessman, who was an Indian citizen, uncovered an elaborate plot to filter funds to fundamentalist organizations in the Middle East. Rajkumar Naraindas Sabnani was suspected of transferring profits from the sales of pirated products from the Pacific Rim. Orders for weapons, authorization to use US$30 million for the transaction, and a stash of bomb-making material were found in his possession while he was under house arrest in Ciudad del Este for money laundering and tax evasion. Sabnani reportedly was sending US$200,000 per day to the Hezballah's chief of military operations, Assad Ahmad Barakat.[19] A 2005 Department of Justice report also refers to Barakat as a "Hezbollah financier."[20] He is a local businessman and part owner of The Galeria Page shopping mall in Ciudad del Este. Investigations of the 1992 bombing outside the Israeli embassy in

Buenos Aires and a 1994 car bomb attack on the Jewish-Argentine community center implicated the mall as a front for operations. In all, these two incidents took the lives of 116 people and resulted in hundreds of injuries. These cases offer some evidence that cooperation between crime and terrorism can be transnational and the use of violence, corruption, and illegal methods is not restricted by culture or organizational structures or goals.

These cases also suggest that the nexus between Chinese criminal organizations and Middle East terrorists might be something more than an *ad hoc* relationship. The link between Hezbollah and Hong Kong based crime groups is "clear" according to the DoJ report. Another report on transnational Chinese crime claims that international intelligence agencies describe the relationship between Chinese criminal groups and the pro-Iranian Hezbollah as being "strong."[21] Proceeds from the sales of pirated software and music albums manufactured in the Rim countries have been finding their way into the coffers of Hezbollah for years.[22] From that point they may transit to anywhere in the world.

Other extremist Islamic groups having dealings with Hong Kong criminal organizations include Hamas and Gamaa Islamiya. In some cases the transactions involved munitions rather than consumer products. A frequently cited example involves a transaction between Gamaa Islamiya and a Chinese crime family Sung-I. Labeling the shipment as medical equipment, the Sung-I attempted to transfer arms and munitions to Gamaa Islamiya. In a separate arrangement another Chinese crime organization, the Ming, manages Gamaa Islamiya funds via a financial circuit that passes through Guyana and the Cayman Islands.[23]

There has been a strong surge in Chinese immigration into Paraguay and the TBA since the 1980s. A large Cantonese population of nearly thirty thousand has insinuated itself into the Ciudad del Este community and provides excellent cover for crime groups.[24] These criminal elements feed off the local Chinese community and their businesses. They are well established, run large-scale smuggling and protection operations, and believed by some to be the main criminal force in the TBA. As described below, their business plan is basic:

> The Chinese groups specialize in providing "protection" to the local Chinese people and imposing "taxes" on the containers imported by the Chinese businesses from Asia. When the groups import goods directly from Asia, the Chinese business community is obliged to purchase that merchandize, or suffer the consequences of not doing so. In this way, the criminal groups gain monopoly control over the import of particular types of merchandise.[25]

Many outlaw groups use the TBA as a station for illegal trade in small arms, drugs, counterfeit goods, and human trafficking that includes immigrants, minors, and prostitution. The Chinese triads are involved deeply. The most active ones in the TBA go by names such as Sun Yee On (New Righteous-ness), Big Circle Boys, Flying Dragons, and Fuk Ching. Triads represent a criminal culture with roots, which date back over centuries of Chinese histo-ry. Their network spans the globe and their operations in the TBA represent a major outpost.

Because of a failure to adjust traditional perspectives on organized crime and terrorism, law enforcement and the national security establishment sometimes locks into a mindset of an earlier system of governance, proto-cols, and jurisdictional and philosophical boundaries. The old assumptions about the organizational nature of organized crime and terrorism also inhibit prosecution. The large-scale, pyramidal structures of a previous era rarely exist in today's underworld. However, security and law enforcement agen-cies are often most comfortable working against a rival whose structure mirrors their own. Adding to the disorder is the obsolescence and uncoordi-nated arrangement of international legal codes. Although transnational, the decision-making process is highly decentralized. Rather than operational units in the service of some grand strategy or acting on orders from a remote headquarters, criminal and terrorist groups are mostly entrepreneurial. They are best viewed as simply a range of actors responding to market forces or local political opportunities—acting semi-autonomously or autonomously.

The forces of globalization, persistent hatred, and an environment of eco-nomic and democratic deficits have created a new security threat. While the nation-state still dominates, the above elements have not only created a new arena of conflict on the interstate level, but also opened up a front involving non-state actors that is rapidly becoming non-asymmetric. The TBA, Chech-nya, parts of southeastern Europe, and the border areas around Central Asia are geographic spaces where crime, terrorism, and corruption can not only nest and operate, but also expand and export their pestilence. As mentioned above, areas such as these can become microcosms for further analysis. To use a simple metaphor—understanding the origins of a disease by observing such factors as organization, milieu, and behavior within populations helps to anticipate its outbreak and track its transmission. Minus those reflections, a treatment will be hard to foresee.

> . . . it is not inconceivable that the major global divide will be caused not by
> competing ideologies, the struggle for power . . . but by clashes between states
> that uphold law and order and those that are dominated by criminal interests
> and criminal authorities.

Recalling Phil Williams's words, which introduced this chapter, his com-ments may unveil to us an emerging paradigm whose threat exceeds our current security structure and mindset. As we assess the dynamic taking place in the TBA, we should consider the changing orientation of the security threat posed by the potential of crime-terrorist nexus and its increasing ability to occupy organs within the state, legitimate society, geographic territory, and daily life.

THE CHINESE TRIADS

Secret societies have long been a part of the larger tradition of Chinese culture and history. Legend holds that the secret societies known as triads first appeared as organizations founded by monks and scholars with political and patriotic objectives.[26,27] Most place their origins at the seventeenth century during the attempt to overthrow the Qing Dynasty; others trace the triads' beginnings back as far as the twelfth century. The dates and exact inspirations for their emergence are obscured by time and lore, but their presence today is worldwide and their impact is undeniable. Not all triads evolved into criminal gangs. However, the ones who did are prime movers of contraband trade throughout the world and their force is dynamic.

Triads have a history as having roles in political movements, labor associations, and as aid organizations serving Chinese communities in hostile environments.[28,29] Despite these examples of activism, they are known mostly (and more accurately) as criminal gangs. Loosely connected and lacking any hierarchical command structure, triads accompanied the Chinese diaspora over time and territory. They insinuated themselves as neighborhood gangs at the local school level, took on roles as protection forces of Chinese-owned businesses, and ultimately became predatory transnational crime organizations with global reach. Their association with official corruption is well documented within the PRC and abroad.

When the Communist Party took control of the mainland in 1949, many triad members fled to Hong Kong and established a major base for criminal operations. Once the former British colony was united with the PRC, many believed these groups would disperse. However, Bertil Lintner writes in *Global Crime* that it was the reverse, which was the actual case.

> Not only did the Hong Kong Triads make arrangements with the territory's new overlords, but in Chinatowns all over the world, close links were also forged with mainland Chinese interests. In China, itself, where "cutthroat capitalism"' has replaced the old austere socialist system, new secret societies, both Triad-linked criminal groups and various syncretic sects, are expanding at a breathtaking pace.[30]

The end of the Cold War era and the ascent of the global economy opened China to the world, and on a lesser scale, the ruling Communist Party to opportunities for further corruption. The freedoms also created ideal circumstances for crime and corruption to merge more adeptly. The term *baohu-*

sang, or "protective umbrella," refers to a government official who offers cover and protection for criminals and their operations in exchange for bribes. The term is not a recent one. Even Mao Zedong reportedly had close criminal associates to help him finance and attain political goals.[31] Sun Yat-sen and Chiang Kai-shek also had underworld connections.[32] The father of China's economic reforms, Deng Xiaoping, once declared in 1984 that "some of them [triad members] were good and patriotic."[33] Deng may have overstated his case. At one point collusion between state officials and criminal elements became so intertwined that the CPC even feared a loss of control. The shift to a market economy proved too inviting for "artful opportunists" and eventually required the government to institute a campaign against rampant crime in the 1990s.

Lintner's account of the details of a corruption scandal in 2000[34] illustrate how the boundaries between crime and officialdom often blur. Reportedly, an influential businessman on the mainland across the Taiwan Straight used connections within the Communist Party of China (CPC) in an attempt to build a smuggling empire. Lai Changxing's plans, which went awry, included the trade of crude oil, cars, electronic equipment, rubber, appliances, tobacco, etc. Having escaped a conviction and sentencing by fleeing to Canada, Lai told reporters that China had a network of spies in North America planted to steal industrial and military secrets. Many regarded this as a ploy to gain special treatment and escape extradition rather than the statements by an insider with connections in the People's Liberation Army. However, his knowledge of intelligence operations proved more precise than false. Lai's accusations were found to be very similar to an earlier investigation, which the Canadian intelligence services uncovered. "Sidewinder" was an alleged operation involving the Chinese businessmen, their criminal counterparts, and PRC intelligence agencies. The basis for the allegations gained traction when FBI agents in New Jersey arrested three Chinese-born scientists on charges of corporate espionage. They were accused of stealing software from Lucent Technologies in order to help create a joint venture with a Chinese data-network supplier. Most marriages between official corruption and triads do not end in an ugly separation, as did Lai's. The new economic era of market reforms offered triads an important and, perhaps, an elevated place in the new order. One report claims that according to Taiwanese officials one-third of local politicians are gangsters. In the Jilin Province on the mainland, the mayor of the city of Meihekuo, Tian Bo, was bold enough to say: "During the daytime, someone else is the mayor. At night I am the mayor . . . in this city, I am more effective than the mayor or the police chief, and that's because I can deal with people from both the ordinary world and the underworld."[35]

In China, as in Russia and to a degree in Western countries, the relationship between the state and crime can be simultaneously in consort and conflictual. The addition of failed states and terrorism create a labyrinthine array of questions concerning legitimacy and claims of authority. Pressures from above in the form of national policy and grand strategies clash with life on the ground. As James Mittelman noted, globalization in its spasmodic complexity

> problematizes the border between "legal" and "illegal" by positing a space between the state and nascent civil society filled by the "covert world": intelligence services, organized crime, terrorist groups, the arms trade, money-laundering banks, hermetic religious cults, and secret societies. [36]

A result of the changing order has been the acknowledgment by many that transnational crime is now evolving as the most serious security challenge. The additive of political terrorism could raise the potency of the crime-terrorist formula to a level beyond the capacity of state-based agencies and current countermeasures. Triads offer only a single glimpse at the problem. The full picture of the challenge is far more Byzantine, and perhaps even inscrutable. When we consider the range of scrambled variables and the competitive and complementary forces simultaneously at play a complicated specter appears. As criminals and terrorists find homes in legitimate commerce, sovereign domains, and under the protection of official auspice their prospects will increase—as will the price of dislodging them. The monopolies that were the exclusion of the state, might ultimately be ceded or expropriated.

GLOBALIZATION OF CRIME AND TERROR

Many population segments are not only vulnerable to poverty, but poverty as a result of economic globalization policies from above, such as structural adjustment programs, privatization strategies, and other IMF and World Bank imposed reform projects. The debt trap now being experienced by the developing world has unleashed global migration on a mass scale. Today, many aid recipient nations pay more than 50 percent of government revenues toward debt service. The onerous financial liability has led to bankruptcy, unemployment, and poverty and has forced many in the developing world to seek opportunity in developed countries. [37] It has become a win-win situation for organized crime and terrorism. Drug trafficking, human trafficking and prostitution have become more lucrative as the demand and labor pool grows, and less risky as concerns for economic accountability wither away.

The challenges from communities who strive to regain the resources needed to survive in their environment and retake the decision-making process offer crime and terrorism an instinctual and convenient outlet for plunder. In the instances of failed states where the security apparatus and infrastructure have malfunctioned or collapsed, the void has opened a breach in the system for advantage taking by criminal elements. Rather than pay taxes to guarantee safety and equity, citizens pay protection money and rely on the black market as an alternative allocative mechanism for goods and services. Additionally, criminal groups exploit marginalized populations as prey and as a source of labor. *Kryshi* and *baohusang* thrive on these conditions to further their interests and erode the rule of law.

As noted earlier, the recent international development has ushered in a realignment of post-Cold War power relations and set into motion a shift in the arena of conflict defined by advancements in technology. In this information-based arena enemies are not as identifiable and can be asymmetric. Lawful society now faces a more uncertain environment, where bides a host of new threats as a result of a hyper-connectivity of populations and systems. The end of old power alignments, the emergence of neo-liberal trade policies, and the impact of technology have unleashed powerful forces. How to transform notions about law enforcement and national security and reinvent policies and institutions into a new security framework will be the challenge.

In assessing some options it might be wise to consider three areas of cooperation. Although these offerings are more heuristic assumptions rather than proven methods, they are, hopefully, at least grist for debate. First, there should be a simple and straightforward commitment to security. Since over 85 percent of the infrastructure is in private hands, the onus obviously falls on the back of private enterprise to protect these assets. With regard to this item, there are both obstacles to cooperation and precedents for success.

Corporate strategy groups might no longer afford to view security operations as cost center items. Rather, they are strategic investments and another cost of doing business. This is not only true for the individual firm, but also for venders and service providers who comprise the extended supply chain. The first and last mile of the supply chain are the most vulnerable and under the most economic and financial pressure to implement security countermeasures. Therefore, facilitating the choice to invest in security without sacrificing trade and commerce must be addressed in a way that neutralizes cost or competitive disadvantages for the investor of an effective security regime. Despite increased overheads, the fear of compromising competitive, market information, and the threat to unfettered trade, these commitments will most likely have to be made across a broad landscape. Government can offer assistance, if not in the form of direct subsidy then perhaps through fiscal policies that provide tax incentives. A solution might lie with some combination of policy mechanisms, which simultaneously match the differing circumstances of global corporations and small to medium size enterprises (SMEs).

Several U.S. government and UN programs, discussed earlier, are already addressing this issue. The U.S. Customs Border Protection (CBP) agency's

Customs-Trade Partnership Against Terrorism (C-TPAT) program was an example. The program nests within a layered defense strategy that enlists the cooperation of members in the private sector trade community to achieve the twin goals of security and frictionless trade. By enrolling in the program and agreeing to C-TPAT security measures and standards, companies receive benefits. As certified participants, companies enjoy the advantages of reduced inspections and shorter delay times of U.S.-bound shipments.[38] It hinges its success on the notion that the "trusted shipper" will act in the best interests of itself and a secure global supply chain. As compliant traders, these private-sector actors will theoretically build an efficient supply chain to better secure and manage private and public infrastructure assets in return for privileges and benefits. Initial critics of C-TPAT complained the program was ineffective because it was voluntary and conceived as a way for the shipping trade to avoid government regulation following 9/11. It was also under-funded and under-staffed, which limited the ability to ensure the integrity of certification and validation processes (many early certifications were based on an honor system of compliance reporting). However, despite these and other flaws, most agree the concept of the trusted shipper is the correct path toward a security framework that serves security and commerce.

The World Customs Organization established the Framework of Standards to Secure and Facilitate Global Trade (SAFE Framework), which extends C-TPAT and other CBP programs beyond the sphere of U.S.-bound trade. One of the primary objectives of SAFE is to foster closer cooperation among national and regional customs administrations by integrating supply chain management of transport nodes. According to its literature, SAFE Framework rests upon its twin "pillars" of (1) customs-to-customs network arrangements and (2) customs-to-business partnerships.[39] It is also a demonstration of how an effort of cooperation might extend beyond national borders and result in some success as well as a step toward some sort of governance over the anarchic realm and global good—the world's maritime supply chain.

Cyberspace, similar to the global supply chain, shares the same properties and, thus, the same language to express its nature and the challenges for its security. Vast, anarchic, and dense, there is no consensus on what constitutes a criminal act and what can be regarded as an act of war amid these uncharted oceans of data, confluences of authority, and army of actors. Inference and evidence are the component parts of attribution. Problems such as collective security persist, not only between national borders but also stakeholders segregated by corporate or parochial interests. Aside from isolated efforts at self-regulation there is little indication that a serious ambition is underway on a global scale to even define cyber crime let alone establish a political framework for cyber arms control.

Second, therefore, state-to-state cooperation is required if the spread of transnational crime is to be controlled. Despite some instances such as the agreement between C-TPAT and SAFE, examples of interoperability and universally accepted policy are scant. The jurisdictional voids discussed above are being filled through treaties and conventions that reduce the number of safe havens that these organizations exploit and depend upon for their existence. A broader span of jurisdiction might result. This means agreement by states to observe and enforce a body of standards and norms by which national regulatory and law enforcement agencies can operate. The definition of "criminal" must be consistent and convergent on a more global scale. Procedural laws such as search and seizure, rules of evidence, and electronic eavesdropping must be reappraised to reflect the times and technologies that define our daily life.

The G-7 Financial Action Trade Force (FATF) is an outcome of such an effort. This initiative, launched in 2000, is an attempt to set norms that aid governments and financial institutions to develop anti-money laundering and transparency laws on the national level. Regulatory, legislative, and law enforcement mechanisms would synchronize with mutual legal assistance treaties (MLAT) to heighten and equalize risks for transnational crime across jurisdictions. It also serves to facilitate investigations as well as extraditions.

Another example of cooperation is in the oil industry. Despite their intense competitiveness, oil companies have established information sharing arrangements and close working relationships with the law enforcement community.[40] In order to succeed in minimizing infiltration and exfiltration of organized crime elements, these companies and government agencies have created a bond of mutual trust that allows them to partner successfully in the war on transnational crime and terrorism. Not only are the structures of cooperation a breakthrough, but also is the organizational spirit of commitment.

Adding to the difficulties of standardizing appropriate responses to threats, subject matter experts from every technical niche invent terms and buzzwords to describe their perception of the environment. Therefore, not only absent is a common framework for ethics and values in establishing and enforcing laws, but also a standardization for language. The "terminological inconsistency"[41] of politicians, lawyers, military experts, computer scientists, network operators, law enforcement, and the public create barriers to interoperability and deter analysts and policy makers from all disciplines and competing interests from working together outside their individual comfort zones. Hopefully, through earnest interaction we can generalize the discourse and keep the technologists (legal, political, and scientific) from hi-jacking the discussion and debate via a parlance based upon a specific specialty.

CONCLUSION

There has been much mentioned in this discussion of neoliberal economic policy. Technology and free, unfettered markets have combined to unleash powerful forces and unprecedented amassing of wealth. The result has been a process we call economic globalization. However, the faith in the market implied by neoliberalism must assume a level playing field where competition thrives, information is perfect, and property rights are clearly established and enforced. Without these assumptions Adam Smith's "invisible hand" is not efficient, let alone perfect. Furthermore, the corruption, crony capitalism, cutthroat capitalism, and rent-seeking activities that have emerged out of the chaos of transition economies and the developing world provide the criminal world with laboratories, proving grounds, and fields of operation where they can practice their craft and test the limits of the system they intend to exploit. In a world where market forces are politically unaccountable, crime will prosper, and its linkage to organizing social structures will be organic. The shortcomings of global economic policies are vast, structures of global governance are in the formative phases, the role of the state is in transformation, and the chasm between the rich and poor is widening and deepening. At the same time, technology is driving the process forward at a breathtaking pace. Under these conditions, the prospects for transnational crime and terrorism seem bright. The linkage between national security and human security is drawing tighter. Populations will expand, trade will increase, and human migration is gaining in velocity. Unless policy makers can focus their resources and resolve on reversing or amending some of the above economic trends, the major global divide between lawful and non-law-abiding states of which Phil Williams warns may be an ultimate consequence.

As the world becomes a more violent place, as the democratic deficit grows beside the imperatives of global commerce, then, the emergence of multinational firms, the creation of trading blocs, the implementation of privatization programs, the rise of civil society, the unbundling of borders will all contribute to the momentum and, wittingly or unwittingly, the politicalization of transnational crime. Terrorism can provide the amalgam with ideological justification, material, and logistical and personnel support. If this continues to occur, circumstances may force security establishments to reassess not only their infrastructures, but also the once popular assumptions about governance and the institutions that provide its structure. Relying upon preconceived accepted wisdoms while disregarding or denying contradictory signs while trying to navigate the uncharted seas where crime and terrorism now flow and perhaps meet would be like, as Coleridge wrote, "a lantern on the stern, which shines only on the waves behind us."

NOTES

1. Rex Hudson, "Terrorist and Organized Crime Groups in the Tri-Border Area (TBA) of South America," Library of Congress, Federal Research Division (July 2003), p. 6.
2. Louise I. Shelley, *et al.*, "Methods and Motives," p. 64.
3. *Ibid.*
4. Mark Steinitz, "Middle East Terrorist Activity in Latin America," Policy Paper on the Americas, Center for Strategic and International Studies (July 2003), p. 8.
5. The Paraguayan President, Julius Stroessner, was an original promoter and developer of the project. Stroessner, himself, is suspected of being involved in drug trafficking operations. He is often credited with turning the TBA into a haven for fugitives. Such individuals include the Nazi war criminal Josef Mengele as a former resident.
6. Shelley "Methods and Motives," p. 60.
7. *Op. cit.*, p. 3.
8. *Ibid.*, p. 2.
9. *Ibid.*
10. Vanessa Neumann, "The New Nexus of Narcoterrorism: Hezzbollah and Venezuela," *Foreign Policy Research Institute* (December 2011).
11. Steinitz, p. 8.
12. Shelley, p. 60.
13. Hudson, p. 69.
14. *Ibid.*, p. 53.
15. *Ibid.*, p. 27.
16. *Ibid.*, 67.
17. *Ibid.*, p. 48.
18. Shelley, p. 43.
19. *Ibid.*, p. 78.
20. *Ibid.*, p. 63.
21. "Transnational Activities of Chinese Crime Organizations," Federal Research Division of the Library of Congress (April 2003), p. 22.
22. *Ibid.*, p. 62.
23. *Op. cit.*, p. 23.
24. *Ibid.*
25. *Ibid.*, p. 22.
26. Rose, M. Miller, "The Threat of Transnational Crime in East Asia" (U.S. Army War College, Carlisle Barracks, PA, March 2002), p. 8.
27. Bertil Linter, "Chinese Organized Crime," *Global Crime*, Vol. 6, No 1 (February 2004), p. 87.
28. *Ibid.*
29. Miller, p. 8.
30. *Op. cit.*, p. 85.
31. *Ibid.*, p. 7.
32. Ko-Lin Chin, and Gordon, Roy Godson, "Organized Crime and the Political-Criminal Nexus in China," *Trends in Organized Crime*, Vol. 9, No. 3 (Spring 2006), p. 6.
33. Linter, p. 90.
34. Miller.
35. Chin, p. 10.
36. James H. Mittelman, *The Globalization Syndrome* (Princeton University Press, 2000), p. 204–205.
37. Saskia Sassen, "Global Cities and Survival Circuits," in Barbara Ehrenreich and Arlie Russell Hochschild (Ed.), *Global Women: Nannies, Maids, and Sex Workers in the New Economy* (Henry Holt & Co., New York, 2003), p. 266–67.
38. "Customs-Trade Partnership Against Terrorism (C-TPAT) Strategic Plan" (U.S Border Customs Protection, Washington, DC, 2004).
39. *The WCO's Framework of Standards to Secure and Facilitate Global Trade* (24 June 2005), http://www.wcomd.org.

40. Phil Williams, "Organized Crime and Cybercrime, Synergies, Trends, and Responses," Global Issues (U.S. Information Agency, 2001).

41. Paul Cornish, David Livingston, Dave Clemente, Claire Yorke, "On Cyber War" (Chatham House Report, November 2010), p. 36.

Chapter Eleven

Chemical Biological Radiological & Nuclear: The Chemical Threat

French soldiers blinded, coughing, chests heaving, faces an ugly purple color, lips speechless with agony, and behind them the gas-soaked trenches, we learned they had left hundreds of dead and dying comrades. It was the most fiendish and wicked thing I had ever seen.
Description of German chlorine gas attack at Ypres, April 22, 1915.

—O. S. Watkins

The history of chemical agents in warfare is ancient. The annals of Egyptian, Babylonian, Indian, Chinese, and Greek civilizations contain accounts of plant poisons' use in battle to induce nausea, choking, sleep, and also blindness. "Greek fire" broke the Muslim siege of Constantinople in 677. The concoction of resin, pitch, sulfur, naphtha, quicklime, and saltpeter ignited on impact with the water surface and burned enemy ships. The weapon allowed the Byzantine navy to dominate the seas and the empire to rule for years.[1] Renaissance armies employed incendiary shells and toxic smoke projectiles during sieges, for use as smoke screens, against navies, and to attack water and food supplies. Chemical weapons also found their way to the Americas, possibly, against the English colonists by their empire-building Spanish rivals. During the American Civil War the offices of the Union forces were flooded with proposals and suggestions for the use of chemical weapons, primarily, chlorine bombs and chloroform gas sprays. Whether for humanitarian reasons or practical concerns, the U.S. Secretary of War, Edwin Stanton, dismissed the submissions.[2] However, in World War I the German and French armies and, eventually, the British, revived such tactics with vigor and investment in research programs and weapons factories. Chlorine gas was the principal weapon, but an arms race soon accelerated and the combatant forces rushed to mobilize phosgene, cyanide chloride, diphosgene, and mustard agents to enhance their attack effort.

The effectiveness of these chemical weapons (CW) was unpredictable, outcomes were often times doubtful or adverse, and the consequences were terrible. Regardless of whichever the results, the impact of these weapons was both devastating and demoralizing. Internal and external blistering, pulmonary failure, influenza, and panic ensued on both sides of the battle lines. The onslaught to dislodge the opposing combatants in trench warfare was merciless during World War I. Yet, according to one German general, in view of the high goals at stake, despite the repugnance—any personal revulsion to the use of chemical weapons against the enemy "had to be silenced."[3]

France initiated chemical warfare, but Germany intensified the arms competition through the momentum of its advantages in the dye and chemical industry. The main figures of science in this warfare were Francois Auguste Victor Grignard, a Frenchman, and Germans Walther Hermann Nernst and Fritz Haber.[4] There was an ironic twist to their careers in the years following the war. All three scientists won Nobel Prizes in chemistry. Haber's fortunes later declined, however, when he became a victim of anti-Semitic Nazi policies during World War II and eventually died in exile.

The French, British, and Germans exchanged barrages of hydrogen cyanide, chlorine gas, phosgene, chloropicrin, and mustard agents by tens of thousands of tons. At the end of World War I, more than 100,000 deaths resulted from the use of chemical weapons.[5] Revulsion to their use forced a ban on chemical weapons at the Geneva Convention of 1925. However, the treaty did not exclude the production or possession of such weapons. Many countries considered a reliable stockpile of CW as insurance against a potential attack and an effective form of deterrence. Despite the Geneva Convention and the fear of retaliation, CWs were deployed again in Libya, Sinkiang, Ethiopia, China, Vietnam, Yemen, and the Iran-Iraq war.

Chemical weapons were not employed on a large scale in World War II (exception being the use of poison gas in the Nazi death camps). Aside from their use in the extermination camps and Japanese experiments on prisoners of war, there was no military application of chemical warfare during World War II. Fear of retaliation suppressed any eagerness by strategists to consider their utilization. After World War II the United States demobilized its Chemical Warfare Service, which it had established in 1918 as part of the Army Corps of Engineers within the War Department. As the "nuclear age" evolved, chemical warfare became obsolete in the opinion of many military planners. The Chemical Warfare Service (CWS) was renamed the "Chemical Corps" in 1946 and under its new heading expanded its mission to include radiological and biological research and planning.

During the Cold War the threat of chemical war and an atmosphere of distrust between the United States and the USSR simultaneously drove and inhibited efforts by both sides to conclude an agreement on a large-scale chemical weapons destruction program. After years of frustration, the Chemical Weapons Convention (formally known as the Convention on the Prohibition of the Development, Stockpiling, and Use of Chemical Weapons) was finally signed and entered into force in April 1997. Yet, parallel to these events, interest and concern in chemical warfare was undergoing dramatic change. The use of limited chemical weapons in Afghanistan by the Soviets and by both sides in the Iraqi-Iranian war during the 1980s had set the tone of apprehension. Terrorists and insurgent groups were learning how easy access to chemical agents and the vulnerability of potential targets created a tactical environment ripe for exploitation for chemical weapons use. As the superpowers were signing treaties, the capability to inflict at least moderate damage and widespread panic was gaining in appeal among non-state actors.

Among the asymmetric episodes was the attack on the Tokyo subway system in 1995 by the Japanese cult group calling itself Aum Shinrikyo (Supreme Truth). The Tokyo Metro is one of the biggest commuter systems in the world. Cult members unleashed their attack during rush hour hoping to produce optimum impact. Sarin was the deadly nerve gas used to kill twelve people, injured 6,000, and forced thousands more into panic. Five attackers entered separate train cars with packets of liquid sarin. They exited the cars after having punctured the bags and allowing the liquid toxin to leak out and quickly evaporated into a lethal gas. Emergency services were strained, diagnosis was delayed, and antidotes were in short supply. Physical harm to the metro system was only slight, however. Cleansing of the surfaces repaired most damage and service was restored the next day. Eventually, members of the group were apprehended. One interesting observation by analysts was the conclusion that, scientific skills notwithstanding, the plotters were limited in their ability to transition their work from laboratory to production scale for the purpose of mass destruction. On the other hand, analysts also noted that, based on Aum Shinrikyo's experience, the capability to develop a chemical weapon was more accessible than the capability to develop a biological one.[6]

Several years later the 2002 attack by Chechen terrorists in a Moscow theater illustrated, with tragic irony, how lethal and aleatory CW attacks can be. Chechen terrorists armed with guns and explosives held nine hundred theatergoers hostage for two and a half days. When their demands for immediate withdrawal of Russian forces from Chechnya went unmet, the terrorists began executing their captives. As the executions were being carried out Russian police filled the theater with a "non-lethal" incapacitating agent—fentanyl. A firefight ensued when police stormed the theater. The attack resulted in over 118 deaths due to exposure to the chemical agent. Thus, in addition to the murders committed from gunfire, hostages were also poisoned by the attempts of their own security forces to rescue them. The use of this gaseous substance in the counterassault sealed the fate of those who had survived death at the hands of their terrorist assailants, only to perish from the attempts of their rescuers.

During the war in Iraq insurgents used makeshift chlorine bombs on civilian and Allied military targets. From October 2006 through June 2007 a series of attacks occurred using explosive devices and car bombs as platforms. Unlike the artillery shells of World War I, these stationary and vehicular methods were less lethal. The heat from the blast probably diminished the toxicity of the gas. In all, slightly over 100 died and hundreds more were injured. The assaults were basically crude and proved not an effective means of inflicting casualties on a large scale. However, panic was widespread and the attack demonstrated the opponent's resourcefulness and ability to adapt to conditions on the ground in order to maintain their struggle. These incidents illustrate the potential that chemical weapons hold for terrorists as well as the potential for major escalation. Their danger may not be from a fear of widespread death and destruction, but rather from the ensuing panic, which eventually would cause a disruption of commerce, a distrust of the security community, and the capability of the asymmetric force to extend the conflict.

CHEMICAL AGENTS

Obviously, chemicals are available for both useful and destructive purposes. By definition, chemical terrorism is when a chemical substance reacts with living processes to cause intentional death, temporary loss of performance or permanent injury to humans, animals, or plants.[7] We assume here that the use of chemicals in warfare is only relevant to a discussion on terrorism since conventional warfare bans the use of CW. However, states that sponsor terrorism still have a role.

As opposed to biological weapons, chemical weapons are not naturally occurring. Weaponization takes place as a result of scientific research and production and mostly under the sponsorship of government programs. Additionally, terrorists are not likely to have access to weapons delivery platforms such as artillery, aircraft, and missiles. The threat mostly comes from the panic and disruption they create disproportionately to the casualties that might result.

Despite the strong predisposition toward state production, many hazardous materials and deadly chemical compounds are obtainable using widely available household ingredients and formulas, which can be found on current Internet sources. For example, the plotters of the Oklahoma City bombing in 1995 combined 5,000 pounds of ammonium nitrate fertilizer and fuel oil to destroy the Alfred P. Murrah Federal Building. Over three hundred buildings in downtown Oklahoma City were also destroyed or damaged. The cost of human life amounted to 168 deaths, nineteen of which were children under

Characteristics of Chemical and Biological Agents							
Agent	*Found in Nature*	*Speed of Effects*	*Contagious*	*Odor*	*Visual*	*Stability*	*Toxicity*
Chemical	No	Fast (seconds to hours)	No	Yes (some)	Yes (usually)	Hardy	Generally less toxic than biological
Biological Pathogens	Yes	Slow (hours to weeks)	Yes (some)	No	No	Not hardy	May be lethal
Biological Toxins	Yes (but must be isolated)	Moderate (minutes to hours)	Yes	No	No	Moderately hardy	Generally most lethal

Table 11.1. Characteristics of Chemical and Biological Agents

the age of six. The toxic industrial chemicals (TIC) below have the potential to cause mass casualties if weaponized. They include:

- Insecticides and herbicides
- Industrial chemicals
- Riot control agents

The following list compares the agents which can be used in chemical attacks and how they are grouped according to their classifications.

Asphyxiating or choking agents inflict injury through the respiratory tract. They are among the first agents produced in large quantities for use as chemical weapons. Effective in trench warfare, both sides used them extensively during World War I.[8] Because of their weight they seek depressions in the earth. Therefore, they were particularly deadly and efficient in spreading panic and forcing victims out into higher ground where they are vulnerable to gunfire. These chemicals irritate the throat and can lead to pulmonary edema and death by asphyxiation. Phosgene, chlorine, diphosgene, and chloropicrin are chemicals that fall within this class of weapons. In the treatment of choking agent victims, decontamination is critical.

Blood agents/systemic poisons are cyanide compounds. These gases can be inhaled, ingested (as solid salts), and absorbed through the skin in liquid form. Hydrogen cyanide is the main blood agent. The more stable cyanogen chloride can be equally deadly. Both formulations affect the cells' ability to utilize oxygen absorbed in the blood stream. Gases tend to evaporate quickly. However, they can be very lethal if released in confined areas. The United States produces approximately 2 billion pounds of hydrogen cyanide a year.[9] The substance is used in various industries such as metallurgy and electroplating. Cyanide can be extracted from as varied a range of sources as burning cigarettes, wool, silks, cherry and apricot pits, and the roots of certain cassava plants. Zyclon B was the cyanide used in the Nazi death camps during the Holocaust. Until 1999 the United States used cyanide to execute prisoners.

Blister agents (vesicants) burn the skin and cause extreme irritation to the eyes and lungs. The basic agent is mustard gas. Diphosgene is a member of this class of compounds, which was used extensively during World War I to incapacitate more often than kill. A blister agent attack forces troops to wear full protective equipment and thus lowering their fighting efficiency.[10] Vesicants such as this can also be thickened to contaminate ships, vehicles, and terrain. Sulfur mustard (HD) and nitrogen mustard (HN) are stable and persistent and present a potential serious threat of terrorism. Production of mustard agents is relatively easy. To date, no effective therapy is available. Furthermore, decontamination can be problematic. A feature of vesicants is their long-term morbidity.

Nerve agents are the most poisonous of synthetic chemicals.[11] They inhibit enzyme activity, which is essential for the proper functioning of the nervous system. The use and development of nerve agents occurred immediately prior to World War II. They are chemically related to the group of organophosphorus compounds commonly used as insecticides. Sarin, the chemical used in the attack on the Tokyo metro, is a member of this group. Large quantities of sarin were produced and stockpiled in the United States and the USSR/Russia.[12] Nerve agents are not only stable, but easily dispersed. Effects are rapid when absorbed through the skin or via respiration. In addition to sarin, other agents include tabun, soman, cyclosarin, and methylphosphonothioic acid. VX is the most toxic chemical known.[13] A single mg can be lethal.

Incapacitating agents include a group of substances that disturb the central nervous system and disrupt cognitive ability. Their effects are usually reversible. However, fentanyl, the agent allegedly used by Russian security forces during the Moscow hostage siege in 2002 is a member of this group. The DoD developed BZ (3-quinuclidinyl benzilate) as an incapacitating agent to induce temporary disability and as an alternative to lethal chemical warfare. During the 1960s BZ was weaponized in bomblets at the Pine Bluff

Arsenal.[14] In the late 1980s military stockpiles were dismantled, and presently there are no incapacitating munitions within the U.S. armamentarium.[15] Today BZ is known as QNB and is used in pharmacology.

Lacrimators or tearing agents are another group of chemicals whose effects are reversible and non-lethal. Extreme ocular (eye-related) irritation, blepharospasm (eyelid spasm, involuntary blinking), and skin irritation are the effects of exposure. Coughing, shortness of breath, and, occasionally, vomiting are additional disabling reactions. Lacrimators are riot control agents not usually in the category of chemical warfare weapons. Chloroacetophenone (CN) and orto-chlorobenzylidenemalononitrile (CS) are the most widely used forms of "tear gas."

Sternutators, or vomiting agents, are similar to lacrimators. They are non-lethal and produce temporary irritation of the nose, throat, and eyes. However, extreme exposure in enclosed areas can cause death. As their name designates, vomiting and nausea are the resultant effects. The human body will normally detoxify after exposure. Depending upon the length of time and volume of concentration, most victims will recover within several hours or less.[16] High explosive shells are the usual delivery method. Surprise is an important element to an attack for this type of gas. When troops are subject to inhalation prior to detection, protective masks become uncomfortable and often prematurely removed. Combatant forces used the vomiting agent diphenylchlorarsine extensively during the First World War.[17] Currently, Adamsite (DM) is the most common.[18]

Defoliants, desiccants, soil sterilants, and plant growth inhibitors can also be used as weapons. The destruction of crops, degradation of soil, and/or contamination of the water supply represent real threats. These compounds are also available to terrorists and their pursuits.

Chemical weapons are similar to biological weapons (discussed below) in several respects. Despite not naturally occurring, the materials used to produce chemical weapons are, nevertheless, ubiquitous and easily accessible. As with biological and radiological materials chemicals also have many dual use applications and are commercially available. Additionally, unlike fissile material, no adequate detection devices yet exist, which would raise suspicions or alert authorities during the production process or while being stored. Even during use CWs can be difficult to sense and identify. Research on trace chemical detectors show promise, but is still in development. The early detection of a chemical weapon is fundamental to the failure or success of an attack. The consequences for the target population can be life or death.

Finally, sophisticated computer modeling and the same sequence technology methods used in creating new strains of pathogens can apply to the synthesizing of advanced chemical structures. Therefore, with these tools, any skilled chemist can potentially create a higher generation of chemical weapons—more efficiently and of greater toxicity. The evolution of information/communication technology has had unimaginable impact on the advancement of science. The skills, tools, and information to create, not only a better world but also a more perilous one, are available and advancement in these fields will continue to accelerate. The result is the potential for more lethal bio-chemical weapons, greater accessibility to precursor materials and knowhow, deadlier weapons of mass destruction, smaller teams of experts required to create weaponized compounds and pathogens—all at less expensive financial costs.

THREATS, COUNTERMEASURES, AND DISARMAMENT

Without access to military grade weapons, terrorists would most likely depend upon their own resources to manufacture CWs. Alternatively, an attack on a commercial site or a supply of hazardous materials during transport might also fulfill their aims. Toxic industrial chemicals are effective attack agents even though they are not specifically designed for military operations. Dual use technology and the relative small amount of substance needed to create a strategic effect make TICs an attractive terrorist tool. These weapons are difficult to detect and their capabilities are complicated to evaluate.[19] Production of TICs has increased unabatedly over the decades of expanded industrial development. In 1999 the Environmental Protection Agency approximated that over 850,000 facilities in the United States were working with as many as 50,000 different commercial products that pose physical or health hazards to humans.[20] It is impossible to control and track the annual movement of millions of tons of chemicals. The globalization of the industry and the commoditization of chemicals make vulnerable the transportation of these materials and create a threat to public safety that requires attention and a concern for national security.

In 1984 a Union Carbide insecticide plant in Bhopal, India, began leaking a plume of toxic gas—methylisocyanate. Two thousand died almost immediately, and within a week a total of 8,000 people perished. Eventually, officials put the total of those affected at 578,000. The chemicals produced at the plant were similar to those used to produce chemical warfare agents.[21,22] The incident illustrated the potential for disaster that a commercial facility can pose from accidental release, and also what possibilities might exist from a sabotage or terrorist attempt.

Despite government reporting requirements and those set by the Chemical Weapons Convention, the procurement of small amounts of precursor chemicals for weapons' production can escape suspicion and detection. Small-scale production sites present a degree of threat from fires, explosion, and leaks on a scale similar to planned unconventional dissemination methods using crop dusters, canisters, fire extinguishers, impact from vehicular crashes, and simple backpack platforms. Heavy metals, volatile toxins, pulmonary agents, dioxins, furans, polychlorinated biphenyls, and industrial compounds such as cyanides, nitriles, and corrosive acids and bases are among the list of poisons commercially available. If the acquisition of weaponized chemicals by theft or largesse from a sponsoring state is not an option, terrorists also have these commercial avenues at their disposal. [23]

In the event of a state sponsored attack, several governments would be prime suspects. Countries who possess CWs and are not signatories to the Geneva Convention include North Korea, Egypt, and for the time being, Libya. Iraq was a suspect. However, weapons inspectors found no evidence that Saddam Hussein had "reconstituted his [chemical and biological] weapon program" following the Gulf War despite the assertion by the Bush administration. [24] The Iraq Survey Group, the international fact-finding team organized to locate alleged WMDs, determined that Iraq unilaterally dismantled and destroyed its undeclared chemical munitions program in 1991. [25] The non-member states of the Organization for the Prevention of Chemical Warfare (OPCW), the organization formed to monitor compliance with the Chemical Weapons Convention, are Angola, Egypt, North Korea, Somalia, and South Sudan. [26] Israel and Myanmar are signatories but their legislatures have not ratified the agreement. Syria became a member in September 2013 due to international pressure during its civil war. Regardless of the impracticality and low probability of state involvement in a CW event, it is a scenario that must not be totally dismissed. Corruption, security lapses, and the lure of a black market for these materials re-intensify the concern as one considers the panorama of possibilities.

Whether state sponsored or a plot by an "entrepreneurial terrorist," a chemical attack on a transportation hub could have grave consequences for commerce. A study conducted by Lawrence Livermore National Laboratory concluded that a closure of San Francisco International Airport could cost $85 million per day and the cascading effect would extend into the entire air transportation network. [27] The report warned that recovery from a toxic chemical release is time critical and challenging. Contamination of closed and open spaces, sensitive equipment, and structural and non-fixed materials raises a set of complex problems. "Waiting for the agent to naturally dissipate will not be an option" [28] Once the compound is identified, responders must activate an effective decontamination strategy as quickly as possible. The undertaking might be complex as chemical toxins penetrate materials below their surface and become trapped within the object and begin outgassing slowly and dangerously. Technicians would have to decide among the various options of (1) using more concentrated disinfectants to remove the substance from porous surfaces, (2) removing the contaminated objects all together, or (3) applying sealants to contain further releases. Each option comes with its own set of risks and cost consequences. No single approach is likely to be satisfactory.

According to the National Academy of Sciences and the Department of Homeland Security, the list of methods for delivery of a toxic chemical attack include the following:

- Ventilation systems of a building
- Misting, aerosolizing devices, sprayers
- Passive release (container of chemicals left open)
- Bombs, mines, or other explosive devices that contain chemicals other than those used to create the explosion
- Improvised chemical devices that combine readily available chemicals to produce a dangerous chemical
- Sabotage of plants or vehicles containing chemicals
- Introduction of toxins into the food or water supply

Any comprehensive chemical weapon counterterrorism strategy involves an array of constituent elements. The most effective preemptive tool is a combination of production monitoring and a well-organized and resourceful intelligence program. Verification activities by OPCW track chemical production of its 188 member states. The destruction of chemical weapons and the control of their proliferation, in accord with the Chemical Weapons Convention, is the primary work. However, weapons destruction and removal is costly.

Not only is weapons destruction expensive, but also the process is very technical. Removal, transportation, and destruction are managed with specialized equipment and facilities. Destruction costs are ten times the cost of production. In the United States, the estimated expense would be $10 billion with an additional levy of $17.7 billion to unearth and destroy previously buried CW.[29,30] The CWC prohibits sea dumping. The sanctioned methods for chemical weapons destruction are with heat, chemicals, and super-critical water and wet air oxidation (the combination of high temperatures and intense pressure).

Preemptive countermeasures to chemical terrorism include several analytical tools referred to as "signatures." Signatures help in the detection of CW development and production by red flagging any suspicious pattern indicating the presence of potential weapons production or intentions to develop these compounds (the term is also relevant to nuclear production and the detection and attribution of cyber attacks). These analytical methods can alert the watchdog communities. For instance, since developing a weapons program cannot occur without the assistance of industrial nations, signature evidence that a country has an interest in investing in a CW program can be uncovered by monitoring trade. Procurement, design, and equipment installation and start up require a dependency on advanced states. Therefore, export controls of instruments and precursor chemicals are important to the demilitarization of the chemical industry. The Australia Group (AG) is an informal forum of countries that work together to coordinate national export-control regulations "to ensure exports do not contribute to the development of chemical or biological weapons."[31] The AG, with the OPCW, assures their members fulfill obligations under the Chemical Weapons Convention. Both organizations work with the international community to function as focal points for harmonizing the effort to prevent chemical weapons use and proliferation.

Other signatures include data obtained by aerial photography, remote sensing, or covert intelligence gathering. In the global war on terror, counterintelligence has undergone a transformation and taken on new roles. As discussed above, counterterrorism policy after 9/11 led to the reorganization and overhaul of the intelligence community. In addition to introducing stricter security measures at ports, borders, infrastructure, and transportation nodes, the Bush administration approved drastic changes in the way the CIA, FBI, other intelligence agencies, and law enforcement authorities interoperate to gather, share, and analyze information (see chapter 1). The intelligence community's work in monitoring activity relative to the production and movement of toxic chemicals is vital. In pursuit of these goals, non-cooperative data collection depends upon several methods of intelligence gathering, which are applicable to all areas of national security concern and inquiry, including biological terrorism, nuclear and radiological terrorism, and any violence against the United States:

- **Human intelligence** (HUMINT)—using human sources by covert or overt means
- **Open source intelligence** (OSINT)—information from print and broadcast news, academic publications, and Internet sources with the aid of advanced analysis tools in data extraction, inference enrichment, and knowledge application and sharing methodology
- **Signals intelligence** (SIGINT)—a category which includes communications intelligence (COMINT), electronic intelligence (ELINT), and foreign instrumentation signal intelligence (FISINT) or what is described as the interception of instrumentation signals such as radio commands[32]
- **Measurement and signature intelligence** (MASINT)—relating to acoustic, optical, thermal, radio frequency, seismic, and material data collection
- **Imagery intelligence** (IMINT)—data collected from space-based satellite sources (non-air breathers) and aircraft (air breathers) with surveillance equipment

- **Geospatial intelligence** (GEOINT)—the combination of imagery intelligence and geospatial information to produce analysis and visual representation of targets relative to security-related targets and issues

Intelligence gathering, homeland security preparedness, and the international cooperation from which the United States benefits and seeks forms the defensive perimeter against terrorism. The overwhelming technological superiority of U.S. military forces creates another deterrent to state and non-state actors who may contemplate any terrorist exploit against the American public. Finally, consequence management and emergency response are not only key to prevailing in the global war on terror, but also in the mitigation of loss in the event of natural disasters and the rampages of the excesses in the overuse of the earth's resources.

NOTES

1. Corey J. Hilmas, Jeffery K Smart, Benjamin K. Hill, "Medical Aspects of Chemical Warfare" (U.S. Department of Army, Surgeon General, Borden Institute, 2009), p. 11.
2. *Ibid.*, p. 11–12.
3. *Ibid.*, p. 14–15.
4. Haber's wife reportedly committed suicide after witnessing the effects of chlorine gas at the Battle of Ypres. Clara Haber, a fellow chemist, opposed her husband's work despite being a party to it.
5. *Encyclopedia of United States National Security* (Sage Publications, Inc., 2006), p. 115.
6. Richard Danzig, et al., "Aum Shinrikyo: Insights into How Terrorists Develop Biological and Chemical Weapons" (Center for a New American Security, July 2011), http://www.cnas.org/files/documents/publications/CNAS_AumShinrikyo_Danzig_1.pdf.
7. Dabir S. Viswanath, and Tushar K Gosh, "Chemical Agents: Classification, Synthesis, and Properties," in *Science and Technology of Terrorism and Counterterrorism*, ed., Ghosh, Prelas, Viswanath, Loyalka, (Marcel Dekker, Inc., 2002).
8. Organization for the Prohibition of Chemical Weapons, http://www.opcw.org/about-chemical-weapons/types-of-chemical-agent/choking-agents/.
9. Federation of American Scientists, http://www.fas.org/programs/bio/factsheets/cyanide.html.
10. *Ibid.*
11. Viswanath, p. 326.
12. *Ibid.*, p. 334.
13. David L. Ormerod, "Chemical Agents: Toxicity and Management" in Ghosh, p. 353.
14. Noblis.org. http://www.noblis.org/MissionAreas/nsi/BackgroundonChemicalWarfare/ChemistryofOtherMilitaryCompounds/Pages/261.aspx.
15. James S. Ketchum, M.D., ABPM; Sidell, Frederick R. M.D. "Chapter 11, Incapacitating Agents," in *Medical Aspects of Chemical and Biological Warfare* (Office of the Surgeon General at TMM Publication, 1997), p. 302.
16. Viswanath, p. 327.
17. "Medical Aspects of Gas Warfare," in *The Medical Department of the United States in the World War,* Vol. XIV, Government Printing Office, 1926.
18. *Op. Cit.*
19. "Counter-Chemical Biological Radiological and Nuclear Operations" (Air Force Doctrine Document 2-1.8, 26 January 2007), p. 4.
20. Ormerod, p. 436.
21. *Op. cit.*

22. Breaking Bhopal News, *New York Times* (13 January 2011), http://topics.nytimes.com/top/news/international/countriesandterritories/india/bhopal/index.html.

23. Ormerod, p. 434–45.

24. Interview with Vice-President Dick Cheney, NBC, "Meet the Press " (Transcript for March 16, 2003), https://www.mtholyoke.edu/acad/intrel/bush/cheneymeetthepress.htm, National Broadcasting Company, Inc.

25. CIA website, https://www.cia.gov/library/reports/general-reports-1/iraq_wmd_2004/chap5.html#sect0.

26. OPCW website, http://www.opcw.org/about-opcw/non-member-states/.

27. "Responding to a Terrorist Attack" Lawrence Livermore National Laboratory (S&TR, March 2010).

28. *Ibid.*

29. M. Renner, Bonn International Center For Conversion (Brief 6, Bonn, Germany, 1996).

30. Viswanath, p. 412.

31. Australia Group website, http://www.australiagroup.net/en/index.html.

32. Amos A. Jordan, et al., *American National Security, Sixth Edition* (Johns Hopkins University Press, Baltimore, MD, 2008), p. 148–51.

Chapter Twelve

Chemical Biological Radiological & Nuclear: The Biological Threat

BIOLOGICAL WARFARE

Because of their relative ease of purchase and development, biological weapons have been called "the poor man's nuclear bomb."
—Aspen Institute Report, 2005

After the sword, the spear, the axe, boiling oil, and anything you can hurl, drop, or stick into someone, the use of biological agents is the oldest form of warfare. During medieval wars, placing rotting corpses in your enemy's drinking well assured you some appalling results. In 1347 Mongol invaders launched remains of their own plague victims over the Crimean seaport walls of Caffa (now Flodosia, Ukraine) to encourage the defenders to abandon the city. Succumbing to the onslaught and pestilence, many survivors of Caffa returned to their homes in Genoa where the contagion spread and may have ranged out into the interior of Europe. Often historians attribute a Black Death epidemic, which eliminated at least a third of the continent's population to this single event. Other early examples of germ warfare include the British army's use of smallpox-infected gift blankets to native North Americans in the eighteenth century. The transmission of smallpox and other diseases also played a significant role in the Spanish conquest over the native populations of Mesoamerica and South America. It was said that the disease path moved much faster than the advancing Spaniards. Some experts claim the indigenous populations in central Mexico may have shrank by over 90 percent by the late sixteenth century due to the introduction of these human-borne pathogens.[1]

Twentieth-century counterparts to these early combatants discovered and deployed advancements in microbiology on the battlefield in World War I and World War II. During World War I the Germans tried to infect U.S. Army horses and mules with glanders, a disease infectious to humans as well as dogs, goats, and cats. The Japanese, however, raised investment in these tactics to a new level by its "'experiments" on Chinese populations. Reputedly, ten thousand prisoners died during Japan's occupation.[2] The invaders also targeted the general population with attacks on food and water supplies with the use of plague-infested fleas. Japanese forces became their own victim in 1941 when these operations reportedly backfired.[3]

The end of World War II marked the end of biological warfare, but not a halt to large state-sponsored programs to develop and produce biological weapons, unfortunately. Despite the Geneva Protocol of 1925 and the Biological Weapons Convention (BWC) of 1972 (known as the Biological and Toxins Weapon Convention by the time it was completed), the lure from advancements in biotechnology and microbiology for military potential loomed too irresistible. The BWC specifically banned the production, development, acquisition, storage, shipment, or deployment of the entire class of offensive biological weapons.[4] Yet, by the United States' own account, between one dozen and two dozen countries around the world were in violation. The treaty was a landmark, but it stood without any authority to monitor, investigate, or otherwise police for noncompliance.

Washington's allegations were eventually confirmed with startling alarm upon the defection of a Soviet scientist in 1980. Vladimir Pasechnik divulged to Western intelligence the details of a program called *Biopreparat*. More than a program, the effort was on the scale of a small industry. According to Pasechek, it involved hundreds of research facilities and production plants, employed tens of thousands, and operated with a budget between 100 and 200 billion rubles per year.[5] Commenting on Pasechnik's revelations, a British report noted:

> The information was stunning: a whole ministry exposed; billions of rubles spent; a complete organization shown to be a front; and there was a clear involvement of Gorbachev, this friend of the West.[6]

Gorbachev's successor and President of Russia, Boris Yeltsin, confirmed the existence of *Biopreparat* and ordered the program ended. Although Yeltsin opened the sites for inspection, Kanatjan Alibek, another witness who defected in 1992, expressed concerns that many of the facilities remain in operation.[7] Among the lineup of weaponized biological agents was an inventory of anthrax, brucella, tularemia, Q-fever, Lassa fever, glanders, plague, monkey pox, Ebola, Marburg variant U, and smallpox.

Since his election, several accusations of bio-terrorism have been laid directly at the feet of Vladimir Putin and his regime. However, not for the purpose of national defense, but rather for reasons related to political convenience. In 2003 a reporter and deputy of the State Duma died of an apparent rare allergic reaction to medication. Yuri Shchekochikhin was investigating an alleged corruption case involving a Russian importer and the government. His cause of death was deemed due to an unidentified allergen. Since no traces of the medication were found in his system during the autopsy many of Shchekochikhin's colleagues regard his demise as murder. [8]

By definition, biological warfare is the use of microorganisms and their toxins to produce death and disease among humans and human, animal, and plant food supply sources. [9, 10] Obviously, as was the case during medieval times, such impact during times of conflict can be devastating. During the twentieth century the science of microbiology allowed for technological advancement and development in methods for using microbes for creating weapons of mass destruction, heretofore undreamed. That research spawned national weapons development programs across the planet. The list of countries to have admitted to such military pursuits during the Cold War includes the United States, the United Kingdom, France, the Soviet Union, Iraq, and South Africa. Iraq admitted to producing botulinum toxin and anthrax for use in scud missiles. They also conducted research on camelpox, a form of smallpox. [11] Past and present, self-declared and suspected states are Russia, Cuba, Iran, Syria, Israel, China, Taiwan, Libya, and North Korea. According to U.S. government estimates, the total number of suspected states involved in the illegal development of biological weapons is well over a dozen countries.

Some sources claim that only states have the capacity and resources to develop a sophisticated biological weapons (BW) program. It is purely the specialty of nations, they reason, which have the financial and technical resources needed to create a biological weapon and execute a large-scale attack. However, others argue that the same rationale that makes BW programs attractive alternatives to investment in state-sponsored nuclear and conventional arms also appeals to non-state actors.

Since pathogens occur in nature, biological weapons are relatively inexpensive and easy to produce. They may be harvested from sources such as diseased animals or contaminated soil. After learning from a published news or industry report that an outbreak has occurred, a weapons producer could collect samples from the outbreak site. [12] These disease outbreaks occur throughout the world. Hence, the locations are geographically dispersed and producing large supplies of agents usually requires a supply of only a small amount of biological material.

Of course, these lethal biological agents are bountiful outside nature. Pharmaceutical firms, agricultural facilities, research laboratories, hospitals, and breweries provide "natural" settings for pathogens. Furthermore, dual use applications of bio-related equipment and technology are commonly obtainable and on hand, legally. Also accessible is the expertise. Life sciences researchers and competent graduate students exist in nature and in clinical settings worldwide. Thus, the combination of available professionals and materials make acquiring and purifying biological material for weapons grade use comparatively easier than refining fissile material for the production of nuclear devices. According to a 1986 article in *International Combat Arms*: "Manufacturing a lethal bacterial disease agent requires little more than chicken soup, a flat whiskey bottle and an available source of seed culture."[13] This widespread availability of material and know-how to manufacture biological weapons is only another disquieting threat for global security. The skills and tools for such undertakings are becoming even more easily acquired due to the advancements in life sciences research and its intersection with the globalization process and evolution of information/communication technology.[14]

Since biological weapons do not have to be produced in large quantities in order to generate high impact events, costs of such exploits can be low and require no highly specialized or extravagant facilities.[15] Yet, the chaos and mass panic of even a low casualty attack could have serious consequences. The plot in 2001 to mail anthrax packets to two U.S. Senate offices and several New York media outlets killed five. Although the attack was basically foiled, due to decontamination procedures, it took months before normal operations were restored to congressional offices.[16] Moreover, the effect on the public psyche was momentous. Adding a sense of frustration to the overhanging fear, attribution attempts failed. Despite being the largest epidemiological investigation of an infectious disease outbreak,[17] authorities never identified the perpetrators who remained at large. The example only demonstrates another reality about BW attacks. BW covert assaults are easy to conceal and implement. Owing to the inherent open architecture of typical BW targets (often, public areas), these exploits are not only easy to conduct, but also can offer the attacker low risk of capture.

BIOLOGICAL AGENTS

More than twenty pathogens are suitable for biological warfare.[18] (NATO lists thirty-nine agents as having the potential for BW.)[19] Despite the relatively long list, only several categories of pathogens represent a potential large-scale threat to sizable urban or regional populations. Well-financed states and less resource-rich terrorist groups are subject to differing circumstances and, hence, unequal levels of frustration in launching a successful BW attack. Nevertheless, the relationship between the potential for infectivity versus the quantity of the agent is at the heart of the calculus for the state and non-state actor alike. The following criteria distinguishes pathogens and their potential to inflect the most harm:

- Lethality
- Communicability
- Ease of production in terms of cost, technology, and equipment
- Ability to produce large quantities from small amounts of material
- Aerosol infectivity and toxicity
- Absence of treatment or vaccine

Anthrax and smallpox are the agents that present the greatest peril. The plague, botulinum toxin, hemorrhagic fever virus, and tularemia complete the list of biological agents in the highest category of virulence and potential for weaponization and priority for the Centers for Disease Control (CDC). These substances are considered and known as "Category A Agents." Anthrax holds the record in popularity. There are more examples of its use as a biological weapon than by other agent.[20]

Contact with the microbe is through ingestion, inhalation, or direct contact. Livestock and workers in the trade, such as farmers, herders, wool handlers, butchers, taxidermists, etc., are at risk. However, general populations are susceptible through contact and contaminated foodstuffs. If not treated, the fatality rate is high. Inhalational anthrax can have a fatality rate of 80 percent. The gastrointestinal form of the disease has a fatality rate between 25 and 60 percent, while skin infections are 20 percent fatal. According to an early World Health Organization study, 50 kilograms of anthrax spores distributed over a 2-kilometer dense swath of urban area could result in 100,000 infected and as much as 95,000 dead.[21]

In addition to its lethality, the rate of transmission and the lack of a reliable and significant supply of vaccine make the weaponized adaptation of this biological agent a potential terrorist tool. The vaccine for anthrax, licensed in 1970, exists. However, production ceased in 1998. Aside from being nearly fifty years old, the vaccine can have serious side effects and is not approved for use in children.[22] Therefore, it is not available for civilian use (with the 2001 U.S. mail attack the notable exception) and is mostly reserved for persons of high risk (see above) and for use by the military. Furthermore, its efficacy in inhalational cases lacks the certainty of exhaustive trials. Production of weaponized anthrax, most likely, requires the resources of a nation-state. Iraq and the former Soviet Union are the two countries cited most as example research and production sites. According to the United Nations Special Commission, Iraq manufactured 84,250 liters of anthrax spores and the Soviet Union produced 30 metric tons.[23,24] Yet, the production of weapons grade anthrax has its barriers for the state as well as the non-state organization.

Assuming the procurement phase of weaponable anthrax material is complete, the following stages become complex and problematic. Purification, storage, and effective dispersal by any BW weaponeer plotting a large-scale attack have some significant obstacles. The challenge arises with the collection of a multidisciplinary team of subject matter experts (SMEs) trained to work with anthrax agents. This process has proven difficult for even military programs.[25] For terrorist groups it entails recruiting SMEs and providing adequate research and development facilities. Communication and other logistical issues surface as program managers work to align research silos and establish linkages between the laboratory and the field of battle.

> Even BW programs in the United States and the former USSR had remarkable multidisciplinary teams, but, nonetheless, they encountered significant issues that in many cases entailed the failure of some lines of research. In the case of locally autonomous terrorist cells without links to each other, the probability of establishing these multidisciplinary teams is much lower.[26]

The terrorist group the Popular Front for the Liberation of Palestine–General Command (PFLP-GC) had ties and access to Syria's military research. Yet, the group never assembled a threatening biological program despite its active agenda of terrorist attacks in the 1970s and 1980s. Analysts believe the fear of military retaliation against Syria inhibited cooperation and collusion between that state and the PFLP-GC.[27]

Before one becomes comforted by the Syrian/PFLP example it is prudent to be mindful, again, that the skill revolutions in microbiology and information/communication technology are constantly altering the threat vector. An additional backdrop to these facts is the reality that seventy thousand research scientists and technicians lost their jobs with the *Biopreparat* weapons program after the fall of the Soviet Union. Their whereabouts and the warehouse of pathogens they created are not completely known. As a footnote of further unease, North Korea and Iraq were the accused illegitimate heirs to part of this inventory.

Aside from anthrax, by the 1990s, the USSR reportedly produced 20 metric tons of the weaponable **smallpox** material. With *Biopreparat* it was possible in 1987 for the USSR to produce eighty to one hundred tons of smallpox per year alone.[28] Smallpox is transmissible from person to person—unlike anthrax, by which infection spreads solely through direct contact with the microbe. Smallpox transfers via aerosolized saliva or contact with the fluid released from the symptomatic exanthem, or viral rash. In the transmission of smallpox, virions (viral particles) from saliva or the fluids that ooze from ruptured vesicles, or fever blisters, leave behind traces of contamination. The contaminated sites are transmittal points. The incubation period is between twelve and fourteen days. The formation of exanthem coincides with the height of disease commutability. There is a 30 percent fatality rate from the most virulent strain, Variola major.

The devastation of smallpox epidemics has been catastrophic. Its scourge has left behind a trail of death that exceeds any other calamity of the twentieth century. Marc Ostfield of the Office of International Health and Biodefense at the U.S. State Department writes:

> Approximately 500 million people died in the century that just ended. This compares with 320 million deaths during the same period as a result of all military and civilian casualties of war, cases of swine flu during the ruinous 1918 pandemic, and all cases of AIDS worldwide. [29]

Happily, smallpox was officially eradicated in 1972 and only two known seed samples of the live virus exist. The legal owners and custodial locations are the United States and Russia. As noted above, it is possible there are live samples elsewhere. If these infective agents fall in the hands of terrorists the consequences, unhappily, could be quite dire. According to many, the virus is available on the global black market and, some regard its BW potential "as the greatest threat if acquired by bioterrorists." [30]

Routine vaccinations ceased with the declaration that the disease was extinct. Therefore, the natural resistance to the virus is weak because vaccinations do not offer life-long immunity. It is highly communicable. Ten to twenty secondary cases occur for every primary case in non-immunized populations. [31] The current stock of the old vaccine covers between seven and fifteen million doses. The CDC estimates, through dilution, coverage might extend by as much as five to ten times that mark. [32] However, given the intensity and velocity of modern travel, a coordinated program of quarantine and vaccination would be logistically daunting. Even more distressing is the prospect of a more virulent strain of the disease. Such a deadly concoction is possible through genetic engineering. Reportedly, the Soviet Union combined smallpox cell tissues with the Marburg virus. The resultant chimera was mousepox. This recombinant occurred accidentally in a state laboratory and the regretful consequence brought into flower a pathogen with 100 percent mortality rate among mice. [33] Mousepox does not affect humans but the incident lays bare how simply a new form of virulence can materialize, either with intent or by caprice.

Not only are most health systems ill prepared to deal with evolving generations of the smallpox virus it is quite possible that most may never have that capability. [34] Because of its rapid rate of transmission, the time lag between the eruption of an outbreak and the introduction of a vaccine affords a dangerously short time window. Even if current supplies were on hand and adequate, a national distribution mechanism might not. The incubation period for smallpox is twelve to fourteen days. An additional delay may be the risk of misdiagnoses. During this span a victim may be assumed to have influenza since the symptoms are malaise, fever, vomiting, and body ache. Once the reality sets in that, indeed, a smallpox epidemic has struck, the proceeding events would most likely include an overwhelmed public health system, a depletion of medical supplies and hospital beds, disrupted transportation and communications networks, and mass panic. In the extreme, the situation could produce swarms of refugees and a collapse of civil order.

The Marburg virus, used in the inadvertent creation of mousepox, falls under the class of **hemorrhagic fevers** (HF). Clinically speaking, HF is a RNA (ribonucleic acid) virus. It transfers its genetic information in viral envelopes, which fuse with the host cell. This is a common mechanism for viral infection.

These pathogens, unlike smallpox, exist in the wild rather than solely laboratory environments. Therefore, their accessibility is nearly as facile as is their ability to move through populations. HF does not require weaponization. It merely needs harvesting from infected specimens and a means of transferral. It mostly commutes between wild animals, particularly, rodents. However, human beings are at risk. Human HF infection usually occurs through close contact with infected animals, particularly, through consumption, slaughtering, or with the bite from a mosquito or tick. Otherwise, the disease transfers from human host to human host via infected tissue or blood. Although not as contagious as other agents, it can be quite deadly. Ebola virus, a class of HF, has a mortality rate between 50 percent to 90 percent.

Fortunately, as the contagion spreads it tends to abate. The transmission loses its efficiency from case to case and, therefore, outbreaks may promptly dissipate.[35] For this reason HF viruses are usually geographically restricted.[36] Their naming reflects the regionalism in their identification.

Travel from an outbreak or infection site into population centers would spread the disease as well as the attendant public panic once there was mass

HEMORRHAGIC FEVERS			
Arenaviridae:	*Bunyviridae:*	*Filoviridae:*	*Flaviviridae:*
Lassa fever	Rift Valley fever	Marburg virus	Yellow fever
Argentine fever	Crimean-Congo HF	Ebola virus	Dengue
Bolivian HF	Hantavirus		Kyasanur-Forest
Brazilian HF	Korean HF		Omsk HF
Venezuela HF			

Table 12.1 Hemorrhagic Fevers

official, or unofficial, notification. A successful terrorist attack would involve a team of suicidal members willing to offer themselves as vectors. There are no documented cases of an attempted HF terrorist plot; however, the Japanese religious-terrorist group Aum Shinrikyo fielded a team of members to collect samples in Zaire (now the Democratic Republic of the Congo) in 1993. The exact details of any further plans were unclear.

If a biological attack using HF were implemented the reaction to infection may be initially misdiagnosed as influenza, malaria, or sepsis. As the disease moves into advanced stages, blood cells that promote clotting dwindle causing spontaneous hemorrhaging from mucosal surfaces and punctures to the skin. Shock and kidney failure can result. Often there is severe damage to the liver, lungs, and nervous system.

Aside from yellow fever, there is no effective vaccine for hemorrhagic fevers. As with all viruses, there is no complete cure. A weaponized version of the agent is expensive, however, and most experts consider the primary terrorist aim would be general chaos and terror as opposed to inflicting widespread death. Regardless of the obstacles to terrorists, an attack with an HF agent must be considered credible and taken seriously.[37]

Plague, or *Yersinia pestis* bacterium (so named for the French Swiss bacteriologist Alexandre Yersin), has a long history of deadly and explosive outbreaks. It appeared in the sixth, fourteenth, and twentieth centuries with cataclysmic consequences involving millions of deaths. In fourteenth-century Europe, the plague was particularly virulent. Fulminant occurrences erupted periodically across the continent reducing the population by one third. Historians estimate the plague claimed at least seventy million lives. Owing to the litany of epidemics, England's population in 1300 (estimated at five million) was not restored, again, to that level until 1430. In addition to the death toll, the plague's impact was transformative to the degree that many scholars maintained it contributed to the change of the social structure of Europe. It depleted the *First Estate* (the clergy), redistributed wealth, and is credited with having helped arouse the iconoclasm and spirit of dissent, which stirred the rise of the Protestant movement and the Renaissance.

Today, plague epidemiology is more comprehensible than it was for the ancients. It is endemic to Europe, Asia, and rural areas of North America. The plague moves through populations along two paths. A common vector is the bite from infected rodent fleas, which spread the disease to human populations. A single bite from an infected flea can transmit 24,000 organisms. Less than ten organisms can infect a human host. Microbes introduced through the skin produce toxins that attack the lymph nodes. Contact with infected animal tissue can also be a gateway to contagion.[38,39] As the organisms multiply, symptoms manifest and tissue destruction occurs. After a two or three day incubation period, acute symptoms of high fever, chills, headache, malaise, vomiting, and myalgia develop. The painful swelling around the lymph node area gives us the term *bubonic plague*. These raised lymph nodes are known as bubos, which appear between one and eight days following the flea bite and, hence, identify the disease while lending its name to the illness.

Human to human transferal only occurs via inhalation of respiratory discharge. This pneumatic (lung infection) form is the most deadly and most suitable for weaponization. In the case of pneumonic plague, treatment must initiate within twenty-four hours of the onset of symptoms.[40] Otherwise, mortality is high. Treated pneumonic plague cases have a 15 percent fatality rate. Untreated cases have 100 percent mortality. In these inhalation cases, the victim has contracted organisms, which have already become more virulent by virtue of the time period spent in another human host. During these periods, bacteria transforms into the more virulent type. By the time it comes in contact with its new host, the agent is in an altered and advanced state.

Yersinia pestis appears naturally in many parts of the world, including North America. The World Health Organization reports between one thousand and three thousand cases per year. These outbreaks occur in mostly rural areas where humans come in contact with wild rodents.[41] In the United States the last urban epidemic was in Los Angeles in 1924–1925. Only a handful of cases are reported annually in the United States. Parts of California, southern Oregon, northern Arizona, and New Mexico, and adjacent regions in Colorado and Nevada are areas where incidences usually appear.

Attempts at weaponizing plague have not yielded much actionable results. Because heat, drying, and ultraviolet light destroy the bacteria, direct weaponization is difficult. Japan experimented with a bubonic form during World War II. The release of billions of infected fleas over northern Chinese cites resulted in a number of epidemics. Since then, the area has been an endemic locale for the plague.[42] However, for further use in modern warfare, the technology and logistics required to harvest, maintain, and launch an effective and well-organized attack appears out of reach.

In the theoretical realm of biological warfare, expert consensus favors the aerosolized option. The United States and the USSR researched the possibilities and potential for pneumatic plague during the Cold War. That effort ended, evidently, without any useful data with respect to a prescribed lethal dose or the quantity of agent required.[43] Thus, there is no empirical evidence for judging the infectivity of a weaponized plague agent. An accurate assessment of a plague cloud's behavior or real-world tendency and lethality is impossible. All that is certain is, because of its potential for disaster, upon its onset decisions about whom to quarantine and treat must be made immediately. As mentioned above, plague symptoms manifest between one and six days after infection. These symptoms may be confused with influenza, pneumonia, or, in light cases, with the common cold. Streptomycin and other

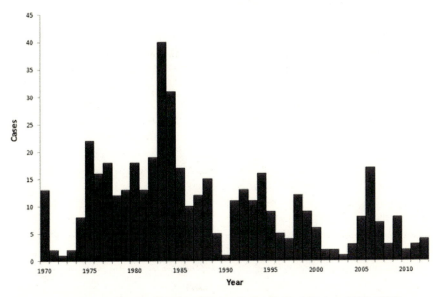

Map 12.1. Reported Cases of Human Plague in the United States, 1970–2012
(Source: Centers for Disease Control and Prevention)

antibiotics are efficient management tools,[44] but no current effective vaccines against aerosol agents exist.

Despite uncertain data, in 1970 the World Health Organization (WHO) estimated an aerosol of 50 kilograms over a city of 5,000,000 would produce 36,000 deaths out of an infected population of 150,000. The infection zone would last an hour and be 10 kilometers long.[45] A simulated U.S. government exercise in 2000 further revealed that public health facilities and agencies were ill prepared to react to a plague attack. The Top Officials Exercise Series (TOPOFF) assessed that the distribution of needed medical supplies was inadequate. As the disease spread, state and local jurisdictions would be unable to stay apace with the advance of the illness. For these reasons, and the fact that it is widely available and contamination requires a low infectious dose, a biological attack using *Yersinia pestis* must also be considered a realistic threat.

Tularemia is one of the most infectious pathogenic bacteria known.[46] As little as ten organisms can cause an onset. Depending on how the bacteria enter the body, the symptoms and indicators of tularemia will differ. Portals for infection are the eyes, lungs, skin, throat, and mouth. The more common and less acute type, oropharyngeal tularemia, is usually contracted by the consumption of contaminated water, vegetation, or food products. All forms of the disease are accompanied by fever. Illness ranges from mild to life threatening. Although a vaccine exists, it is currently under review by the

Food and Drug Administration and not available in the United States.[47] Fortunately, most infections can be treated successfully with antibiotics.

Small mammals, such as rabbits, squirrels, moles, rats, mice, etc., are the natural reservoir of infection. Insects can also transmit the disease to humans. *Francisella tularenis*, named for its discoverer Edward Francis, can spread through direct contact with infected tissue by handling diseased animals or carcasses. Therefore, laboratory workers, farm workers, and even pet handlers can be at risk. It is not communicable from human to human.

Inhaling dust or aerosols produces the most severe form of the disease—pneumonic tularemia. (A "typhoidal" form of tularemia can result as a general infection in addition to the local lung infection case.) In the argument about a presumed terrorist attack, an aerosol release would be the most preferred mode. Such a strike method would have the greatest adverse effect on the target population and its public health system. If untreated, fatality rates could range between 30 and 60 percent. Survivor incapacitation may last several weeks or months. Moreover, proper diagnosis may not be immediate. Diagnosis of tularemia can be problematic. Because of the rarity of the disease the symptoms can be mistaken for other more common illnesses. Routine examinations are too unspecific and, consequently, the organism might escape detection. Once detected, an outbreak of inhalational tularemia in an urban setting should trigger a high level of suspicion of an intentional or terrorist event, since most all reported inhalational tularemia outbreaks have occurred in rural areas.

Although most patients completely recover, as mentioned above, treatment usually lasts several weeks depending on the stage of illness and the medication used. In the event of a terrorist attack experts assess that 50 kilograms of tularemia spread over a population of five million could amount to 250,000 infected. The death toll might approach 20,000.[48] Similar studies reveal similar statistics.[49] Comparable attack rates across sex and age groups would uphold. Risk would be related to degree of exposure to the point source. In the instance of a wide scale terrorist attack, the CDC also assessed the economic impact of bioterrorist attacks and estimated the total base costs to society of an *F tularensis* aerosol to be $5.4 billion for every 100,000 persons exposed.[50] The political costs and toll from public panic may be unquantifiable. Adding to the inscrutability is the somber fear that a drug-resistant organism might be engineered as part of the weaponization process. Such re-engineering could defeat attempts at diagnosis and treatment of tularemia.

According to a 2001 article in the *Journal of the American Medical Association*, Ken (Kanatjan) Alibek maintained the Soviet Union took those exact steps. While the U.S. military was producing and stockpiling stores of tularemia, "a large parallel effort by the Soviet Union continued into the early 1990s and resulted in weapons production of *F. tularensis* strains engineered to be resistant to antibiotics and vaccines."[51] Alibek also suggested that during World War II outbreaks of tularemia on the eastern European front might have been the result of biological warfare. Tens of thousands of Soviet and German soldiers were affected and, as asserted in a book by Alibek, this may have been the outcome of a deliberate act of a war using a biological weapon.[52]

Tularemia attacks were the subject of research by the Japanese in Manchuria between 1932 and 1945. The United States also examined its warfare potential after World War II. In the 1950s and 1960s, the U.S. military continued research in the pathophysiology of tularemia and the development of weapons, which would dispense *F tularensis* aerosols. The United States began terminating its biological weapons development program in the late 1960s, however, and by 1973 had destroyed its entire biological arsenal in accord with the BWC strictures.

Francisella tularensis has long been judged a viable agent in the biological warfare arsenal. Its communicability, accessibility, and infectivity and toxicity through aerosol methods make it a viable, if latent, threat. Although tularemia may have a slower progression of illness and a lower case-fatality rate than either inhalational plague or anthrax, its potential as a biological weapon is quite real.

Botulism is a serious, but rare, paralytic illness caused by a bacteria known as *Clostridium botulinum*. The bacteria exist in untreated water and soil sources around the world. Improperly preserved or canned foods are the usual agents of infection. The disease was not obvious until the nineteenth century when food preservation methods first appeared.[53]

Clostridium botulinum produces the botulinum toxin. Botulinum is the only biotoxin (any poisonous substance produced by a living organism) included among the Category A agents. As opposed to the other Category A agents, the botulinum toxin is a product of the microbe, not the microbe itself, that causes the disease. It is also the most toxic naturally occurring substance known.[54, 55] The estimated toxic dose is 0.0001 micrograms/kg of body weight.[56] In an ideal situation, 1 gram could kill over a million people.[57] Its potent toxicity, ubiquity, ease of production, and ability for dispersal via aerosols or food contamination make it a robust biowarfare threat. For these reasons botulism has been a potential agent in modern war game models and scenarios.

The history of its use and availability in warfare is fairly well documented. During World War II the Japanese fed it to their Chinese prisoners of war. Fearing the prospect of biological war once the allies opened their attacks on the European continent, the U.S. military vaccinated soldiers prior to the D-Day invasion. The USSR and Iraq maintained research and development efforts during the period of the 1970s and early 1980s. Presently, Iran, North Korea, and Syria are on the list of suspected governments possessing and/or producing the botulinum agent. Prior to the U.S. invasion of Iraq, Saddam Hussein's government was also on the list of "state sponsors of terrorism," which was producing and developing botulinum toxins as biological weapons.

Following the 1991 Persian Gulf War, Iraq was forced to admit to the United Nations that it maintained an arsenal of 19,000 liters of the concentrated toxin. A report prepared for the UN Security Council stated that more than half that inventory (10,000 liters) was loaded into military weapons. The full accounting of Iraq's complete stock was never given. What experts in biological warfare do know is that a 19,000-liter quantity of concentrated botulism toxin constitutes "approximately 3 times the amount needed to kill the entire current human population by inhalation." [58]

Inhalation is the more rapid method of infection and, thus, the aerosolized form of the toxin offers the greater threat from a bioterrorist perspective. A faster onset is possible because of a slower absorption rate of sporadic botulism through the intestinal mucosa compared to respiratory intake. Large quantities of botulinum can be produced using automated processes. However, aerosolization has limitations. The toxin's stability and its inability to resist standard water treatment methods affects its effectiveness as a weapon. At present, despite its potential as a bioweapon, there is no evidence that an engineered aerosol form exists. Hence, deliberate contamination of food sources poses an equally viable option if not the terrorists' preferred one. [59]

There are three naturally occurring forms of botulism: foodborne, wound, and intestinal. The toxin does not penetrate intact skin surfaces. It relies on absorption into the blood system through wound surfaces and ingestion. Although inhalational dispersion has its inefficiencies, food contamination is not without serious obstacles. Wide-scale attacks depend upon the number and distribution of various food products. Any attempt to poison the water supply would most likely be defeated by existing purification treatment systems, which inactivate the toxin. Furthermore, botulism is not communicable between humans. One acquires the disease not through infection, but rather by intoxication. Initial symptoms include paralysis of the skeletal and neck muscles. As the condition deteriorates, limbs and trunk areas become affected. Difficulty chewing, swallowing, speaking, and seeing are other outward signs that the disease is progressing. The most severe cases may require mechanical breathing support. Death usually results due to upper airway and respiratory muscle paralysis. [60]

Recuperation may require extensive care over a period of months. An assault upon a large population might overwhelm medical personnel and facilities. Because of the prolonged care needed to restore public health, authorities fear the consequences of a planned terrorist biological attack involving botulinum. Such acts have occurred, notably in Japan. Aum Shinrikyo conducted three failed attempts on U.S. and Japanese military bases.

Using clostridium cultures grown from local soil samples the cult successfully created an aerosolized toxin but, fortunately, failed to produce the disease.[61,62]

Fortune, however, cannot be an elemental factor in the defense against a terrorist biological attack. The accessibility of material and expertise is in a constant state of progress and development. The advancements in life sciences proceed at an ever-accelerating pace. Some claim the microbiology sciences equivalent of "Moore's Law" in computer science is even more dynamic and irresistible.[63] (See box below.)

In the case of botulism, the substance is an example of the dual-edged sword of modern technology. The authors of an article in a 2001 issue of the *Journal of the American Medical Association* write:

> It is regrettable that botulism toxin still needs to be considered as a biological weapon at the historic moment when it has become the first biological toxin to become license for the treatment of human disease.[64]

The toxin has licenses for treatment in a variety of medical applications. Such conditions include tetanus, blepharospasm, strabismus, and in cosmetic surgery. Additionally, "off label" (not FDA approved) use of the botulism toxin to treat migraines, chronic back pain, achalaisa, stroke, cerebral palsy, traumatic brain injury, and other conditions has been successful.[65] However, on the reverse side of the double-edged blade, in the event of malevolent use the kill rate is between 5 and 10 percent. Once established, there is no antidote or vaccine available.

DNA: The next big hacking frontier
By Vivek Wadhwa, *Washington Post*, December 7, 2011
Imagine computer-designed viruses that cure disease, new bacteria capable of synthesizing an unlimited fuel supply, new organisms that wipe out entire populations and bio-toxins that target world leaders. They sound like devices restricted to feature-film script writers, but it is possible to create all of these today, using the latest advances in synthetic biology. Just as the personal computer revolution brought information technology from corporate data centers to the masses, the biology revolution is personalizing science.

In 2000, scientists at a private company called Celera announced that the company had raced ahead of the U.S. Government-led international effort decoding the DNA of a human being. Using the latest sequencing technology, plus the data available from the Human Genome project, Celera scientists had created a working draft of the genome. These efforts cost over $1 billion, combined.

That speed and cost has since been significantly reduced, at double the rate of Moore's Law, and the process can be done by a variety of companies. Today, it is possible to decode your DNA for a few thousand dollars. Expect the price to drop to the cost of a regular blood test within five years and, shortly thereafter, a cup of coffee.

But this process is about "reading" DNA. It is now possible to "write" it—a revolution in biology.

Craig Venter, who led the research at Celera, announced a decade later, in May 2010, that his team had, for the first time in history, built a synthetic life form—by "writing" DNA. Christened Mycoplasma mycoides JCVI-syn1.0, also known as, "Synthia," the slow-growing, harmless bacterium was made of a synthetic genome with 1,077,947 DNA base pairs.

The technology that Venter used to "boot up" this new organism was the equivalent of a laser printer that can "print" DNA.

There are a number of DNA "print" providers, such as DNA2.0 and GeneArt, which offer DNA synthesis and assembly operations as a service. Current pricing is by the number of base pairs—the chemical "bits" that make up a gene—to be assembled. Today's rate is about thirty cents per base pair. Prices are falling exponentially. Within a few years, it could cost a hundredth of this amount. Eventually, like laser printers, DNA printers will be inexpensive home devices.

Andrew Hessel, co-chairman of bioinformatics and biotechnology at Singularity University, where I currently serve as vice president of academics and innovation, predicts that within ten years, it will be possible to search for genetic designs on the web, download them to your computer, and modify and adapt these to your needs. He predicts that cold and flu vaccine designs will be spread quickly over social media and that the process will be as easy as downloading an app on a smartphone. This technology will, ideally, make it possible for us to print our own treatments.

All of this opens up a Pandora's box of problems. Security futurist Marc Goodman says that synthetic biology will lead to new forms of bioterrorism—opportunities for the bad guys to create never-before-seen forms of bio-toxins. These bio-threats might be nearly impossible to detect because they can be customized to the genome of a certain person or groups of people. Goodman, who has long worked on cyber crime and terrorism with organizations such as Interpol and the United Nations, believes the potential bio-threat is greatly underestimated.

"Bio-crime today is akin to computer crime in the early 1980s," said Goodman at the Singularity University executive program this week. "Few initially recognized the problem, but one need only observe how the threat grew exponentially over time."

In the future, as the price drops and the technology becomes more commonplace, criminals and terrorists will be able to exploit synthetic biology not only to drive large-scale outbreaks. They will also be able to create targeted attacks against a single individual based on his or her own unique biology.

We will need anti-virus software and defenses just as we have for computer software. But although we can reformat our hard disks to remove a computer virus, we can't reformat our genomes ... yet.

As described above, unlike nuclear weapons, the materials to manufacture biological weapons exist in nature. Not only are the materials ubiquitous, producing large supplies of biological agents from very small source amounts is quite achievable. "Bacteria, viruses, and toxins occur naturally in the environment" and "are relatively easily obtained either as a WMD or for more limited terrorist attacks."[66] However, although the fabrication of biological agents is possible at low costs, the properties with respect to lethality, range, and shelf life of a crude biological weapon are variable and may be erratic.[67]

Table 12.2 on the following page is the list of organisms described above and deemed to pose the greatest risk for biological weaponization. The CDC gives them the highest priority, Category A, for national security based upon their ease of dissemination, mortality rate, impact on the prevailing health system, and potentiality for public panic.

Of the above category, the only medical countermeasures in the national stockpile are for anthrax and smallpox-based biological agents. According to a 2013 report by the Alliance for American Manufacturing, the United States is dangerously under prepared for a large-scale biological attack and there are no new medical countermeasures in development. Meanwhile, industry has no interest in developing any new antiviral or antibiotic vaccines, which require sizable investment, and whose demand and ROI are unpredictable.[68]

BIOSECURITY POLICY

As discussed above, pathogens exist in nature and can be widely harvested from assorted sources worldwide. Pharmaceutical firms, agricultural facilities, research laboratories, hospitals, and breweries also supply the market (and black market) with pathogens. In addition to the material for manufacturing biological weapons, expertise is also abundant. Life sciences research-

Category A Biological Agents			
Agent:	*Fatality Rate:*	*Transmission:*	*Vaccine:*
Anthrax *	25% - 80%	Inhalational and gastrointestinal.	Vaccine available, but no longer produced
Smallpox	30%	Contact with contaminated fluid or aerosol saliva	Vaccine available, but limited
Hemorrhagic Fever	50% - 90%	Contact with infected tissue, blood, mosquito bites, and close personal contact	No effective vaccine available
Plague	15% Treated 100% Untreated	Contact with infected tissue, flea bites, and inhalation	No effective vaccine available
Tularemia *	30% - 60%	Contact with infected tissue, fly and tick bites, and inhalation	Vaccine available, but limited and efficacy is unknown
Botulism *	5% - 10%	Food-borne – intestinal and inhalational in lab environments.	Vaccine unavailable in the US, currently undergoing FDA trials

Table 12.2. Category A Biological Agents

ers and expertly trained graduate students are part of a growing global industry in microbiological science. Advancements in *de novo* research and synthesis allow for the creation of new strains of viruses and organisms, which outpace the efforts to develop vaccines, antidotes, and the efforts to control their proliferation. Consequently, the combination of available know-how and materials make acquiring and purifying biological material for weapons grade use is comparatively easier than the production of other weapons of mass destruction. However, current biosecurity policy relies heavily upon the same strategic approaches and techniques used to safeguard society from terrorist chemical and nuclear attacks.[69] Non-proliferation strategies mostly drive policy and are at the core of most national and international programs and agreements.

Because biological weapons are often considered part of the CBRN panoply, the conventional logic is to view the threat with the same gaze as chemical and radiological-nuclear WMDs. In truth, these are fundamentally different weapons and pose different exposures of risk. By not accounting for the ubiquity of material and personnel available to the production of biological weapons, the effectiveness of these nonproliferation approaches has stark limits. Marc Ostfield goes on to warn that

> advocates of pathogen security are promoting what may only be an *illusion of security*—creating the false impression that such [nonproliferation] measures will meaningfully prevent or substantially reduce the risk of a bioterrorism attack.[70]

In actuality, these classes of WMDs differ in their essence and in the trajectory of their specific attack surfaces. Controlling the access to pathogens as we do the access to chemical and nuclear material is merely part of the solution. Ostfield describes the emphasis on nonproliferation for biosecurity as analogous to a person intent on looking for their lost car keys only under the area below a street lamp. The rationale is that the light is better under the street lamp and, therefore, overrides the fact that the keys may be elsewhere. Although nonproliferation treaties and initiatives may provide an initial framework for international agreement, the solution offering is incomplete. Ostfield identifies several points that would make biosecurity programs more efficient, workable, and scalable with an ever-advancing technological variable. They include:

- Developing early detection for biological outbreaks
- Creating a mechanism for cross-border information sharing
- Constructing an operational framework for international investigation
- Establishing and harmonizing international standards
- Building preparedness mechanisms
- Enhancing and expanding medical countermeasure development and stockpiles
- Creating response and mitigation capabilities

The points Ostfield raises only further demonstrate how bound security policy is by an Industrial Age system of protocols and approaches, which has yet to adapt to the complexities and re-orientations of an information age. Due to decades of development and cultivation, these nonproliferation strategies have become household to policy makers and, therefore, harbor an inertia resistant to change. Their theoretical approaches have become realities. The realm of "guards, gates, and guns" is limited territory in the biosecurity expanse. Its value is similarly curbed. Unless the security establishment finds a proper balance between the obvious mechanisms involving physical security and the more difficult task of building a system of preparation and response—biodefense strategy might be inadequate against future challenges. The analogy between cyber attacks and biological terrorist attacks are no longer simply metaphoric—it is becoming actionable. The future ability of individuals to decode their own DNA through the aid of sequencing technology will intersect with the ability of terrorists to create new forms of biotoxins. These developments are foreseen and their consequences require concern and attention.

NOTES

1. S. F. Cook, W. W. Borah, *The Indian Population of Central Mexico* (Berkeley: University of California Press, 1963).
2. Gordon D. Christensen, "Biological Agents: Effects, Toxicity, and Effectiveness," *Science and Technology of Terrorism and Counterterrorism,* ed., Ghosh, Prelas, Viswanath, Loyalka (Marcel Dekker, Inc., 2002).
3. *Ibid.*
4. http://www.opbw.org/.
5. Michael Moodie, *The life Sciences, Security, and the Challenge of Biological Weapons: an Overview* in Bio-inspired Innovation and National Security, ed., Armstrong, Drapeau, Loeb, Valdes (for Technology and National Security Policy, National Defense Press, Washington, DC, 2010).
6. *Ibid.*
7. Mark A. Prelas, "Weaponization and Delivery Systems," in Ghosh.
8. David Satter, "Russia's Looming Crisis," *Foreign Policy Research Institute* (March 2012), p. 22.
9. Christensen.
10. Moodie.
11. Mark G. Kortepeter, Gerald W. Parker, "Potential Biological Weapons Threat" (U.S. Army Medical Research Institute of Infectious Diseases, Fort Derrick, MD, 1999).
12. R. M. Salerno, and L. Hickok, "Strengthening bioterrorism prevention: global biological material management," *Biosecurity and Bioterrorism* (Vol. 5, 2007), p. 107–16.
13. E. K. Roosevelt, "Germ Warfare," *International Combat Arms* (July 1986).
14. M. Stebbins, "Technicalities prevent bioterrorist attacks for the moment," *Federation of American Scientists* (17 February 2006).
15. According to a study by the Stockholm International Peace Research Institute, the cost per death/per kilometer to inflict civilian casualties is: $2,000 with conventional weapons, $800 with nuclear weapons, and $1 using biological weapons.
16. Marc Ostfeld, "Pathogen Security: the illusion of security in foreign policy and biodefence," *International Journal of Risk and Management,* Vol. 12, Nos. 2/3/4 (2009).
17. Larry M. Bush, Maria Perez, "The Anthrax Attacks: Ten Years Later," *Annals of Internal Medicine* (2012), http://www.annals.org.
18. *Globalization, Biosecurity and the Future of the Life Sciences,* IOM/NRC, Institute of Medicine/National Research Council, Committee of the Advances of Technology in the Prevention of their Application to the next Generation of Biowarfare Threats, Washington, DC (The National Academies Press, 2006), in Christensen.

19. *NATO Handbook on the Medical Aspects NBC Defensive Operations*, Departments of the Army, Navy, and Air Force (Washington, DC, 1996).

20. Christensen.

21. *Health Aspects of Chemical and Biological Weapons*, WHO Group of Consultants (Geneva, 1970).

22. John Adams, "Remaking American Security: Supply Chain Vulnerabilities and National Security Risks Across the U.S. Industrial Base," *Alliance for American Manufacturing* (May 2013), p. 307.

23. C. Davis, "Nuclear blindness: An overview of the biological weapons programs of the former Soviet Union and Iraq," *Emerging Infectious Diseases* (1999).

24. Ostfeld.

25. Rene Pita, Rohan Gunaratna, "Anthrax as a Biological Weapon: From World War I to the Amerithrax Investigation," *International Journal of Intelligence and Counterintelligence* (2009).

26. *Ibid.*

27. Adam Dolnik, *Understanding Terrorist Innovation: Technology, Tactics, and Global Trends* (Oxon, UK, Routledge, 2007) p. 102–103.

28. Prelas.

29. M. T. Osterholm, J. Schwartz, *Living Terrors: What America Needs to Know to Survive the Coming Bioterrorist Catastrophe* (Delacourt Press, New York, 2000), p. 17.

30. Ronald Atlas, "Bioterrorism: From Threat to Reality," *Annual Review of Microbiology* (2002).

31. Christensen.

32. *Ibid.*

33. Atlas.

34. *Ibid.*

35. "Management of patients with suspected viral hemorrhagic fever," *Morbidity and mortality weekly report* (CDC, 1988).

36. Christensen.

37. *Ibid.*

38. CDC website, http://www.cdc.gov/ncidod/dvbid/plague/.

39. Christensen.

40. Atlas.

41. CDC website.

42. Heather Brannon, "Plague as a Bioterrorism Threat: Bubonic Plague and Pneumonic Plague," http://dermatology.about.com/cs/bioterrorism/a/plague.htm.

43. Anthony H. Cordesman, "Defending America, Asymmetric and Terrorist Attacks with Biological Weapons," Center for Strategic and International Studies (Washington, DC, 2001).

44. *Ibid.*

45. T. V. Inglesby, D. T. Dennis, D. A. Henderson, "Plague as a Biological Weapon, medical and public health management," *Journal of the American Medical Association* (2000).

46. T. V. Inglesby, D. T. Dennis, D. A. Henderson, et al. "Consensus Statement: Tularemia as a Biological Weapon: Medical and Public Health Management," *Journal of the American Medical Association* (6 June 2001), vol. 285, no. 21: 2763–2773.

47. http://www.cdc.gov/tularemia/faq/.

48. *Op. cit.*

49. Atlas.

50. A. F. Kaufmann, M. I. Meltzer, G. P. Schmid, "The economic impact of a bioterrorist attack: are prevention and post-attack intervention programs justifiable?" *Emerg Infect Dis.,* 1997; 3:83–94.

51. Alibek K. Biohazard (Random House, New York, NY, 1999:29–38. in http://jama.ama-assn.org/content/285/21/2763.full#ref-24.

52. *Ibid.*

53. J. L. Middlebrook, D. R. Franz, "Botulism Toxins," in Sidell, F. R., TakaFuji, E. T., Frans, D. R., eds. "Medical Aspects of Chemical and Biological Warfare," Washington, DC:

office of the Surgeon General (TMM Publications, Borden Institute, Walter Reed Army Medical Center, 643–54, 1997).

54. Christensen.

55. Atlas.

56. *Ibid.*

57. Michael R. Grey, Kenneth R. Spaeth, *The Bioterrorism Sourcebook* (The McGraw-Hill Companies, Inc., 2006).

58. Stephen S. Arnon, Robert Schechter, et al., "Botulinum Toxin as a Biological Weapon: Medical and Public Health Management," in *JAMA* (28 February 2001), vol. 285, no. 8.

59. *Ibid.*

60. *Op. cit.*

61. Christensen.

62. Grey.

63. Moore's Law suggests every eighteen months the number of transistors on a computer chip doubles driving the expansion of functions on a chip at a lower cost per function; thus, making technological growth in the computer sciences field exponential.

64. Arnon.

65. *Ibid.*

66. Ostfield.

67. Christensen.

68. Adams, p. 307.

69. *Ostfield*

70. *Ibid.*

Chapter Thirteen

Chemical Biological Radiological & Nuclear: The Radiological Nuclear Threat

Oh, you want to build a bomb, too?
—University Librarian to John Aristotle Phillips, undergraduate thesis author of "An Assessment of the Problems and Possibilities Confronting a Terrorist Group or Non-Nuclear Nation Attempting to Design a Crude Pu239 Fission Bomb"

As a junior at Princeton University in 1977 John Aristotle Phillips bemoaned: "if I flunk another course, I'll be bounced out of Big U right on my ass."[1] The former Princeton tiger mascot and aerospace science major determined he needed an extraordinary thesis project in order to remain in school. He submitted his proposal, "How to Build Your Own Atomic Bomb" to his project mentor. His mentor was the noted mathematician and physicist Freeman Dyson. Dyson agreed to be his academic advisor whose academic advice included burning the paper as soon as his grade was registered. The advice proved unnecessary since other faculty members who had worked on the Manhattan Project believed Phillips's bomb design workable and, therefore, confiscated his paper and turned it over to the U.S. government. The U.S. government took possession of his research, classified it as "secret," and, happily, Phillips eventually passed his course and graduated.

His undergraduate thesis project not only offered startling evidence that one could build a Nagasaki-class nuclear weapon within a year and at a cost of $2,000, but that the feat could be accomplished by using information from publicly accessible sources that included college textbooks, government documents, and industry sources. The National Technical Information Service, a central source of government-funded scientific and technical information, provided research papers and lectures. Among them was *The Los Alamos Primer: The First Lectures on How to Build an Atomic Bomb*. When he needed information on explosives, he contacted DuPont Company to learn which materials would be useful for compressing high-density metals. An engineer suggested a detonator DuPont had sold the government "for use in nuclear weapons."[2] Phillips also found a way to get around the sticky issue of obtaining plutonium-239. Despite industry denials, he learned an accessible source was reprocessed plutonium from nuclear power plants. Reprocessing refers to the extraction of plutonium-239 from spent reactor fuel. The end product of his research would have been the size of a beach ball with a 10 kiloton yield. Graham Allison, founding dean of Harvard's John F. Kennedy School of Government and former Assistant Secretary of Defense, described the device as "the perfect terrorist weapon."[3]

John Phillips is, today, founder and CEO of Aristotle International, a strategic political consultancy on technology applications. In an interview years after he submitted his thesis he remarked: "I would never have thought we have gone twenty-five years without a terrorist getting a nuclear device; I'm surprised it hasn't happened. I still do expect it."[4]

WHAT IS RADIOACTIVITY?

Everything in our world is radioactive to some degree. Naturally occurring radioactivity, or what is also known as background radiation is all around us. Human activity, as well, creates radioactivity for curative and destructive purposes. Therefore, the term radiation refers to a broad range of definitions, phenomena, and applications. It includes the experience of sunlight, the glow of a fire, the health benefits of modern miracle drugs and medical treatment, and the blast of a nuclear device. The spectrum has two major divisions:

Non-ionizing Radiation has insufficient energy to separate an orbital electron in an atom. This activity generates only enough energy to move atoms in a molecule around or cause them to vibrate, but not enough to release electrons and emit excess energy. Examples of this kind of radiation are sound waves, visible light, and microwaves. These low and medium range energy waves produce sonar, radar, and visible waves. Above this energy spectrum level electromagnetic radiation creates the energy required to achieve ionization.[5]

Ionizing Radiation, on the other hand, has enough energy to remove tightly bound electrons from atoms, thus creating two charged particles—the molecule with a positive charge and the free electron with a negative charge.

These particles are known as ions. This type of radiation is the subject of the following discussion (see below).

Understanding the nature of radiation begins with the basic structure of an atom, which is simply a nucleus of protons and neutrons with electrons orbiting the nucleus. In more stable, lighter elements there is a one-to-one ratio of protons to neutrons. Generally, when the nucleus is stable, meaning ratios are maintained, there is no measurable radioactivity. However, *radioactive decay,* or radioactivity, occurs when nuclei are unstable and attempt to move from a proton-to-neutron unstable ratio to a proton-to-neutron ratio that is stable. The transition emits energy.

We measure radioactivity as the rate by which radioactive nuclei decay, or disintegrate. Half-lives are the measurement units that mark the level of this process of self-destruction and the degree of radioactivity. The term *half-life* expresses the amount of time it takes for one half of the radiation to decay. Therefore, as time passes radioactive material diminishes but their radioactivity is never zero. Radioactivity introduced to the body for diagnostic purposes might have a half-life of a few hours and decrease to negligible traces within a few days. Radioactive treatment of such ailments as thyroid conditions has longer half-lives and patients have been known to trigger nuclear detection devices. Other radioactive elements, which occur naturally, have half-lives in the billions of years. Plutonium-239, the primary element used for nuclear weapons, has a half-life of 24,100 years.

The process of radioactive decay releases about 33 electron volts (eV) of energy per ionization. The resultant ionization radiation deposits a large

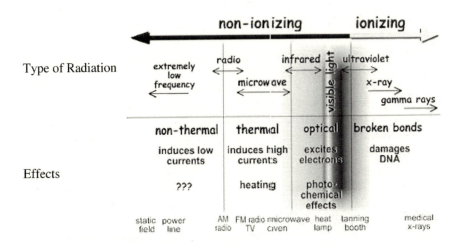

Figure 13.1. Non-ionizing and Ionizing Radiation *(Source: Environmental Protection Agency)*

amount of energy into small areas. There are three main types of ionizing radiation. *Alpha particles* are two protons and two neutrons. *Beta particles* are basically electrons. *Gamma rays* and *X-rays* represent pure energy. We benefit by the properties found in the freeing of electrons and other subatomic particles to generate electric power, to kill cancer cells, and in many manufacturing processes.[6] We also take advantage of this process in producing weapons of mass destruction.

SO YOU WANT TO BUILD A BOMB?

Nuclear fission is the essence of an atomic weapon. It occurs during a nuclear reaction or a radioactive decaying process, which forces atomic nuclei to split into smaller parts releasing neutrons and photons (elementary particles) in the form of gamma rays. Large amounts of energy discharge, causing a chain reaction as neutrons split more atoms. The cascading effect releases more energy, and the explosion time is a matter of microseconds. The power density is extremely high. Plutonium-239, mentioned above, is an isotope[7] of plutonium and the main fissile isotope used for the production of nuclear weapons (Uranium-235 is another, but a secondary alternative). It takes approximately 9 pounds of plutonium to achieve a nuclear explosion as compared to 35 pounds of highly enriched uranium.

The event begins with a critical mass of fissile material. Critical mass is the minimal amount needed to sustain a chain reaction. During the chain reaction the process reaches the supercritical stage as the fission rate and the energy release rate multiply. Achieving critical mass is done by compressing the mass by either using chemical explosives, or firing one mass into another. In the case of the latter, a "gun-type design" can be used. This is a relatively simple and inexpensive method for creating and detonating a fissile weapon. It is the sort of device within the grasp of a resourceful terrorist group or curious undergraduate science majors.

Using this crude schematic and a gun tube similar to the barrel of an anti-aircraft gun, scientists from the national laboratories created such a device in 2004. They presented their model to Joseph Biden, who at the time was the ranking Democrat of the Senate Foreign Relations Committee. In testament to the argument in Phillips's college paper, the weapon was built within several months with off-the-shelf materials. The parts for the entire structure of explosives and firing system are available from commercial sources, which sell the same equipment for the purposes of demolition work, boring holes for oil wells, and in icebreaking operations.[8]

The device works by using one quantity of fissile mass as a bullet and firing it through a gun tube at another fissile mass. When the bullet collides with the target, the masses fuse together to form a dense supercritical mass and detonate. As the compression continues, the release of energy doubles with shorter increments of time. This all occurs during a span of microseconds. Although the explosive part of a nuclear weapon can be only a mere few centimeters in diameter,[9] the devastation is vast. As the scientists from the national labs demonstrated, assembly is possible with accessible and inexpensive parts and equipment.

The reality of nuclear weapons production is that since the first deployment of a nuclear bomb over sixty years ago, "The fundamentals of crude nuclear weapons production are reasonably well understood and publicized."[10] *The Los Alamos Primer* used by Phillips and another declassified document, *Atomic Energy for Military Purposes,* are available on Amazon.com.[11] A *Washington Post* article in 2004 further claims there exists a sophisticated black market in "weapons designs, real-time technical advice, and thousands of sensitive parts."[12] The authors of the piece also report that much of this equipment may have been manufactured at secret factories.

At the time of its collapse, the former Soviet Union possessed tons of fissile material and, eventually, an unaccounted number of dispossessed elite weapons designers. By most expert analysis it had 140 to 160 tons of plutonium, an even higher inventory of HEU. The leakage of material and expertise from bankrupt nuclear munitions facilities in Russia creates the same concern for global security as posed by the former Soviet bio-chemical sectors as discussed above. Powerful computers and sophisticated programs dealing with such topics as neutronics, fluid dynamics, heat transfer, and structural issues abound. A team of three to five scientists and engineers with backgrounds in nuclear physics, metallurgy, explosives, and electronics could provide the staff. Laboratories and machine shops would be manufacturing facilities.[13]

Fortunately, unless stolen or illegally purchased, plutonium and uranium fissile material is a difficult acquisition. Its production is technically complex and comes at a high capital expense. It demands an array of plant, equipment, and a well-educated pool of technical experts. Nuclear weapons production is not simply a matter of a few manufacturing facilities and projects. It is an industry that relies upon infrastructure and long-term governmental investment for its support. Plutonium is synthetic material. It involves nuclear reactors and neutron accelerators for its production. Natural uranium must be enriched via a technically complex and extensive process. After being extracted from rock, uranium ore is milled, soaked in sulfuric acid, and leached to produce "yellow cake." Following some additional filtration, the powdery yellow cake is chemically converted into a gaseous substance called hexaflouride to produce a high content of U-235. The uranium hexa-flouride gas then undergoes centrifugation, electromagnetic, diffusion, nozzle flow, or laser processing for further enrichment. It should be noted that if the developer only requires a limited amount of weapon grade uranium, laser and electromagnetic separation are relatively inexpensive techniques. [14]

States seeking nuclear capability also need substantial military resources such as delivery systems. However, rather than sophisticated guided missile programs, terrorists merely need cargo containers, barges/ships (see chapters 5 and 6), vans, or trucks as delivery platforms. Terrorists also have short-term or immediate time horizons. Crude and unreliable devices suffice when the objective is political chaos and upheaval as much as it is utter destruction. Furthermore, tactics and methods of non-state actors differ wildly from states when the attacking community is virtually immune from retaliation and the notion of national defense policy is irrelevant.

THE DIRTY BOMB ALTERNATIVE

A radiological dispersion device (RDD), or what is commonly called a "dirty bomb," is an alternative weapon if attackers do not have the technical means or the ambition to detonate a nuclear explosion. Rather than causing mass destruction, a dirty bomb will result in mass disruption. Simply, a RDD uses conventional explosives to disperse radiological material mostly causing radiation sickness and mass panic. Other direct and indirect damage includes heavy financial costs due to evacuation and resettlement, healthcare, decontamination services, insurance industry fallout, and future investment in security. Non-radiological substances, such as anthrax, can also be used in a dirty bomb attack.

Although necessary to create a nuclear explosion, fissile material such as plutonium-239 and HEU are not practical for use in a dirty bomb. Their particles would not travel far as a result of a detonation of a conventional explosive device. Neither isotope is radioactive enough to penetrate the skin and clothing. Alternative radioactive substances, which emit gamma rays, are far more effective. The major options for use in a dirty bomb include the following:

- **Cesium** (chemical symbol Cs) may be non-radioactive or radioactive. The most common radioactive form of cesium is cesium-137. Cesium-137 is a significant environmental contaminant as well as being very useful in industry for its strong radioactivity.
- **Strontium** (chemical symbol Sr) is found naturally as a non-radioactive element. Strontium has sixteen known isotopes, twelve of which are radioactive. Strontium-90 is the main radioactive isotope in the environment. Strontium-89 can be found around reactors. Strontium-85 is common for use in industry and in medical research.

- **Americium** (chemical symbol Am) is a man-made radioactive metal produced when plutonium atoms absorb neutrons in nuclear reactors and in nuclear weapons detonations. Americium has several different isotopes, all of which are radioactive. The most common use (americium-241) is as a component in household and industrial smoke detectors.
- **Cobalt** (chemical symbol Co) is a metal that may be non-radioactive. If radioactive it may be naturally occurring, or synthesized. The most common radioactive isotope of cobalt is cobalt-60. Cobalt-60 is used in many common industrial applications, such as in leveling devices, thickness gauges, and in radiotherapy in hospitals.[15]

Material such as cesium can be used with extreme effect. Cesium emits gamma rays and causes radiation poisoning. Exposure to radiation from cesium-137 causes an increased risk of cancer. If close to the detonation point, serious burns and death can result. By comparison, it would take 1,460 tons of low-enriched uranium to contaminate the same area as 1.4 ounces of cesium-137.[16] This would equal, roughly, the size of Manhattan.

If a dirty bomb dispersed a cloud of cesium or other high concentrations of radiological material such as cobalt, large swathes of neighborhoods and residents would be affected. Concrete, asphalt, vegetation, and soil would need to be decontaminated or removed. Depending upon the amount of the radioactive substance, population density, and atmospheric conditions—areas may depopulate.[17] There are also accusations that radiological weapons can be used for purposes other than mass disruption. Assassination is a possibility according to some experts. A highly publicized account raising such suspicions occurred in 2006. Alexander Litvinenko was a former Russian spy turned journalist. While investigating the murder of another journalist and Putin critic, Litvinenko was fatally poisoned by a radioactive substance. John Henry, a British toxicologist, examined Litvinenko before his death and said the substance, polonium, was involved and lethal dosages are "only found in government-controlled institutions."[18] Similar questions have circulated over the circumstances of Yasser Arafat's death. Traces of Polonium were also found among his possessions shortly before his end. Authorities exhumed his body in 2013 and forensic teams from Switzerland, France and Russia spent months examining his remains for traces of polonium. The findings conflict as to whether Arafat died of natural causes. At the time of this writing, no explanation has yet been offered as to why and how three teams reached separate conclusions.

Part of the problem and threat of a radiological attack is the ubiquity of highly radioactive substances, or radionuclides. Radionuclide sources are everywhere. There are many civilian uses and supplies are often unsecured. Radioactive materials have wide and varied use. Hospitals, laboratories, doctors' offices, and mining operations have minute and ample quantities of cesium and cobalt. Electrons, alpha-particles, neutrons, X-rays, and gamma rays are types of nuclear radiation found across the arc of applications in industry, medicine, agriculture, and scientific research. If not managed safely and securely during their production, use, transportation, storage, and disposal, a security and public health threat looms from potential accidental events or terrorist exploits.[19]

Authors in a 2012 GAO report claim that federal regulators have been unsuccessful in implementing the necessary safeguards to secure radiological materials, which could be used to produce a "dirty bomb." Such failures occur at nearly four out of every five high-risk hospitals and medical facilities nationwide.[20] The GAO assessed the efforts by the Nuclear Regulatory Commission and the National Nuclear Security Administration and determined that only 321 of 1,503 medical facilities and hospitals identified as high risk fully complied with the security upgrade standards. The report also claimed that because the security requirements were too broad and merely voluntary, serious effort on behalf of these high-risk facilities was lacking. These findings also draw attention to the larger problem. Diagnosis and treatment of cancer and other diseases often requires radioactive material. Yet, the storage and tracking of nuclear materials are generally, at best, less than adequate—worldwide. Given the array of sources for obtaining harmful radionuclides and the spectrum of potential methods and devices for use as platforms, several experts at Los Alamos National Laboratory wrote in a 2003 research paper: "a RDD attack somewhere in the world is overdue."[21]

CONTROLLING PROLIFERATION

Since 1968 the Nuclear Proliferation Treaty (NPT) has been the chief legal framework and basis for international cooperation in halting the spread of nuclear weapons and weapon technology. At that time, sixty-two nations signed the pact and agreed to abide by its provisions. Today 190 countries are party to the treaty. NPT promotes efforts in support of nuclear disarmament and upholds the right for nations to develop peaceful, energy-related uses. It fulfills its mission by obligating its members to the following simple (and perhaps utopian) terms:

- Prohibit nuclear weapons states (NWS) from transferring nuclear weapons or nuclear explosive devices to any other state.
- Prohibit non-nuclear weapons states (NNWS) from acquiring or manufacturing such weapons or explosive devices.
- Demand NNWS abide by the International Atomic Energy Agency's (IAEA) standards, guidelines, and safeguards.

- Encourage NWS and NNWS, alike, to share in the exchange of equipment, scientific information, and material to develop nuclear energy for peaceful purposes.
- Require all parties to pursue good faith negotiations in order to terminate the nuclear arms competition and to eventually achieve total disarmament. Partly due to this effort, bilateral and multilateral agreements exist around the world.

There are five authorized nuclear weapons states: United States, United Kingdom, Russia, China, and France. Other national nuclear weapons programs are in states that are non-signatories: India, Pakistan, and Israel. Following the collapse of the Soviet Union, Kazakhstan, Belarus, and Ukraine surrendered their weapons to the Russian Federation in 1996 and added their names to the list of parties as non-nuclear weapons members. In 1993 South Africa became a member after having developed a nuclear weapons program and eventually dismantling it as a result of international pressure. North Korea, which has a nuclear arsenal and is working on a quick launch response system, withdrew its membership in 2003. Many still suspect Syria and Iran as having nuclear capability. Despite the lack of verifiable evidence to support the accusation, the contention refuses to fade. In summary, regardless of the treaty's landmark beginnings, the growth of its membership, and the consensus that the need for such legal framework is vital to global security—nuclear weapons have proliferated to other nations who have refused to sign the agreement, and the goal of total nuclear disarmament does not appear a reality of the near future.

In 2007, the United Nations General Assembly approved the International Convention for the Suppression of Acts of Nuclear Terrorism. After resolving contentions over the definition of the term "terrorism," the treaty joined the twelve previously existing anti-terrorism conventions as another effort to counter the spread of these tactics.[22] There are 115 signatories and 79 parties. Primarily, the treaty establishes a broader definition on nuclear materials and facilities related to military and peaceful applications. It also requires states to criminalize acts of terrorism through their national legislatures and set conditions under which states institute jurisdictions for these offenses. Importantly, as well, the convention establishes guidelines for extradition and measures of punishment.

STATUS	STATE
NPT States	U.S., UK, Russia, China, France
Non-NPT States	India, Pakistan, N. Korea
Unacknowledged	Israel
Suspected	Iran, Syria
NATO Sharing	Germany, Italy, Turkey, Netherlands

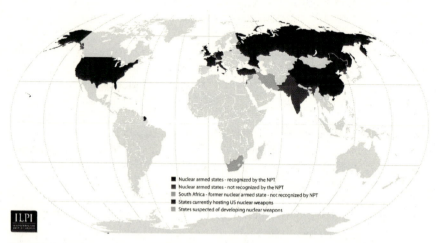

Map 13.1. Status of States with Nuclear Capability *(Source: International Law and Policy Institute)*

Former Programs	Belarus, Ukraine, Kazakhstan, S. Africa

Undercutting all efforts to control the spread of nuclear and radiological devices is the universal accessibility of materials, information, and expertise for creating weapons of mass destruction and mass disruption. The distributional mechanism of a vast underground economy facilitates the risk further. Legitimate players have a role in these circumstances as well. During the Cold War, powers like China, India, and Pakistan developed these weapons programs to enter the nuclear club. By the late 1960s Israel had a nuclear arsenal of at least two warheads.[23] North Korea entered the club in 2006 with an underground test of a single kiloton bomb. Whether these governments see it today as a way to counter the U.S. conventional military advantage or as a means to gain dominance in their regions, these states (and very possibly other countries) gladly embrace the risk of a potential escalation of violence.[24] Additionally, the sale of nuclear reactors by the United States and other developed countries for "peaceful" nuclear energy purposes (in accord and with the encouragement of the NPT), aside from being an obvious benefit for countries seeking an alternative energy source also creates opportunity for abuse of good intentions by bad actors.

Paul Bracken, of Yale University, warns of a more disorderly second nuclear age. The stage no longer belongs to Washington and Moscow. Now a cast of several state actors comprises a "multi-polar nuclear order." This new power arrangement defines the tension and frames the global nuclear security paradigm. With the bloc discipline of the Cold War withered away, the superpower monopoly over nuclear weapons use broke, and the authority and right to wage nuclear war devolved to regional actors and conflicts. China, Pakistan, and India have been developing a new class of battlefield nuclear weapons, and road-mobile and submarine-based missiles.[25]

As these revolutions in global politics occur they demand a new approach to observing and assessing problems. In chapter 1, the discussion included the topics of containment and rational deterrence theory. Bracken comments that these theories "have a powerful grip—so much so that we don't even see them as theories but reality."[26] A challenge is to break free of old mindsets and open the analysis and debate to new directions and ways of thinking.

CONCLUSION

The discussion of the chemical biological radiological nuclear threat appears after a review of the supply chain, cyber war, and the crime-terrorist nexus. The preference in the organization of the book is to present the national security issues, which are most immediate and discuss those topics in the earlier sections. The danger from CBRN attacks represent impending threats but the placement of their discussion at the end of the book does not imply that they are less serious issues. If Timothy McVeigh had chosen to include radioactive material as part of his ammonium nitrate bomb in Oklahoma City, the devastation would have been worse and state of national alert and the realm of public discourse would have had a different skew and atmosphere. The same can be said if the 9/11 bombers had chosen a nuclear reactor as one of their targets. James Holmes used small arms weapons on moviegoers in an Aurora, Colorado, theater to kill twelve and wound fifty-eight. If his ambition to commit murder matched his derangement, he might have considered using his training in neuroscience or work at the Salk Institute for Biological Studies to rain death on a much larger victim population.

Fortunately, these were not the course of events. That does not preclude incidents such as these occurring at any time in the future. Controlling the manufacture, storage, sale, and shipment of these materials is critical. The system's ability to respond to a CBRN event and restore services and ordinary life is equally vital. Unfortunately, some of the same economic imperatives that inhibit the ability to manage and contain the attack surface of cyber crime and warfare and the corruption of the supply chain apply to this arena. The similarities in the threat to the supply chain, from cyber intrusions, and from CBRN attacks, curiously, share a kindred vernacular (virus, bacteria, Trojan horses); detection methodology (tracking and sensor technology, development of algorithmic theory, conical analysis, etc.); and involve a need for interoperability and partnerships between the separate sectors of society. Therefore, the chapters, simultaneously, are separate discussions as to the character and nature of the threat and linked with respect to the way we express risk, lethality, and apply defense mechanisms. The need for a private sector–public sector partnership is just as urgent along these attack fronts as the others. Yet, the capability to provide national security while enabling commerce is still an underdeveloped art. We may have been managing the CBRN threat from the time of the last world war. However, since then the dis-aggregation of the Soviet Union's military industrial complex and the explosion of the global black market have altered the threat matrix.

A great challenge in this area is that these CBRN materials are the DNA of daily life. Their use in medical treatment, industrial processes, and in the household is ubiquitous. They exist naturally or can be harvested, refined, and created in laboratory environments as well. As scientific discovery advances and intersects with breakthroughs in ICT technology, the threat vector for misuse takes on a new potency. While this occurs, national security policy still relies upon the same strategies of nonproliferation that were the guiding elements of the Cold War. Today these approaches have limits and future agreements and international regimes will have to take into account the current inadequacies. New threats, power alliances, and new partnerships are taking shape and test the national security establishment's ability to adapt. As defense systems adjust to the revolutions in politics and technology, it is important to understand the nature and potential of the risk.

NOTES

1. Paul Collins, "The A-Bomb Kid" *Village Voice*, (2003), http://www.villagevoice.com/2003-12-16/news/the-a-bomb-kid/.

2. John A. Phillips, David Michaelis, "Mushroon: The Story of the A-Bomb Kid" (William Morrow, 1978).

3. Graham Allison, *Nuclear Terrorism: the Ultimate Preventable Catastrophe* (Henry Holt & Co., New York. 2004). p. 88.

4. Collins.

5. William H. Miller, "Nuclear Terrorism: The Nature of Radiation," in Ghosh, p. 263.

6. Environmental Protection Agency, http://www.epa.gov/radiation/understand/ionize_nonionize.html.

7. Atomic nuclei can be altered and isotopes formed through natural processes or through human/laboratory manipulation. Isotopes are different forms of a single element. They differ structurally by having the same number of protons but with a varying number of neutrons. Plutonium 239 is also one of the three main isotopes usable as fuel in nuclear reactors, along with uranium-235 and uranium-233.

8. Allison, p. 97.

9. Sudarshan K Loyalka, "Nuclear Terrorism: Nuclear Weapons," in Dabir S. Viswanath, and Tushar K Gosh, "Chemical Agents: Classification, Synthesis, and Properties," in *Science and Technology of Terrorism and Counterterrorism*, ed., Ghosh, Prelas, Viswanath, Loyalka (Marcel Dekker, Inc., 2002).

10. *Ibid.*, p. 283.

11. Allison, p. 93.

12. Joby Warrick, Peter Slevin, "Probe of Libya Finds Nuclear Black Market," *Washington Post* (24 January 2004).

13. Sudarshan, K. Loyalka, Mark, A. Prelas, "Nuclear Terrorism: Threats and Countermeasures," in Gnosh, p. 287.

14. *Ibid.*, p. 286.

15. Environmental Protection Agency, http://www.epa.gov.

16. Joe Cirincione, "Dirty Bomb, Muddy Thinking," *Foreign Policy Magazine* (18 September 2012), http://www.foreignpolicy.com/articles/2012/09/18/dirty_bomb_muddy_thinking.

17. Allison, p. 59.

18. Mary Jordon and Peter Finn, "Radioactive Poison Killed Ex-Spy," *Washington Post* (26 November 2006).

19. International Atomic Energy Agency, http://www-ns.iaea.org/security/dirty-bombs.asp?s=4.

20. Anne Gearan, "Dirty Bomb Threat at Hospitals Remain, According to GAO Report," *Washington Post* (11 September 2012), http://www.washingtonpost.com/world/national-security/dirty-bomb-threat-at-hospitals-remains-gao-report-says/2012/09/10/976214f6-fb53-11e1-b2af-1f7d12fe907a_story.html.

21. Gregory J. Van Tuyle, et al., "Reducing RDD Concerns Related to Large Radiological Source Applications," Los Alamos National Laboratory (September 2003), in Allison, p. 8.

22. Nuclear Threat Initiative, nti.org, http://www.nti.org/treaties-and-regimes/treaties/.

23. Paul Bracken, "The Bomb Returns for a Second Act," *Foreign Policy Research Institute* (November 2012).

24. *Ibid.*

25. *Ibid.*

26. *Ibid.*

Part III

Policy Implications and the Public—Private Partnership

Chapter Fourteen

Industrial Policy and Defense Policy

Why Do We Have Brakes?—So We Can Go Faster!
—Nicholas Benvenuto, Former Managing Director, Protiviti Consulting

Put forth in the initial chapters was the concept of an integrative management approach to enhance national security. The concept relies upon a public sector–private sector partnership. It requires that government, industry, and the consumer realize that their interests in a reliable national security framework are of universal benefit. The idea is easy to explain, but difficult to put into practice. The issues of government regulation and intrusiveness, rights of privacy and private property, and financial obligation are contentious matters but need addressing. It is difficult, particularly, in difficult economic times for a business to justify the case for corporate security investment.

To review some earlier points, as mentioned above, the pressures of just-in-time processing often crowd out the concerns for security. Financial constraints and the absence of a perceivable, overt threat leave fallow the will and actions to commit resources. However, our infrastructure is aging. The threat is growing and morphing. Despite the global alarms set off over a decade ago on September 11, much has not changed in our current security structure and mindset. We are locked into an industrial age system of governance, protocols, and jurisdictional and philosophical boundaries. In the age of information we are still organized to fight Industrial Age conflicts. The forces of globalization and international trade, persistent hatred, and an environment of economic and democratic deficits have created a security threat whose total depth and scope we are still troubling to fully assess.

The decades of deregulation and privatization have put a considerable inventory of public good assets in private hands. Therefore, national defense, the textbook example of a public good, is mostly in the form of a private asset. Today, the private sector owns most of the critical infrastructure and if it breaks or is destroyed—who is accountable for its restoration? It is easy to say that the onus is with the owner. However, the threat is shared, and so should the responsibility be shared. Society will be served and protected when security becomes a part of the core business process. However, the incentives for this are still lacking. Security investment does not directly convert into earnings. Government does not mandate as it once did because of decades-long and fractious political debate over its appropriate role. In many cases, the actual loss of an asset due to theft, sabotage, or electronic exfiltration is a more acceptable cost of doing business than the investment to defend against the loss. That cost may now be too high. The array of actors, the advantage of offense, and the failings of legal systems may have raised these issues and stakes to a point of crisis. Meanwhile, the amount of data and intellectual property extracted grows and the war of economic espionage intensifies.

In addressing the possibility of crisis and to help share that responsibility, the outline below is a mere suggestion for considering how government and industry might collaborate through a blend of fiscal policy and strategic defense policy. The gauge of its success depends upon the degree to which it helps stir debate. A national dialogue on security is overdue. It is a subject too critical to be left to the so-called experts. Our daily lives and routines are at stake and without public engagement, the solutions we come by will lack the relevance and durability required to meet the challenge. We are all susceptible to praise for our ideas. However, in this case criticism is most welcomed.

TOTAL QUALITY CONTROL AND SECURITY

The frictionless commerce/secure commerce issue may be viewed as a dilemma or an opportunity to facilitate, both security and trade. Those who would see it as a dilemma regard security measures and the unencumbered flow of trade as mutually exclusive. The examples discussed earlier demonstrate their point. The higher inspection rates for cargo are prohibitive for enterprises, which base their business models on just-in-time processing. The costs associated with cybersecurity upgrades means expenses due to technology purchases, labor, and downtime. The traditional financial gauge of return on investment (ROI) assigns security a negative measure. Justifying the allocation of resources for security is a difficult sell when those divisions must compete against business units that contribute to the profitability of an organization. However, those who view it as an opportunity see it as a way of converging two distinct business imperatives into a single, seamless process harmoniously linking security, production, and distribution. Furthermore, because of the rising risks, particularly due to the cyber threat, the traditional assessments may be undergoing change in many corporate boards.

The enactment of the Sarbanes-Oxley Act in 2002 introduced major changes to the regulation of corporate governance. In response to a loss of confidence by American investors the bill imposed stiff penalties for corporations failing to meet transparent accounting standards and applied the force of its rule to firms attempting to conceal information about financial or business operations. Disclosure of losses due to the diversion of funds or theft of intellectual property applies. Therefore, the law also has direct applicability and implications for corporate security. It was intended to force into practice ideals associated with corporate responsibility to the shareholder and, as well, its larger social responsibility. In consequence, when the nation's vulnerability is interconnected and depended upon the preservation of corporate assets, Sarbanes-Oxley is very relevant in a discussion on national security.

It follows that the onus of defending global trade's supply chain and cyber network must most likely fall upon those that own and maintain it and less upon the protection force of a national military. Militaries are nationally based—commerce is global. In the international system of governance, overlapping jurisdictions and rights of sovereignty have boundaries and are bounded by territory. In global commerce, territories are virtual and boundaries are permeable. Security investments may become more than simply the cost of doing business, as is marketing, R&D, employee benefits, etc. It may be an operational driver. According to Brad Minnis, Director of Environmental, Health, Safety and Security for Juniper Networks, a primary reason for security investment is to increase corporate efficiency.[1]

> It is the responsibility of the corporate Security department to demonstrate the benefits of good security programs and the contributions to the bottom line, as well as to integrate security components into business processes and make security a part of the business model, not something that is added after the fact. Part of that responsibility is to educate senior management in these areas and be able to articulate with metrics the contributions of the security program.[2]

Improvements in asset management, trade efficiency, and market response can be indirect, or "collateral" benefits of a well-designed and integrated security program. In much the way Total Quality Management (TQM) provides an overarching approach to internal discipline, security investment is adding a formal, systematic layer of control for organizations who seek to enjoy such collateral benefits as inventory and asset visibility, time to market advantages, improved customer satisfaction measurement, lower costs related to conveyance expenses and safety stock, and the minimizing of business and political risks.

TQM is a management concept with striking relevance for a current discussion involving the topics of security, governance, efficiency, and overall good corporate citizenship. A concept introduced following World War II, TQM seeks to institutionalize higher standards of quality, consistency, and ethics throughout the organization, its partners, and eventually, society. It is an approach dedicated to total quality, not only to an organization's internal operations, but also relies on the upstream and downstream participation of its suppliers and customers. It is through such collaborative efforts and shared culture along the business chain that enterprises strive to excel within their markets.

Similarly, enterprise security seeks to insinuate itself and offer commerce a panoply of defense, quality, and control. These improvement processes, whether directed at product quality or supply chain security, are designed to go beyond the enterprise and extend to the suppliers. The participation of upstream and downstream partners in an open and cooperative culture is crucial to success of either paradigm. To quote a CEO of an international supplier of defense and security technology products: "for success [of the vender security company and its customers], we need to combine security with operating processes."[3] The future quality of security may well require an expanding network of trusted shippers and partners, and with it, a global effort of cooperation.[4] Cyberspace would require a network of trusted information senders. However, in much the same way that many firms have found TQM too elusive, operationally and conceptually, security has also suffered from frustrations due to embedded corporate cultures and the inertia to think and act anew. A commitment to a thorough security structure requires a significant commitment to planning and change management. Without these requirements being met, the collateral benefits that are the harvest of security ROI will go unrealized.[5]

The present unspoken practice of under-reporting intrusion events cannot be a long-term strategy either. Section 409 of the Sarbanes-Oxley Act specifically requires public firms to disclose any information on material changes in their financial condition or operations. We already know that groups like Anonymous and LulzSec make public their hacktivist successes while their victims remain silent. The savings attained by absorbing these losses, and thereby deferring higher insurance premiums and onerous legal fees, may be ultimately offset by the incurred losses of the same expenses for concealing these events. If the crimes are made public, shareholder outrage, consumer boycotts, and government lawsuits extract their pounds of flesh in ample portions. Not the crime, but the cover-up has been the undoing of many in the high profile world. In an age when information is more powerful and harder to control than any time in the past, corporate executives, audit committees, and boards must consider which policy approach is the more prudent.

Additionally, since the current voluntary initiatives, such as C-TPAT, Fast and Secure Trade, and the World Customs Organization's SAFE Framework, target large multinational firms (LMFs), truer vulnerability may arise from the smaller firms who fall out of the reach and scope of these programs. In this case it will be in the interest of the LMFs to imbed a TQM program and work with their smaller partners to lessen supply variability, and assure business continuity and resiliency. Where programs such as C-TPAT and the SAFE Framework fall short, the concept of the trusted shipper should, somehow, extend its reach and apparatus. This problem for small businesses, which do not have the financial resources or competitive advantages of large organizations, is a glaring weakness in the defense shield. The same dilemma applies to technology upgrades. A sense of urgency aside, these firms may not have financial means to deploy security measures. Brad Minnis comments on C-TPAT's compliance costs:

> Costs to comply are insignificant for companies who have established security programs. [The same costs] may be prohibited for smaller businesses without a solid security infrastructure."[6]

Faced with the option of investing in corporate security or maintaining employee benefits at higher premium rates, small and medium size enterprises (SMEs) may see themselves as having no choices. Therefore, if a TQM program is to extend across all commerce, a private/public sector partnership of mutual assistance and collaborative policy design will be needed in order to establish a "normalcy" in international trade.[7] This means standards being established to create interlocking processes and procedures. They will most likely include effective and accessible technologies for archiving, mining, sharing, and safeguarding information. At the nodes and inter-modal connections, special design codes to expedite throughput (whether it be cargo or information) will be necessary, while a common platform for personnel training and security clearance may span the system. The entire set of arrangements will also have to be cost effective—for all. The argument, which pushes back against the demand to limit such expenses, is that without these initiatives firms may not only be vulnerable to disaster and disruption, but also lose a competitive advantage in the marketplace. Yet for smaller firms, unfortunately, it may be not only the cost of doing business, but the price of staying in business. Their options may be to either invest in security and compete, or find another way to survive. In these cases, dependency on market forces is not enough. Craig Shau, Manager of International Trade Compliance for Parker Hannifin Corporation realizes the financial problems compliance costs may create for firms:

Funding needs to be shared through the use of federal assistance in the form of
grants or tax relief for those participants who are expending significant sums
of money to increase the security of their portion of the supply chain. [8]

The question of regulation versus non-regulation is the concern and an issue
of contention for cybersecurity. Under the Bush administration, the first National Strategy to Secure Cyberspace attempted to give the quietus to any
calls for regulation: "federal regulation will not become a primary means of
securing cyberspace . . . the market itself is expected to provide the major
impetus to improve cyber security."[9] The usual fears of regulation include
questions over who should be subject to regulation, how to adapt mandates to
the changing times and evolving technology and the financial burdens of
compliance. Despite the legitimacy of these concerns many experts now
agree that without some regulation cyberspace cannot be secured.[10] James
Lewis's 2008 project report for the 44th presidency recommended an approach which would allow the private sector to identify a best practices
standard for flexibility and government regulatory authority for enforcement.
In today's political climate, despite the evidence of persistent cyber threat,
involvement by government for the purpose of cybersecurity can still be seen
as intrusive and anathematic. Whether seen as a hindrance to commerce or an
invasion of privacy, across the spectrum, resistance will be the natural response from many who fear the potential for abuse. The past discourse and
vitriol over a national healthcare plan may offer a glimpse of the quality of
debate, which might ensue.

Yet, without some enforcement mechanism or some way to recover the
cost, there is little incentive for companies to invest in their own security and
contribute to the greater national defense. In the meantime, incremental and
ad hoc upgrades to our security and commercial infrastructures leave us more
vulnerable not only to terrorist attacks, but also natural disasters. As our
systems become more automated, they become more complex and interconnected. Therefore, the threat of cascading failure increases. The need for
"baking in" security defenses and adding system resiliency is sine qua non
for the goals of remaining globally competitive and assuring our future.

An alternative may have to be in the form of tax credits that offer some
percentage of cash equivalents in return for outlays on security. The most
efficient solutions to the problems faced by supply chain and industrial control system integrity perhaps exist in the form of tax relief. Financial burdens
to such firms may be eased by some package of fiscal incentives or investment tax credits. This also applies not only to those of small businesses but
also small business states.

TAX CREDITS

The mechanism of tax credits for firms who invest in their own security infrastructure is a provoking discussion topic, not only for small business but also for industry in general. Tax credits, or what economists often refer to as Pigouvian subsidies,[11] were initially suggested as an alternative to transfer payment programs during periods of macro-economic market or demand shock.[12] These "negative" income taxes were programs directed to adjust and smooth the impact of market externalities on household incomes. The Kennedy administration, however, introduced the first tax credit for business in 1962. The Investment Tax Credit (ITC) appeared after the trough of the 1961 recession at 7 percent and was adjusted frequently in response to perceived economic conditions.[13] It was strengthened in 1964, suspended in 1966, repealed in 1969, and resurrected in 1971. During the oil shock of the mid-1970s, investment tax credits rose to 10 percent and seen as a way to encourage conservation and develop alternative energy research and use. As the 1974 example demonstrates, aside from being an instrument to help stabilize the system from market externalities, ITCs are a way to incentivize socially valued behavior. It is this latter instance that concerns the focus of discussion on what might be called a "Security Investment Tax Credit," or SITC.

The notion of a tax credit for firms who invest in their own security is a way of shifting the direct costs of defense away from the strains of a federal government budget deficit and an overextended military and into the hands of the owners of these strategic national assets—namely, the commercial infrastructure. Moreover, with the aid of such fiscal policy, businesses can contribute to national defense, while improving their organizational efficiency. Government recognizes these efforts with tax equivalents. Federal policy makers are pro-business, the firm is a good corporate citizen, and both can claim to be forward thinking on national defense. Hence, the public/private partnership forms a tighter union, structurally, operationally, and in their efforts at capacity building. The policy is politically viable and, at least theoretically, should enlist bipartisan approval.

Because ITCs are inherently elective they are an alternative to regulation, which has been an anathema to pro free trade forces for the past several decades. Government regulation and security controls have always been viewed as twin obstacles to frictionless commerce. The availability of tax credits would ease concern about adverse regulatory intrusion, particularly for small and medium size businesses on the outer edges of the supply chain or on places within the Internet where vulnerability is the most critical. Additionally, the economies of small business states and regions can suffer negative consequences as a result of mandated security measures and their attendant regulatory compliance costs. An elective alternative that offers tax relief would allow businesses and authorities in those areas to bear the burden of helping to pay for security financially and politically, despite their remoteness from commercial and transportation nodes.

This would also allow programs such as C-TPAT to extend its reach and effectiveness. C-TPAT has received criticism for working exclusively with large companies while leaving small businesses outside the collaborative process of setting security guidelines. Big government is better scaled to big business. Involving companies at the lower end of the full range of actors is often difficult. This "difficulty" does not change nor mitigate the fact that it is the first and last mile of the supply chain that harbors the greatest risk of compromise. In the case of cyberspace, local area networks (LANs) are the first and last mile equivalents in terms of vulnerability. Therefore, a system of self-regulating and self-motivating internal levers may be the most effective way of attempting to create an integrated defense system that is whole cloth and yet voluntary.

Other than the pressure of competition, small firms have little inducement to subtract from their bottom line by investing in their security divisions. A SITC may make the above option not only less difficult, but rather obvious. Depending on macro-economic conditions and the cycles of market disruptions, at certain times such a fiscal policy may be even more justifiable. Furthermore, the decision to opt out of implementing security standards may result in severe business risk. SMEs, which decide that added security is not a viable cost of doing business, may soon realize with that decision there comes a competitive disadvantage. On a global scale for developing countries, which do not conform to a more precise security regime, the consequences might be negative trade bias. The United States, with its dominance in the global market and the reach of the U.S.-based international corporate community, can urge, if not impose, its policy. Either way, these entities may run the risk of being forced to exist along the margins of mainstream economy as a result of their lax security schemes. As has been with past periods of economic evolution, the motto remains: "adapt or die." The SITC may help ease the adaptation process.

Tax credits may also help address the inconsistencies and shortfall of the legal process. Despite Sarbanes-Oxley, the threat of civil suit against a firm that has not taken the necessary precautions against a terrorist attack lacks incentive as well. The current U.S. laws that determine civil liability in the event of a terrorist attack are vague and fragmented.[14] Aside from specific contract terms, only a standard code of business practices could exert proper pressure on many businesses to adopt stricter security measures. Legal proceedings would also most likely involve a range of jurisdictions and statutes and legal interpretations before cases were decided. Since the nature of the justice system involves precedent, the absence of adequate historical benchmarks of terrorist events and their sequelae of damage deprives courts a reasonable basis for culpability and reward.[15] Until the unblessed time that these precedents evolve, firms have little motivation to upgrade security when it is unclear as to whether they carry any legal or financial onus.

The lack of substantial historical data on terrorist attacks also inhibits agencies from drafting and enacting regulations. Since the Reagan administration all agencies have been required to conduct cost/benefit impact analysis to determine the net social costs associated with a regulatory statute. If alternative methods could achieve the same regulatory goal, then the regulation would be deemed unjustified. The Office of Budgetary Management reviews these studies before the proposed rule could be issued. Under conditions when the direct impact between a regulation and its impact can be quantitatively assessed, these evaluations are difficult. Under the conditions of trying to assess the damage from a significant terrorist attack, these judgments are purely speculative and can also be arbitrary. Losses in these cases are profound. Furthermore, the impact of cascading economic loss, psychological damage, and political instability is incalculable. Although they represent the collateral damage of an assault rather than direct losses, these objectives are also the main targets of terrorism. The result is the regulatory process alone is not conveniently disposed toward addressing and managing the threat posed by terrorism. As Rob Strayer, former Director of Homeland Security Affairs, Senate Committee on Homeland Security and Governmental Affairs comments:

> DHS has trouble evaluating the costs and benefits of proposed regulations and specific policy choices necessary to implement those regulations. In a 2003 report to Congress, OMB reviewed 69 homeland security regulations issued as of May 2003, noting that only 20 included a cost estimate and only 2 had a quantified benefit assessment.[16]

As mitigation to the above problem, a Security Investment Tax Credit might also add impulse for the need to establish codes, best practices standards, and maturity and success benchmarks to an emerging security industry that generally lacks such measurements. Qualifying for tax relief will require filers to fulfill some set of standards and guidelines. The dual pressure of fiscal policy and defense policy should force activity and make this proposal highly actionable. For the supply chain industry and the cyber-infrastructure sectors, such countermeasures against the terrorist, criminal, or natural event threat are an opportunity to organize themselves and, perhaps, institute the level of governance the system has been lacking. If authority and oversight over these vast, complex, and unsystematic networks can be established, the first steps toward securing the critical infrastructure will, perhaps, have been set. Hopefully, the thrust generated from support of these measures will not only impact industry standards, but technology, research, and business models for future circumstances.

As the system lacks a body of benchmarks for best practices standards, so too does it want for a set of guidelines sensitive to investment decisions and resource allocation. Government is not suited for such undertaking, particularly when the assets requiring investment are privately owned and, therefore, subject to the owner's unique business and commercial risk circumstances. As an example, the Homeland Security Presidential Directive-13 (HSPD-13) requires the coordination of U.S. maritime security policy be the subject and responsibility of the National Strategy for Maritime Security. A GAO criticism of the National Strategy for Maritime Security reports that there is no investment strategy for implementing the strategic plan or mention of how costs will be borne and who will bear those costs. A section of the plan merely calls for action to "Embed Security into Commercial Practices," but offers no specifics. In its commentary, GAO submits the following assessment:

> Without guidance on resources, investment, and risk management, implementing parties may find it difficult to allocate resources and investments according to priorities and constraints, track costs, and performance, and shift investments and resources as appropriate. [17]

This is an even more sensitive issue for cyberspace. Innovation occurs at a pace that requires flexibility in standards for countermeasures and investment into new resources and technologies. The only parties qualified to establish such guidelines and monitor efficiencies are the actual network operators. Government's aptness and effectiveness to regulate on these investment matters would be limited. A SITC may help sharpen the relief of various indistinct issues as government and industry collaborated to set security and investment benchmarks. The incentive of tax benefits may create a natural order for stakeholders to work toward optimizing rather than maximizing their positions. Working with an integrative approach may allow representatives in industry and government to achieve a "common good" whose payoffs exceed parochial interests and the tendency to view goals as distributive and mutually exclusive.

The regulatory and legal authority of the Internal Revenue Service can be the sharpened point of the sword in the tax program's incentive plan. Additionally, the "stick" of potential board liability can also accompany the "carrot" of tax relief. As Joseph McGrath, former CEO of Unisys Corporation explains:

> It is the Board of Directors Audit Committee's responsibility to ensure the Enterprise Risk Management Framework includes adequate controls and tools to monitor for, and defend against cybercrime and cyberterrorism. The Chief Risk Officer and Chief Security Officer in turn have an obligation to ensure

the Board is fully aware of the Corporation's risks and have implemented the internal controls required. [18]

In other words, Sarbanes-Oxley holds responsible the Board of Directors and specifically the Corporate Risk Officer and the Audit Committee for establishing oversight mechanisms. One of the major purposes of the legislation is to require these corporate executives file reporting instruments on the behalf of investors. If board members do not exercise their responsibilities or do not have the expertise to understand the complexities of the businesses, they may be liable. The consequences can be dire if fraud is involved. Section 802 of Sarbanes-Oxley "imposes penalties of fines and/or up to 20 years imprisonment for altering, destroying, mutilating, concealing, falsifying records, documents or tangible objects with the intent to obstruct, impede or influence a legal investigation. This section also imposes penalties of fines and/or imprisonment up to 10 years on any accountant who knowingly and willfully violates the requirements of maintenance of all audit or review papers for a period of 5 years."[19] Concealing a serious security breach or the loss of assets that increases a firm's commercial risk or negatively affects its market price is a grave matter. Once board members and corporate executives realize their personal liability is at stake, the problem of security takes on a higher priority. The threat of a security breach now is viewed less as an abstraction and more of an issue that needs addressing. Directors and officers liability insurance may cover short-term events involving lawsuits, but the damage to personal and corporate reputations can be long-term and, in some cases, nonrecoverable. These disincentives in combination with a strong tax incentive such as a SITC, might provide the necessary inducement for firms to invest in a comprehensive security framework.

Conceivably, once these policies yield benefits a path toward some set of operational and ethical norms between the private sector and the public sector may be established. At some point a sunset provision may allow for disappearance of the credit as the new business model and public mindset take root. Hopefully, government, business, and the economy will realize self-evident efficiencies. All companies who are eligible and take the SITC election will enhance their bottom lines with, initially, tax equivalents and, ultimately, with improved asset and inventory management. They can hone their competitive edge while, at the same time, provide a vital public good. Furthermore, the revenue loss to the Treasury may be offset with a gradual withdrawal from expensive weapons programs, offensive military activity, and rescaling for combating asymmetric wars. The savings gained from less investment in offensive weapons and operations could be used to fortify support for the defense and reconstruction of the nation's critical infrastructure. These tax incentives would allow government and industry to partner in sharing the burden. Only private-sector firms whose business is directly linked to the national critical infrastructure would qualify for the tax credit. However, that is a grand swath of enterprise and the economic stimulus would be relayed to ancillary sectors of the economy. A separate stimulus package would not be required, as some have suggested.

Although the benefits of such a proposal are only speculative, past examples of the applicability and effectiveness of the role of the investment tax credit exist. Yet government incentives for the private-sector investment in critical infrastructure protection are presently insufficient. Merely raising awareness of this option is perhaps, in itself, a valuable service.[20] Any provocative discussion that helps keep alive public discourse about national security lessens the tendency to think too abstractly. Hence, an active, broad-based dialogue may make officials and stakeholders less prone to act or reflect dismissively about our vulnerability. Often daily routines get in the way of our attempts and obligation to plan and think long-sighted. A debate among private-sector stakeholders, policy makers, and elected officials helps to serve the purpose breaking through the inertia and taking seriously the system's vulnerability. Although our vital national interests have fundamentally not changed, the nature of conflict, warfare, and competition has. It would seem the opportunity is here to reassess and exert all the resources and prudent policy options available to assure the nation's security and continued history of ascent.

The benefits of a Security Investment Tax Credit seem rational and attainable. In summary, those calculated benefits include, but are not restricted to, the following:

1. An alternative to regulation due to the inherent elective feature of a tax credit
2. Political viability and bipartisanship potential since it would serve the purpose of national defense and offer some economic stimulus while acknowledging participating businesses with tax relief
3. Recognition, promotion, and reward for good corporate citizenship for those firms who take advantage of the tax benefit
4. Extension of programs such as C-TPAT to small businesses while enlisting the involvement of SMEs who might otherwise not participate without the tax incentive because of financial constraints
5. Add impetus in the effort to establish best practices codes and standards in the security industry by requiring IRS conditions for qualification purposes of filers
6. An additional stimulus to technological research and development, and once standards were set, help counter the tendency for the security industry to be "vendor driven"
7. Promotion of a new business model based on more efficient and secure management of assets

8. Reorientation and rescaling of the national defense establishment to the new arena of asymmetrical warfare against terrorist and criminal gangs rather than large-scale military interstate conflicts
9. A stimulus to the economy under macro market failure conditions which could be offset by a draw-down in traditional offensive operations

SECURITY BENEFITS BUSINESS

President Obama's proposed 2012 defense budget was approximately US $671 billion. Currently, nearly 750 U.S. foreign military bases circle the globe. Despite the devotion of these resources to national defense, according to Chathamhouse.org, "it would take two years and cost less than $50 million a year to prepare a cyber attack that could paralyze the United States," and this effort could involve fewer than 600 people working to infect computers."[21]

National security aside, the financial benefits to business, though perhaps difficult to approximate, are easy to discern. The cost to legitimate international business resulting from cargo theft is estimated in the fifty billion dollar range.[22] The losses due to cyber crime are far more staggering. The UK's National Security Strategy 2010 report estimates the cost to be as high as $1 trillion per year, globally.[23] As well as limiting these unprofitable statistics, other direct benefits are foreseeable, such as reduced insurance premiums.

There are more indirect payoffs for commerce. The benefits of a visible and secure international supply chain, although difficult to calculate, are obvious as well as predictable. While helping to avert a catastrophic global incident, advantages to multinational firms may also include the following:

- Increased shipment visibility, accuracy, and efficiency
- Reduced cycle time and faster speed to market
- Better asset control (product specialization, inventory, and warehousing improvements)
- Enhanced customer service/satisfaction
- Optimization of promotional activity and new product launches
- Protection from contamination or infiltration/exfiltration
- Improved supply chain management

A study at Stanford University by Peleg-Gillai, Bhat, and Sept, although qualitative and directional in its findings, revealed substantial collateral benefits to firms as a result of supply chain security investments. Study participants experienced a 90 percent reduction in theft/loss/pilferage and in tampering, 50 percent reduction in damages, 75 percent reduction in inventory, and 90 percent cost savings due to improved visibility.[24] Although the authors of the report caution against expectations for immediate return on investment, their study strongly suggests that such expenditures net significant business value and eventually a higher rate of profitability.

Furthermore, of the above items, "improved supply chain management" is a key element of today's business model. Many executives of larger multinationals worry that mid-market companies outside the direct control of their organizations leave their supply system open to vulnerability and disruption. Outsourcing raises a complex set of issues for firms active in emerging or developing countries.[25] Not only are comprehensive employee background checks a concern, but LMFs may be unaware of political risks to which their business may be subject if they are not aware of what sources participate in their supply chain and from what regions they are located. As discussed in chapters 7 and 8, this is a particularly sensitive issue for ICT companies involved in developing markets. Computers and servers can be accessed and exploited from anywhere in the world. The same can be said of production facilities. The pace of cyber weapons development is exponential. New malware signatures are identified at a rate of one every eight seconds. Misuse of the Internet and technical computer science skills are growing. The same has been said about the pace and potential for malicious exploitation in the field of biological sciences.

Smaller players in the commercial network could be drawn into participation. Programs such as C-TPAT and SAFE would allow large multinational firms to assert control. The guidelines that C-TPAT "recommends" to its members could, in turn, be demanded along the extended enterprise as the cost of doing business. Because major firms regard their supply and distribution chains as critical components of their own risk profiles, they are demanding that smaller companies satisfy certain minimums and baseline security standards. However, without the influence of a SITC, the security requirements to compete for business may be all the incentive available to force mid-size companies and the "first mile" and "last mile" suppliers to upgrade security operations.[26] The same might hold true for LAN and subnet operators along the ICT network. Failing that, a Security Investment Tax Credit may be the leverage the system needs to set in motion a positive chain of events toward building a global security ecosystem, or megacommunity (see chapter 3).

Critics of C-TPAT may complain that certification costs may be substantial. Compliance costs can range from $40,000 for smaller firms to hundreds of thousands for larger companies.[27] Owners of industrial control systems fear losses due to downtime and implementation costs. However, a package of tax incentives would alleviate these costs and further establish the rationale for such trusted shipper and trusted sender programs. Against the backdrop of over $40 trillion total world gross domestic product, the cost benefit tradeoffs seem more than reasonable, if not imperative. Hence, adding support to the argument that well-envisioned security measures are essential to the survival of today's global economy is the evidence that these precautions can even assist the movement of world trade and boost global commerce. If allowed to reach these logical conclusions, the new business model could displace the opaqueness with transparency, improve organizational efficiency, and make a significant contribution to national defense.

The discussion about national defense also comes at a time when our critical infrastructure is on the verge of obsolescence. There is a serious underinvestment in our network of roads, water supply, energy grid, inland waterways, waste water systems, and communities. If we continue to lag in this area our future will be at an even greater risk. The United States spends less than 2 percent of its GDP on infrastructure. Meanwhile, the emerging economies of Asia have raised the stakes. India's allocation is 5 percent and China's is 9 percent.[28]

Experts estimate that the U.S. government, alone, needs to appropriate $48 billion annually for infrastructure.[29] The total underinvestment, however, equals $129 billion per year.[30] These U.S. rates of investment are not only substandard in proportion to the scale of the nation's economy, but also insufficient to maintain the current dismal ranking of 24th in the world in the quality of infrastructure.[31] The U.S. infrastructure is not only aging, in many areas it is near the point of collapse. The facts are even more distressing when we are forced to admit to ourselves that these systems not only sustain our way of life, they define it. Therefore, they are the most highly strategic targets. A security investment includes an investment in these structures. An upgrade of these systems is well overdue, as is the need to rethink our notions of national defense. The functional purposes, designs, and needs of national security and infrastructure have overlap. These environments are converged and national industrial and security policy have reached an inflection point. We may be at a moment in the history of a nation when ideology must adapt to necessity. Mark Gerencser, of Booz Allen Hamilton, writes about the need, at times, for the United States to retool its infrastructure and the requirement of "varying degrees of investment, management and maintenance on behalf of what was well understood to be critical to both our economy and national security."[32]

The pace of technology, the fragile hyper-connectivity of the global system, deregulation, and the preference for shorter-term profits over long-term benefits has destabilized the planning process. Today, rather than representing a unity of command, the role of government is under debate as to its very purpose or intrusion upon society. In addition, the complexity of the debate is compounded by the privatization of public assets and services. The strength of a nation will depend upon the efficiency of its critical infrastructure and its ability to secure it. To this end, government and commerce must find a way to partner. The convergence of functions should reflect a confluence of policies—industrial, defense, fiscal, and diplomatic. As Jonas Grätz of the Swiss Center for Strategic Studies remarks:

> Military power will not be sustainable without independent economic might— even more so as key allies like Japan or the UK are being weakened economically as well. The prime challenge to US power is thus economic, not military.[33]

The responsibility of national defense is a shared one. The United States, too, long has been a nation of interest groups. The end of the Cold War may have deprived the country of a common enemy and an identity of who we were and for what we stood. The new enemy is ill defined, without a native territory of its own and, therefore, enigmatic to us. For over a decade we were involved in the nation's longest offensive war. It has been a war of dubious cause, with tentative mission, and void of a specific goal. Somehow, we should find a way to return to a sense of mission that placed partisan politics and parochial interests in subjugation to the welfare of the nation. Past conflicts provided the rationale for marshaling such ways of thinking and some understanding of the purpose of sacrifice. Sacrifice, today, would be in the form of long-term investment in upgrading and securing the critical infrastructure. During the Cold War era, this sort of sacrifice was relatively easy to command. The National Security Report, NSC-68, called for and set in motion the military buildup that marked an entire generation. With the challenges ahead, there appears to be the need for a new call for another generation of Americans to shape not only national security, but also the quality of daily life.

CONCLUSION

Incentives can help ensure the integrity of the supply chain network, communications, and trade. The tax incentive discussed above could be a step toward a means to ensure verification without imposing regulation. Trusted shipper and trusted sender mechanisms are technologically and materially available. In the policy area they are nascent. It is the political will that is lacking. If the political system and commerce will not accept regulation as a means of assuring the protection of the supply chain and cyberspace and a significant reinvestment in the critical infrastructure, then national security requires some alternative action. Action may require economic incentives since the field of battle is more over the economy rather than over territory. The immediate reward of the incentive program would be the cash equivalents from tax credits, and the longer-term form of business and market efficiencies. Ultimately and hopefully, it will be an environment of a more secure nation and a safer world.

In the meantime, the United States should assess its security with a sense of urgency. As long as it remains the premier economic and technological power the United States must make use of its hegemonic influence to help cast a global security framework appropriate for the post-Cold War paradigm of power relations. Economic gain or political instability may be enduring enticements for the adversaries of legitimate stakeholders. As legitimate entities work to counter the offensive against them, they will also continue to be encumbered by traditional protocols, outdated legal codes, and abiding rivalries within and outside government.

Furthermore, those who celebrated the attack on September 11 and regenerated into hostile cells, new organizations, and random groups of "entrepreneurial terrorists" may by now, or at some point in the future, have their own sense of urgency. Another demonstrative, high impact event might be viewed as necessary in order to remain creditable with their world and able to attract sympathy, funds, and recruits.[34] Therefore, the threat of a serious terrorist attack, either electronic or kinetic, whether out of ideological motivation or economic incentive, must be more than an abstract fear. Rival states and non-state actors can be the sources of attack. As the United States considers policy and resource options, finally puts aside the post-Cold War "triumphalism," and prepares for a future of uncertain power arrangements, there is also one more consideration to keep in mind. There are and will continue to be attempts of attack, either successful or failed. To constantly hope for the latter outcome by writing them off or bureaucratically defining problems away could be fatefully dangerous. A series of half measures or toothless programs with no regulatory authority does not work. The world has always been a perilous place. Simply waiting for the threat to subside and abiding by previously accepted norms and aging institutions of organization and thought makes it only more perilous.

The recurring theme throughout this book has been the transformation wrought and forced by globalization. The process has offered up a new mode of existence with the similarities of a single space where market relations and political responses intensified and create a new geography. Within this space no market or military target is inaccessible or beyond reach at any time, and commerce and national defense is under constant pressure to respond effectively and efficiently. Meanwhile, the world becomes a more uncertain and violent place. The imperatives of global commerce are unforgiving. Failed states offer safe havens for transnational crime and terrorists. As criminals attempt to exploit these weak states politically, terrorists are becoming more entrepreneurial. In this transforming world we are all more interconnected than any time in history. The new security environment calls for a re-envisioning, an ability to abandon comfortable assumptions and practices of the past. Otherwise, eventually one day if a disaster overwhelms our defenses and relative peace, the lessons of history will be as Coleridge once warned— and we will be obliged to admit that "the light which experience gives us is a lantern on the stern, which shines only on the waves behind us."

NOTES

1. Brad Minnis, Director, Environmental, Health, Safety and Security Juniper Networks, Inc., from dissertation interview (July 2008).
2. *Ibid.*
3. Gianni Arcaini, CEO, Duos Technologies, Inc., Interview (June 2008).
4. David J. Closs, & Edwin F. McGarrell, "Building Security into the Supply Chain" (Michigan State University, April 2004).
5. James B. Rice, & Philip W. Spayd, "Investing in Supply Chain Security: Collateral Benefits" (Massachusetts Institute of Technology, May 2005).
6. Minnis.
7. *Ibid.*
8. Brad Schau, Manager of International Trade Compliance for Parker Hannifin Corporation from dissertation interview (July 2008).
9. "The National Strategy to Secure Cyberspace" (February 2003), p. 15.
10. "Securing Cyberspace for the 44th Presidency," Center for Strategic and International Studies Commission Report, Washington (December 2008), p. 50.
11. Arthur Cecil Pigou (1877–1959) was the Chair of Political Economy at Cambridge who helped pioneer the idea that government, through the use of fiscal policy could help correct market failures.
12. Lily L. Batchelder, Fred, T. Goldberg, Peter, R. Orszag, "Efficiency and Tax Incentives: The Case for Refundable Tax Credits," *Standford Law Review* (October 2006).
13. Alan J. Auerbach, "The Effectiveness of Fiscal Policy as Stabilization Policy" (July 2005), available at http://emlab.berkeley.edu/users/auerbach/effective.pdf.
14. Michael D. Greenberg, *et al.,* "Maritime Terrorism: Risk and Liability," Center for Terrorism Risk Management Policy (RAND Corp., Santa Monica, CA, 2006) p. 136–37
15. *Ibid.*
16. Robert Strayer, Director, Senate Committee of Homeland Security and Governmental Affairs, unfinished article (2008).
17. GAO Report (June 2008, GAO-08-672), p. 18.
18. McGrath, Joseph, interview (20 July 2001).
19. "A Guide to Sarbanes-Oxley," http://www.soxlaw.com/index.htm.
20. Stephen Flynn, e-mail communication (12 March 2008).
21. Paul Cornish, *et al.*, "On Cyber War," Chatham House Report (November 2010), p. 28.
22. Closs.
23. *Op. cit.*, p. 9.
24. Peleg-Gillai Barchi, Gauri Bhat, and Lesley Sept, "Innovations in Supply Chain Security: Better Security Drives Business Value" (Stanford University, the Manufacturing Institute, July 2006).
25. Thomas Cavanagh, "Threat, Vulnerability, and Consequence: A Framework for Managing Security Risk," The Conference Board (June 2006), p. 46.
26. Thomas Cavanagh, "Corporate Security Measures and Practices: An Overview of Security Management Since 9/11," The Conference Board, June 2005, p. 45.
27. Pierre Martin, "The Mounting Costs of Securing the Undefended Border," Policy Options (July-August 2006).
28. Mark Gerenscer, "Re-imaging Infrastructure," *The American Interest Magazine* (March 2011).
29. Keith Miller, Kristin Costa, Donna Cooper, "Creating A National Infrastructure Bank And Infrastructure Planning Council" (Center for American Progress, September 2012).

30. John Craig, e-mail communication with co-author of "Accelerating Infrastructure Improvements With Better Public Policies That Tap Private Investment" (17 April 2013).

31. *Op. cit.*

32. *Ibid.*

33. Grätz .

34. Victor Renuart, Gen. USAF Chief of U.S. Northern Command in Associated Press interview (7 March 2008).

Glossary of Terms

Anthrax: A highly lethal biological agent, which can be weaponized. Contact with the microbe is through ingestion, inhalation, or direct contact.

Arsenal of Democracy: Franklin Roosevelt's term to describe the partnership of science, industry, and the military to defend the United States and advance its interests.

Asphyxiating Agent: Chemical agents that inflict injury through the respiratory tract. They are among the first agents produced in large quantities for use as chemical weapons.

Asymmetric Conflict: A conflict in which the relative military power between combatants differs significantly.

Attribution: Determining the source of Internet and network threats.

Aum Shinrikyo: "Supreme Truth"—Japanese religious-terrorist group, which conducted a sarin attack in the Tokyo subway system. Also known to experiment with biological attacks.

Australia Group: An informal forum of countries to coordinate national export-control regulations to ensure exports do not contribute to the development of chemical or biological weapons.

***Baohusang*:** In Chinese meaning "protective umbrella," refers to a government official who offers cover and protection for criminals and their operations in exchange for bribes.

Biopreparat: A massive Soviet biological warfare program that existed after the collapse of the USSR.

Blood Agents/Systemic Poisons: Cyanide compound gases inhaled, ingested (as solid salts) and absorbed through the skin in liquid form, which can be very lethal if released in confined areas.

Botnet: Short for robot network, they are large numbers of computers infected to perform automated tasks to attack other networks with spam, denial of service commands, viruses, and other forms of malware.

Botulism: A potential bio-weapon. In an ideal situation, 1 gram could kill over a million people.

CBRN: Chemical Biological Radiological Nuclear material which can be used in a violent attack.

C4ISR: Command, control, communication, computers, intelligence, surveillance, reconnaissance—combines information collection, analysis, and transmission and weapons systems into a wholistic mission.

Cesium-137: A significant environmental contaminant as well as being very useful in industry for its strong radioactivity.

Cobalt: The most common radioactive isotope of cobalt is cobalt-60, which can be used in a dirty bomb as can cesium-137.

Computer Network Exploitation: Collection of information via computer networks to exploit data gathered from target or enemy information systems or networks.

Containment: A strategic foreign policy application of hard and soft power to contain Soviet world ambitions.

Courtesan State: The corruption of a state structure serving the interests of globalizing crime organizations or non-criminal actors.

Crime-Terrorist Nexus: Interactions between international terrorists and criminals to commit crime or terrorism for mutual benefit.

Cyber Riots: A form of Internet warfare where hackers disable or deface targeted websites.

Democratic Deficit: The lack of democratic accountability and control over decision-making process.

Desiccants: Chemical agents used in the destruction of crops, degradation of soil, and/or contamination of the water supply.

Deterrence: The use of primarily military threats as a means to deter international crises, conflict, and war.

Electro-magnetic Spectrum: The combination of electric and magnetic fields. The reciprocal relationship between electricity and magnetism form the medium for transporting information in cyber.

European Recovery Act: Known as the "Marshall Plan" it offered faltering European economies financial aid for economic recovery following World War II.

Exabyte: One billion billion bytes of data.

Exfiltration: The loss of confidential data or information due to cyber attack.

Exploit: Packets of computer code that take advantage of software flaws and allow hackers to infiltrate computer systems

Extended Enterprise: Multinational corporations that employ disaggregated production schemes to take advantage of lower costs of capital, economies of scale, and more highly organized inventory and asset management control.

Fusion Center: Sub-federal intelligence gathering centers that concentrate on identifying precursor crime and activity relative to emerging terrorist threats; they also work with private-sector personnel and public safety officials on critical infrastructure protection.

Globalization: The highly interconnected state or process that links populations. Usually used in reference to economic affairs.

Hawala: An honor-based transfer system of funds in, primarily, the Arab world. An alternative system to traditional banking.

Hegemony: From Greek, hegemon or "leader," the predominant influencer of a state through culture or ideology in political or economic affairs.

Hemorrhagic Fever: A pathogen, which can be quite deadly. Some classes of HF have a mortality rate of 50 percent to 90 percent.

Homeland Security Council: Advisory body that meets at the discretion of the president. Its function is to advise the president on all matters relevant to homeland security.

Idealists: Foreign policy strategists who felt containment did not go far enough in meeting the Soviet challenge and believed in greater militarization.

In-Bond Cargo: Refers to merchandise that has not yet officially entered into the U.S. commercial stream and is covered by a bond agreement.

Incapacitating Agent: A group of chemical substances that disturb the central nervous system and disrupt cognitive ability. Their effects are usually reversible.

Intelligence Cycle: The process for converting raw information or data into actionable intelligence for use by policy makers in decision making.

Ionizing Radiation: A type of radiation that emits enough energy to remove tightly bound electrons from atoms.

Jurisdictional Arbitrage: Using legal discrepancies between jurisdictions or states in order to have advantage over government law enforcement agencies.

Just-in-Time Process: Producing with a minimum of waste of time and resources while meeting exact market quality and price demands.

Kinetic Warfare: Refers to movement, velocity, and mass to disable an opponent rather than through electronic means.

Krysha: In Russian "roof"—a term for "protection" and a means of extracting revenue.

Lacrimators: Chemical tearing agents whose effects are reversible and non-lethal.

Logical Security: The use of logic-based methodology to secure physical or intellectual assets and environments. The term is used in contrast to physical security, as referred to as "guards, gates, and guns."

Machtpolitik: Power politics; the use of force to impose will.

Malacca Max: The designation given to the dimensions of a ship too large to pass through the vital shipping lane between Malaysia and Indonesia.

Malware: Short for malicious software or any programming designed to disable, deny, or disrupt operations.

Monopoly of Violence: A term used by Max Webber to express the states exclusivity to raise an army or protection force for the purpose of applying force.

Moore's Law: Axiom that suggests every eighteen months the number of transistors on a computer chip doubles driving the expansion of functions on a chip at a lower cost per function.

National Hactivism: The use of computers to break into a system for political motives and in the interest of one's country.

National Security Council: A forum to assist the president in coordinating defense policy and foreign policy. The NSC was part of the defense reorganization following World War II.

National Security Strategy: The document, approved by the president and outlining the nation's worldwide interests and foreign policy.

NATO: North Atlantic Treaty Organization—a collective security arrangement where an attack on any member would be viewed as an attack upon all. It institutionalized containment as policy.

Natural Language Processing: A computer science field concerned with the interactions between computers and human (natural) language. NLP develops programs that allow computers to extract meaning from texts as it moves from lexical to relational context.

NSC-68: A report within the U.S. Government at the onset of the Cold War to raise defense spending far above the levels originally set and committed to by the Truman Administration to contain the Soviet Union.

Neo-Liberalism: A market-driven approach to economic and social policy, which assumes the efficiency of markets and the restriction of intervention by government.

Nerve Agents: The most poisonous of synthetic chemicals. They inhibit enzyme activity, which is essential for the proper functioning of the nervous system.

Net Force: Networks of loose horizontal coalitions engaged in conflict using some common identity as an organizing mechanism.

Nomenklatura **Capitalism:** The governance system of preference and nepotism, which prevailed in the Soviet era and survived the transition to the present economic and political environment.

Non-ionizing Radiation: A type of radiation that has insufficient energy to separate an orbital electron in an atom.

Nuclear Proliferation Treaty: The chief legal framework and basis for international cooperation in halting the spread of nuclear weapons and weapon technology.

Office of Management & Budget: OMB assists the President in preparing the national budget and measures the effectiveness of agency programs, policies, and procedures to see if they comply with the President's policies.

OPCW: Organization for the Prevention of Chemical Warfare.

PATRIOT Act: Providing Appropriate Tools Required to Intercept and Obstruct Terrorism Act was implemented after 9/11 to grant the government new security and surveillance powers.

Plague: A bacterium with a long history of lethality. It can be weaponized and potentially effective in an aerosolized form.

Plutonium-239: An isotope of plutonium and the main fissile isotope used for the production of nuclear weapons.

PPBES: Planning, Programming, Budgeting, Execution System analyzes the value of fund allocation on force structure, weapons procurement, and mission objectives for defense.

Public Good: A good or service consumed by society as a whole. Its use presumes "non-excludability" and "non-rivalness." National defense is often cited as a textbook example.

Quadrennial Defense Review: The document based on the National Security Strategy, which provides recommendations for federal budget planning for the Department of Defense. By law, the DoD conducts studies and releases the QDR findings every four years.

Radioactive Decay: Occurs when nuclei are unstable and attempt to move from a proton-to-neutron unstable ratio to a proton-to-neutron ratio that is stable. The transition emits energy.

Radionuclide: A highly radioactive substance.

RAND Corporation: United States' first think tank founded to connect military planning with Research & Development in weapons production and strategy.

RDD: Radiological Dispersal Device, or "dirty bomb" is a conventional explosive device that includes radioactive material.

Rent Seeking: Obtaining economic benefits through the political arena.

Resilience: The ability of an organization to adapt and survive fluctuations and disruptions and restore its operability.

Revolution in Military Affairs: The application of information/communication technology to weapons and warfare.

SCADA: Supervisory Control and Data Acquisition computer systems, which automate, monitor, moderate, and control industrial plant functions and critical infrastructure.

***Shashoujian*:** In Chinese: "assassin's mace," the name given to defense projects and a response to America's lead in RMA.

Smallpox: A pathogen, which can and has been weaponized. There is a 30 percent fatality rate from the most virulent strain. The devastation of smallpox epidemics has been catastrophic.

Social Media: Also known as social software and Web 2.0, it refers to networks where people create, share, and exchange information and ideas in virtual communities.

SOX: Sarbanes-Oxley Act was legislation introduced in 2002 in response to a spate of corporate scandals. The act made major changes to the regulation of corporate governance and financial practice.

Sternutators: Chemical vomiting agents are similar to lacrimators. They are non-lethal and produce temporary irritation of the nose, throat, and eyes.

Stuxnet: Stuxnet virus preys on widely used Siemens industrial control software and databases and Vacon and Fararo Paya controllers. It disabled the Iranian nuclear program at Natanz.

Trojan Horse: A computer program appearing to be useful but conceals a harmful code. It also refers to a method of attack with a WMD hidden in a cargo container.

Tularemia: One of the most infectious pathogenic bacteria known, tularemia can be weaponized for a bioterrorist attack.

Uranium-235: An isotope of uranium and alternative to plutonium-239 as the main fissile isotope used for the production of nuclear weapons and nuclear fuel.

Vesicants: Chemical agents that burn the skin and cause extreme irritation to the eyes and lungs. The basic agent is mustard gas.

Yellow Cake: Yellow cake is used to produce hexafluoride, which is necessary to the process of enriching uranium.

Zero Day Event: The moment a cyber weapon activates and becomes operational. Prior to this point victims have no awareness of the malicious code's existence.

Index

Abu Sayyaf Group, 103
Acheson, Dean, 3, 7
Al-Awlaki, Anwar, 57
Alfred P. Murrah Federal Building, 10, 206
Al Qaeda, 57, 58, 59, 147, 164, 171, 183, 189; Maritime capability, 60, 66, 75, 90, 110
Anthrax, 200n17, 200n25, 218, 221–222, 222, 229, 233, 244; US attack in 2001, 220; Use in scud missiles, 219
Anti-terrorism, 247
ANZUS, xi, 21
Arafat, Yassar, 242
Army of National Liberation (ELN), 181
Arsenal of Democracy, 4, 30, 34, 275
Asymmetric Conflict, xxii, 22, 58, 156
Asphyxiating Agent, 275
Attribution, xix, 132, 158, 197, 212, 220, 275
Aum Shinrikyo, 125, 142n5, 205, 214n6, 224, 230, 231, 275
Australian Group, xiv, 212, 214n3, 275
Authorized Economic Operator, 86
Automated Targeting System, xii, 87

Baohusang, 193, 195, 275
Bin Laden, Osama, 56, 59, 164, 169, 171, 184n8
Biological agents, 218, 219, 236n2; Description and categories of, 220–233; Historical use, 217

Biological terrorism, 213, 214n7, 219, 222, 225, 228, 229, 232, 235, 236n2
Biological Weapons Convention, 218
Biopreparat, 218, 222
Blister agents, 208
Booz Allen Hamilton, 52, 92, 102n50, 109, 269
Blood agents, 208
Botnet, 141, 145, 147, 154, 156
Botulism, 229, 230, 231, 237n53, 275
Brzezinski, Zbigniew, 7
Bush administration, 7, 12, 69, 126, 211; Cyber policy, 129, 260; Intelligence agencies, 213
Bush, George, W, 10, 22, 23, 25, 35n19, 35n20, 62, 215n24
Business Executives for National Security, xii, 48

C4ISR, xi, 24, 25, 276
Cali drug cartel, 226
Cargo screening, 84, 101n30
CBRN - Chemical Biological Radiological Nuclear weapons, xii, xxii, xxiii, 10, 53, 235, 249–250, 276
Center for Disease Control, xiv, 222, 223, 228, 233, 237n35, 237n38, 237n41, 237n47
Center for Risk and Economic Analysis of Terrorism Events, xiii, 165

Central Asia, 56, 65, 81, 185, 185n27, 192;
Drug trafficking, 169–174, 174, 175, 183

Central Command, xii, 146

Central Intelligence Agency, 7, 12, 16n27, 41, 44, 51, 53n1, 147, 213; 11n24; Director of, 10, 11; Establishment of, 6; Website destruction, 37, 39

Cesium, 244, 245, 276

Chemical terrorism, 206, 208, 212, 212–213

Chemical warfare, xxii, 204, 208–209, 210, 211, 279

Chemical weapons, 211, 212, 214n6, 214n8, 275; Description and categories of, 206–209; Historical use, 203–206

Chertoff, Michael, 82, 126

Chinese triads, 191, 193–195

Chlorine, 203, 204, 206, 207

Cobalt, 245, 276

Cocaine, x, 181, 183; *Shining Path* trafficking activities, 182–183; Trafficking routes, 182

Cold War, xvii, xxi, 4, 8–9, 10, 13, 20–22, 22, 60, 153, 155, 177, 182, 183, 207, 225, 226, 248, 270; Alliances, 21, 56, 115, 135, 138; Apparatus, 9, 10, 11, 20, 250; Post- Cold War, xix, 18, 22, 23, 26, 30, 32, 33, 49, 51, 55, 62, 67, 115, 131, 132, 156, 168, 174, 193, 196, 271; Return to, 138–139, 156

Commercial Off-The-Shelf (COTS), xiii, 149

Computer Network Exploitation, 276

Computer Security Incident Response Team, xii, 47

Container Security Initiative, ix, 87, 89

Container Evaluation Facilities, xii, 82

Containment, 18–19, 21, 22, 33, 72n29, 249, 276, 277, 278

Corporate Social Responsibility, xii, 47

Counterintelligence, 37, 38, 136, 143n43, 152, 213, 237n25

Counterterrorism, 80, 87, 88, 100, 101n38, 111, 213, 214n7, 236n2, 250n9; Strategy against a chemical weapon attack, 212

Courtesan State, 165, 276

Crime-Terrorist Nexus, 158, 164, 165, 184n1, 184n17, 184n24, 185n26, 185n33, 185n39, 185n42, 189, 195, 198, 199, 249; Central Asia and the Balkans, 172–174; Conditions for collaboration, 190–192; Evolution of, 167–168; South America, 180–184

Critical infrastructure, xviii, xxi, 25, 29, 30, 45, 69, 121, 122, 127, 133, 147, 149, 151, 255, 263, 265, 269, 270, 279; Dependency on electronic networks, 149–151, 152–156; Vulnerability, 45, 50, 65, 269

Critical Infrastructure Protection, xii, 13, 48, 266, 277

Customs Border Protection, xii, 81, 85, 196

Customs-Trade Partnership Against Terrorism, xii, 51, 85–86, 88, 89, 111, 196–197, 198, 200n38, 259, 262, 266, 268

Cyber attacks, xviii, 41, 130, 131, 132, 139, 147, 212, 235

Cyber crime, 48, 141, 148, 155, 157, 158, 232, 249; Legal issues, 131, 134, 147–148, 197

Cyber riots, 41, 276

Cyberspace, 39, 136, 139, 141, 145, 197; Militarization, 130–134

Cyber-terrorism, 121, 142n1, 157, 264

Cyber warfare, 38, 121, 134, 135, 136, 139, 141, 154

Defense Advanced Research Projects Agency, xiii, 125

Defense Contract Audit Agency, xii, 31–32

Defense Contract Management Agency, xii, 31–32

Defense Intelligence Agency, xi, 6, 11

Democratic Deficit, xxiii, 52, 68, 107, 192, 199, 255, 276

Denial of service attacks, 41, 140, 276

Desiccants, 209, 276

Deterrence, 20, 21, 22, 33, 39, 153, 157, 204, 276

Deterrence theory, 20, 21–22, 249

Director of National Intelligence, xi, 7, 11, 12, 16n30, 38

Dirty bombs, 90, 93, 244, 245, 246, 251n16, 251n20, 276, 279

Domain Name System, xiii, 125
Drug trafficking, 67, 93, 108, 132, 164, 174, 185n30, 185n45, 189–190, 200n4; Link to terrorism, 58, 115, 169, 170, 173, 182, 185n26, 195
Drug Tracking Organization, 164
Duel use, xxii, 47, 135

Eisenhower, Dwight, 7, 22, 30
Ejercito De Liberacion National (ELN), xi, 181
Electromagnetic spectrum, xii, 122, 134, 142n2
Electron Volt, xiv, 241
European Recovery Act, 20, 276
e-Verify, 104
Exabyte, 57, 276
Exfiltration, 154, 198, 255, 267
Exploit, 276
Extended Enterprise, 64, 65, 80, 136, 268, 277

Federal Bureau of Investigation, 10, 13, 48, 131, 147, 194, 213
Federal Emergency Management Agency, xi, 10, 100n4
Financial Action Trade Force, xiii, 198
Flynn, Stephen, 89, 91, 100n2, 100n5, 101n24, 101n39, 101n41, 102n45, 117n4, 118n31, 119n46, 151, 160n44, 160n51, 272n20
Former Soviet Union, 21, 60, 110, 147, 171, 177, 221, 237n28, 243
Foreign Terrorist Organization, xiii, 181
Fusion center, 13, 16n31, 16n33, 277

Gama'a al-Islamiyya, 110, 189
Geospatial intelligence (GEOINT), xi, 12, 214
Globalization, xviii, xxiii–xxiv, 17, 40, 56, 58, 62, 71n5, 72n24, 72n42, 107, 118n14, 132, 145, 184, 192, 194, 195, 200n36, 236n18, 255, 271, 277; Crime and facilitation of, 51, 52, 65, 67, 70, 107, 158, 168, 183; Definition of, xvii; De-borderization driver, xix, xxiii, 24, 34, 49, 56, 58, 68, 77, 116, 130; Economic, 17, 63, 65, 72n25, 77, 113, 130, 179, 183, 195, 199, 210; Impact of

technology on, xxiii, 49, 55, 57, 65, 219, 237n28
Global war on terrorism, xi, 11, 12, 21, 23, 33, 38
Golden crescent, 174
Gorbachev, Mikhail, 218
Gulf War, 23, 211, 230

Hamas, 109, 147, 189, 191
Hawala, 277
Hegemony, xvii, xix, 18, 30, 68, 75, 82, 134, 135, 141, 271
Hemorrhagic Fever, x, xi, 221, 224, 225, 237n35, 277
Heroin, x, 164, 169, 170, 171, 172, 185; Amount of traffic through Central Asia, 171; Trafficking routes, 172, 174
Hezbollah, 110, 145, 164, 183, 189, 190, 191
Highly enriched uranium, xiv, 60, 242
Hizh ul Tahrir (HT), xiii, 171, 185
Homeland Security Council, xi, 10, 102n45
Human intelligence (HUMINT), xi, 12, 213
Human trafficking, 168, 191, 195

Idealists, 19, 277
In-Bond Cargo, 81, 101n22, 277
Incapacitating agent, 205, 208, 214n15, 277
Imagery intelligence (IMINT), xi, 12, 213
Improvised explosive devices, xiii, 164
Information-Communication Technology, xiv, xxii, 219, 222, 250, 268, 279
Information Sharing and Analysis Centers, xii, 47
Information warfare, xi, 41, 143n43
Intelligence and National Security Alliance, xii, 49, 121
Intelligence cycle, 3, 277
Inter-continental ballistic missile, xii
International Atomic Energy Agency, xii, 60, 246, 251n19
International Monetary Fund (IMF), xii, xxiii, 63
Internet, ix, 38, 53n9, 57, 67, 71n8, 77, 104, 121, 124–125, 128, 129, 130, 137, 139, 141, 144n62, 145, 146, 147, 206,

213, 261, 268; Creation of, 125–126; Vulnerability for SCADA systems, 149, 151, 152

Internet Corporation for Assigned Names and Numbers, xiii, 125

Internet Services Providers, 126

Investment Tax Credit, xi, 50, 260, 261, 263, 266, 268

Ionizing Radiation, x, 240, 241, 277, 279

Iraq War, 204

Islamic Movement of Uzbekistan, xiii, 170

Jemaah Islamiya organization, 60, 164

Jurisdictional arbitrage, xix, 56, 277

Just-in-time process, xviii, xxiii, 63, 256

Kennan, George, 4, 18

Kinetic warfare, 46, 133, 138, 271, 277

Kissenger, Henry, 3, 7

Krysha, 176, 277

Kosovo Liberation Army, xiii, 169

Lacrimators, 209, 277, 280

Logical Security, 278

Liberation Tigers of Tamil Eelam, xii, 66, 72n38, 111

Liquefied natural gas, xii, 95, 185

Local area network, xiii, 262

Machtpolitik, 138, 278

Malacca max, 79, 278

Malicious code, 137, 140, 280

Malware, 101n30, 136, 140, 148, 152, 154, 276, 278; Black market availability, 156; Emission rate, 154, 268; Use by China in cyber attack, 149–153

Man-Portable Air-Defense System (MANPADS), xii, 61, 72n24

Measures and signatures intelligence (MASINT), xi, 12, 213

Monopoly Of Violence, 17, 278

Moore's Law, 231, 232, 238n62, 278

Mumbai attacks, 42

Mutual Legal Assistance Treaty, xiii, 198

National Hactivism, 278

National Infrastructure Protection Center, xii, 48

National Cyber Security Division, xii, 92

National Reconnaissance Agency, xi

National Security Council, xi, 7, 8, 10, 12, 35n38, 38, 278

National Security Council / Principals Committee, xi, 29

National Security Council / Deputies Committee, xi, 29

National Security Council / Interagency Working Group, xi, 30

National Science Foundation, xiii, 125

Natural Language Processing, 43, 278

Neo-Liberalism, 62, 63, 77, 196, 278

Nerve agents, 208, 278

Net war, 145, 276

911 attacks, 196, 213

911 Commission Report, 9, 11, 17, 29, 55, 58, 68, 71n1, 71n7, 82

Nomenklatura, 177, 178

Nomenklatura Capitalism, 178, 278

Non-ionizing Radiation, 240, 279

Nongovernmental organizations, xii, xix, 45, 49, 105, 158

Non-Intrusive Inspection vehicle, xii, 82

North American Aerospace Defense Command, xii, 32

North Atlantic Treaty Organization, xi, 20–21, 48, 56, 138, 220, 237n19, 242, 278

NSC-68, 17, 19, 20, 34, 270, 278

Nuclear Proliferation Treaty, xiv, 246, 247, 248

Nuclear terrorism, 60, 71n15, 242, 250n3, 250n5, 250n9, 250n13

Nuclear Weapons States, 246, 247

Office of Homeland Security, 10, 11, 92

Office of Management and Budget, xiii, 23, 27

Oklahoma City bombing, 206

Open source intelligence (OSINT), xi, 12, 213

Opium, 164, 170, 173, 174, 185

Organization for Economic Cooperation and Development, xii, 58, 67, 72n20, 77, 90, 100n6, 104, 112, 118n20, 119n45

Organization for the Prevention of Chemical Warfare, 211, 212, 214n8, 215n26

Organized crime, 17, 56, 71n2, 153, 159n3, 168, 171, 174, 184n13, 184n17, 184n24, 185n26, 185n41, 192, 195, 198, 200n1, 200n27, 200n32, 201n40; Links to terrorism, 172, 184n17, 184n24, 185n26; Relation with the state, 107, 166, 187

Pakistan, 42, 60, 66, 67, 68, 84, 164, 171, 247, 248
PFLP-General Command, xiv, 111, 222
People's Liberation Army of China, xiii, 136, 152
Piracy, 21, 108–109, 189
Planning Programming Budgeting Execution System, xi, 28, 279
Plague, x, 134, 217–218, 218, 221, 225–226, 226, 227, 229, 237n38, 237n42, 237n45
Plutonium, 239, 279, 280
Policy Coordinating Committee, xi, 30
Private Military Army, xii, 32
Provisional Irish Republican Army, xii, 111
Public Good, xxiv, 25, 45, 46, 65, 69–70, 125, 127, 130, 255, 265, 279; National defense as a, xxiii, 34, 45, 50, 52, 69, 71
Public Telecommunications Network, xiii, 126
Putin, Vladimir, 180, 186, 219, 245

Quadrennial Defense Review, xi, 23, 26, 35n20, 35n31, 279

Radioactive Decay, 241, 242, 279
Radio Frequency Identification, xii, 96
Radiological Dispersal Device, or "dirty bomb", 90, 93, 244, 245, 246, 251n16, 251n20, 276, 279
Radiological terrorism, 213
RAND Corporation, 4, 53n5, 95, 97, 279
Radionuclide, 245–246, 279
Rent Seeking, 179, 199, 279
Resilience, 22, 153, 279
Revolution in Military Affairs, xi, 23, 24, 25, 135, 279, 280
Revolutionary Armed Forces of Colombia (FARC), xiii, 42, 180–181, 182, 183
Ridge, Tom, 10

Rocket Propelled Grenade, xiii, 111
Roosevelt, Franklin, 4, 30, 236n13, 275
Russian organized crime, 176, 178–179, 180, 184n13, 185n27

Sarbanes Oxley Act, 50, 257, 258, 262, 265, 272n19, 280
Sarin, 207, 208, 275
Secretary of State, 7
Signals Intelligence (SIGINT), xi, 12, 213
Shashoujian, 135–136, 143n35, 280
Shining Path, *Sendero Luminoso*, 182–183
Smallpox, 217, 218, 219, 221, 222–223, 223, 224, 233, 280
Social Media, 41, 44, 54n16, 232, 280
Southeast Asian Treaty Organization SEATO, xi, 21
Soviet Union, xx, 3, 5, 19, 21, 62, 170, 174, 176, 178, 181, 247, 278; Development of CBRN weapons, 10, 57, 60, 219, 221, 222, 223, 228, 237n23, 243, 249
Standards to Secure and Facilitate Global Trade (SAFE), 84, 86, 111, 197, 198, 259, 268
Standoff weapons, 24, 35n26
Sternutators, 209, 280
Stuxnet, 147, 154, 156, 280
Surface to Air Missile (SAM), xii, 61
Supervisory Control And Data Acquisition System (SCADA), xiii, 149, 151, 152, 155, 279
Syria, 41, 139, 183–184, 219, 222, 229, 247

Taliban, 164, 171, 184n8
Terrorism, 151, 158, 160n36, 188, 194, 195, 214
Total Quality Management, xii, 47, 118n10, 257–258, 259
Transnational crime, 60, 71n2, 130, 166, 193, 195, 198, 200n26, 271; And terrorism, 65, 67, 107, 115, 145, 158, 164, 165, 166, 184n1, 184n11, 188, 199
Trans-International Routier, xii, 96, 111
Transmission Control Protocol/Internet Protocol, xiii, 124, 125, 126
Transportation Security Administration (TSA), 92

Index

Tri-Border Area, x, xiii, 187–189, 200n1
Truman, Harry, 4, 5, 7, 9, 20, 278
Trojan Horse, 111, 136, 137, 140, 249, 280
Tularemia, 218, 221, 227, 228, 228–229, 237n46–237n47, 280

Uniform Resource Locator, xiii, 125
Union Carbide, xxii, 210
Uranium, xiv, 60, 189, 242, 243, 245, 280
USA PATRIOT Act, 11, 12, 279
US Central Command, xiii, 146
US Department of Defense, ix, 7, 8, 11, 16n16, 26, 30, 32, 38, 42, 92, 125, 126, 131, 133, 137, 146, 156, 208, 275; Budget, 4, 26–33; Organization, 6, 9, 15
US Department of State, 7, 8, 15, 19, 121, 137, 146, 181, 223
US Department of Energy, 152
US Department of Homeland Security, xii, 13, 16n31, 16n33, 42, 47–48, 82, 101n35, 104, 105, 165; Creation of, 9, 10–11
US Department of Justice, 38, 184, 185, 187, 190
US-CERT, 47, 54n21
USS Cole, 10, 60, 110

Vehicle and cargo inspection system, xii, 82
Vesicants, 208, 280
Vietnam War, 23, 204
Virtual private networks, xii, 124
Voice over Internet Protocol, xiii, 126

Weapons of mass destruction, xii, 25, 26, 34, 75, 81–82, 89, 105, 111, 114, 211, 215n25, 233, 235, 280
World Bank, xxiii, 63, 72n37, 131, 195
World Trade Center, 9, 10, 58, 59, 68–69, 110
World War I, 4; Bio-chemical weapons use, xxii, 203–204, 204, 207–208, 209
World War II, xxi, 4, 6, 17, 18, 20, 34, 50, 64, 77, 203, 204, 206, 209, 237n25, 258, 276, 278; Bio-chemical weapons use, xxii, 204, 208, 218, 226, 228–229, 229
World Wide Web, 41, 151

Yellow Cake, 243, 280
Yeltsin, Boris, 178, 180, 218
Ypres, 205

Zero day event, 153, 280

About the Author

Dr. Jack Jarmon has taught international relations at the University of Pennsylvania, the John C. Whitehead School of Diplomacy and International Relations at Seton Hall University, and Rutgers University where he was also Associate Director of the Command, Control and Interoperability Center for Advanced Data Analysis—a Center of Excellence of the Department of Homeland Security, Science and Technology Division.

He was USAID technical advisor for the Russian government in the mid-1990s. During its economic transition period he worked for the Russian Privatization Committee, and with such organizations as the U.S. Russia Investment Fund, European Bank of Reconstruction and Development, and various money center banks. His private-sector career includes global consultant firms, technology companies, and financial institutions. He was a manager with Arthur Andersen in Moscow and Director of Strategic Alliances at Nortel Networks, Brampton, Ontario.

He studied Soviet and Russian affairs at Fordham University and the Harriman Institute at Columbia University. He is fluent in Russian and holds a doctorate degree in global affairs from Rutgers.